W9-AJK-084

Please Return To

John Rogers

1160 S. E. LakeWay Blvd.
Port Orchard Wa, 98367

(360) 895-8233

Gipp's
Understandable
History
of the BIBLE

Gipp's

Understandable
History
of the BIBLE

by

DR. SAMUEL C. GIPP, TH.D.

DayStarPublishing

P.O Box 587 • Northfield, Ohio 44067-0587

First Edition, Copyright, 1987
Second Edition, Copyright, 2000
Dr. Samuel C. Gipp Th. D.

No part of this book may be reproduced in printed form, electronically, or by any other means without the express written permission of the author. Said letter of permission must be displayed at the front of any electronically reproduced file.

(Think about it! You spend years writing a book and **thousands** of dollars to have it printed. You then rent warehouse space for the copies until they're sold. Then somebody puts it on the Internet and it gets copied free of charge. **It's not a question of getting rich!** If the books don't turn a profit, no more books can be written and all the money is rotting in some warehouse.)

First Edition Printings
1st Printing 1987
2nd Printing 1990
3rd Printing 1994
4th Printing 1997

Second Edition Printings
1st Printing 2000

ISBN
1-890120-13-8

Library of Congress Card No.
00-091647

By the Same Author

The Answer Book

A Practical and Theological Study of The Book of Acts

A Practical and Theological Study of The Gospel of John

Living With Pain

Job

Answers To the Ravings of a Mad Plunger

Reading and Understanding the Variations
Between the Critical Apparatuses of
Nestle's 25th and 26th Editions of
the Novum Testamentum-Graece
(With updated information on the 27th edition)

How To Minister To Youth

Life After Y2K

For His Pleasure

Selected Sermons (Vols. 1 - 10)

(Christian School materials)

Dedication

This book is dedicated to
Matthew 7:17, 18

*After you read it you
will understand why.*

Contents

Preface

Where is the Bible?

How did we get it?

These questions, though simple, have baffled the mind of man for centuries. Today even Christians wonder if we **really** have the Word of God. Most Christians are interested is finding out how the Bible came to us through history.

Many authors, in an attempt to explain how we got our Bible, have clouded the issue in the gray fog of the language of the scholar's union. This has resulted in more puzzled looks than answered questions.

You will find this book is, as its name implies, **An Understandable History of the Bible.** For almost fifteen years it has been "field tested" in the hands of the common man. From steel worker to Greek scholar, from housewife to missionary, all have been impressed by its easily understood style. In one case a 71-year-old lady who had just trusted Christ as her personal Saviour asked her son, "Where did we **get** the Bible from?" In response he gave her a copy of this book. He says that three months later, **she** was teaching **him** about the history of the Bible!

You, dear reader, may find the answer to many of the questions you have about the Word of God. You will certainly find it educational. After all, **it was written just for you.**

Introduction

(By Dr. David Otis Fuller)

There are just two kinds of Christians. (Are all saved or not? We cannot tell; only God knows the heart.)

One kind is that earnest, honest number who are ever anxious to have the FACTS of a vital issue so they may talk intelligently and for the TRUTH.

The second kind are the multitude of Christians (Fundamentalists for the most part) who just do not wish to be confused by the FACTS.

Lenin, one of the founders of communism, for **once** told the truth when he said, "Facts are stubborn things." Indeed they **are**. There are so many plain FACTS favoring the King James Version as being nearest **by far** to the originals (which it **IS**) and far, FAR more accurate and authoritative than **all** the modern versions **combined** (which it **IS**), **that it is indeed** "a riddle wrapped up in a puzzle" how so many truly born-again, blood-bought Christians, when presented with the FACTS, become angry or sarcastic and just do not wish to be confused by the FACTS.

IF, kind reader, you are the latter, may I be so bold as to suggest, if not urge, that you waste no time reading further. This book is filled from end to end with FACTS that are fully documented and they bring the whole Bible version issue into clear-cut focus. There are no "gray" sections to it, it is all black and white.

ii

I confess there was a time in y ministry when I extolled, read from, and recommended from the pulpit some Bible version that had just been published, solemnly stating , "This is the nearest to the originals...easier to read...clarifies difficult phrases that are weighed down with archaic words which need to be eliminated so the sense will be better understood." When the Holy Spirit convicted me of this sin, I asked His forgiveness, and He gave it.

I keep always in mind, and Remind as many as possible, that we face as of **NOW** the most vicious and malicious attempted assassination of the character, the name, the Word of God ever done on planet Earth since those blasphemous words were first uttered in Eden, "YEA HATH GOD SAID?"

I have spoken to many in meetings in this country and Canada and have stated flatly that this is a life and death matter, for IF we do have an infallible, pure, inerrant, Holy Word of God NOW (**NOT** in the originals which have been lost forever centuries ago) to rest our weary souls for time and eternity, **THEN** we have but one alternative or option, "Let's eat, drink and be merry, for tomorrow we die and go to hell."

I also keep issuing a friendly warning — IF you **SEE** this issue and take your stand openly and unashamedly for the King James Version as being your final, absolute Authority, and true Holy Word of God, **THEN** you will lose friends and make enemies. I gladly add that I keep on finding **NEW** friends I have made because of this issue, I would not exchange for the old friends I have lost— **FOR ANYTHING!**

Some fifty years ago or more when I entered the ministry, I knew **THEN** as I know **NOW** I had he final absolute Authority from God Himself to guide me through this dark tunnel called LIFE, beset on ever side by Satanic traps. If I had not known this for sure, I **NEVER** would have been a minister. I refuse to play the hypocrite.

iii

Without God's true, inerrant Word and His eternal Son, the Lord Jesus Christ, "GOD MANIFEST IN THE FLESH", Who has saved me by His grace and has done so mush for me, and still does, and will do throughout the long reaches of eternity, I say without these two ironclad, life-giving FACT, **THEN** the Bard of Avon would be absolutely right when he defined LIFE in one of his plays;

"LIFE IS A TALE TOLD BY AN IDIOT,
FULL OF SOUND AND FURY,
SIGNIFYING--NOTHING!"

Introduction
to the
Second Edition

The first edition of *An Understandable History of the Bible* was enthusiastically welcomed by Christians, whether Bible believers or not. Thousands of copies were sold and many churches utilized it as a text to help bring new converts "up to speed" on the Bible issue. Further, it has been used in Bible colleges around the world as an easily understood textbook. Many pastors have used it in their Sunday School classes to help their congregations to be able to refute the criticisms of Bible correctors they come in contact with. So why a second edition?

The answer to that question is a simple one. There was just so much more material to inform people of. I wanted readers to understand what "The Oxford Movement" was and that it was a pattern for how apostasy is introduced into New Testament churches. I wanted to review the arguments of current scholarship. I wanted to try to get the truth that the King James Bible was written in **modern** English, not Old English. I had planned to add a couple of pages on King James to one chapter but there was so much information that needed to be conveyed that those few pages expanded themselves into a complete, independent chapter. The first edition had ten chapters. The second has eleven. I had planned on adding a few paragraphs of additional information about

King James to an existing chapter. The "few paragraphs" grew into a free-standing chapter. The new chapter concerning King James has been made chapter ten and the former chapter ten formerly entitled "Vindication" has been expanded and re-titled "Considerations, Conclusions & Vindication" and has become chapter eleven. Also added are several more Scripture comparisons to further arm the Bible believers against their foes. There will be new material found in almost every chapter. So I would advise you to read the entire book even if you have already read the first edition.

In addition to the above, I felt the book sorely needed an Index. I read volumes of books and always appreciate a good index. In this case I added not one, but four, an index of: Scripture references, people and a general one and one for Bibles versions. Also, there were no personal computers when I first wrote *An Understandable History of the Bible* and much to my dislike the footnote documentation was listed by chapters in the back of the book. A very frustrating, if not useless, arrangement. This new edition places the footnotes at the bottom of each page where they belong. I believe it will help the reader tremendously in utilizing the information found in the text. Even the Table of Contents has been expanded with more detailed information to act as a crude index.

Furthermore, the type has been enlarged slightly to make the book easier to read. This need came home to me when I met a sheepherder in New Zealand who had to read his copy by candlelight because his shepherd's hut lacked electricity. I aim to please!

If you are a new reader I hope that the information found within will help you to understand the battle over the Bible and why you should hang on to your King James Bible. If you have already read the first edition I hope you will find the added material even more informative.

Why the name change? Well, many, many years ago, before I

was saved, I lived an ungodly life in a small town in Ohio. My father was a honest, hard-working steel worker. My ungodly life greatly grieved him. One day, after another one of my brushes with the law my father blurted out in angry frustration, "I'm doing everything I can to make the name 'Gipp' stand for something good in this town and you're doing everything to bring it down!" I've never forgotten those words. Therefore I am endeavoring to uphold **my father's** name for **good** to make up for the years of grief I caused him. He's in Heaven now. I hope I've made him happy.

About the cover. The cover to the first edition was done in 1987 by a great man who was a member of the church I used to pastor. He has a knack for graphics arts and did the work by hand. He would later end up with his own sign business. When I needed a cover for the second edition I turned his way again. (And for several other of my books.) He leaped to the task. You see the finished product on the cover of this edition. I liked the journeyman on the original cover and was thrilled to see he had remained. Thank you, Gary.

I have toyed with the idea of really "pouring it on" and doing a volume that I would entitle "A **Complete** History of the Bible." Unfortunately there are multitudes of other projects to do first. This work should fulfill the need until such a time as that dream becomes a reality.

Dr. Samuel C. Gipp Th. D.

Chapter 1

Time Trip!

IMAGINE for a moment that we are in a different time period. We have gone back thousands of years. There are no cars. There are no airplanes. There are no modern conveniences. No means of mass communication. We are in primitive times.

We take a look around us. There is no Bible. We know nothing about the universe around us. We have no knowledge of there being a "God." We don't know how mankind got here.

Then we look around us again. We see a seed fall from a tree and (from the **top** of the soil) plant itself, tend to itself, raise itself up into a seedling, and mature into a tree, only to repeat the cycle all over again. And we wonder.

Now we go to the ocean. We study the tides and discover that they are used to clean the waters, making it impossible to support life without them. We look and ask ourselves, "Was this planned?"

We look beneath the surface of the water, to the depths below. We find **life**. Strange creatures! Some which breathe water and some which breathe air like us. Some that spawn eggs. Some that give birth to living young. We see creatures of all different shapes and sizes.

Some are very small. Some are so huge that they weigh many tons. Some go fishing with a worm attached to their own fishing pole. Some have no eyes. Some have their eyes perched out on long stalks. Some carry their own lights with them. Some move very slowly. Some dart about almost too fast for our eyes to follow. Again, we wonder and we ask ourselves, "How did this come into being?"

Next we look overhead. We see the birds. They know how to fly, yet are never taught. They move through the air with grace and precision. Their bones are hollow to give them the light weight suitable for flight. Their feathers all grow in the proper places. They migrate to the same place every year. They possess innate abilities and characteristics required for their survival. And again we wonder. Could this "just happen"?

Finally we look at ourselves, at our bodies. We study the intricacies of the eye and how it works. We examine the complex mechanisms of the ear. We marvel at our ability to keep our balance; to speak; to walk. We look at the heart, that marvelous muscle whose valves know when to open and when to close. It starts functioning without our help and stops itself in spite of all we can do to prevent it. We look to the nervous system and the brain. **How** did all of this come about? Are we to believe that it all happened by accidents?

We put forth our questions to our contemporaries. They have no satisfactory answers. Theories, conjectures, wild sounding hopes, but no answers that can bring peace to our wondering hearts.

WHERE IS GOD?

Through this all, perplexing questions come to mind, "Could there be a 'Being' greater than we are? One who designed and created

—

all of these marvelous things that we have looked at? If there were a 'Being' greater than we, where would He be?"

We look to the ground. No, He would not be there. We scan the oceans. He is not there either. Both of these are limited, and they could not contain so great a "Being." Anything that could create the marvelous works that we find all around us could only come from...(and we look upward)... from the seemingly unlimited sky!

We look to the sky. Is there Something up there? Something that is watching us even now? Something that has created this whole universe and set it in motion? Something that created **us**?

But wait! If there is Something up there, if there is a "Supreme Being," He must know us! He must know what is happening on this earth at this very moment. He must know all of our problems and have the answers for every one of them. And if this is so, and He sees our helpless state, He is indebted to us, His creatures. As our Creator, He must help us with our troubles, assist us through this life, and see to it that we find a way to reach Him. **He must communicate!**

THE COMMUNICATION!

We can call to the heavens. We can climb the mountains in an attempt to be nearer. We can pray. But in all of this, we can only send words in one direction. **He** must communicate **with us!** He must send words to **us.** He must establish reliable communications with us. But how?

One day it suddenly happens. As we walk down the road toward home, far down in the distance we see a figure. That figure is shouting and causing a stir. He has an air of excitement about him. A crowd of curious onlookers has gathered around him to see what has him so excited. As we draw nearer we can hear him shouting, and as we get closer still we can make out what he is saying.

"Make straight the way of the Lord!"

We stop him. "What did you say?"

"Make straight the way of the Lord!"

"Who is the Lord?" we ask.

"The Lord, the Lord God of heaven...".

Of heaven! Quickly we glance up. He has sent someone! We must find out more!

"Tell us more about this 'Lord,'" we ask.

"The Lord God of Heaven! **The Creator of the Universe!**"

We look to the heavens again. We fall on our knees. **God has communicated!** We grasp this figure and desperately demand that he tell us more!

"Tell me! Tell me of this God! Tell me of this Creator!"

"Tell you? You have no need that I tell you, for it is written right here in this Book. For if all you ever knew about God was what I said, there would be no way to verify it. But if God is God, He must put His words in writing, so that we may have it long after His prophets are gone."

Then he pulls from his belongings a volume of a book. We look at it. Writing! Our God writes!

"How did these things come to be?" we ask.

"Holy men of God wrote as they were moved by the Holy Ghost," he replies.

Now we hold in our hands our **communication from our Creator.** He has spanned time and space and worked through men. He has communicated! He had a message for us but did not keep it locked in heaven, for He sent it to earth. He has sent that message in plain black and white so that we could keep it and study it. His obligation to us was to communicate with us. Now our obligation is to accept that communication; to read that communication; to obey that communication. Without that communication, we have no connection to this God Who is the Creator of the universe. If these are not His words, we have no hope.

We have known that He existed for so long. But now we hold in our hand His Word. He has communicated!

THE QUESTIONER

But wait! No sooner do we acquire this precious communication than a shadowy figure arrives on the scene.

"Yea, hath God said? That **isn't** the Word of God. That only **contains** the words of God. That only holds His thoughts, not His very words. Oh, there may be a few fundamental doctrines that you can pretend to believe. But surely you don't believe that these are God's very words? Don't be a fanatic. Settle for just a few accurate passages."

We find ourselves shocked. Our new-found faith assailed! Our confidence in our God's communication shaken! Then our true prophet turns to us and explains.

"He is an unbeliever. He does not believe that God has the power to write this Book perfectly. And even worse, he is struck with fear when he discovers anyone who does, so he tries to destroy their faith in it."

"Why doesn't he just give in and believe it?" we ask.

"Pride," explains our prophet.

BACK HOME

Now, with this Grand Communication tucked safely under our arm, we are transported back to our present day. Times and surroundings have changed. The tattered old volume we held in our hand has become a black, leather-covered book with gilt-edged pages and two precious words printed on the cover, "Holy Bible."

Our prophet now stands before us. He wears a suit and tie now, but he still has a copy of that precious Book in his hand. With a look of determination on his face, he speaks.

"This is the Bible. This is God's Word and God's words. Believe it. Read it. Practice it. This Book will lead you; strengthen you; empower you. It is God's Word."

We open it up and look gratefully at its pages. It is so much easier to read now. So orderly. The books have been divided into chapters and each chapter is subdivided into numbered verses. Everything is now so much easier to find. **And we have our very own copy!** The Word of God. My, how He must love us to have written all of this. My, what power He must have to have brought it through a history that has always been hostile to it, preserve it perfectly, and put it here in our hands!

THE QUESTIONER RETURNS

Suddenly someone speaks.

"Yea, hath God said?"

"What?" We look up. He is a fine looking man, well dressed and obviously quite educated. A look of cynical confidence is in his eye.

"I hate to disillusion you, but actually that is **not** God's Word. That only contains a mere translation of the Word of God, and a poor one at that. Oh, you can find the fundamentals in it, but surely you don't believe that those are God's very words? Please, your lack of proper education is showing. I'm embarrassed for you. So don't be a fanatic. Settle for a few accurate passages, but don't be a fool and hurt the cause of Christ by saying that God preserved His very words. Grow up!"

We find ourselves shocked. Our faith is being assailed. But wait a minute. As our verbal intruder walks away, the lesson that we learned earlier strikes home.

"Wow! Those unbelievers are everywhere," we say to our prophet with a sigh of relief. "They certainly are quick to try to destroy a person's faith in the Bible. I hope he gets saved some day."

"What do you mean?" replies our prophet. "That guy was a **Christian**, a Bible college graduate. He believes that God wrote this Book perfectly a few thousand years ago but then **lost it**. He doesn't believe that God had the power to preserve it through the centuries and give it to you and me perfectly in English. What's worse yet, he is struck with fear when he finds someone who does believe it's perfect, so he tries to destroy their faith in it."

"But why doesn't he just give in and believe it?"

"Pride."

Chapter 2

Where Do We Go From Here?

THERE is a controversy raging today across America and around the world. Where is the Word of God? This is the most important question in life. This is the most important question in eternity!

There are a multitude of answers to that question. They come in all shapes and sizes. Some say that we do not have the Word of God anywhere in this world. Others say that it is found in the Bible but it is only those portions that "speak" to the individual. Some say it lies hidden, locked up in the ancient languages in which it was originally written. Some say we have every word wrapped up in one volume. Still others say that our English translations, though reliable, are faulty at best. Where is the Word of God?

We live in an age of change and confusion. The world without Christ is lost in a turmoil of fear and indecision. Yet to this world, we Christians, who have trusted Christ as our personal Saviour, are taking, and have been taking for many centuries, a message of hope. That message is that **there is salvation in Jesus Christ.**

We make many claims for this Saviour of all mankind. We claim that He was all man, and yet that He was every bit God. We claim that He was begotten by God through a virgin. We claim that He lived among men for over thirty years but never once committed a sin. We all know of His death on the cross. It is we Christians, however, who claim that His death was not simply a symbolic gesture of a rebel dying for a "cause," but instead we say that it was part of a masterful plan by God Himself through which He could make us acceptable in His presence. We claim that the blood shed by Jesus Christ on that terrible old wooden cross was God's own blood, and that it made the divine and complete atonement for the sins of all the world.

But our seemingly outlandish claims do not stop at the cross. We claim still further that this same Jesus Christ was removed dead from that cross and then buried, only to raise Himself from that grave three days and three nights later. Then we claim that this supposed "dead" man walked this earth for an additional forty days. This visit was climaxed, we say, when He, in plain view of His disciples, rose bodily into Heaven to be seated at the right hand of God.

Yet we bold sounding Christians don't stop there. For added to all of this, we claim that Jesus Christ has not left this world without a hope. We say that He is calling out a people to Himself in this generation. We claim that through faith in His atonement, by simply "calling upon the name of the Lord," we shall be eternally saved from the hopelessness of a burning Hell. Not to be stopped yet, we go on to say that we can predict future world events, including what we call "The Rapture" of the believers. We say that still later this same Jesus Christ will return bodily to Jerusalem to set up His kingdom on earth and reign one thousand years.

THE QUESTIONER

—

"Wild claims! Outrageous! Unfounded superstitions!" shout our critics. Our critics are quick to attempt to disqualify our claims-to disprove them-for these claims are completely contrary to the humanistic philosophy through which mankind is attempting to "bring in the kingdom."

Our critics continue, "If the claims of these peculiar people-these Christians-are correct, then there is no excuse for not accepting Jesus Christ and repudiating the misguided philosophies of all the humanists, the politicians, and the socio-religious community. **They can't be right!** There is too much to lose." So they seek to discredit our claims.

WE HAVE PROOF!

Wild claims? Seemingly. Outrageous? No more than some of the theories put forth by the scientific "freethinkers" of our day. Unfounded superstitions? **Never!**

And this is where the battle has raged for centuries and will continue to rage. Now, if all we had to back up our claims was our multiplied words expressing nothing more than our opinions, then we would be no different than our "scientific" adversaries. No, these are not vain words or trumped up theories that we believe. **We have a Book!** Oh, what a Book! Every claim that we make concerning Jesus Christ and future world events is contained in it.

We open it and let the arguments of our critics do battle against it with spears made of putty, on horses with feeble legs. They are repulsed; defeated; humiliated. They regroup and send in artillery, mortars, and missiles only to find that the Word of God is better fortified than a concrete bunker. Then suddenly it strikes back and cuts them to ribbons, and they retreat wounded, grumbling, and fear-bound to their havens of "higher learning."

What was it about this Book that so aptly handled them and yet remains unharmed by their attacks? It was **its words!** For this is not a novel. This is not a fictional "techno-thriller." This is not just another "science" book which must be rewritten every few years to "keep up with the changing theories of the times." No, this is God's Book, **the Bible.** This is God's Book, filled with God's words. They are immortal, indestructible, infallible, immovable and unchanging. What a marvelous Book! What power! What an fearful enemy to the silly theories of mankind.

The Bible. It stands tall, towering high above its enemies. And it is ours!

MY CONVERSION

I shall never forget the day I trusted Jesus Christ as my own personal Saviour. I was twenty years of age. I was wild, rebellious, and unhappy. I was lost and on my way to Hell. I knelt at an altar where a great man of God took the Bible and leafed through it, showing me the truths of salvation. Just before he led me in prayer, he, in his wisdom, played a trick on me, a trick that God used to set the course for my life. He looked over at me and asked,

"Do you believe that Jesus Christ paid for all your sins?"

I replied, "Yes."

"Do you believe that He will save you if you ask Him to?"

"Yes."

Then the trick! "How do you know it?"

—

"Because you told me!" I replied somewhat impatiently and a little put out. I had come to get saved, and I felt like I was getting the run around. I saw no need at all for that last question.

"NO!"

What! No? What was going on here? I had come to get saved, and now I was being made to look like a fool. I had been intentionally set up just so that I would give the wrong answer! I was angry! I was embarrassed! If his telling me how to be saved wasn't how I knew it, then **how** was I supposed to know? I looked him dead in the eye and blurted out my response almost demandingly, **"Then why?"**

His next action took me completely off guard, but it plainly answered my question and set the course for my life. He held that open Bible up in front of me with one hand and tapped its open pages with one finger of the other and said with grave finality, **"Because this Book says so!"**

I was shocked! I remember looking at that precious open Bible, and while trying to fathom this great truth that had just been expounded before me, I said to myself, "You mean that Book has that much power?" I knew the answer was "Yes." Then I humbly bowed my head and my heart and put my faith and trust in Jesus Christ, accepting His payment as my own. I have never forgotten the lesson taught to me so powerfully on the day of my salvation.

WHAT A BOOK!

The Bible. What a powerful Book! It needs no man's approval to assert its authority. The Bible. The Book that no man can conquer. The Bible. That faithful message from God. Never changing; never weakening. Standing defiantly as perfect, as authoritative, in a world that claims nothing can be perfect and that rebels at the thought of any authority, especially that of a **book**. The Bible. It is God's Book.

Yet a Book with such a powerful Creator is bound to have a tenacious adversary. It is the actions of this adversary and his consistent humiliation at the hands of the Book's Creator that we will now study. We will examine the tactics he uses in his never ending campaign to destroy man's faith in God's Book. We will note what and what kind of people he uses to help accomplish his vile purpose. We will behold God's miraculous faithfulness in providing us with a flawless copy of His divine Book.

Come along. For now the journey really begins!

Chapter 3

The Ground Rules

ANYONE who has ever played a game, been involved in any kind of competition, or conducted any type of scientific investigation knows that "ground rules" must be established at the beginning. It is far better to know the rules before you begin an investigation than to try to establish them as you go.

If we are going to make a study of the preservation of the Word of God, the rules we shall follow must be established now. The rules we establish now will have a direct effect on the conclusion we reach at the end of our investigation. We must be cautious as we seek to found these rules. We must free ourselves from prejudice that would taint the outcome of the investigation. We must establish rules which, firstly will not contradict each other and rules that, secondly can and will be applied fairly to all evidence examined.

As in any issue with two sides, the conclusion cannot please all. Those to whom the conclusion is favorable will commend the investigation for its fairness, while those to whom the conclusion is unfavorable will obviously seek to discredit the method used to arrive at such a conclusion. Because we know that we will not be able to please everyone, the most important portion of our investigation will not be what evidence we examine, but the rules by which we interpret that evidence.

Much of the material to be examined is not new but holds huge amounts of truth which have been locked up and unusable due to the previously unfair method by which its testimony was evaluated. To insure that this testimony will be thoroughly heard in an unprejudiced court room, this writer seeks to establish plain, unprejudiced, and spiritually sound rules by which to judge the witnesses. The voices of some learned men will no doubt be heard to protest, while the voices of others, equally as learned, will be heard to agree. The writer will not appeal to either of these voices for approval but will seek to establish rules which even those who disagree with the conclusion must admit are fair. By these rules we will judge all the witnesses fairly and completely so as to wring every bit of worthwhile testimony from them. We must deal in facts and deal with the facts fairly. As one scholar so aptly put it, "My leading principle is to build solely upon facts--upon real, not fanciful facts--not upon a few favorite facts, but upon all that are connected with the question under consideration."

First and above all in importance, it must be remembered that the Bible is a spiritual book. If we divorce this fact from our minds, it will be impossible to arrive at a valid conclusion. We simply cannot evaluate the witnesses for the Bible as we would some uninspired secular work. Let me explain.

First, we must accept and believe that God had His hand in the inception of the Bible. The passage that so quickly comes to the mind of all fundamentalists is **2 Peter 1:19-21**:

19 We have also a more sure word of prophecy; whereunto ye do well that ye take heed, as unto a light that shineth in a dark place, until the day dawn, and the day star arise in your hearts:
20 Knowing this first, that no prophecy of the Scripture is of any private interpretation.
21 For the prophecy came not in old time by the will of man: but holy men of God spake as they were moved by the Holy Ghost.

Note that Peter is stating that the **written words** of God are more sure than God **speaking from Heaven**, Whose voice Peter himself had heard (vss. 17, 18) when he witnessed the transfiguration of Jesus Christ along with James and John, as recorded in the 17th chapter of the Gospel of Matthew.

There are many "side-show evangelists" who would have us believe that God authorizes their ministry by assuring us that "God spoke to me last night." Peter says that God's **verbal commands and precepts** are not as sure as His **written words.** Verbal statements are not binding. They cannot be proven. Anyone who has ever bought a car knows that. But written words are not so fluid. When God chose to put His words down in writing, He made an irreversible decision. **We can now hold Him to His words.** Once those words have been written, they are irrevocable. A God who would bind Himself to us so inescapably must love us and truly desire for us to have His words and to be sure of them.

Peter also states that the writers of Scripture did not write under their own power, but *"holy men of God spake as they were moved by the Holy Ghost."* Therefore, we can be certain that the Bible is not simply a collection of the theories and opinions of a select group of people. They are **inspired** by God Himself.

WHY INSPIRE A BOOK?

God wants us to know that He had His hand in the creation of the Bible from its beginning. The words of those original autographs were not the thoughts of God but His very words. This brings to mind a question. "Why did God inspire His Word perfectly?" Obviously the answer comes back, "So that man could have every word of God, pure, complete, trustworthy, and without error." Amen! That statement touches the heart of any fundamental, Bible-believing Christian.

But what would we do if God gave those precious words **only** to those early writers, then **lost them** in the years that followed, allowed them to be diluted with heretical teachings, and then locked them up in a prison where few could visit them and none could trust them? What if these words and manuscripts, which have long passed off the scene, were the only perfect words God ever gave us? What if it was impossible for us ever to obtain those original words for ourselves in this present generation? Why did God inspire them? Why write a perfect Book and then lose it? Why provide those closest to Christ with a perfect Book but us, 2,000 years removed from Him, with a book that is only a shadow of truth at best? A book filled with mistakes, spurious passages, and doubtful readings! This would be inconsistent with God's nature.

The question that **demands an answer** is this: "Could God, who overcame both time (about 1,700 years transpired from the writing of the oldest Old Testament book to the closing of the New Testament in 90 AD[1]) and man's fallible human nature to write the Bible perfectly in the first place, do the same thing to preserve it?"

Let us look to see what The Authority says about such a thing happening. He makes a very clear statement in the twelfth Psalm.

Psalm 12:6,7:
6. The words of the Lord are pure words: as silver tried in a furnace of earth, purified seven times.
7. Thou shalt keep them, O Lord, thou shalt preserve them from this generation for ever.

Psalm 12:6 is God's clear promise that the originals were perfect and free of any error. We need not worry that any of those words were

---

1 Ray, James, *God Wrote Only One Bible* (The Eye Opener Publishers, Junction City), p. 96.

tainted by the opinion of any of the human writers. But the originals have long passed into history and are no longer in existence. What good was God's marvelous act of **inspiration** if He didn't or **couldn't** preserve those same words error free through history?

This is where verse seven comes in. Note that verse seven is an equally clear promise that God would also **preserve** His words throughout all of time: *"THOU shalt keep them, O Lord, thou shalt preserve them from this generation for ever."* The same God Who inspired the words of the Bible would also be in charge of seeing to it that they would remain pure in spite of their long journey through time. The Bible, God's Word, says that God will preserve His words. Verse six mentions the "words of the Lord" and the "them" of verse seven is referring to those "words" of verse six. So, apparently the all-powerful God of creation will not preserve merely His "thoughts" or "ideas," but He will preserve **His very words!** In fact, to inspire the Bible perfect in the originals and then lose it somewhere in history would have made God's initial work all for naught. You see, "inspiration" without "preservation" would be a **Divine waste of time!**

Is God capable of preserving His words? We find the answer stated very plainly in **Jeremiah 32:17, 27**:

17. *Ah Lord God, behold thou hast made the heaven and the earth by thy great power and stretched out arm, and there is nothing too hard for thee:...*

27. *Behold, I am the Lord, the God of all flesh: is there any thing too hard for me?*

Is such a miracle as preserving His words through history too hard for the God of miracles? Was the creation too hard for God? Was the flood too hard for God? Was the parting of the Red Sea too hard for God? Was the 40 years of manna in the wilderness too hard for God?

Was the virgin birth of Christ too hard for God? Was the collection of the 66 books of the Bible written over a period of 1,700 years too hard for God? Was overcoming the human nature of the sinful writers too hard for God? Is preserving the words of those writers too hard for God?

Personally, I think that inspiration would be a far more difficult doctrine to accept than preservation. Think about the different challenges presented by "inspiration" and "preservation." Building a road across a vast wilderness (inspiration) would be much more difficult than patching the holes (preservation) in that same road after it has been built. But if the road **isn't preserved** it will soon deteriorate. That is exactly what non-Bible believers do in fact believe. They believe that God inspired a Book and then cast it adrift in time without any Divine intervention on His part to assure its preservation.

Why is it that men of faith sound out their convictions so loudly on the above mentioned doctrines (and others) in which their faith cannot be pressed to the limit, but suddenly shrink from the thought that God, Who they claim could write His Book perfectly, could also preserve it perfect? Why is it so easy to believe that God's great miracles are all in the past, but He cannot work one now? Where are those "words" that Peter spoke of in 2 Peter 1:19-21? Where are those "words" which David spoke of in Psalm 12:6,7? Where are those "words" which Jesus Christ Himself spoke of in **Matthew 24:35** when He said, ***"Heaven and earth shall pass away, but my words shall not pass away."***?

It is a **coward's faith** that so loudly declares "faith" in something (the originals) that will never be produced so that that faith can be challenged. These "courageous" souls safely put their faith where it will never-**can never**-be assaulted because the evidence can never be produced. But put your faith in **a Bible you can hold in your**

‐

hand and "the fur will fly"! And sadly, your adversaries will be the very "Christians" who claim to "love" and "believe" the Bible!

Have those precious and perfect words from the pens of Moses, David, Isaiah, Daniel, Matthew, Peter, Paul, Luke, John, and others been cast into oblivion? Have they fallen to the ground to be trampled under foot of men, only to be replaced by something not as pure, not as perfect, not as reliable, which we "Bible believers" are forced to **pretend** are the words of God when we are in the pulpit, while in the quietness of our studies or in our private conversations we let our infidelity and fear show as we check off "mistake" after "mistake"?

GOD'S MISTAKE?

Is this God's method? I trow not. For if God wrote the Bible perfectly in the "originals," but we cannot have those same words in a volume of that Book today, then it would seem that He wasted His time inspiring it perfectly in the first place. We who are so far removed from the New Testament times need His every perfect word far more than Matthew, Luke, John, or Peter or the others who saw Jesus Christ in the flesh! They had their memories. They had His touch still on their brow. They had His words still ringing in their ears. All we have is the Book. All we have are the words bound between those black covers. It is essential that they be His every word, for they are all we have!

So well has Wilbur Pickering put it when he said:

"If the Scriptures have not been preserved then the doctrine of Inspiration is a purely academic matter with no relevance for us today. If we do not have the inspired words or do not know precisely which they be, then the doctrine of Inspiration is inapplicable."[2]

Yes, if God has not preserved His words as He said that He would (Psalm 12:6,7), then He has done something which He has never done before. He has wasted His time! The inspiration of the original manuscripts was in vain if we do not have those very same words in English today.

Therefore, we see that it is important to any seeker of truth to always keep in mind that the Bible is different from all other books in that God had His hand in it. It is a **spiritual** book. It is **the only** spiritual book. Anyone undertaking a study of the evidence of the New Testament, or any other portion of Scripture, who does not take this into consideration cannot possibly arrive at the correct conclusion. Nor can he himself be considered completely honest in his supposed search for the truth. On this supposition we base our first of two rules that will guide us in our study.

RULE #1

It is always to be remembered that the Bible is a spiritual book which God exerted supernatural force to conceive, and it is reasonable to assume that He could exert that same supernatural force to preserve.

Such a rule is completely compatible with the power of God as we know it. It is not only a reasonable rule. It is absolutely necessary to believe. To believe that God could **inspire** a Book but couldn't (or wouldn't) **preserve it** is foolish.

---

2 Fuller, David, *Which Bible?*, (Grand Rapids International Press, Grand Rapids, 1973), p. 269.

THE POWER OF OUR GOD

The men who penned the words of Scripture include two murderers, Moses and David; an adulterer, David; a Christ denier, Peter; an idolater, Solomon; some uneducated fishermen, Peter, James and John; and a farmer, Amos. Yet we Christians believe that their humanity did not taint the very words of God as He inspired them through them. We claim that the human nature of the writers was no obstacle for God's great power to overcome. Thus we claim that their finished work, produced by forty different men over a period of 1500 years, is perfectly the Word of God. **Down to the very words!** "God-breathed" bold Christians like to say.

Doubtless such an undertaking took some doing on the part of God. But a God who can breathe the universe into existence, give life to a pile of clay, part the Red Sea, raise the dead and perform other miracles too numerous to mention is not going to find it impossible.

Now, I ask you, "Is **preserving** those same words too difficult of an undertaking for such a God?" Are we to believe that a God who could overcome man's sinful nature in inspiring the Bible **could not** overcome that same nature in **preserving it**? What happened? Has He lost His power? Has He grown senile? Is He sitting in a divine wheelchair in the **geriatric section** of Heaven?

No! Never! He hasn't lost **anything!** He is the same as when He spoke the world into existence. The God of **inspiration** is also the God of **preservation**.

So why do some Christians voice such rock-solid faith in God's ability to **inspire** His Book perfect in the originals and yet **vehemently** deny Him the ability to **preserve** that same Book. "God-breathed"? Sure. But these anemic Christians believe that **God has bad breath**.

It is a plain, undeniable fact: **the God that inspired the Bible perfect can preserve it perfect!** To deny that truth is infidelic.

This brings us to our second Ground Rule:

RULE #2

Satan desires to be worshiped. He has the ability to counterfeit God's actions and definitely will be involved actively in attempting to destroy God's Word and/or our confidence in that Word while seeking to replace it with his own "version."

THE GREAT COUNTERFEITER

This brings us to our next logical step. If God, the supreme force for good, was active in the conception and preservation of the Bible, then **the supreme negative force** in nature must be active against it.

This Book has an adversary. Satan is against it!

The Bible is a tangible item. Like most books, it is printed on paper with ink. As mentioned above, however, it must be remembered that **it is a spiritual book** in which God has had a positive and an active part. It must also be remembered that there exists in the world a supreme negative power, Satan.

One general truth that we all know concerning Satan is that he at one time had a position in Heaven. Iniquity was found in him, and he was cast out of Heaven and will one day end up in Hell. What was his offense? He wanted to be worshiped as God. Remember that! The Bible records in **Isaiah 14:12-14,**

12. How art thou fallen from heaven, O Lucifer,[3] son of the morning! how art thou cut down to the ground, which didst weaken the nations!

13. For thou hast said in thine heart, I will ascend into heaven, I will exalt my throne above the stars of God: I will sit also upon the mount of the congregation, in the sides of the north:

14. I will ascend above the heights of the clouds; I will be like the most High.

Satan wanted to be worshiped as God! He has not changed his goals. He still desires to be worshiped as God. In order to be worshiped as God, **he must imitate God.** Satan is the great counterfeiter. From beginning to end, the Bible records Satan's constant efforts to imitate and replace God. In Genesis Chapter 3, we find Satan implying that he knows more than God, and from this point, he influences mankind to obey him. When Moses displays the miracles of God through the plagues of Egypt, Satan's magicians counterfeit as many plagues as they possibly can.

Monasteries, mosques and huge cathedrals cover the globe as a testimony to his religious fervor and as clear evidence of his ability to extract worship from his followers. Call him Lucifer, Baal, Ashteroth, Mary or any other name, but allow him the liberty and he will take a portion of truth and twist it in such a deceitfully convincing way that if possible he could "deceive the very elect" (Matthew 24:24).

In Matthew 4:9, we find Satan's last desperate plea to Jesus Christ was that He *"fall down and worship me."*

---

3 "Lucifer," the name used for Satan as early as the third century, has been removed from this passage in the New International Version.

Satan is the great counterfeiter. He has always attempted to counterfeit God's actions in every aspect. For every genuine manifestation of God, Satan produces hundreds of carbon copies. Look at the record:

1. One God -- many "gods"

2. One Christ -- many "christs"

3. One Gospel -- many "ways to heaven"

4. One following: Christianity -- many religions, denominations, cults

5. One Bible -- ? [4]

Whenever God manifests His power through some positive action resulting in a miracle, Satan manifests his power in a counterfeit, and deceptive, way in an attempt to "steal" God's deserved reverence.

Note in Revelation Chapter 13 how many times the word "worship" occurs in reference to Satan in the form of the Anti-christ. Notice also that this worship comes as a direct result of Satanic, counterfeit miracles which are all imitations of similar true miracles performed by God, by His prophets, or by Jesus Christ which resulted in God being worshiped.

---

4 For years I have maintained the belief that the Bible of the Anti-christ would be called the "New Authorized Version". The July 19, 1999 edition of The New American had an article about a new version of the Bible entitled the Third Millennium Bible (TMB). On the cover of this version it says, "New Authorized Version of the Holy Bible." Could this "bible" become known as the "New Authorized Version" (NAV). Is it the "bible" of the Anti-christ. Only time will tell.

—

Think about it. Satan has tried to corrupt and counterfeit every work of God. Are we to be so naive as to believe he would leave the Bible alone? The Bible, our communication from God. The single most important Book ever written and Satan is going to consider it "off limits"?

The sad fact is that he has so muddied the waters of Scripture that **he has more bibles than God has!** He has been so successful at this "bible business" that he now has the faculty of most "Bible" colleges and universities and the sales staff of most "Christian" bookstores doing his work for him. He has actually been able to "deceive the very elect"!

GOD'S WARNING

God knew of Satan's "standard operating procedure" and He tried to warn Israel of his ability to counterfeit God's miracles.

In **Deuteronomy 13:1-3** we read:

1. *If there arise among you a prophet, or a dreamer of dreams, and giveth thee a sign or a wonder,*
2. *And the sign or the wonder come to pass, whereof he spake unto thee, saying, Let us go after other gods, which thou hast not known, and let us serve them;*
3. *Thou shalt not hearken unto the words of that prophet, or that dreamer of dreams: for the LORD your God proveth you, to know whether ye love the LORD your God with all your heart and with all your soul.*

Notice that God is aware of the false miracles of Satan and is awaiting the outcome. To resist Satan's false miracles is to turn your heart toward God. This is what happened with Job. This is what would have happened with Eve if she had rejected his counsel. By **rejecting** modern versions we actually please God.

SATAN'S DESIRES

As stated before, Satan desires to be worshiped. This is the motive for his actions. Let us look briefly at a scriptural record of the methods he used in dealing with his arch-enemy, Jesus Christ.

1. Satan makes a direct approach to achieve his goal (Mat. 4:1-11). Satan fails at his attempt to get Jesus Christ to worship him. In fact, Jesus foretells that it will be Satan who in fact will be forced to worship Jesus Christ (Mat. 4:10).

2. He produces many "christs" to God's one Christ (Mat. 24:23, 24). Satan has had much more success dealing with the **creatures** rather than the **Creator**. Millions of people have been swept into Hell through the "ministry" of such false christs as: Buddha, Mohammed, Mahatma Gandhi, Joseph Smith, Martin Luther King and many others.

3. At the trial of Jesus Christ, Satan can produce only two false witnesses to refute the testimony of many, and their witness does not even agree (Mat. 26:60, Mark 14:50). (The **real** Christ had many witnesses. Even after death there were over 500 witnesses of His resurrection appearances [1 Cor. 15:16.])

4. He produces a lie attempting to prove that the original Christ has been lost and is nowhere to be found. This leaves the field open for his anti-christs (Mat. 28:13, 14).

Now, you must remember, Satan desires to be worshiped as God. You must also remember that he is "the great counterfeiter." The

—

methods he used to attack Jesus Christ are the same methods he uses to attack the Bible.

GOD'S THREE GIFTS

Now look at the three most important things God has given to the world.

1. Jesus Christ - Through Jesus Christ, God's plan of salvation has been wrought, God has displayed His love to the world and His plans for the future and the coming King. Jesus Christ is now in Heaven waiting to return. If Satan is to be worshiped he must both attack and replace Jesus Christ with his own christ.

2. Christianity - These are those individuals who are born-again believers, who have been regenerated by the power of God upon their accepting Christ's payment for their sins. The Christians reside on earth, physically separated from their Saviour. If Satan is to be worshiped, these are his mortal enemies. He must attack them and replace them with his own "Christians."

3. The Bible - This is the crowning work of the Holy Spirit. It is the lifeline of the earthbound Christians to the Heaven-seated Saviour. This Book tells us **everything** we know about God. If Satan is to be worshiped he must attack and replace God's Bible with one of his own making.

Think about this for a second. If heaven were real (and it is), if Jesus Christ died for our sins (and He did), if salvation were free (and it is), if Jesus Christ is coming back to get His church (and He is), if He will some day rule on a throne in Jerusalem (and He will), but **if we**

have no Bible to tell us these things, **we would not know them!** Truth does no good if we do not know that truth exists! The Bible is God's medium through which He tells us all that we know about Him. If it is eliminated, we can know **nothing** about God!

If Satan can eliminate the Bible, he can break our lifeline to Heaven. If he can only get us to doubt its accuracy, he can successfully foil God's every attempt to teach us His truths. The Holy Spirit will lead us into all truth, but every truth He leads us to will be in the Bible. If Satan is going to be consistent with his nature, he must attack the Bible, the Word of God.

It would not be foolish, but **insane** to believe that Satan would adopt a "hands off" attitude concerning the Bible. The single most important thing you can do to your enemy is to destroy his ability to communicate clearly with his troops. Are we to believe that the devil would choose not to try to hamper God's communication with His saints? (Would you like to buy a bridge in Brooklyn?)

When the United States (I **didn't** say "Coalition") opened the Gulf War of 1991 to liberate Kuwait, it did so by first attacking Saddam Hussein's **communication facilities**. It doesn't matter how mighty an army is in the field. If it never gets the order to attack, it is useless. Hussein's much vaunted Republican Guard was "blind, deaf and dumb" because they were unable to receive orders from Hussein. That attack was a stroke of military genius.

Imagine, then, the importance Satan must put on destroying God's Word or destroying man's confidence in it. If he can convince Christians that the Book they hold in their hands **is not perfect**, then it **will not matter** that it is perfect. Christians won't have confidence that it is, and so it will be useless to them.

—

To illustrate the importance of communication, imagine the following scenario: three hundred enemy soldiers are surrounded by five companies of one hundred men each. The outcome is obvious, five hundred should defeat three hundred. Now, the Supreme Commander sends the order to attack to his five individual companies. But something goes horribly wrong! The first company **never gets the message**, so they don't attack. The second gets the message but doesn't get the part that tells **when** to attack, so they wait for further orders. The third gets nothing more than a few garbled words which make no sense, so they don't attack. The fourth company gets the message perfectly clear but thinks that it is a fake, sent by the enemy in an attempt to get them to attack alone. The fifth company gets the message, believes it, and follows it - **and is wiped out** by the 3-to-1 odds.

If the devil can achieve the same kind of confusion among God's people, he can pick us off one-by-one while we run around trying to find out what our orders are. **But!** If **all Christians** simply **believe** that the Bible is **perfect** and follow it, **the devil is in big trouble!**

Therefore, it is plain to see that causing confusion among God's people concerning the word of God would be one of the devil's highest priorities. To leave the Bible unmolested would be foolish on his part.

THE RULES REVIEWED

The two rules which we must keep in mind at all times are:

1. It must always be remembered that the Bible is a spiritual book which God exerted supernatural force to conceive; and it is reasonable to assume that He could exert that same supernatural force to preserve.

2. Satan desires to be worshiped. He has the ability to counterfeit God's actions, and definitely will be involved actively in attempting to destroy God's Word and/or our confidence in that Word, while seeking to replace it with his own "version."

We will now examine the methods Satan has used in trying to accomplish his multiple purposes of destroying God's Bible and gaining the worship of His creatures.

Chapter 4

The 100 Year War

FOR approximately one hundred years now, a battle has been raging over the answer to the question, "Where is the Word of God?" The opposing sides in this war are extremely loyal to their respective positions. At times this battle has been vicious, with some rather scurrilous tactics used by both sides. Since the tactics and attitudes of both sides have been known to leave a little to be desired, if we are going to find who is right and who is wrong we need instead to focus our attention on **"who started it."**

Surely we Christians cannot expect a Christ-rejecting world to accept our Book as its authority. We can just naturally expect rebellion. We can expect the world to make attempts to discredit the Bible's reliability. The battle of the lost theologians against the Bible has been waged since the Garden of Eden.

But the war that I am referring to is not the war between the lost world and born-again Christians. For the last one hundred years the same kind of war has been raging **within Christian ranks!** We need to find out why people who called themselves "**Christians**" would be so vehemently opposed to the concept that God has divinely preserved His words.

From its publication in 1611, the King James Bible slowly overtook and replaced every translation that had preceded it. This was not accomplished by some "Madison Avenue" advertising campaign. Nor was it the result of an organized group of Christian colleges forcing it on a reluctant student body. It can only be ascribed to **the approval of the Holy Spirit.**

Although the Pilgrims who landed in America in 1620 had their favorite (Geneva) Bible under their arms as they disembarked from the Mayflower. But by 1776 the King James Bible had supplanted it to become the Bible on which America was founded. It was the Bible used by the nation's early evangelists as they preached across the young nation.

Until the late 1800's there was, generally speaking, only one Bible, the Authorized Version. There had been others, but the translation instituted by King James I in 1603 A.D. had become known not just in England but throughout the entire world as the "Authorized" Version. Some people mistakenly think that the King James Bible became known as the "Authorized" Version because King James had decreed that it become the Bible of the Church of England. But this is incorrect. It is a historical fact that the King James Bible had become known as the "Authorized" Version due to its universal acceptance among Christians of the world, and not due to a proclamation from King James himself.

Edward F. Hills states:
       "Although it is often called the 'Authorized Version,' it actually was never authorized by any official action on the part of the Church or State. On the contrary, it's [sic] universal reception by the common people of all denominations seems

clearly to be another instance of the providence of God working through the God-guided usage of the Church."[5]

Peter Ruckman points out:
"As anyone knows, the AV 1611 had no royal backing, no royal promoting, no act of Parliament behind it, and the University Press was allowed to print any other version of the Bible along with it."[6]

Alexander McClure states concerning the King James Bible:
"Its origin and history so strongly commended it, that it speedily came into general use as the standard version, by the common consent of the English people; and required no act of parliament nor royal proclamation to establish it's [sic] authority."[7]

As well, the footnote from the above reference in McClure's work tells us:
"Says Dr. Lee, Principal of the University of Edinburgh: 'I do not find that there was any canon, proclamation, or act of parliament, to enforce the use of it. "The present version," says Dr. Symonds, as quoted in Anderson's Annuals, "appears to have made its way, without the interposition of any authority whatsoever; for it is not easy to discover any traces of a proclamation, canon or statute published to enforce the use of it." It has been lately ascertained that neither the King's private

5 Hills, Edward F., *Believer's Bible Study*, (The Christian Research Press, Del Moines, 1967), pp.120-122.

6 Ruckman, Peter S., *Christian's Handbook on Manuscript Evidence*, (Pensacola Bible Press, Pensacola, 1970), p.24

7 McClure, Alexander, *Translators Revived*, (Maranatha Publications, Worthington), p.61.

purse, nor the public exchequer, contributed a farthing toward the expense of the translation or publication of the work.'"

God used the King James Bible to establish both England and America as two of the greatest nations the world has ever known. Because of this blessing, it has been these two nations that have been the most instrumental in carrying the Gospel of Jesus Christ around the world through their various missionary efforts. You can only imagine the **grief** this must have been to the devil. Therefore, we can be sure that it would be a priority for him to want to destroy these nations' faith in the Book God was using, the King James Bible.

So all was fine until the mid to late 1800's. It was then, after two hundred years of preparation that the devil was ready to make his move. Just as the devil used a **theory** (evolution) to overthrow the authority of the Bible years later in America, in England he also used a **theory** that was invented by two English scholars. These men, Brooke Foss Westcott and Fenton John Anthony Hort, were used to usurp the authority of the King James Bible. The theory that was used is called "The Conflate Theory." This is the assertion that the Traditional Greek Text of the King James Bible was a "conflated" text produced by a group of editors in the fourth century and not really a copy of the manuscripts as they were. Over the years their theory has remained- as Darwin's theory of evolution has remained- **just a theory**. It has never been proven and has in fact **lost support** over the years. Dr. David Otis Fuller confirmed this when he recorded Martin's statement that "the trend of scholars in more recent years has been away from the original Westcott-Hort position."[8]

8 Fuller, David, *Which Bible?*, (Grand Rapids International Press, 1971), p. 254.

—

Kurt Aland is much less kind in his Introduction to the 26th edition of the *Nestle-Aland, Novum Testamentum-Graece* when he flatly declares, **"The age of Westcott and Hort...is definitely over!"**[9]

Their theory will be looked at in depth in a later chapter of this book.

REVOLUTION

By 1870 England was ripe for Westcott's and Hort's radical ideas. Higher education had been casting doubt on the King James Bible for years. Their Greek Text, based on a handful of poor quality Egyptian manuscripts rather than the **irrefutable majority** was used by the Revision Committee of 1871 in an effort to supplant the King James Bible. It, or a variation of it, has been the text used by almost every revision and version ever since. This text of theirs, which is entirely Egyptian in origin, relies on nothing more than a handful of inferior Egyptian manuscripts which had already been rejected centuries earlier by the Church as a whole. They had languished unused and neglected until these two apostate scholars took up their cause and foisted them on Christianity.

So the battle began! Which text is closest to the "originals"? Which manuscripts are "most reliable"? And, of course, the ultimate question: "Do we have a perfect Bible in English today?" Dazzled by Westcott & Hort's slight-of-hand, Bible colleges and learned men all over England jumped on the Egyptian bandwagon and faithfully promoted the Westcott & Hort theory while heaping scorn on the God-honored text of the King James Bible. Young ministerial students had

---

9 Nestle, Eberhard, *Novum Testamentum Graece*, (Deutsche Bibelstiftung, Stuttgart, 1979), p.43*

their faith in God's ability to preserve His words assailed and then finally had their perfect Bible replaced with an inferior English copy of the African text. As young pastors, these deceived young men occupied pulpits across the country and around the world and immediately began to parrot their professors, seeking to dislodge the King James Bible from the hearts, minds and hands of believers.

Today, as we enter the Twenty-first Century, Christianity is still divided over the question, "Do we have a perfect Bible in English today?" This battle will probably continue in this century as it did in the 20th, if the Lord tarries His coming.

DO WE HAVE A PERFECT BIBLE?

Do we have a perfect Bible in English today? This is not an amazing question at all. In fact, it is a quite natural question that comes to every Christian at one time or another. Surely a naive babe in Christ would never approach an unbelieving scholar with this question and then lay his Bible in his hands so that he may do with it as he pleases. Surely he would not leave God's book at the mercy of man's opinion. If he would, he should not be surprised when the scholar's answer comes back, in terms not easily understood, "No!" **Nothing** scares a scholar more than the thought that the Bible might be perfect! Unbelieving scholarship is its own authority. It does not need any competition from a book!

Unregenerate man goes about believing a theory that man has evolved and was not created. Yet when this theory is examined scientifically and logically, it cannot be proven to be true. Does this upset the unbeliever? No. He just sets about to believe his theory, for he knows that believing it allows him to be his own final authority. He also knows that to reject the theory of evolution means he must accept

Creationism as true, and this he has vowed in his heart not to do. He does not want to be associated with a few fanatics!

But why is it that this same type of reaction is also found in Christian scholarship concerning the Bible? If you ask a Christian scholar to tell you where the Word of God is, and he will tell you, "in the Bible." Yet hand him an English Bible, **any** English Bible, and he will reply, "It's not there." The "Bible" that he refers to **does not exist** anywhere on the face of this earth. He only pays English versions "lip service" so that his congregation will not discover his infidelity to the Word of God. He cannot point to a copy of Scripture anywhere on earth and say, "**That** is perfect." And the **last thing** he wants anyone else to do is to believe that **any copy** of the Bible is perfect. He will stop at nothing to destroy the faith of every Christian he meets in the infallibility of Scripture.

How can we, as fundamental Bible-believers, declare to people from our pulpits that the Bible is "infallible, without error, the very words of God" and then step **out** of the pulpit and allege to be able to find even one mistake in it? This contradiction would not seem so serious if the infallibility of "the Word of God" was not one of the doctrines that separates us from the world. We take pride in thundering forth that we are not as the unregenerate world, without an absolute guideline. We have a guideline. We have **the** guideline, the Word of God! Then we hold our open Bible up for all to see and shout, "This is God's Word! It's perfect, infallible, inerrant, the very words of God!" Yet in our hearts we are saying, "I believe all this about the original; this is really just a mistake-filled translation."

A great many of today's fundamentalists vehemently reject the thought that God has truly preserved His words in English. We have "the Bible," they say, but it isn't in any one English version. They believe that any version of the Bible is only the "Word of God" where it has been correctly translated. But such a "safe" stand is really a deadly trap in disguise. For that statement is **the eighth tenant of the Mormon church!**[10]

These men **really believe** that the "perfect" Bible that they refer to is long lost and cannot be possessed by anyone on this earth. But they know if they actually tell their congregations that, they will be run out of their churches.

Most fundamentalists never truly realize the weight of their statements when they say that we have no perfect English Bible. Anyone who has studied even a little about Greek manuscripts knows that the Word of God isn't to be found in any of the Greek texts when they are translated literally. They may find one Greek text that they prefer over another. But they **do not believe** that that text is infallible. They have no "perfect Bible" and don't want anyone else to have one either. They simply leave us with **no authority but themselves**. A convenient coincidence!

Who started this controversy? From whence has this division of the brethren come? To keep from condemning an innocent party we need to examine who is accused of being "the Problem" and who truly is. You may be surprised when you see the difference between the two groups. Then you will need to see **where you are.**

THE PROBLEM?

The first answer that comes to the mind of some Christians is that this division has been caused by a small group of fanatics who

---

10 The 8th Tenant of the Mormon Church reads, "We believe the Bible to be the word of God as far as it is translated correctly; we also believe the Book of Mormon to be the word of God."

—

think that only the King James Bible is the infallible Word of God and who refuse to face the facts that the oldest and best manuscripts support the new translations flooding Christianity. It is stated that if these few fanatics were not "so divisive," a great deal more could be done for the cause of Christ. They are told that they can use their King James Bible all they want, but they should quit calling it **"the only"** Bible. There are plenty of other "good translations" out there. But the fact is that none of these version are considered to be the **infallible Word of God**.

In spite of being blamed for starting the battle over Bible translations, the King James Bible believers **are not** the culprits who really did it. Strangely enough, history points to just the opposite being true. The Greek text used by the Authorized Version had been **the only text** used by Christians for centuries before the invention of any of the modern Greek texts. It has been used from the time of the early church until today by true Christians. It is supported not only by the vast majority of manuscripts existent today but also by those of the highest quality and oldest reading. It has been used throughout history with the blessing of God among His born again believers.

This text was the basis of all popular English translations prior to the King James as well. The King James Bible was the Bible upon which America was founded. It was the Bible that was used by God during the great modern mission movement that saw the Gospel carried all the way around the world by English-speaking missionaries. Up until very late in the Nineteenth Century, everyone just used and believed a King James Bible. It was the "Common Bible" that was used at home, public school, government functions and in Christian colleges and seminaries. Thus, whoever it was who tried to get Christianity to use **any other version** is the party who has **truly** caused all the division in the cause of Christ.

A simple parable will illustrate this truth. Imagine for a moment that a sweet, godly old grandmother is sitting in her rocking chair reading her Bible. She has a King James Bible just as her parents used and as their parents before them. She loves the Lord and loves to sit for hours reading His words.

One day a college professor comes into her livingroom and snatches the King James Bible out of her hands and replaces it with a "more modern" translation. He tells her, "Read **this!** It's easier to read than your old, archaic King James Bible."

She looks up, bewildered, then meekly pleads, "But I want to use my old King James."

Suddenly her antagonist goes into a rage and screams, "You're causing division in the cause of Christ!"

Now who was **the real problem** here?

THE PROBLEM!

The **real problem** is that Christians have been either deceived or intimidated into abandoning the God-honored, God-used King James Bible for something inferior. Like "the Emperor" who was deceived by charlatans into thinking he was wearing beautiful new clothes when he was actually naked, these Christians come away from modern scholarship with a new version tucked under their arm, confident that they are arrayed in apparel that only the truly wise can appreciate. Instead, they are parading their ignorance for all to see. They too have been deceived by some fast talking swindlers.

It is only a recent occurrence that biblical Christianity has been beguiled into thinking that the inferior Greek text of Egypt is superior to that used by the King James translators. This text is found in Roman Catholic manuscripts and asserted to be better than the Majority Text

–

used for the King James Bible. This is the mistake garnered by the errant "scholarship" of Westcott and Hort. These men represent the new young sect of Christianity who will not accept the oldest and best. Modern Christians are unsuspectingly beguiled into supporting manuscripts which are decidedly Roman Catholic in doctrine and history. These manuscripts form a text that is used to produce inferior translations which in turn result in weaker Christians who have no confidence that the Bible is infallible. It is we King James Bible-believers who are sure we hold the true words of God brought down through the centuries by the blood of our martyred Christian brethren. We are the ones who **truly believe** that our Bible is perfect.

Ironically, those that take up the "new" versions, with their "better" Greek text are voluntarily taking up the Bible which their early Christian brethren refused to use. When the Roman Church produced a translation based on this inferior text, early European Christians turned their corporate backs to it. It was a refusal that brought the wrath of the Roman Catholic Church, the historic enemy of the Truth, crashing down on them. Christ-loving Christians were literally driven to living in catacombs to escape this vicious enemy. This same Roman Catholic Church is still active against the Truth today. Only now, due to the deceptive practices of modern Christian scholarship, many Christians are using her bible and helping her cause.

I know that these are strong statements. I intend throughout this work to prove their truth, but I state now that I do not intend to bring railing accusations on those brethren who do not agree with me. I will state that they are wrong, prove that they are wrong, and attempt to point out their position in regard to God's revealed word. I do not intend, however, to forget that they are my brethren (those who have trusted Jesus Christ as their own personal Saviour) and will treat them as beloved. Some of these opponents are innocent and need only to see the facts in order to correct their errant position. Unfortunately, some know exactly what they are doing and for one reason or another have given their energy to promoting Satanic perversions of Scripture.

THE SHOT HEARD 'ROUND THE WORLD

This one-hundred-year-long war of words started in the mid-1800's in England. By that time infidelity to the Bible was the norm in institutions of "higher" education. The leading university of England was Oxford. It was imperative to Bible rejecters that Oxford be won over to the forces of biblical infidelity. The vehicle they used would become known as "The Oxford Movement." The Oxford Movement was the instrument used to reintroduce Roman Catholic practices into the Church of England. We will review the origin of the Church of England and how the Oxford Movement influenced it back into the fold of Rome.

THE BATTLE FOR ENGLAND

England had been languishing under the iron hand of Roman Catholic tyranny for centuries when **Henry VIII** took the throne in 1509. He ruled until 1547. Born just a year before the discovery of the New World, Henry was destined to alter English history permanently.

Henry VIII was a gifted scholar, linguist, composer and musician. He was the second son of his father, Henry VII. His elder brother, Arthur, destined to replace his father on the throne, died in 1502, leaving Henry as the heir apparent.

Shortly after ascending the throne he married Catherine of Argon. Their union produced six children. Five of these died in their youth, leaving one sickly girl, Mary. It was not known at the time if a woman could succeed to the throne of England. Henry sought to

—

remedy that by having his marriage to Catherine annulled by the Roman Catholic Church. Pope Clement VII refused to do this, so Henry broke all ties with the church of Rome. He closed the Roman Church's monasteries and confiscated the property. He forbad the ascetic practice of self-flagellation (the practice of whipping oneself as an atonement for sins). Furthermore, he eliminated the Roman Catholic sisterhoods. He then established the Church of England, which was to be Catholic in practice with the exception that its head would be the ruling monarch of England rather than the pope. He forbad appeals to the Roman pope, ceased payments to Rome, and imprisoned Cardinal Wolsey. In 1534 the "Act of Supremacy" made the ruler of England the official head of the Church of England. The Bible was translated into English and a copy was placed in each church to give the people access to it.

But in all this there was a flaw that three centuries later would prove fatal to his new church. Henry's church remain **"Catholic" in spirit and doctrine**. It retained the priesthood, the belief in baptismal regeneration and many of the damning doctrines of Romanism. It was to be the **"English"**Catholic Church as opposed to the "**Roman**" Catholic Church. For this reason Henry was as much an antagonist of Protestantism as he was of Rome. Earlier he had written a book opposing Luther's Reformation. For this the pope had bestowed upon him the title "Defender of the Faith." A title still held by the British monarch today. But Henry wanted no part of **biblical** Christianity. He wanted a "catholic" church which **he** ran rather than some "pope" in far off Rome.

Following his divorce from Catherine, Henry sought another wife, hoping their union would produce a male child to succeed him on the throne. His choice was Anne Boleyn. She also gave birth to a daughter, Elizabeth. Being unsuccessful he next married Jane Seymour. This union produced a son, Edward. In all, Henry had three children who eventually sat on the throne of England. Each was to leave their individual mark on English history.

Henry's immediate successor was his son Edward, born from his third marriage to Jane Seymour. **Edward I** reigned only from 1547 to 1553. To his credit he steered the Church of England farther from Rome. But he died before his purifying work was complete. His death led to the ascension of his half-sister Mary, the sickly little daughter of Catherine of Argon.

Mary I, a staunch Romanist, tried in vain to force the Church of England back into the Roman Catholic Church. She mercilessly persecuted Protestants, spilling their blood so freely that to this day she is better known in history as **"Bloody Mary."** Thousands died in England due to her hatred for anything non-Catholic. Bloody Mary's reign ended in just five short years. She was replaced on the throne by her half-sister Elizabeth, daughter of Henry and his second wife Anne Boleyn.

Unlike her predecessor, **Elizabeth I,** known as "The Virgin Queen," redirected the Church of England back toward Protestantism. The nation she inherited had been devastated by Mary's cruel ways and was in grave financial straits. Because she was only 25 years old, it seemed doubtful that Elizabeth was up to the task. Yet she amazed her detractors by taking the government firmly in hand and steering it in a positive direction. In a desperate attempt to intimidate the English Queen, in 1570 pope Pius V (now **there's** a "humble" title!) issued an interdict that declared that English Roman Catholics owed no allegiance to the English throne. But the pope's hasty interdict backfired, driving Elizabeth and the Church of England further from the fold of Rome. Unable to intimidate the English Queen into submitting to it, in 1588 the Roman Catholic Church next tried military might. Spain attempted to invade England, unseat Elizabeth, and install Mary Stuart as Queen. The English were outnumbered and outgunned. Yet God turned the battle into a fiasco for Spain, whose armada was so soundly defeated that she never regained the naval might she had once known. England in turn became the world's preeminent sea power.

–

Elizabeth died in 1603 at age 69. She was followed by James VI of Scotland who became **James I** of England, the "King James" of the King James Bible.

Though son of the Catholic Mary Stuart, James was a devout Protestant. He had been raised a Presbyterian after the teaching of John Knox. Upon ascending the throne He immediately sanctioned the translation of the Bible into English so that the every Englishman could have a copy in his native tongue. In 1605 the Roman Church tried to murder him and all of Parliament by blowing it up in "The Gunpowder Plot." (More on that in a later chapter.) James united England and Scotland and laid the foundation for what was to become the British Empire. When he died in 1625 he was succeeded by his son **Charles I**, who ruled from 1626 until he was beheaded in 1685. He was replaced in turn by his son, **James II**.

This second James differed greatly from his magnificent grandfather of the same name. James II was a devout Roman Catholic who unashamedly (and unsuccessfully) tried to re-establish the authority of the Roman Catholic Church in England. He went too far when he placed Roman Catholics as bishops in the Church of England. William of Orange, son of Mary the daughter of Charles I and husband of James' elder daughter Mary, was asked to leave Holland and come to England and claim the throne. When William landed in 1688, James' support evaporated and he fled to France as William was crowned **William II**. The bloodless "Glorious Revolution" ended with a Protestant once again on the throne of England. William and Mary, his wife, ruled England jointly until her death in 1684. He ruled on until he died in 1702.

Immediately upon ascending the throne he saw Parliament pass the "English Bill of Rights," which required that all future rulers of England must be a Protestant. 1701 saw the "Act of Settlement," which further required that the British monarch also be a member of the Church of England.

Thus ended the great battle for religious pre-eminence in England with the throne firmly in the hands of the Church of England and the Church of England decidedly Protestant. But if the Roman Catholic Church is anything, it is patient and calculating. It would now begin another war against English Protestantism. Not an open, physical rebellion as it had tried and so miserably failed at in the past. This time it would seek to capture **the minds** of English Protestantism. Once that was accomplished, England would fall into its hands like an over ripe fruit.

In a later chapter we will chronicle the deceit, intrigue and wickedness used to destroy England's faith in its own Bible. We will see how the Church of England was conquered **from within** through the "Oxford Movement", a process that has left England a second-rate world power which is teetering on the brink of becoming a Moslem nation.

BLIND RAGE!

Today, on both sides of the issue, men are called "fanatic," "heretic," "cultist," "Bible-rejecter," "demon-possessed" and more. These two sides have viciously fought until the facts about which they fight are obscured by the dust of the battle. They call each other names until the student of Scripture finds reputable men on both sides of the controversy damaging their potential influence by using some adjectives which, indeed, are very descriptive but totally unnecessary. I am not a soft city gentleman who thinks we should all sit around and talk in quiet tones while sipping tea and eating "brunch." I am a militant Bible-believer who hates the devil, sin, heresy, and apostasy.

—

Yet I think it is time that we who claim to be "fundamentalists" step back and look to see who our enemy really is!

THE REAL ENEMY

The subtle Roman Catholic Church has assumed the position of the lad who told two of his enemies, "You and he fight...I'll hold the coats!" After all, is not "divide and conquer" one of the oldest military strategies known to men? The fundamentalists have laid their coats at the feet of the so-called "Holy Mother Church" and for the past 100 years proceeded to "knock each other's block off." Is it any wonder that the pope smiles so much? Who is our enemy? Let's find him and fight him. Today it seems that on both sides we are concerned more with finding fault with the people that we disagree with rather than what they teach. Let me make this statement: if what I believe about the King James Bible can be disproved, I will gladly trade it in for the "right" Bible. But because I'm a **thinking** Christian, it will take **facts** to change my mind, not ugly names!

We have an enemy, and I believe we should be verbal and active against that enemy, but I feel it is time that we realize that our enemy is not our brother. It is the one holding his coat! We need to join together to fight this common, historic enemy of Truth.

The Roman Church benefits greatly from our internal battles. Battles, incidently, which **it** has provoked. We rage, lie, cheat and who knows what else to overcome our **perceived enemy**, our brother in Christ, while Rome looks on eagerly. On occasion she sends in fresh troops. **Disguised as Christians** (2 Cor. 11:13-15) with "ministries" that are supposed to help Christians combat cults, they attack all but Rome, with a **special vengeance** toward King James Bible believers. They attempt to isolate Bible believers with the charge of "Cult!" and warn Christians not to read any of their material. Ignorance of **the facts** has always been Rome's greatest ally.

The part of the Roman Catholic Church in the affair is similar to that of a soldier attacking an enemy position. He leaps into the foxhole of the enemy, only to find that all of the enemy soldiers have strangled each other! Rome laughs while we expend our energies destroying each other and each other's ministries, thus saving them both time and effort.

Occasionally on either side we will be forced to face a railer, but instead of "writing him off" we will have to be charitable and look past his railing to see what his facts say. If we can disprove his facts, we need not worry about his mouth!

Am I therefore become your enemy, because I tell you the truth? Galatians 4:16.

THE TEST

What we must do as men of understanding is look into these statements and the questions which they naturally provoke. We must examine the **internal evidence** of Scripture to see just what we really should believe concerning inspiration and preservation. Once that goal is achieved, we should hold true to Scripture no matter what some educated "expert" says to the contrary. And we should **resist being intimidated** by those who like to think that they are higher than we are and that the average Christian is an uneducated bumpkin who is to be talked **at** not **to**.

There are two bedrock questions that **must** be addressed in seeking the truth. The first is.

1. Did God inspire His Word perfectly in the original autographs?

The answer is childishly simple to find:

For the prophecy came not in old time by the will of man: but holy men of God spake as they were moved by the Holy Ghost. **(2 Peter 1:21).**

If Peter's testimony isn't clear enough, God placed another witness, just as dogmatic, in **Psalm 12:6**

The words of the Lord are pure words: as silver tried in a furnace of earth, purified seven times.

There can be **no doubt** then that the original autographs were divinely inspired and perfect, free from any tainting by their human writers. God simply overcame their humanity with His divinity!

But, as stated earlier, **"inspiration" without "preservation" is a Divine waste of time!** Why should God bother inspiring a Book that He was going to allow to get "lost"? Why give first-century Christians a perfect Bible, while those of us who are almost two thousand years removed from Christ are expected to get along with an error-riddled translation?

If God really did intend for those with access to the original autographs to be the only people in history to profit from a flawless Bible, there must be a logical reason. Several scenarios must be examined to explain why God wrote a perfect Book in the originals and then allowed it to become a victim of history:

1. Did God feel that only those who would come in contact with the originals needed a perfect Bible? Was He doing a particular work at that time which required a perfect Book, (a work that is apparently no longer going on since He cut this generation off from any contact with that perfect Bible)?

This can not be! It is simply implausible to believe that God's divine plan centered only around those who had access to the original Old Testament and New Testament autographs. By allowing His **perfect** Bible to pass into oblivion, would God be telling us that His goal, whatever it was, had been reached?

2. Did God intend for the Bible to be transported through time perfectly but His plan was thwarted by the devil?

If this was true, then it would mean that the devil would be more powerful than God! The devil could claim that he had been able to overcome God's efforts to preserve His Book throughout time without any errors.

Anyone who believes this is, **in practice**, a devil worshiper, no matter **what** he claims to believe about Jesus Christ.

3. Did God intend for the Bible to be transported through time perfectly but that desire was thwarted by the man?

This couldn't possibly be true! God had overcome the sinful nature of the men who wrote the Bible. Are we to believe He had now **lost the ability** to overcome their nature in preserving it?

4. Did God possibly preserve His Book perfectly across time, but it simply hasn't been found yet and is patiently waiting in some dark cave in the Middle East to be discovered?

Actually, this foolish belief is very similar not only to what Bible rejecters believe but to what they claim has happened! They truly believe that the Bible was "lost" for literally **centuries!** Then one copy was found in a wastebasket in a monastery and another mysteriously appeared **in the Vatican library!** Anybody who believes that **this** is how God preserved His words has been reading too much science fiction!

All this leads us to the second important question:

2. Did God promise to preserve His words perfectly throughout history?

The answer to this question is no more difficult to find in Scripture than is the answer to the first one. All we need to do is to read the verse following Psalm 12:6...verse 7.

> *Thou shalt keep them, O Lord, thou shalt preserve them from this generation for ever.* [11]

You then need to follow that up with the testimony of none other than Jesus Christ Himself as found in **Matthew 24:35.**

> *Heaven and earth shall pass away, but my words shall not pass away.*

We need to face the very real question, do we have Christ's words, or have they "passed away"? If they have "passed away," then

---

[11] The Hebrew word translated "them" in verse seven is a **third person plural** pronoun. In an effort to get rid of the doctrine of Preservation, the translators of the New International Version and several other modern translations have altered the verse to read, "You will keep **us**...," even though there is absolutely **no Hebrew authority** for this translation. This is very poor translating!

Jesus Christ didn't know what He was talking about when He made this statement.

The first verses referred to, 2 Peter 1:21 and Psalm 12:6, guarantee that God was active in originating His Word in the first place. "Inspired" we call it. Inspired perfectly, without any error. God was the all-powerful agent in seeing to it that sinful man wrote down His words flawlessly. Because of this Divine intervention, the words written were the very words of God.

The second reference, Psalms 12:7, claims that God was not only the agent in writing His words (verse 6) but is also the primary agent in **preserving** His words. Note that the subject is God's words, not His "thoughts."

In the next reference, Matthew 24:35, we find that Jesus Christ, God in the flesh, reinforces what Psalm 12:7 has already said. Christ said that Heaven and earth would pass away before His **words** would. Heaven is still above us, and I am relatively sure that the earth is still beneath our feet. Therefore, the very words of God must be here, within our grasp **somewhere.** If His words are to be found only in Greek, then He has restricted their usage to an elite number of scholars who, I might add, are doing **absolutely nothing** in fulfilling the Great Commission! This, however, was never Jesus Christ's method when He was on this earth. He always went past the religious, scholarly minority and took His words to the common people. Until then, only the Pharisees had possessed God's words in the form of the completed, accepted Old Testament books, and although they were well educated and very religious, they were found to be taking advantage of the common people. Christ eliminated this problem by going directly to the common people of His day.

The Gospel is meant for all. God gave His Word to every person and gave the Holy Spirit as a guide to all truth (John 16:13) in spite of

—

the Roman Catholic teachings that only the "clergy" are allowed to interpret the Scripture.

If God's words are locked up in the "Greek Text," then once again education is a prerequisite to having the Word of God and knowing what it says. This type of philosophy would have eliminated Peter and John from the ministry, for they were "unlearned and ignorant men." They were unlearned, and the Bible states that they were ignorant as though incapable of learning. Yet "they had been with Jesus" (Acts 4:12,13)! Jesus Christ made the difference, giving Peter a greater understanding of Scripture than the "educated" Pharisees! Notice his delivery in Acts 1:15-22, 2:14-36 and 4:8-12. He understood the Scripture, though "unlearned and ignorant." Education, though beneficial, is not a necessity for being used of God. I am not anti-education or anti-college, but the first requirement for God to use someone is that a person has "been with Jesus" (Acts 4:13) and that they realize and believe that the written Word which they have in hand is "more sure" than God's spoken words.

Now, today we know that it is easy to "be with Jesus." The Bible says in **Romans 10:9,** *That if thou shalt confess with thy mouth the Lord Jesus, and shalt believe in thine heart that God hath raised him from the dead, thou shalt be saved.* **John 14:20** says, *At that day ye shall know that I am in my Father, and ye in me, and I in you.*

THE "DUMB GOD" THEORY

I have often told those who believe there is no perfect Bible **that you can hold in your hand** in existence today that I do not agree with them because I do not subscribe to the "Dumb God" theory.

You see, **they** believe that God is **so powerful** that He could overcome man's sinful nature and **inspire** a Book with no errors. But then He was **so dumb** that **He lost it!**

We Bible-believers simply believe that the God who was **so powerful** that He could **inspire** a Book with no errors also **has the power** to **preserve it.** He simply is not so "dumb" that He lost it.

So where is that perfect Book? Where is that written Word that we can be confident is "more sure" than God's speaking from heaven? A Word which the Bible claims God has exalted above all of His name (Psalms 138:2)? Do we have God's words today in our common language?

THE COMMON LANGUAGE

While on the subject of a common language, let me point out that many opponents of the infallibility of the Authorized Version say that if God provided a perfect Bible in English, He is also obligated to furnish such a translation in every other language in the world. They claim that there must also be a perfect Bible in German, French, Japanese and all of the other languages of the world. Unfortunately for them, the answer to this argument is embarrassingly simple to even a casual student of history. It is simply that God did nothing different by putting His words in one language (English) than He did when He inspired the Old and New Testaments. God has **always** used only **one language** in which to have His words to be found perfectly.

HEBREW, GOD'S DIVINE CHOICE

There were many languages on this earth at the time that **God chose to inspire His Old Testament in Hebrew.** This was the language of His chosen people, the Jews. He did not bother to inspire a perfect copy of His Book in Egyptian, Syrian, Ethiopian, Greek, or any of the languages in existence at that time. During Old Testament times if someone wanted access to the perfect Bible, **he had to learn Hebrew**. God did not feel obligated to provide every other language with a perfect copy of His Word.

It may be said that this was unfair. **It doesn't matter** what is said about it. It is **still** the method that God chose to use in providing the world with a **written** message. And **God is never wrong!**

GREEK, GOD'S DIVINE CHOICE

There were also hundreds of languages on this earth when God chose to inspire His New Testament in Greek. Matthew 13:18, Acts 13:46, 28:28, and Romans 11:11 show that this time God was going to be taking His message to the Gentiles, so He furnished it in the common language of the day-Greek. Think about it. Not only did God not feel it to be necessary to inspire a copy of His Book in any of the other languages of the day, but He didn't even feel it was necessary to inspire a copy in Hebrew, the language of His chosen people! If the Jews wanted access to the perfect words of God **they would simply have to learn Greek**.

It may be said that this was unfair. **It doesn't matter** what is said about it. It is **still** the method that God chose to use in providing the world with a **written** message. And **God is never wrong!**

ENGLISH, GOD'S DIVINE CHOICE

Question: When would the two Testaments be combined into one perfect Book?

Answer: As soon as God chose a language to become common to the entire world.

Before combining His two Testaments, God would have to choose which language He was going to make the world's most common language. Germany, Spain, France and almost all of Europe were soon to be overly influenced by Rome. No useful language to be found there.

French, though fairly common at one time, has just about disappeared outside of France and few portions of Canada. I once heard of a professor at the University of Paris who asked each of his students to write a paper explaining why they thought French was a dying language. Of fifty-two papers, **fifty** of them where turned in **written in English!** This, in the capital of France! French isn't a "dying" language. It's dead!

There had been great Latin and Syrian translations of the New Testament, but these languages **never became common to the entire world**. The Roman Catholic Church adopted Latin as its official language. This action destroyed any hope of it ever becoming accepted by the world.

What God needed was an island of purity, a nation not shackled by Romanism. A nation with a language so descriptive and simple that it could best deliver His message. Both of these needs were satisfied in England. Here was a people who had thrown off the bondage of Rome and had a young language which was to find its way into every corner of the world; from the Arctic to the Antarctic, from England and America to Moscow and Peking. **English is the language of this world!**

–

Today English is taught to Russian pilots, because it is universal. It is learned by Oriental businessmen, because it is universal. It was the first language spoken on the moon! English is spoken the world over. This is the language God would use.

Being a God of purity, He would want to use this language in its purest form. The English of the King James Bible has been known to be the finest form of the language ever used. McClure praises the Authorized Version in this manner:

> "The English language has passed through many and great changes, and had at last reached the very height of its purity and strength. The Bible has ever since been the great English classic. It is still the noblest monument of the power of the English speech. It is singularly free from what used to be called 'ink-horn terms' that is, such words as are more used in writing than in speaking, and are not well understood except by scholars."[12]

THE DEVELOPMENT OF ENGLISH

Many people are under the false impression that the King James Bible is written in **Old** English. This is due to three things. First, the original King James Bible was set in **Gothic** type face. This font is sometimes even referred to as "Old English". It is very ornate and equally difficult to read. Roman type was in use in 1611 and subsequent editions of the King James were changed to that. Second, some folks think that the use of "thees" and "thous" indetifies the English of the Authorized Version as "Old." This is incorrect. The use of "thees" and "thous" was in use in common speech in 1611 and is not at all

---

12 McClure, Alexander, *Translators Revived*, (Maranatha Publications, Worthington), p.61.

associated with either "Old" or even "Middle" English. Third, many not-so-well-meaning critics like to make the assertion that the English of the King James Bible is "Old" English in order to mislead their congregations and further alienate them from God's perfect Bible.

The English language developed over approximately 1000 years. It passed through three distinct segments known as, Old English, Middle English and Modern English.

Old English was spoken from 449 AD to around 1100 AD. When the Angles, Saxons and Jutes invaded England in 449 AD, they brought with them their own individual languages. Over the years these languages combined to form Old English which utilized six vowels rather than the five of Modern English. The sixth being similar in appearance to a lower case **e** and **a** superimposed over one another. Old English was further divided into four distinct dialects by geographic location. These were, Northumbrian, Mercian, West Saxon and Kent. Old English looked nothing like the English of today and could not be read, spoken or understood by someone who speaks Modern English as the following example will illustrate.

Example #1
> **Modern English** - "The man saw the woman."
> **Old English** -   "se guma geseah þa cwen."

Example #2
> **Modern English** - "The woman saw the man."
> **Old English** -   "seo cwen geseah þone guman."[13]

Example #3

---

13 *The Cambridge Encyclopedia of the English Language*, (Cambridge University Press, 1995), p. 20.

–

Modern English - "When this answer was received he began immediately to sing in praise of God the Creator, with verses and words that he had never heard." (Translated.)

Old English - "he ða þas andsware onfeng, þa fers ond þa word þe he naefre gehyrde."[14]

Thus, it is obvious that the King James Bible was **not** written in **Old** English as some would have us believe. Bible critics may wear this transparently false argument out but **the facts** prove that is simply isn't true.

Middle English was the second step in the development of the English language and was predominant from around 1100 AD to 1450 AD. It began to develop in 1066 AD when the Norman's invaded England. The French language was forced upon many of the inhabitants, but it was absorbed into English rather than replacing it. In 1362 AD the "Statute of Pleading" made English the official language of Parliament. French had lost the battle for supremacy and English took another crucial step in its development.

Middle English also would not be readily understood by those of us who speak Modern English. It would be as foreign to our eyes and ears any other foreign language is today. The following example is an excerpt from *The Peterborough Chronicle* as written in 1154 AD. It rehearse methods of torture used in monasteries. It is considered by some to be the earliest surviving example of Middle English. For ease of comparison it is presented in an interlinear format.

[Me dide cnotted stenges abuton here] haeued and uurythen it dat it
[One placed knotted cords   about their]   heads   and twisted   it that it

gaede to pe haernes. Hi diden heom in quarterne par nadres and snakes

---

14 Ibid., p. 20.

entered to   the brains They put them   in cell   where   adders and snakes

and pade waeron inne, and drapen heom swa. Sume hi diden
and toads were in,   and killed   them so.   Some they put in

in crucethus, dat is in an cest pat was scort, and nareu, and undep,
   torture box,   that is in a chest   that was short,   and narrow and shallow,

and dide scaerpe stanes perinne and prengde pe man paer-inne dat him
and   put   sharp stones   therein, and   pressed the man   therein[15],   that

braecon alle pe limes.
they broke   all the limbs.[16]

These examples make it plain that neither "Old" nor "Middle" English was the language used for the King James Bible. Anyone who teaches anything different is either mistaken or dishonest.

Modern English came into existence around 1450 AD and was basically solidified by the end of the 16th century. In about 1500, major changes in vocal pronunciation, inflection, and spelling simplified and helped solidify the language.[17] This was all in preparation for the ultimate work of the English language, the Authorized Version of 1611.

The greatest works in English, those of the "Golden Age" of English literature, are all in Modern English. William Tyndales' translation, the works of William Shakespeare and, of course, the **pinnacle** of the English language, The King James Bible.

The English language is made up of elements of Danish, Old Norse, Latin, Greek, French, German and many other dialects. Today

---

15 Note the two different ways of spelling "therein." Spelling was still fluid in the English language into the eighteenth century. Noah Webster and his dictionary had a great deal to do with the standardization of spelling.

16 *The Cambridge Encyclopedia of the English Language*, (Cambridge University Press, 1995), p. 33.

17 *New Standard Encyclopedia*, (Standard Educational Corporation, 1977), Vol. L, p. 64.

—

we use words such as alcohol and assassins (Arabic), coffee (Turkish), mammoths (Russian), robots (Czech), shampoo (Hindi), ketchup (Malay) and thousands of others which have come to us from all around the globe. No language is more complete or descriptive than our own marvelous English!

Many claim today that since the Authorized Version was printed in the common English of that day, the Bible should be retranslated into the common English of today. This is not a valid claim. It must be remembered that the English used in the Authorized Version was not only the common language, but it was also the English language in its purest form. The English language has degenerated from what it was in 1611 to what it is today. Those claiming to put the Bible in "modern English" are actually, though possibly not intentionally, trying to force the pure words of God into the degenerated vocabulary of today! What a disgrace to God's Word! What a shame to those who propose such a thing!

It is also thought by some that the King James Bible is written in "Old" English. This is because the first few printings were set in Gothic type which is very ornate looking. Actually the King James Bible is one of the first to be printed in **"Modern"** English. As previously mentioned, Old English looks completely foreign to anyone who speaks English today. But the English of the King James Bible is basically the same as that which is spoken today. You see. The King James Bible **is** a "modern" translation!

THE ARCHAIC CON-JOB

A charge often brought against the Authorized Version is that it is full of "archaic" words. But are we to make the Bible pay the penalty of our own irresponsibility in not keeping our language pure and descriptive? Would we not be richer to learn the meaning of those nasty old "archaic" words and add them back into our own vocabulary? Would we not be making the Bible poorer by depriving it of its descriptive style? Are these words truly "archaic"? I have seen stores today that still advertise "sundry" items. Perhaps the store owner didn't realize that it was supposed to be archaic. Perhaps it is like the coelacanth caught off the coast of Africa more than sixty years ago; the fish was supposed to have been extinct for millions of years. Of course it was extinct! It just didn't know it! Science said it was extinct, so it must be. (They first had better prove that the world was here millions of years ago.)

For example of an "archaic" word in the King James Bible take the word "conversation" as used in Philippians 1:27 and see how God chose the most descriptive word He could. Is not "conversation" a much more descriptive term than "life?" When we realize that our life **speaks** to people as a "conversation," then we must live our Christianity, not just talk it. It has often been said, "I can't hear what you're saying because what you're doing is speaking too loud." So we see that the Authorized Version obviously gives us a deeper meaning.

The question arises, "What about words whose usage has definitely been dropped from today's English? Those words which are just not used any more? What shall we do with them?" In answer to this question, let us remember that the Bible is the Word of God. We "Bible people" claim to accept its authority as **final** in **all matters** of faith and **practice**. But do we? Do we accept the biblical practice of how to deal with situations today? Would we be willing to accept the biblical example of how to deal with words whose meanings have changed?

It just so happens that there is a perfect example in the Bible of how **God** handles archaic words. Let's remember that **we** can't come up with a better way of handling archaic words than **God** can. Let's look **and learn and follow the Bible example** of handling, "archaic" words. Surely the Bible, God's Word, cannot be wrong! Let us look at **1 Samuel chapter 9.**

—

1. *Now there was a man of Benjamin, whose name was Kish, the son of Abiel, the son of Zeror, the son of Bechorath, the son of Aphiah, a Benjamite, a mighty man of power.*

2. *And he had a son, whose name was Saul, a choice young man, and a goodly: and there was not among the children of Israel a goodlier person than he: from his shoulders and upward he was higher than any of the people.*

3. *And the asses of Kish Saul's father were lost. And Kish said to Saul his son, Take now one of the servants with thee, and arise, go seek the asses.*

These verses give us the circumstances involved. After searching fruitlessly for his father's asses, Saul decided to give up, fearing that his father Kish might begin to worry about him and his servant.

6. *And he said unto him, Behold now, there is in this city a man of God, and he is an honourable man; all that he saith cometh surely to pass: now let us go thither; peradventure he can shew us our way that we should go.*

7. *Then said Saul to his servant, But, behold, if we go, what shall we bring the man? for the bread is spent in our vessels, and there is not a present to bring to the man of God: what have we?*

8. *And the servant answered Saul again, and said, Behold, I have here at hand the fourth part of a shekel of silver: that will I give to the man of God, to tell us our way.*

Now let us watch very carefully, for an "archaic" word is about to make its appearance in verse eleven. But before it can, God inserts a note to the reader in verse nine!

9. *(Beforetime in Israel, when a man went to enquire of God, thus he spake, Come and let us go to the seer: for he that is now called a Prophet was beforetime called a Seer.)*

Notice what God has done here. Verse 9 is in parenthesis. **It is a note to the reader from God!** God note wrote us a Book. But He even inserted a few notes to us to help clear up what might seem to be a problem!

God knows that the word "seer" is no longer in common usage; it is archaic. At the time that Saul was looking for his father's asses it was in common usage. But by the time this story is written down it has passed from common usage. So God defines it so that we will better understand His choice of words. Is this changing the text? No! Look at the following two verses.

10. *Then said Saul to his servant, Well said; come, let us go. So they went unto the city where the man of God was.*
11. *And as they went up the hill to the city, they found young maidens going out to draw water, and said unto them, Is the seer here?*

Notice in verse eleven God leaves the "archaic" word in the text! He does not change "seer" to "prophet." He does not change the text. God gives us a definition of the word which He chose to use in the text, but He does not give us a "modern" or "updated" edition. This is the **biblical method** of how God handles an "archaic" word without rewriting the text. Anyone who claims that the archaic words should be replaced is claiming that they have **a better method of dealing with archaic words than God does!** Are **you** smarter than God?

We Bible-believers like to say, "We fundamentalists accept the authority of the Bible in all matters of faith and practice." I suggest we practice this method. Define what a word means if its definition has become cloudy through the changes in the English language. I am not advising "running to the Greek." I am advising "running to the dictionary" and letting the text stand as it reads without the derogatory remarks about "archaic" words and "out of date usage." Let us respect God's text more than that.

READ THE BOOK!

–

God has given us every word; we do well to accept them from Him as they are and not attempt to "improve" on them. As one great preacher said, "The Bible doesn't need to be re-written, it needs to be re-read." I concur. Born-again Christians are intended to be "Bible people." Are we not expected to read the Book we claim so loudly to believe?

Upon receiving a lengthy letter from home, does a lonely soldier proceed to the third page to begin his reading? After page 3 does he "speed read" page 4, skip page 5, and read half of page 6? Does he attempt to understand the last page and then proceed to the first? Ridiculous, isn't it? Yet it describes the Bible reading habits of many of God's people. Obviously, our soldier, so far away from the home he loves and the writer of his letter, is going to devour **every word** of this letter and upon finishing it, he will read it again-every word.

God sent us, His homesick soldiers, a "letter from home," yet we steadfastly refuse to read it. He didn't give us the **whole** Book just so that we could read the Psalms. We are expected to read Leviticus, Numbers, and Deuteronomy as well as John, Acts, and Romans. The same author who inspired 1 and 2 Corinthians placed every bit as much inspiration into 1 and 2 Chronicles. We are to read Malachi as well as Revelation. God has given us every word of the Bible. We are to start at the beginning and read every word! Upon reaching Revelation 22:21, we are not expected to quietly lay the Bible aside as if our work has been done. We are to begin afresh at Genesis 1:1. There are only two events that should stop a Christian from reading through his Bible continuously, cover to cover: **death** and **the Rapture**. All other "reasons" are really just weak excuses. We are to read the Book!

Many exclaim, "But I can't understand it! There are portions with deep and difficult meanings." These people find a difficult passage, give God approximately five minutes to deliver the answer, and then turn to a "better translation" or a Bible commentary if the answer isn't quick in coming. They are like the four-year-old child who wishes to drive a car. He sincerely wants to drive a car. His motive for wanting to drive may be pure. He believes that he can handle the job, and he wants the answer **now**. He will not only be refused permission to drive the car, but he as yet won't even be allowed on a bicycle. He cannot handle anything larger than a tricycle. As he matures, he will "graduate" to bigger and more complicated things.

This is true with our English Bible. We begin to read through it for the first time and ask God a question, the answer to which we just cannot handle until our fourth or fifth or thirtieth time through it. Just like the four-year-old child, we sincerely want the answer. Our motive may be pure. We believe that we can handle the answer, and we want it **now**. God will not show us on our first time through the Bible what He has ready for us on our tenth or eleventh time through. **We must grow up.** There are no shortcuts to maturity . A shelf full of Bible commentaries and other translations is an attempt at a shortcut, but it will not work. I am not opposed to Bible commentaries. I am opposed to their de-emphasizing the Bible and replacing the Holy Spirit. I am in favor of intensifying our reading time in the only authority we have, the Authorized Version!

It never fails to amaze me how willing we are to read books **about the Bible, but not the Bible** that those books are written about! Take this book for an example. I **want** it to be a help to you understand more clearly how God inspired and preserved His Book. But if you read **this book** but don't read **the Book** that it is written about, you have cheated yourself.

I strongly recommend everywhere I go that Christians read a Proverb that corresponds to the day's date **everyday** and a **minimum of ten pages of their Bible everyday.** Start reading at Genesis 1:1 and read straight through the Book to Revelation 22:21. When you finish, **go back and do it again.** You should read your Bible **everyday** till you die or the Lord comes back. And make sure that the Bible you read is a King James Authorized Version.

—

Why the Authorized Version? Who says we have to use only this particular translation? Why couldn't some other version be perfect in English instead of the Authorized Version?

To get answers to these questions, we will have to take our hands off each other's throats long enough to examine the evidence which has come down to us through history. First, let's study where the manuscripts come from.

Chapter 5

The Localities

THE manuscripts and their classifications and readings will be studied in later pages. What we shall do now is closely scrutinize the two primary centers from which our extant manuscripts have originated. It will be revealed by further study that biblical manuscripts are divided into two general groups. These two groups have been found to disagree with each other in many areas. Every English Bible in existence today will be found to proceed more or less from one of these two groups. The fact that there is one God plainly tells us that there can be only one correct reading concerning any given discrepancy between these two groups. We aim to identify which location for Bible manuscripts is to be trusted.

FAMILY FEUD

Obviously, before someone compares readings, it will be beneficial for him to investigate the ancient centers from which our two basic groups proceed.

Earlier, we established two "ground rules." It will be relevant to our study to review those rules at this point, and to keep them in mind as we continue.

Firstly, we established that, **The Bible is a spiritual book which God exerted supernatural force to conceive, and it is reasonable to assume that He could exert that same supernatural force to preserve it.**

Secondly, that, **Satan desires to be worshiped. He has the ability to counterfeit God's actions and definitely will be involved actively in attempting to destroy God's Word and/or our confidence in that Word while seeking to replace it with his own "versions."**

We must **never** forget the truths embodied in these two simple rules. No matter what we look at throughout the long history of the Bible, we will find that these two rules successfully define the battle that has been fought for the Bible.

As mentioned already, there are basically only two locations that Bible manuscripts originate from. The fact that a great many of the disagreements between these two families is centered around points of deity or doctrine tells us that one of them must be the preserved text, as found in the original manuscripts, while the other is a Satanic forgery. Satan attacked Jesus Christ (Mat. 4:1-11) and will try to replace Him with himself in the future (Rev. 13:1-8). This is no different than what he has been trying to do with Scripture for centuries.

Stop and think. Are we to believe that Satan, a sworn enemy of Truth, is not going to attempt to disrupt the travel of God's words through history? Would he dare let **the only tangible item** which God has left us remain free of his Satanic attacks? No! Satan cannot afford to allow the Holy Scriptures to pass through history unmolested. He will obviously be heard to be its loudest textual critic and will attempt to eliminate God's true Word while replacing it with his own Satanic counterfeit.

With this great truth in mind, we shall begin our investigation with a look at the original autographs and trace the history of how theses two families of manuscripts came into being. One must good and one must be bad.

THE BEGINNING

During His earthly ministry Jesus Christ worked through His followers. The New Testament was originally written by followers of Christ as they were inspired by God. Therefore it is only logical that He would look to His followers as being instrumental in the preservation of His words. By "followers" I mean those who had forsaken their own lives and taken up His cross and "followed" Him. These were the disciples of His day. They were also the early Church Fathers of the first few centuries whose lives were in jeopardy due to their resistance to Rome and their fervent desire to propagate the Gospel **personally.** It is certainly not a reference to an elite cadre of air conditioned "scholars" who wouldn't be found door-knocking to save their lives!

It must be understood that the New Testament was a paradox. It was completely foreign to anything that the world had ever known. Until the time of Christ, the world was biblically divided into two groups.

One group was the Jews. They were known as God's "chosen people." Their religious practices were founded on the teachings of the Law, the Prophets, and the Writings (thirty-nine books which comprise our present Old Testament). Guided by Scripture they lived lives that were different and separated from the Gentile world around them. In accordance with that Scripture, they awaited their Messiah, the ruler who was expected at any time to come to earth and set up a Jewish kingdom based in Jerusalem.

The other group spoken of in Scripture is the Gentile population of the world. The Gentiles are also referred to as a group in Scripture by the term "Greeks." They were very religious but heathenistic in practice. This is noted by the Apostle Paul. When in Athens he mentioned that the city was "wholly given to idolatry" (Acts 17:16). After seeing them carry out their religious duties, he concluded, *"I perceive that in all things ye are too superstitious"* (Acts 17:22). The Gentile world was caught up in the fantasies of Christless education, philosophy and religion not unlike the world in which we now live.

In addition to the pagan center of Athens, another location of pagan religious practices was Rome. In Rome were found temples built for the worship of many pagan gods and goddesses. A few of these were Jupiter, Apollo, and Minerva.

Still another pagan city known for its education and philosophy was Alexandria, Egypt. Famed for its library and school, it was a center of education during the centuries prior to the New Testament era. It was known to have received much of its philosophy from Athens about 100 BC. It was therefore thoroughly steeped in the philosophy of the pagans.

In those first few centuries after the Christian church appeared, made up of born-again believers, it was looked upon by the world around it as a rather strange group of people. The Jews rejected it because its patrons claimed that Jesus Christ was the Jewish Messiah. The Gentiles rejected Christianity because of the Christians' claims that salvation was complete and that one could know without a doubt that he had eternal life. This ran contrary to the teachings of pagan philosophy that nothing can be known for sure. Christianity also rejected the use of statues and images as "aids" to worship. This made the heathen religious practices of the Gentiles worthless, not to mention all of their beautiful temples.

The New Testament church needed its own unique geographical location to establish itself and grow. It needed a location that was far away from the prejudices of the Jewish religious community centered in Jerusalem and the Gentile philosophical communities. It needed a location that would be advantageous to the spreading of the Gospel.

Just such a location was realized when, after the death of Stephen in Acts chapter 7, the believers traveled to Phenice, Cyprus, and **Antioch** (Acts 11:19). All three of these were Gentile cities, but it was Antioch that the Holy Spirit had chosen for the base of Christian operations.

Antioch was founded by Seleucus I about 300 B.C. Its location was of prime importance to the Gospel since it was built at the crossroads of ancient trade routes from Mesopotamia to the Mediterranean and from western Arabia to Asia Minor. Although located inland of the Mediterranean Sea, it still boasted a great seaport on the Orontes River. History records that by the end of the first century there were over 100,000 Christians living in Antioch.

In addition to the secular history of these two areas, we need to examine what **the Bible** says concerning them. We Christians claim to accept **the Bible** as out **final authority** in **all matters** of faith and **practice.** Therefore, the information that the Bible gives us concerning the two sources of New testament manuscripts will be far more important than the opinion of any humans.

In examining the two prime sources of Bible manuscripts, the "Law of First Mention" is important. This law is an observation of the simple fact that the first mention of a subject in the Bible usually sets the light in which that subject shall reside in the Bible narrative. Sometimes it is negative. Sometimes it is positive. We will see what the Bible thinks of the two locations of Bible manuscripts.

EGYPT

Since one of the two families of manuscripts originated in Alexandria, Egypt, we shall first look at Egypt. We will look at the way Egypt is presented in the Bible.

1. The **first mention** of Egypt in the Bible is found in Genesis 12:10. *"...Abram went down into Egypt to sojourn there...,"* but verse 12 says, *"Therefore it shall come to pass, when the Egyptians shall see thee, that they shall say, This is his wife: and they will kill me, but they will save thee alive."*

So in the Bible's first mention of Egypt we immediately find a negative air about Egypt. Notice that Abram's fear concerns the line of Christ, Satan's first enemy.

2. *"And the Midianites sold him into Egypt unto Potiphar, an officer of Pharaoh's, and captain of the guard"* (Genesis 37:36). Here we find that Joseph was sold into slavery in Egypt. This also is negative.

3. *"Therefore they did set over them taskmasters to afflict them with their burdens. And they built for Pharaoh treasure cities, Pithom and Raamses"* (Exodus 1:11). In this verse we find Israel, the people of Abraham, Isaac, and Jacob, persecuted in Egypt, a type of the world. Jacob's descendants had become slaves in Egypt.

Verses 15 and 16 show that Pharaoh wanted all the male children born to the Jews killed. This was a Satanic attack which was once again directed at the seed through which the Lord Jesus Christ would come.

4. In Exodus 20:2, Egypt is called *"the house of bondage."* In Deuteronomy 4:20, God calls Egypt *"the iron furnace."* The outstanding fact here is that these are the very words of God as they were "breathed" by Him. This is not the "twisting" of Scripture done by some "King James fanatic" in an effort to prove a point. These two titles clearly display **God's** opinion of Egypt.

5. While Israel is in the wilderness after leaving Egypt yet before entering the Promised Land, God gives them instructions on how their future king should behave. In Deuteronomy 17:16 God forbad Israel to carry on commercial activities with Egypt. ***"But he shall not multiply horses to himself, nor cause the people to return to Egypt, to the end that he should multiply horses: forasmuch as the Lord hath said unto you, Ye shall henceforth return no more that way."*** Notice this final sentence gives the solemn warning, ***"Ye shall henceforth return no more that way."*** Think about it! If we shouldn't go to Egypt for a **horse**, should we go there for a **Bible?**

6. In Jeremiah 46:25 we find God promising punishment on Egypt. ***"The Lord of hosts, the God of Israel, saith; Behold, I will punish the multitude of No, and Pharaoh, and Egypt, with their gods, and their kings; even Pharaoh, and all them that trust in him:"*** Not hardly a "positive" outlook on Egypt.

7. Look at Ezekiel 20:7: ***"Then said I unto them, Cast ye away every man the abominations of his eyes, and defile not yourselves with the idols of Egypt: I am the Lord your God."*** Here we find that God commanded Israel not to be associated with Egypt's idolatry.

8. The last of our references compares Jerusalem in apostasy to Sodom and Egypt. During the Tribulation Moses and Elijah will be killed in Jerusalem. God wants Jerusalem to know how low His opinion is of that city when He says, ***"And their dead bodies shall lie in the street of the great city, which spiritually is called Sodom and Egypt, where also our Lord was crucified"*** (Rev. 11:8).

This is only a small cross section of the biblical references to Egypt, but I believe we see that **God's attitude towards Egypt is not positive.** We as Christians should do all we can to avoid any association with a location for which God has such disdain.

Now let's zero in on the city of Egypt which will concern our study, Alexandria.

ALEXANDRIA

The city of Alexandria, Egypt, is mentioned only four times in Scripture. We will examine all four and note the opinion of Scripture as being far more significant than the opinions of scholar, most of whom got their education from there.

1. The **first mention** of Alexandria is found in Acts 6:9. ***"Then there arose certain of the synagogue, which is called the synagogue of the Libertines, and Cyrenians, and Alexandrians, and of them of Cilicia and of Asia, disputing with Stephen.***

Here we find that Jews from Alexandria were partially responsible for the stoning of Stephen. Thus we see that the blood of the Church's first martyr was shed by people from Alexandria.

It must also be noted that this is the "First Mention" of Alexandria and must be noted for the fact that it is negative just as the "First Mention" of Egypt was.

2. Later, in Acts 18:24 we learn that Apollos was from Alexandria. ***"And a certain Jew named Apollos, born at Alexandria, an eloquent man, and mighty in the Scriptures, came to Ephesus."***

Here we find that an unsaved Jew from Alexandria named Apollos was fervent in spirit but was misinformed concerning the Gospel. Not knowing the true Gospel of salvation by faith through the death, burial and resurrection of Jesus Christ he went to Ephesus and preached instead the baptism of John the Baptist as the way to salvation, (Acts 18:25). In Acts 19:3 we find some of his "baptized believers" who were no more saved than he was. Apollos was not saved and neither were his converts.

Later in the passage we see that Apollos is intercepted by Aquila and Priscilla (verse 26) and led to Christ. How do we know he got saved? Look at the radical change in the message he preached. In Acts

18:25 Apollos is preaching "salvation" through the baptism of John. In Acts 18:26 he gets saved. And in Acts 18:28 we find that his message had changed from preaching John's baptism to "preaching Christ."

But we must take note that in its second mention we find that Alexandria is synonymous with **bad Bible teaching.**

3. The **third** and **fourth** mentions of Alexandria are very similar.

After Paul is arrested in Acts 21 and appeals his case to Caesar, he is sent to Rome, (and eventual death) on a ship from, of all places, **Alexandria** (Acts 27:6). *"And there the centurion found a ship of Alexandria sailing into Italy; and he put us therein."*

Someone might say that using this reference is stretching things to prove a point. That might be true if it were not for the **fourth** mention of Alexandria.

4. While sailing to Rome, Paul's ship is sunk by a tempest. After spending three months on the island of Melita (modern day Malta) he is sent on his way to eventual death on another ship. And where is this second ship from that is so ready to carry Paul to Rome and his death? Acts 28:11, *"And after three months we departed in a ship of Alexandria, which had wintered in the isle, whose sign was Castor and Pollux."*

We have now looked at what **the Bible** has to say concerning Egypt in general and Alexandria in particular.

Since we accept the Bible as our **final authority** in **all matters** of faith and **practice**, we should take care to remember that God takes a negative approach to Egypt and Alexandria. Do we have any right to ignore God's displeasure and approach Egypt or Alexandria in a "positive" manner? I can safely tell you, "No!" But there is an even stronger witness to the folly of turning to Egypt in spite of the biblical warnings we have seen

DANGERS OF IGNORING THE BIBLE'S WARNINGS

Solomon was by far wiser than we are, yet he ignored God's clear warnings in these matters. He paid a terrible price for his actions.

In Deuteronomy 17:16 we saw that Israel's future king was warned not to return to Egypt to buy horses. Yet in 1 Kings 10:28 we find that *"... **Solomon had horses brought out of Egypt, and linen yarn: the king's merchants received the linen yarn at a price."*** Solomon did this in direct disobedience to a plain Bible teaching.

Furthermore, we find in Deuteronomy 17:17 that Israel's future king was not supposed to multiply **silver** and **gold** to himself. But 1 Kings 10:27 tells us that, in spite of this admonition, Solomon *"...made silver to be in Jerusalem as stones...".* And if you will read the entire passage of 1 Kings 10:16-25 you will find that Solomon multiplied, *"...gold...gold...gold...".* How much *"gold"* did Solomon gather to himself in just one year's time? 1 Kings 10:14 tells us, *"...six hundred threescore and six talents of gold,".* That's **666** talents of gold in one year. (Any warning bells going off?)

But sadly that is far from the end of the matter. For Deuteronomy 17:17 also told this king not to *"multiply wives to himself"*. How did Solomon handle that little problem? We find the answer in 1 Kings 11.

1. *But king Solomon loved many strange women, together with the daughter of Pharaoh, women of the Moabites, Ammonites, Edomites, Zidonians, and Hittites;*
2. *Of the nations concerning which the LORD said unto the children of Israel, Ye shall not go in to them, neither shall they come in unto you: for surely they will turn away your heart after their gods: Solomon clave unto these in love.*
3. *And he had seven hundred wives, princesses, and three hundred concubines: and his wives turned away his heart.*

4. *For it came to pass, when Solomon was old, that his wives turned away his heart after other gods: and his heart was not perfect with the LORD his God, as was the heart of David his father.*

Solomon not only married Pharaoh's daughter (Now really! If you shouldn't go to Egypt for a **horse**, should you go to Egypt for a **wife?!**), but 999 other women. What was the result? Verse four says, *"his wives turned away his heart after other gods:"*. In fact, Solomon, the wisest man that ever lived, ended up sacrificing his own children to Moloch. **That's** how far you can go when you defy the clear teaching of Scripture. Now, do you want to go to Egypt for a Bible?

Certainly, if a man as wise as Solomon could fall by accepting Egypt in spite of God's clear condemnation, we would do well to take care before we buy any "horses out of Egypt." God may not be pleased with such actions.

It must also be noted here that Alexandria was a center of education and philosophy. (Col. 2:8) It received these terrible twins from Athens about 100 BC. (Acts 17:16). There was also a school of the Scriptures founded there by one Philo, who was an unsaved philosopher. Philo did not believe that the Bible was the inspired word of God. He interpreted Scripture both **philosophically** and **allegorically**. That is to say that philosophically he believed truth to be relative, not absolute. He did not believe that the Bible was infallible. By looking at the Bible allegorically he believed that men such as Adam, Noah, Moses, and David existed only in Jewish poetry and were not true historical characters. His writings were famous for being repetitious, rambling, artificially rhetorical, having little sense of form and for being completely devoid of humor...in other words **he was the perfect scholar!**

He was succeeded as head of the school by Clement of Alexandria and later by Origen - men who shared his skepticism. These men carried manuscript corruption to new heights - or new **depths**, depending on how you view biblical infallibility.

It was Origen, deceived by **the dual intoxicants of education and philosophy**, who upon receipt of pure copies of Scripture altered them to parallel his twisted thinking.

THE ALEXANDRIAN MENTALITY

Origen is the spiritual father of all Bible critics and is not only responsible for the physical manuscripts which delete such verses as Luke 24:40, Acts 8:37 and I John 5:7, but he is also responsible for the **Alexandrian mentality** parroted by so many of our fundamental scholars who claim that "The Bible is perfect and infallible" with one breath and then state, "The Bible has mistakes and mistranslations in it" with the very next. It is this demented ideology that gave birth to the corrupt Alexandrian manuscripts in the first place. Thus we see that not only are the physical manuscripts of Alexandria corrupt and to be rejected by true Bible-believers, but also the Alexandrian mentality. A mentality that believes the Bible has mistakes in it and must be corrected is even more subtle and dangerous and must also be forsaken by true Bible believers.

The **Alexandrian mentality** can be stated in one sentence. "The Bible **is not perfect** and **can be improved on.**" Any teacher, preacher or professor who makes the statement, "A better translation would be..." has the same Alexandrian mentality that these three Bible rejecters had. Beware! Remember Solomon!

It is to be noted that the five uncial manuscripts which today's scholars have used to supplant the Received Text of the Authorized Version all come from Alexandria. So here you have well over five thousand witnesses, the vast majority of which testify to the authenticity of the King James Bible, and just a **literal handful** of opposing witnesses and yet scholarship, deluded by their infatuation with Alexandria turns a blind eye to them and scurry to Egypt and bow their knees to an tiny gathering that God refuses to acknowledge.

SYRIA

We will now look at the first mention of Syria in the Bible, just as we did Egypt..

1. In Genesis chapter 24 Abraham (who is a type of God the Father) commissioned his servant Eliezer (who is a type of God the Holy Spirit) to go back to his kindred (v.4) to find a bride (a type of Christ's Gentile bride) for his son Isaac (who is a type of God the Son). And where does Isaac get his Gentile bride from? We are told in Genesis 25:20 that he got her from "Laban **the Syrian**." So we see that the **first mention** of Syria in Scripture is in a **positive context**.

2. But there is an **earlier inference** to Syria than this. When Abraham sends Eliezer to **his country** (Gen. 24:4) he is sending him to **Syria**. So in Genesis 12:1, when Abram is told by God to "Get thee out of **thy country**," He is referring to **Syria**. Therefore, Syria is inferred to for the first time (Gen. 12:1) **in the exact same chapter** that Egypt is mentioned its first time! (Gen. 12:10-12) One with a **positive connotation** and the other with a **negative connotation** and **both within ten verses of each other!**

Of course, the Bible critic will immediately try to play these appearances down as a mere "coincidence." Bible critics **claim** to believe in God and His Book. They just don't like to give Him any credit for the **super**natural things that are found in the arrangement of Scripture. And if it were not for what we find when studying Antioch in the Bible their feeble argument might have a chance of holding water. Unfortunately for them, their flimsy ship receives another torpedo below the waterline at the first mention of Antioch also.

ANTIOCH

Let us see what the Bible says about the city of Antioch.

1. The **first mention** of Antioch in Scripture is in Acts 6:5 when Nicolas, a Christian from Antioch, was chosen to be one of the first deacons. So we see here that the first time Antioch is mentioned in Scripture, it is in a **positive light.**

2. Antioch is mentioned again in Acts 11:19. Here it is a refuge for Christians fleeing from the persecution mentioned in Acts 8:1. In the Scripture Antioch represents a "type" of the new life given to believers after they have accepted Jesus Christ as their personal Saviour. It is a location disassociated with their old existence and blessed by God as a place where a new life can be founded.

To fully understand the light in which the Bible presents Antioch in Acts 11, we must look at the context in which chapter 11 is written. In the preceding chapter (Acts 10) God plainly shows that He is calling out a following from among the Gentiles. In the following chapter (Acts 12) God shows that He is not going to use Jerusalem as the center of the New Testament church (Acts 12:1-4). And in the chapter following that (Acts 13:1-4) He shows that He will look to Antioch for Christian soldiers to carry out the work that was neglected by those in Jerusalem.

OUR ANTIOCH

Antioch, the new center of God's dealing with mankind, is away from the Gentile centers of Alexandria, Athens, and Rome and the Jewish center of Jerusalem. Antioch symbolizes the Christian's new life, apart from the heathenism of the Gentiles' religions and the ritualism of Judaism. 2 Corinthians 5:17 says, *"Therefore if any man be in Christ, he is a new creature: old things are passed away; behold, all things are become new."* When a Gentile is saved, he is to leave his heathenistic lifestyle for a new spiritual location in Christ. Likewise, when a Jew is saved, he is to leave his ritualism for a new spiritual location in Christ. In Galatians 3:28 Paul states that *"There is neither Jew nor Greek...for ye are all one in Christ Jesus."* In 1 Corinthians

10:32 he divides mankind into three groups; *"Jews...Gentiles...the Church of God."* As God gives born-again man a new spiritual location, He also gave His new young Church a new physical location.

Please notice that after Acts chapter 12, the other apostles are left alone at Jerusalem and are mentioned only one last time in the narrative. This is in Acts 21:18, where they briefly rejoice in a report of Paul's ministry among the Gentiles **and then get preoccupied with the law!** In Galatians 2:11 Paul had to rebuke Peter of this very thing when he came to Antioch and tried to exercise the same legalistic teaching of Judaism on the New Testament Church there. Obviously God was using Antioch and Antiochan Christians to forge a new practice of worshiping Him, different from the Old Testament Judaism and the Gentile mythology and heathenism.

GOD'S MOVE

3. Acts 11:20 shows the beginning of God's settlement in Antioch. *"And some of them were men of Cyprus and Cyrene, which, when they were come to Antioch, spake unto the Grecians, preaching the Lord Jesus."* We see then that the **first time** that Gentiles got saved in **public preaching** was in Antioch. (Cornelius in Acts 10 got saved in **private** preaching in his home.)

4. In Acts 11:22 Barnabas, one of the most important figures of the New Testament, moves from Jerusalem to Antioch. He is the man who is responsible for Paul being in the ministry. It was Barnabas who went to Tarsus to get Paul (then named Saul) in Acts 11:25. Upon finding him, Barnabas brought him back to Antioch, not Jerusalem (Acts 11:26). So we see that the primary figure of the New Testament church actually began his ministry in Antioch. Paul had visited Jerusalem in Acts 9:26-29 and had even preached there, but his ministry to the Gentiles really began when he departed from Antioch in Acts 13:1-3 with Barnabas.

5. We must also notice that it was at Antioch that the disciples were called "Christians" for the first time (Acts 11:26). Thus, anyone who claims the name "Christian" is claiming a connection to the disciples at Antioch. What is amazing about this is that today we have men who call themselves "Christian" (Antioch) yet espouse an Alexandrian bible and/or mentality in dealing with the Bible. What a contradiction of terms! This is just like someone who claims to be an "American" who then burns the American flag!

6. In verse 27 of Acts 11 we find that the prophets from the Jerusalem church left it to settle in Antioch. If anybody knew where God was working, it would be a prophet.

7. In verse 29 of Acts 11, we even see that it was necessary for the Christians at Antioch to send relief down to their brethren in Jerusalem. This is because the Jerusalem church had never been faithful to the commission given the Apostles in Acts 1:8. God will leave a church that doesn't obey Him and **take His prophets with Him.** Thus, the forsaken church needed help from the church which was obedient to God's direction.

8. As we mentioned before, Paul's first missionary journey originated from Antioch in Acts 13:1-3. The Bible states in verse 2 that the Holy Ghost "called" them. It was in Antioch that God chose these men. Upon returning from their trip (Acts 14:26-28), they came back to Antioch, not Alexandria nor Jerusalem.

9. When some "Christian" Judaizers came up to Antioch from Jerusalem and began to teach the believers there that *"Except ye be circumcised after the manner of Moses, ye cannot be saved"* (Acts 15:1), Paul and Barnabas confronted them. Afterwards, Paul and Barnabas went down and spoke with the apostles concerning this. They formed a council and returned to their beloved Antioch with a written statement to the effect that Judaism had no hold over the New Testament church.

10. Upon returning to Antioch, Paul and Barnabas took with them chosen men of the Jerusalem church, Silas being one of them (Acts 15:22). Once they had accomplished their mission they all returned to Jerusalem but Silas (Acts 15:33,34), and he is the only one whom we find recorded in New Testament history. After Acts chapter 11 and the move to Antioch, God used only those who left Jerusalem and settled in Antioch! Such is the case with Paul, Barnabas, Silas, and Mark. Paul and Barnabas resided at Antioch (Acts 15:35) and departed from there again in verse 40.

Notice that Paul set his mind to go back to Jerusalem in Acts 20:22, knowing that it was against God's will, as we find in Acts 20:23 and 21:4, and again in 21:10-12. He went to Jerusalem in spite of God's warning against it and was seized in Acts 21:30, thus beginning the end of his ministry! This plainly teaches that a Christian is not to return to his "old" life in any way, shape, or form and should stand firm in his "new location" in Christ. It also shows that if there will be any center for New Testament Christianity, it will be found **in Antioch**.

It may well be that many of the "originals" that we have heard so much about were written right there in Antioch! We can be certain that they never came from Alexandria.

Alexandria was not the only location boasting a school of the Scriptures. In the second century, a disciple by the name of Lucian founded a school of the Scriptures at Antioch. Lucian was noted for his mistrust of pagan philosophy. Unlike Philo's school in Alexandria, Lucian's school **magnified the authority and divinity of Scripture** and taught that the Bible was to be taken **literally**, not figuratively as the philosophers of Alexandria taught.

So Antioch is not only the point of origin for the correct family of Bible manuscripts, but is also the source for the ideology that accepts the Bible as literally and perfectly God's words. Very simply stated the two opposing mentalities originating from Alexandria and Antioch are these:

The Alexandrian Mentality: "The Bible is **not perfect** and **can be improved on.**"

The Antiochan Mentality: "The Bible **is perfect** and **cannot be improved on.**"

Egypt is a type of this world, a type of the **old life**. Antioch is a type of a Christian's **new life** in Christ. Which one do you think that God would use to preserve His Word?

God will not do anything contrary to His nature. It would not be consistent with God's nature to use Alexandria, Egypt, to preserve His Word when He paints such a dismal picture of it in Scripture. In fact, there is no record of any of the New Testament Christians ever visiting there.

Antioch, on the other hand, was greatly used by God as the center of New Testament Christianity. Paul never took up residence in Jerusalem, but always returned to Antioch spiritually and practically. Therefore, Antioch would obviously be the logical location of the true Bible text.

Today many well meaning preachers, steeped in the **mentality of Alexandria** are uplifting the Antiochan Bible (King James) but with the Alexandrian conviction that it cannot be perfect. When you hear a preacher says, "A better rendering would be..." or "That word in the Greek means..." or "That word wasn't in the originals..." then you know you are listening to someone who, regardless of what he may **say** about believing the Bible, looks at the Bible in the same way that Philo did; It is **not perfect** and **can be improved on.** In fact, this Egyptian conviction states that there cannot be a perfect Bible on earth, in spite of God's promise in Psalm 12:6,7. Some Alexandrian "bibles" have even gone so far as to alter the words of Psalm 12:7 in an attempt to destroy this reference to God's promise to preserve His words!

To accept the proper Book with an improper attitude will only predestine one to make the same mistakes and corruptions that his Egyptian forefathers did.

Can anyone ignore a Bible admonition and not fall? As seen earlier, Solomon ignored the Bible's directives concerning Egypt and ended up sacrificing his children to Molech. (1 Kings 11:7) Do you think that you can ignore the Bible's directives concerning Egypt and do any better?

Chapter 6

The Witnesses

IT WOULD be extremely beneficial at this point if we could simply produce the original autographs for examination. This would greatly simplify the operation of establishing correctly the New Testament text. But this simply cannot be done. It has long been acknowledged by scholars that we no longer have the "originals." They have long since passed from the scene. This is due to the fact that scribes were known to have destroyed worn out manuscripts after they had copied them. Apparently the early church valued the words of the original more than the original itself. Therefore, the readings of the originals must be preserved with us somewhere, or else God's words have "passed away," which we surely know, from the scriptural record, cannot happen (Psa. 12:6,7 and Mat. 24:35). We must review the witnesses of the Bible record which have come to us across time. We will be required to keep two things in mind:

1. There is a marked disagreement between the two basic families of readings. These two families of manuscripts basically originate in either Alexandria, Egypt or Antioch, Syria. In the previous chapter we looked at the **biblical attitude** we should have concerning these two locations.

2. Due to the above truth, we must remember our spiritual considerations as well as historical. Remember, the Bible is like no other book. All other books are written and then cast adrift on the sea of time; this is not the case with the Bible. We must remember that God had His hand in its inception and will be seen to have His hand in its journey through history to the present day. It must also be remembered that just as God will be active in the preservation of the Bible, Satan will be active in attempting to disrupt or destroy it.

DEFINING THE TERMS

For all practical purposes there are only two Greek texts used today in Bible translation works. The first is the Textus Receptus which was used by the translators of our Authorized Version, the King James Bible. This is the authentic Bible text as preserved in Antioch, Syria, and was the text used almost exclusively (save for the Catholic Church's translations) for all English translations prior to 1881. The other text is much more recent and hails from Alexandria, Egypt. This text, in some form, is the basis for almost every modern translation since 1881. These two localities and their influence on the text of Scripture have already been examined in the previous chapter, so nothing more needs to be said here.

These two basic texts that we possess today are the product of the **"editors"** who have compiled a **"text"** from the available **"witnesses"** that were available to them. Each text then **testifies to their respective localities,** or Alexandrian. The witnesses used to compile these texts consist of **"manuscripts"**. For our study a simple definition of a manuscript is **"Anything that has some portion of Scripture written on it."**

The manuscripts do not necessarily consist exclusively of books of the Bible. Manuscripts also include **portions of sermons** with Scripture references in them, portions of Scripture from the back of hymnals (**lectionaries**), early **Bible commentaries** or other books

–

which quote some portion of Scripture or some other written source that reproduced some part of a biblical passage.

Furthermore, manuscripts can originate from any time period and in any number of writing styles. A manuscript witness can be several hundred years old or just a few years. Its text can be either hand **printed** or written in long hand (**cursives**). The words may be written in block capital letters (**majuscules**) or in lower case letters (**minuscules**). The term "manuscript" can apply to the very writings of one of the inspired authors (**"original autograph"**) or to a **copy** of an original autograph or, for that matter, to **a copy of a copy of a copy...** etc. Manuscripts are even extant in languages other than Greek. These translations are referred to as **"versions."**

Also, a manuscript that is a copy of a particular book of the Bible may consist of the entire book, a few chapters, just a few pages or possibly no more than a scrape of material with only a few words from a verse preserved on it (**fragment**).

The "hard" evidence at hand today which is available for our examination consists primarily of three groups. We will examine each of these groups more thoroughly and explain their importance in the forming of a text. Everything we are going to list will be extant as either a **manuscript** or a **fragment** of a manuscript.

I. THE COPIES

It has long been established - admitted if you please - that the originals are long gone never to be seen again. Since there are no originals, every record of Scripture will be a copy. Copies are produced in Greek and are further divided into four groups:

A. Minuscules - These are by far **the most numerous** of extant copies which we possess. Minuscules in Greek are like the **lower case**

letters of our alphabet and are **hand-printed** rather than written out in longhand as the cursives.

The oldest copies of this type are **papyrus** manuscripts, which is a reference to the material they are written on. Papyrus was made from the stalks of reeds. Sometimes these sheets were sewn together into a **scroll** or bound like a book form, which was called a **codex**. Papyrus was an inexpensive paper somewhat like newsprint.

Since writing materials were hard to obtain, early copies had their words printed end to end with no space in between. There were no capital letters to begin sentences and also little if any punctuation. Nor were there any chapter designations or verse markings to assist in finding a passage. Furthermore words like, "God", "Son", or "Father" were abbreviated in the following manner: God,-gd, Son,-sn, Father,-ftr.

Therefore, a particular verse that we know as **John 1:18** would appear like this:

"nomanhathseengdatanytimetheonlybegottensnwhichisinthebosomoft heftrhehathdeclaredhim"

In like manner, **Ephesians 2:8, 9** would appear:

"forbygraceareyesavedthroughfaithandthatnotofyourselvesitisthegift ofgdnotofworkslestanymanshouldboast"

(Aren'tyouthankfulthatGodgaveuschapterandversemarkingtoclearupt hismess?!)

Later manuscripts separated the words for ease of reading. Thus, John 1:18 would now look like this:

—

"no-man-hath-seen-gd-at-any-time-the-only-begotten-sn-which-is-in-
the-bosom-of-the-ftr-he-
hath-declared-him"

Ephesians 2:8, 9 would now appear as,

"for-by-grace-are-ye-saved-through-faith-and-not-of-yourselves-it-is-
the-gift-of-gd-not-of-works-lest-any-man-should-boast"

When some portion of a **papyrus** manuscript is found by archeologists it needs a name to identify it. Papyrus manuscripts are identified by a number preceded by the letter "p". Thus papyrus manuscripts would be referred to by such titles as: p31, p45, p66, p75 etc.

Other manuscripts in general are designated by numbers with letters preceding them

The Greek used to write most of these manuscripts is known as the **Koine** Greek. It was the **common language** used on the streets in daily life.

B. Majuscules or Uncials - These are equivalent to the upper case or capital letters of our alphabet. Majuscules are capital letters and tend to be very square in form. Uncials are similar to this except that they were formed with more rounded lines than the majuscules. For all practical purposes they are the same. Uncials were not used by "the man on the street" in writing but rather by the scholars of the day.

Most Uncial manuscripts were written on **vellum**. Vellum is made from young calf skins. This was used because of its durability, although it was more expensive than papyrus. The vellum of some of the earliest manuscripts is noted for being the thinnest and whitest in quality, while later manuscripts are recognizable by the thicker, courser vellum used at the time of their writing.[18] These vellum sheets could also be sewn together into a scroll or bound into a **codices** (plural).

If we review the sample verses referred to above if John 1:18 were written in uncial letters of our alphabet, it would appear in this manner:

"NOMANHATHSEENGDATANYTIMETHEONLYBEGOTTENS NWHICHISINTHEBOSOMOFTHEFTRHEWHICHISINTHEBOS OMOFTHEFTRHEHATHDECLAREDHIM."

Ephesians 2:8, 9 would read,

"FORBYGRACEAREYESAVEDTHROUGHFAITHANDTHATN OTOFYOURSELVESITISTHEGIFTOFGDNOTOFWORKSLEST ANYMANSHOULDBOAST"

Majuscules manuscripts did not appear until the 4th Century and are found in far fewer numbers than minuscules.

Uncial manuscripts also need names by which to be identified. They too are designated by a number which is usually preceded by a zero (01, 012, 0227). But a few are also designated by a single letter. Since they are written in capital letters, the names ascribed to them are simply that, capital letters. Thus we would refer to manuscript "A" or "B" or "C" or possibly a letter from the Hebrew or Greeks alphabets.

The Greek used to write Uncial manuscripts is known as **classical**. It was not a spoken language and **was not used by the common Greek-speaking people** in everyday life. It could be viewed as being similar to what we refer to today as "legaleze." A formal way of writing that no one used in public everyday life.

---

18 Frederick Henry Ambrose Scrivener, *A Plain Introduction to the Criticism of the New Testament*, (London, 1894), Vol. I, p. 23.

—

C. Cursives - These are usually later than minuscules and are written out in longhand rather than printed. The vast majority of manuscript witnesses are cursives. Cursives are also designated by numbers but the number is not preceded by a zero.

Thus we would refer to cursive witnesses as: *283*, or *350*, or *427.*

Some scholars claim that cursive writing did not enter popular usage until the ninth century. In this manner they quickly dismiss any cursive manuscript as being of late origin. But F. H. A. Scrivener corrects this fallacy:

> "Cursive letters were employed as early as the ninth or tenth century, and continued in use until the invention of printing superseded the humble labours of the scribe. But cursive writing existed before the Christian era: and it seems impossible to suppose that so very convenient a form of penmanship could have fallen into abeyance in ordinary life, although a few documents have come down to us to demonstrate the truth of this supposition."[19]

D. Lectionaries - These are equivalent to the "responsive readings" found in the back of today's hymnals. These readings came into existence due to the shortage of copies of Scripture. Lectionaries were used to put key passages of Scripture into the hands of the people. A pastor might not preach much out of 1 Chronicles but would commonly use passages from the Gospel of John. These passages would be reproduced in the lectionaries so the congregation would have the most commonly used Scripture texts available to them.

Passages that taught major Bible doctrines would likewise be placed in the lectionaries.

---

19 Ibid. Vol I., p.30.

In this way the congregation, though lacking personal copies of Scripture, would at least have access to the most commonly used passages through the lectionaries. In many cases these readings are very early, i.e., closer to the originals than some later copies of the Bible itself and are therefore an important **witness** to the authentic text of Scripture.

Each lectionary is defined by the letter "l" followed by a number. So we would see "l 72" or "l 171" or "l 738".

Let's just say that somebody 2000 years from now dug up an NASV and a King James Bible. They turn it to John, Chapter 1. In the King James it says, "In the beginning was the Word, and the Word was with God, and the Word was God."

In the NASV it says, "In the beginning was the word, and the word was a god."

Two scholars get to bumping heads on it trying to establish which reading was accurate. They looked for a witness, and they came across a songbook. They come to lectionary 1522, and say, "Look here. This is what the church was singing out of. Don't you think that would be right? This book says, 'In the beginning was the Word, and the Word was with God, and the Word was God.' This thing that says 'NASV' isn't very good."

In this way, lectionaries are valuable witnesses of the text.

2. THE VERSIONS

Our second group of biblical witnesses is the **ancient versions**. God chose to write the New Testament in Greek, but He did not choose to keep it in Greek only. Those early Greek manuscripts were translated into many other languages in order that the true Word of God could be put into the hands of people in other lands. Some versions such as the

Peshitto (or Peschito), a Syrian translation, and the Old Latin Vulgate (vulgate means "vulgar," i.e., "common") are actually older than our oldest uncial manuscripts. The Peshitto was translated from the Greek in about 150 A.D. The Old Latin Vulgate was translated about 157 A.D. Therefore, the testimony of these ancient versions would be very important in verifying the authenticity of a questioned reading.

Other well known versions are the Gothic, Sahidic, Bohairic, and Coptic.

The versions are most often identified by a simple abbreviation of the name of the language in which they are written. Therefore, the "old Latin" (which is known to scholars as the "Italic") is referred to as "it." Jerome's "Vulgate" will be identified by "vg." The numerous "Syrian" translations are all identified by the letters "sy" with the addition of a suffix in superscript to further identify which Syrian it is. Thus the Peshitto Syrian would appear as "sy^p" while the less reliable Siniatic Syrian would appear as "sy^s."

3. THE CHURCH FATHERS

Our third body of witnesses consists of the writings of the **early church fathers**. These are the men who led the Christians in the first few centuries after the New Testament was completed. We have written remnants of their early sermons, books, and commentaries. Obviously, the notes of a church father writing in the second century would carry greater weight than a later copy of Scripture. These writings will be able to provide us with much information on disputed passages. Many early church fathers may have seen and handled the original autographs themselves.

Here we now have our three sources of information or witnesses that will testify to the authentic text of Scripture. They are copies, versions, and church fathers. These three groups combine to give us in excess of 5,250 witnesses.[20] Over 3,000 of these are Greek manuscripts.[21] With this many extant copies, versions, and the fathers for reference, we should have little trouble determining the Greek text of the original New Testament autographs.[22]

The writings of the church fathers are usually identified by an abbreviation of their popular name. Therefore, we will find John **Chr**ysostom reduced simply to "Chr". **Or**igin, in turn, becomes "Or."

What if we were disputing a verse? Let's say 1 John, Chapter 5, Verse 7. Someone says, "Okay, I have a fourth-century Greek manuscript that does not have 1 John, Chapter 5, Verse 7 in it; therefore, when I make my Greek text I'm not going to put it in it."

Then someone roots around and finds somebody's sermon notes. He finds one of the early church preachers in, let's say, 150 AD preaching a sermon on the Trinity out of 1 John, Chapter 5, Verse 7. Do you see where a man's sermon notes just became more authoritative than one of the General Epistles that we have?

We know that 1 John 5:7 isn't found in the fourth-century manuscript, "Vaticanus," that everybody likes so much. On the authority of that, it has been removed from many modern translations. But there's this little thing called *"Tatian's Diateserian."* This was a harmony of the four Gospels written in 150 AD. While dealing with

---

20 Hills, Edward, *The King James Version Defended* (The Christian Research Press, Des Moines, 1956), p. 115.

21 Fuller, David, *Which Bible?*, (Grand Rapids International Publications, Grand Rapids, 1970, First Edition), p. 10.

22 Over the years, through a multitude of sources, I have arrived at the following numbers for most of the extant witnesses. Although each source varies, the approximate numbers I have are, Uncials, 210; Cursives, 2400; Lectionaries, 1678; Papyrus, 92; Peshitta (Syrian), 350; Old Latin, 50; Gothic, 6; Coptic, 5; Bohairic, 80; Old Syrian, 2; and Jerome's Latin Vulgate, 8000. Again, these figures may differ in other sources, but this is a relatively accurate accounting of the existing witnesses.

the Gospel of John, he refers back to 1 John 5:7, thus proving that the existence of 1 John 5:7 **predates** the unreliable Vaticanus.

There's *Tatian's Diateserian*, right in there with all those other Greek manuscripts.

There was also the problem of heresy. Do you realize that before your Bible was even finished being written there were already people spreading heresy and causing problems for the Apostles? Paul mentions this in the book of Philippians and John affirms it in 3 John, verses 9 and 10. There was already trouble way back in the first century. So there were heresies, and those heresies would have to be disputed.

Now if you want somebody to go out and dispute a heretic, you want somebody who knows what he's talking about. That's why the church fathers went out and did that. There were cases when they went out and debated heretics. Some of those debates with heretics were written down. In writing down such a debate, and quoting a verse used in that debate, they may verify in a second century AD manuscript a verse that might not be found in a manuscript that was written in fourth century AD.

In order to reassemble the original text, a man has to take all of the Greek manuscripts for the Gospels, Acts, the Pauline Epistles, the General Epistles, and Revelation and all of the versions, like the Latin, and Syrian, into consideration. Then he has to add the testimonies of the church fathers and the lectionaries to that as well. He has to examine all of these witnesses thoroughly.

THE TEXT: PROBLEMS WITH TRANSMISSION

The journey of Scripture from the inception of the **original autographs** to the pulpit of our churches today has not been all "smooth sailing." There were numerous obstacles that had to negotiated through the centuries. Some were blatant attempts to taint the text while others were merely the natural logistical problem inherit in bringing the text across the centuries intact. If it had not been for the **supernatural intervention** of God (Psalm 12:7), we can be certain that we would not have a Bible to hold in our hands today.

Believe it or not, one of the first things that had to be decided was **the canon of Scripture**. You see, there were many people who took it upon themselves to write down the events of the life and ministry of Jesus Christ. Some of these writers were trying to record the happening of the day as best they could but were simply not inspired of God in their work as the New Testament writers were. These books are called **"extra-canonical"** because they were written **in addition** to those that God inspired.

Others writers were not so sincere. They fraudulently presented their works as though written by one of the apostles or an early church father. These books are called **"pseudepigrapha"** or **"spurious writings,"** because they are were known by the church to falsely claim authorship by someone other than the actual author.

To sort this all out the church fathers (**not the Roman Catholic Church!**) met in the third century to define what was and was not accepted as authentic Scripture. This eliminated such books as, *The Gospel of Peter* and *The Epistle of Barnabus* and verified the authenticity of *The General Epistle of James* and *The Third Epistle of John*.

Thus, within a few hundred years of the death and resurrection of Jesus Christ the **canon** of Scripture had been identified.

Now the holy books continued their perilous journey through time. As the original autographs passed off the scene, they were replaced by copies. In fact, most of the original autographs were intentional destroyed after they had become so worn out as to be

–

difficult to read so as to protect the text from corruption by mistakes in copying. You see, the early church put a premium on **the words** of God and placed no special value on the material on which it was written as most of today's misguided scholars do.

Furthermore, as mentioned earlier, these manuscripts began to be translated into other languages, such as Latin and Syrian. The Old Latin (**not** Jerome's corrupt "Vulgate") swept across Europe and was the heart of the New Testament church there while the ancient Peshitto (Syrian) was used by the church throughout Asia.

About this time there arose horrendous persecution faced by the church, which brought great death and destruction. Many copies of Scripture were destroyed by such demoniac devices. Rome was the leader in wholesale slaughter of God's people. But the faithful Christians continued to copy and translate Scripture faster than it could be destroyed, leaving multitudes of witnesses to undeniably testify of the text of the holy writings.

As the Roman Church increased its political power, it scattered true Bible Christianity to the winds as Europe was overshadowed by the Dark Ages from 475 to 1000 AD. Around 1280 new rounds of persecution were felt by the church at the hands of this same "Holy" Roman Catholic Church.

But a new dawn was breaking. As the sixteenth century dawned, God was preparing to sweep Europe with what would be known throughout history as **the Reformation**. But before He could do that, He first had to reassemble His holy text from the ravages of Rome. The text would have to be identified and separated from the text of Rome that was contaminated by Alexandrian philosophy. He would have to re-establish His text before it could be used to spark the Reformation. This would require **an editor** to review the available witnesses and define the pure text of Scripture.

THE EDITOR: DEFINING THE TEXT

Consider for a few moments, the immense undertaking it is to attempt to compile the sometimes contradictory testimony of thousands of witnesses in order to reassemble the true New Testament text. Imagine trying to put together a huge puzzle. In this case you are working not only with the pieces of several puzzles that have been added to the mix but you also must contend with the existence of innumerable copies of the same correct picture. So here you are with pieces whose shape, size and color closely match the authentic pieces, as well as hundreds of the same original pieces. But most confusing of all is the fact that you have no exact picture of what the puzzle should look like when you are finished.

You have a few factors working in your favor. You know that the original picture had been reproduced hundreds of times. Therefore, you can authenticate a piece by seeing how many copies you have of it. You also have the ability to discern where each piece was produced. Since you know where the authentic picture was made (Antioch), you can discount pieces that originated somewhere else. Also, you have a knowledge of what **would** be in the picture (the deity of Christ, the blood atonement, the virgin birth, etc.) and what **would not** be in it (prayers for the dead, false doctrine, etc.).

This is a simplistic example but it will help acquaint you the complexities of the task. With this in mind, we will examine the job of the editor of the text.

Let's go back five centuries. You're now in the 1500's. Obviously, you don't have a King James Bible. What you have is a vast sea of witnesses, some reliable, some not, from which you wish to deduce the true text of Scripture.

The first thing you need to do is divide the witnesses according to their own individual texts. The extant witness are grouped into certain portions of the New Testament, one being **the Gospels**. These

—

four books are referred to as **"the Evangelists"**. If you deal with any of these manuscripts, they'll be designated by a, **"e."** All "e" manuscripts contain only a text from the four gospels. It may be a copy of one entire gospel or just a few lines from a chapter or two. These witnesses will help you identify the correct gospel text but will be useless in defining the text of other portions of Scripture.

Following the gospels you have the book of **Acts**. Any manuscript that contains some portion of Acts will be abbreviated by an **"a."** Of course, these will be no help in discerning the true text of the gospels, the book of Romans, or any other book in Scripture.

Following Acts you have **the Pauline Epistles**. So scholars use a **"p"** to designate manuscripts which contain text of the Pauline Epistles.

Next you have a **"c"** for **"the Catholic Epistles."** As you know, the word "catholic" simply means "universal." It has nothing to do with the Roman Catholic Church. Rome stole the name later. We sometimes refer the catholic epistles as the General Epistles.

Lastly you have **Revelation**. These manuscripts will be designated by the letter **"r."**

You have to understand that the scribe who copied out Revelation may never have had anything to do with the copies of the Gospels or other portions of Scripture. Therefore, you're going to have different writing forms, different styles and such things.

These letter designations **are not names** for the manuscripts but rather simply define what books will be found in their text.

In order to secure the original test of Scripture an editor will need to examine all of the witnesses and establish which are reliable and which have been tainted. Obviously, the easiest thing to do would be to simply collate them and be done with it. But the job is not as simple as that.

An example of how the collating process would work follows.

Before beginning his task, the editor would assemble all of the extant witnesses that he could obtain. He would then carefully compare their readings and establish which ones possess a reliable text. Then he would slowly reestablish the text. But there would undoubtedly be problem passages to deal with. The authenticity of some portion of Scripture would be disputed, so he would have to study the **oldest readings** (which would **not** necessarily be found in the oldest manuscripts) to confirm or deny the authenticity of a disputed passage.

As stated earlier, some of these are from the fourth century, some are from fifth century, some from the sixth century, some from the ninth century and so on. I'm not talking about just four individual manuscripts: there are hundreds of them that represent just the gospels alone. Hundreds more testify to the text of Acts. You may have a manuscript whose text contains solely that of the gospels and Acts. Another may have just the General Epistles and Revelation.

When you purchase a modern copy of a Greek text, such as Nestle's *Novum Testamentum-Graece,* you will find a small card included with it that gives the number designation that identifies each existing manuscript, along with a note telling you which books of the Bible are contained in each and also what century it was written in. So when you look up manuscript "E," you will see that it contains only the text of Acts. You would see that "D" is the Evangelists, Acts, and the Pauline Epistles. Here's "W," it's just the Evangelists. Here's "X," it's just the Evangelists.

The papyri are also identified by text and date of origin. Examining the card will show you such information as "p1" has just the Evangelists, "p10" which is just the Pauline Epistles. We find that "p45" has the Evangelists and Acts. That's how each manuscript is designated.

So, to reassemble the text the editor has to get all those Greek manuscripts together and combine their texts. But wait! There are going to be a few problems in attempting this. The problems are that the texts from one manuscript may read differently than that of another even though they may be a copy of the same book and even from the same century.

Let's take the Gospel of Mark for an example. Our editor will look at chapter 1 and verse 2, where it says, *"As it is written in **the prophets.**"* Yet in a different manuscript he will find it saying, *"As it is written in **Isaiah the prophet.**"* Now he has two entirely different readings for the same verse. What will he do? He will simply look in his Bible and see that the quotations found in Mark 1:2, 3 are from Isaiah 40 and Malachi 3. Therefore, the reference to *"the prophets"* is correct and the reference to *"Isaiah the prophet"* is wrong.

So we see that your King James Bible **is right** when it says, *"As it is written in **the prophets.**"* The modern translations are wrong when they read, *"As it is written in **Isaiah the prophet.**"* The editor has protected the text from error and defined what the original really said.

What the editor is doing is putting together his own text. He's going to consolidate all of the over 5,000 witnesses into one volume. When he's finished he will have "a text."

Now he comes to another disputed passage. He arrives at Acts 8:37. So he looks at what all of the witnesses have to say about it. Do the most reliable manuscripts contain or omit it? By carefully examining the witnesses, he finds that the **most reliable** manuscripts **contain** the verse. So he includes it in his text. Thus, we find that a "bible" that omits Acts 8:37 is based on manuscripts inferior to those used for our King James Bible.

It must be remembered that there are some other witnesses to the text aside from just the Greek. Some of the other witnesses are versions. There are some Syrian versions. There are old Latin versions. There are old Coptic, Bohairic, Armenian, Ethiopic and Georgian versions, written in many languages other than Greek but just as reliable as the Greek witnesses.

There may be something in the old Latin that gives us some light on the Gospels. We have something over here, some Ethiopic, that answers some of our questions about the General Epistles. One particular version may be older than some of the Greek witnesses.

Your witnesses break down into copies, and they're in Greek. Then you have "versions," and they're in assorted languages. One of the dishonest things that our modern scholarship will try to do is say, "Well, since these are versions, they can't have the authority of an original copy, because a version is just a translation and doesn't carry as much authority as a witness written in the same language as the originals." That sounds logical until you observe **the actions** of scholars rather than merely accepting their **words**. What puts the lie to that statement is the fact that they will all run to what's called the "LXX" or the Septuagint as a legitimate authority. Yet this so-called Septuagint is supposed to be **a translation** of the Old Testament from Hebrew into Greek. If the Septuagint really did exist, then by the scholars' own rule it would be rejected as authoritative because it is "just a translation."

Our editor will also want to consult the Scripture readings found in the lectionaries. The lectionaries contain readings from all through the Bible. You can see where a lectionary covers almost all of our major doctrines. They'll cover the deity of Christ, they'll cover the virgin birth, they'll cover the atoning death of Christ, they'll cover the resurrection, they'll cover the second coming, they'll cover the sinfulness of man. You'll find out that a lectionary covers most of our basic Bible doctrines so that you could teach and preach basic Bible doctrines to people who did not have a Bible.

—

Furthermore, our editor will want to examine the works of the church fathers. If you couldn't find a Bible 2000 years ago but you came across somebody's Bible commentary, you could find the text of that particular book reproduced in it.

Now our editor comes to Luke 24:51, which reads: "*And it came to pass, while he blessed them, he was parted from them,* **and carried up into heaven.**" Those last words, "**and carried up into heaven**," are not found in the New American Standard Version. They have been removed from the text.

In 1898 an editor by the name of Eberhard Nestle published his first Greek text. That text has now gone through 27 editions, each one changed from the previous one in some way. The NASV is an English translation of the 23rd edition of Nestle's Greek Text. The New International Version is a translation of the 26th edition. The 23rd edition of Nestle's *Novum Testamentum - Graece* removed the words "and carried up into heaven" because Nestle relied on inferior Greek manuscripts when producing his text. Therefore, the NASV, which used this flawed Greek text incorrectly omitted the phrase.

Our editor examines Luke 24:51 in all of the available witnesses. He wants to know which manuscripts omit the words and which preserve the words in their text. As a result of his examination he discovers that the words "and carried up into heaven" are **in** the following witnesses: B, C, E, F, G, H, L, S, T, V, Y, Z, Delta, Theta, Psi, Omega and papyrus manuscript p75 and in all of the remaining witnesses that contain Luke 24:51.[23] Ironically, B and p75 are manuscripts that will quite often read contrary to the King James Bible. When they do, scholars like to use them as authorities to alter the King James text. Yet here where they read **with** the King James Bible, they are ignored.

---

23 This information is expanded from the footnotes in the critical apparatus of the 25th edition of Nestle's *Novum Testamentum - Graece*.

What's the manuscript evidence **against** the King James reading? Only Siniaticus, D, 52 and a 5th century manuscript.

It doesn't take long for our editor to realize that he words "and carried up into heaven" **are authentic** and belong in the text.

It is through such a slow, painstaking process that an editor reviews the extant witnesses and then establishes what the original text said. That is what an editor has to do. He has to go through piles of manuscript fragments, plus unroll scrolls, and folio books to examine. He has to reduce that to one single text. When he is finished, he compiles his entire New Testament text and publishes it for the world to use in translating Scripture.

ERASMUS: THE GREATEST OF EDITORS

We have seen what an imaginary editor would go through in the process of examining the extant witnesses and defining the original text. Now we'll study how we got our Textus Receptus, the Greek text that is closest to the original and is the basis from which the King James Bible was translated. When I say that the editor assembled it, you now know what he had to go through to identify it.

The man responsible the Textus Receptus was Desiderius Erasmus (1466 - 1536). He may well be called "the Original Editor." Erasmus was a genius. He was without argument the most learned man of the sixteenth century.

Erasmus was born in Rotterdam in 1466 and died in 1536 at the age of seventy. This is an amazingly long life for someone who lived through the age of the great plagues of Europe. He was the son of a Roman Catholic priest. Both of his parents died from the plague while Erasmus was just a lad. He had a brother and the two boys were placed in the care of an uncle after the death of their parents. The uncle did not want the boys and promptly sent them off to a monastery just to be rid

—

of them. Thus Erasmus' destiny was sealed long before he could ever have a say in the matter.

Destined against his will to be a Roman Catholic priest, Erasmus chose to become an Augustinian on the sole attribute that they were known to have the finest of libraries available in Europe. This was where he could feed his insatiable desire for knowledge.

His behavior was somewhat bizarre by Augustinian standards. He refused to keep vigils, never hesitated to eat meat on Fridays, and (though ordained) chose never to function as a priest. The Roman Church had captured his body, but quite apparently his mind and heart were still unfettered.

He is known to history as one of the most prolific writers of all times and all of Europe hung on his words.

Erasmus was a constant and verbal opponent of the many excesses of his church. He berated the papacy, the priesthood and the monks for their over-indulgences. He stated that the monks would not touch money, but that they were not so scrupulous concerning wine and women. He constantly attacked clerical concubinage and the cruelty with which the Roman Catholic Church dealt with so-called "heretics." He is even credited with saving a man from the Inquisition.

One of his many writings consisted of a tract entitled "Against the Barbarians," which was directed against the overt wickedness of the Roman Catholic Church.

He was a constant critic of pope Julius and the papal monarchy. He often compared the crusade-leading pope Julius to Julius Caesar. He is quoted as saying, "How truly is Julius playing the part of Julius!" He also stated, "This monarchy of the Roman pontiff is the pest of Christendom." He advised the church to "get rid of the Roman See." When a scathing satire in which pope Julius was portrayed as going to Hell, written in anonymity, was circulated, it was fairly common knowledge that its author was Erasmus. Thus, it is plain to see that only a dishonest person would attempt to portray Erasmus as a "good" Catholic.

The pope attempted to bribe Erasmus into silence by offering him a bishopric. The wealth and power of such a position in mediaeval Europe is unimaginable today. Erasmus rejected the bribe flat and continued his attacks undeterred.

The Europe in which Erasmus was raised was vastly different than the one we know today. It was a rigidly classed society. The common people were peasants and served the upper levels of society. Many men entered the priesthood because it afforded them a luxurious lifestyle in spite of their "vow of poverty" and gave them great power over the commoners.

Erasmus was an opponent of this system. He was called a Humanist because he sought to elevate the lowly position of the common man. The term "Humanist" did not carry the same meaning that it does today, when it describes one who exalts man's achievement as opposed to God. This is no different than the change that has taken place in the biblical term "Liberal." A careful reading of Proverbs 11:25, Isaiah 32:5-8 and 2 Corinthians 9:13 will reveal that the term "liberal" in Bible days was a positive title. But it has been stolen and used to describe those who wish to tax, control and oppress the common people of today. These are the very same people Erasmus fought against in his desire to set the common people free.

The only Bible available to Catholic Europe was possessed and controlled by the Roman Catholic Church. This was, of course, a warmed-over edition of the corrupt Alexandrian text. The true text of Scripture had been ravaged by years of persecution by that same Catholic Church. Erasmus sought to correct this deficiency and provide the **common people** with a copy of the true text of Scripture. Erasmus is quoted as saying, "Do you think that the Scriptures are fit only for the perfumed?" He also stated, "I venture to think that anyone who reads

—

my translation at home will profit thereby." He boldly stated that he longed to see the Bible in the hands of "the farmer, the tailor, the traveler and the Turk." Later, to the astonishment of his upper classed colleagues, he added, "the masons, the prostitutes and the pimps" to that declaration. Thus he began a project that he could never know would touch the lives of you and me almost five centuries later!

Before beginning his work, Erasmus collected all the available witnesses to the text. Then, just as our imaginary editor did, he carefully examined them to determine which were reliable and which were to be rejected as tainted.

Erasmus completed his work and published his Greek text in 1516. He later refined this and a second edition was published in 1519.

His first two editions did not contain I John 5:7, although the reading had been found in many non-Greek texts dating back as early as 150 AD. Erasmus desired to include the verse but knew the conflict that would rage if he did so without at least one Greek manuscript for authority. Following the publication of his second edition, which like his first consisted of both the Greek New Testament and his own Latin translation, he said that he would include I John 5:7 in his next edition if just one Greek manuscript could be found which contained it. Two were found and presented to him, so he included the verse in his third edition of 1522. Opponents of the reading today errantly charge that the two manuscripts found had been specially produced just to oblige Erasmus' request, but this charge has never been validated and was not held at the time of Erasmus' work.

He later published a fourth edition in 1527 and his fifth and final edition in 1535, a year before his death.

So steadfast was his stand against the corruptions of the Roman Catholic Church that he even refused to incorporate the official Latin text of Scripture, Jerome's "Vulgate," into his work. Instead, he placed his own Latin translation beside his rendition of the Greek. The Roman

Catholic Church criticized his works for his refusal to use Jerome's Latin translation, but Erasmus was unmoved. He claimed that Jerome's Latin inaccurate. He disagreed with it in two vital areas.

1. He detected that the Greek text Jerome used for his translation had been corrupted as early as the fourth century. He knew that Jerome's translation had been based solely on the Alexandrian manuscript Vaticanus, written itself early in the fourth century. Because Jerome used the corrupted text of Alexandria, Egypt, Erasmus knew that it too was unreliable (just like today's modern translations based on this same corrupted text.)

2. He also differed with Jerome on the translation of certain passages which were vital to the claimed authority of the Roman Catholic Church.

Jerome rendered Matthew 4:17 thus: "Do penance, for the kingdom of Heaven is at hand."

Erasmus saw that this translation added authority to the Roman Catholic practice of confession and instead rendered the verse: "Be penitent for the kingdom of heaven is at hand."

Erasmus was also a staunch defender of both Mark 16:9-21 and John 8:1-12 with a zeal which our modern-day scholars cannot seem to find.

With the publication of Erasmus' Greek text, Europeans now had access to the true text of Scripture. It didn't take long to have a **major** effect on the events of the day. Martin Luther welcomed it with open arms and used in to translate his German Bible. This is the Bible that God used to spark the anti-Catholic Reformation in Europe.

After his death Erasmus' text was revised by men like Robert Stephanus (four editions) and Theodore Beza (ten editions). It was

Beza's fifth edition that was to be the basis for our English King James Bible.

Erasmus' text was so accepted that it was used by the Elzevir brothers in their two editions of the Greek New Testament, published in 1624 and 1633. In the preface of the 1633 edition they wrote, "You have, therefore, the **text** now **received** by all, in which we give nothing changed or corrupt." From 1633 on this text became known as the "Received Text" (or "Textus Receptus" in Latin) and that name has stuck ever since.

Erasmus' Greek text and personal writings were devastating to the totalitarian Catholic Church. He was so hated by his "church" that in 1559, twenty-three years after his death, pope Paul IV put his writings on the "Index" of books forbidden to be read by Roman Catholics!

TAKING SIDES

The surviving manuscript witnesses to the Greek New Testament text which we now possess are found to generally fall into two groups, or "texts." The **vast majority** of manuscripts agree with the Textus Receptus upon which our King James Bible is founded. This is the true text from Antioch which we studied in the previous chapter.

A small group of manuscripts which have proved to be unreliable originate from Alexandria, Egypt and are the general basis for all modern translations.

Some scholars have tried to define a third classification which is called the "Western" family. But most of these manuscripts fit well into one of the two families already mentioned. Therefore, we will dismiss then so-called Western family and deal with the two predominant text families.

This is where we begin to find some major problems. We find that these two texts disagree consistently concerning the major doctrines and minor points of truth. They are found to disagree on readings concerning the virgin birth of Jesus Christ, the blood atonement, Christ's second coming, the deity of Christ, and many other fundamental Christian doctrines. In fact, the alterations are so obviously hostile to the Bible's fundamental doctrines that it cannot be argued that such changes were either innocent or accidental. It is for this reason that we must examine our witnesses to determine if their testimony is accurate (God's text) or if they are fraudulently misleading (Satan's text). Remember our Ground Rules!

THE GOOD GUYS

The first of these two texts which we will examine is the **Majority Text**. This is basically another name for the Textus Receptus which we have just studied. This is the text which will be found to uphold those major Christian doctrines which are so vital to our fundamental beliefs. It is called the Majority Text because it is the text found in the overwhelming majority of extant manuscripts.

The Majority Text has been known throughout history by several names. It has been known as the Antiochan Text, the Byzantine Text, the Imperial Text, the Traditional Text, and the Reformation Text, as well as the Majority Text, to name a few. This text culminates in the Textus Receptus or "Received Text" which is the basis for the King James Bible, which we know also as the Authorized Version.

I do not desire to add one more name to the list, but in the interest of finding the most accurate term to describe this text, and due to its **universal** reception by orthodox Christians throughout history, we shall refer to this text as the "**Universal Text**."

Dr. Edward F. Hills justifies this choice when he states:

"There is now greater reason than ever to believe that the Byzantine Text, which is found in the **vast majority** of the Greek New Testament manuscripts and which was used well nigh **universally** throughout the Greek Church for many centuries, is a faithful reproduction of the original New Testament and is the divinely appointed standard by which all New Testament manuscripts and all divergent readings must be judged."[24] (Emphasis mine.)

We designate this text with the term "universal" because it represents the text found in the majority of extant manuscripts and was used **universally** by the early church. These manuscripts represent the original autographs. Professor Hodges of Dallas Theological Seminary explains,

"The manuscript tradition of an ancient book will, under any but the most exceptional conditions, multiply in a reasonably regular fashion with the result that the copies nearest the autograph will normally have the largest number of descendants."[25]

Even Hort was forced to admit this, as Professor Hodges points out in his footnote,

"This truism was long ago conceded (somewhat grudgingly) by Hort. A theoretical presumption indeed remains that a majority of extant documents is more likely to represent a majority of ancestral documents at each state of transmission than vice versa."[26]

---

24 Fuller, David, *Which Bible?*, (Grand Rapids International Publications, Grand Rapids, 1970, First Edition), pp. 51, 52.

25 Ibid., p. 21.

26 Ibid., p. 21.

Professor Hodges then concludes,

"Thus the Majority text, upon which the King James Version is based, **has in reality the strongest claim possible to be regarded as an authentic representation of the original text**. This claim is quite independent of any shifting consensus of scholarly judgment about its readings and is based on the objective reality of its dominance in the transmissional history of the New Testament text."[27] (Emphasis mine)

What these men are saying is simply that any corruption to the New Testament text would obviously have to begin some time **after** the original autographs were completed, or there would be no originals to corrupt! If the originals and the first corruptions of those originals multiplied at the same rate, **the correct text would always be found in the majority of manuscripts**. Add to this the fact that the orthodox Christian Church would reject the corrupted manuscripts and refuse to copy them, and we would find that the correct text would be in the vast majority of manuscripts, universally accepted as authentic, while the corrupt text would be represented by an elite minority. These are exactly the circumstances which exist in the manuscript evidence available today! Fuller records, "Miller has shown that the Traditional Text predominated in the writings of the Church Fathers in every age from the very first."[28]

The Universal Text traveled north from Jerusalem to Antioch, the "Gateway to Europe" It is quite likely that some of the original manuscripts were even written in Antioch. From there it was translated

---

27 Ibid., p. 21.

28 Fuller, David, *True or False?*, (Grand Rapids International Publications, Grand Rapids, 1973), p. 264.

–

into numerous other languages, such as Syrian[29] and Latin, and crossed into Europe. This text then crossed the English channel. Upon arrival in England it was ready for translation into the language through which God has chosen to spread His Gospel to the entire world...**English**.

THE "ORIGINAL" VULGATE

The true text of Scripture from Antioch was translated into Latin in the second century and spread throughout Europe, rapidly becoming the standard Bibles of European Christianity. It was used by the Christians in the churches of the Waldenses, Gauls, Celts, Albigenses, and countless other early fundamental groups throughout Europe. This Latin version became so used and beloved by orthodox Christianity and was in such common use by the common people that it assumed the term "Vulgate" as a name. Vulgate comes from the word "vulgar" which is the Latin word for "common." The Old Latin Vulgate was the **common Bible** of the Christians in Europe.

The Roman Catholic Church, desperate to replace the true word of God with a copy of its own making, had Jerome translate the corrupt Egyptian text into Latin in 380 AD. Then in a vain attempt at fooling Bible Christians into believing it was the true Word of God they dishonestly named it "The Vulgate" or "common" bible.

But these zealous Christians were not the fools that it was hoped they would be. They so esteemed the "Original" Vulgate for its faithfulness to the deity of Christ and its accurate reproductions of the originals, that these early Christians let Jerome's Roman Catholic translation "sit on the shelf" for almost **eight hundred years!** Jerome's translation was not used by the true biblical Christians for almost a millennium after it was translated from corrupt Alexandrian

---

29 There are still 350 copies of the Syrian Peshitto in existence today as a testimony to this widespread usage in the years since 150 A.D.

manuscripts by Jerome in 380 AD. Even then it only came into usage due to the death of Latin as a common language, and the violent, wicked persecutions waged against true believers by pope Gregory IX during his reign of terror from 1227 to 1242 AD.[30]

CROOKED TACTICS

The Old Latin Vulgate had come into existence no later than 157 A.D. The Latin version of Jerome, translated by order of the Roman Catholic Church, was published in about 380 AD. It was rejected by real Christians until approximately 1280 A.D. The Roman Catholic Church used the tactic of choosing the name "Vulgate" or "Common" for Jerome's translation in an attempt to deceive loyal Christians into thinking that it was the true common Bible of the people. This is the same tactic used today by the New Scofield Reference Bible (1967) and the Common Bible (1973). The former claims to be an Authorized King James Version, when in fact it is not (check the margin). The latter's name falsely implies that it is the Bible in "common" use, when in fact the Bible in common use is the Authorized Version of 1611! It would seem that such deception lacks a little in Christian ethics, if not honesty.

It is plain to see that the Universal Text has not only been universally accepted by the faithful Christians down through the centuries, but it was also responsible for keeping the Roman Catholic Church contained to southern Italy for centuries. It was not until the Roman Catholic Church successfully eliminated this Book through persecutions, torture, Bible burnings, and outright murder that it could capture Europe in its web of superstitious paganism.

Perhaps we should learn a lesson. Where the Universal Text of the King James Bible reigns, God blesses. Once it is eliminated for a

30 Wilkenson, Benjamin, *Our Authorized Bible Vindicated* (Takoma Park, 1930), p. 28.

less "clean" text, God withdraws His blessing. Oh, that America could but look at what has happened to England since the corrupt Revised Version was published! That perversion has been the father of every "revision" since, on either side of the Atlantic. Yes, the sun began to set on the British Empire in 1904, when the British Foreign Bible Society changed from the pure Textus Receptus to the Egyptian text collated by Eberhard Nestle.[31]

Today, the Old Latin Vulgate (as opposed to Jerome's corruption) and the Syrian Peshitto still stand as faithful witnesses to the true text of Scripture being far more reliable than Greek manuscripts of a greater age from Alexandria, Egypt, such as Vaticanus and Siniaticus.

THE BAD GUYS

The other text which we must investigate is the Minority Text. This is the text which is found to be **untrue** to the beloved doctrines of Scripture, such as the virgin birth, the deity of Christ, the blood atonement, the Trinity, and others. This is also the text which has been used for almost every translation of the Bible since the Revised Version of 1881.

There are two outstanding trademarks of this text throughout history. the first is that orthodox Christianity has **never** used it or even recognized it as authoritative. The second is that the Roman Catholic Church has militantly (read that "bloodily") supported it. Strangely and embarrassingly, so-called "Christian" scholars laud this error-ridden text as superior to the Universal Text. We shall say more about this matter later.

---

31 Nestle, Eberhard, *Novum Testamentum -Graece* (Gesamthersellung Biblia-Druck, Stuttgart, 1898), p. 60.

The Minority Text is also known as the Egyptian Text (remember our study of Egypt), the Hesychian Text, and the Alexandrian Text (remember our study of Alexandria), which was the basis for the critical Greek Text of Brooke Foss Westcott and Fenton John Anthony Hort. The Westcott and Hort Text of 1881 was collated with Weymouth's third edition and Tischendorf's eighth edition by Eberhard Nestle in 1898 to become what is known as the Nestle's Greek New Testament.[32] This text has, through twenty-seven editions, been the text used in all "modern" translations. In the early 1970's Nestle's 25th Edition was combined with the 3rd Edition of the United Bible Society's Greek New Testament to create the 26th Edition of Nestle's *Novum Testamentum-Graece*. This 26th reintroduced more than 250 Textus Receptus readings back into the its text. This has since been edited yet again to produce the **27th** Edition. (Do I hear 28th ...28th? Going once! Going Twice! Sold to the man with the most money!)

Ironically, there are **no changes in the text** from the 26th to the 27th editions. Then why produce another edition if you aren't changing the text? Simple. The Majority Text manuscript evidence was weakened by removal of references to witnesses that uphold it. In the Introduction to the 27th edition, its primary editor Dr. Kurt Aland he shamelessly admits this when he declares, "Several uncial fragments are *no longer cited*. For the most part these comprise only small portions of text and are related to the Majority text,".[33] (Emphasis his)

He further admits, "Also omitted are...fragments whose witness in the passage selected for the apparatus of this edition ...coincides with

---

32 Ibid., pp. 59, 60.

33 Nestle, Eberhard, *Novum Testamentum -Graece* (Gesamthersellung Biblia-Druck, Stuttgart. 1993), p. 46*.

—

the Koine text..." and "Finally, the Koine minuscules 28 (in Mk, Lk and Jn) and 1010 are no longer cited consistently.[34]

WITNESS FROM EGYPT

The most notable manuscripts in the Egyptian text consist of a handful of uncial manuscripts of the 4th and 5th centuries. These uncials have been found to be error-ridden and untrustworthy and found not to agree even among themselves.

One of these manuscripts is called Sinaiticus and is represented by the first letter of the Hebrew alphabet, Aleph. This manuscript from all outward appearances looks very beautiful. It is written in book form (codex) on vellum. It contains 147 ½ leaves. The pages are 15" by 13 1/2" with four columns of 48 lines per page. It contains many spurious books such as the "Shepherd of Hermas," the "Epistle of Barnabas," and even the "Didache."[35] Due to exile in the Sinai desert and the fact that no Christian would use it, this manuscript has survived time well, but being in good physical shape by no means makes its contents trustworthy.

The great Greek scholar Dr. Scrivener points this out in his historic work *A Full Collation of the Codex Sinaiticus*. He speaks concerning correctional alterations made to the manuscript:

> "The Codex is covered with such alterations...brought in by at least ten different revisors, some of them systematically spread over every page, others occasional or limited to separated

---

34 Ibid, p. 47*.

35 Ruckman, Peter, *Manuscript Evidence* (Pensacola Bible Press, Pensacola, 1970), pp. 72, 73.

portions of the manuscript, many of these being contemporaneous with the first writer, but for the greater part belonging to the sixth or seventh century."[36]

Dr. Alfred Martin echoes this, "Aleph shows the works of ten different correctors down through the centuries."[37]

The corrections are so obvious as to induce Dr. John Burgon to question therefore Dr. Tischendorf's willingness to exalt this badly marred manuscript: "With the blindness proverbially ascribed to parental love, Tischendorf follows Aleph, though the carelessness that reigns over that manuscript is visible to all who examine it."[38]

May I note here that Dr. Tischendorf was the discoverer of Codex Sinaiticus. He found it in St. Catharine's Monastery in the Sinai desert in February 1859. It was, of all places, in the wastebasket.[39] Why? Because everyone there knew it was of no value!

Scrivener further remarks on Aleph's poor quality with, "From the number of *omoioteleuta* ('similar loosenesses') and other errors, one cannot affirm that it is very carefully written."[40]

---

36 Fuller, David, *True or False?* (Grand Rapids International Publications, Grand Rapids, 1973), pp. 74,75.

37 Fuller, David, *Which Bible?* (Grand Rapids International Publications, Grand Rapids, 1971, Second Edition), p. 272.

38 Ibid., First Edition, p. 61.

39 Burgon, John, *The Revision Revised*, (Conservative Classics, Paradise, 1883), pp. 243, 244.

40 Scrivener, Frederick Henry Ambrose, *A Plain Introduction to the Criticism of the New Testament*, (London, 1894), Vol. I, p. 93.

In fact, Dr. Scrivener further informs us that there is a claim that this so called "ancient" manuscript was actually written in the **nineteenth century!**

> "...Constantine Simonides, a Greek of Syme, who had just edited a few papyrus fragments of the New Testament alleged to have been written in the first century of the Christian era, suddenly astonished the learned world in 1862 by claiming to be himself the scribe who had penned this manuscript in the monastery of Panteleemon on Mount Alto, as recently as in the years 1839 and 1840."[41]

This revelation certainly dismantles the "oldest is best" argument. In fact, scholarship is **forced** to give no more credence to this claim than the myopic evolutionists who realize the injury their religious faith in evolution will receive if they ever investigate the **outboard engine** found in strata claimed to be **millions of years old!**

Since this manuscript had supposedly been written in the fourth century, Tischendorf, deceived by the outmoded philosophy that "older is best," immediately altered the 7th edition of his Greek New Testament in over 3,500 places. He had claimed that this 7th edition (1856-59) had been **perfect** and **could not be superseded**. His 8th edition (1865-72), based primarily on Aleph, was apparently 3,500 times more perfect!

FALSE WITNESS FROM ROME

Another manuscript belonging to minority family is called Vaticanus. It is often referred to by the letter "B." As its name implies, it is in the Vatican library at Rome (remember our enemy). No one knows when it was placed in the Vatican library, but its existence was

41 Ibid., p. 95.

first made known in 1841. This manuscript is also in the form of a book and written on vellum. It contains 759 pages each 10" by 10 1/2" with three columns of 41 lines per page.

This codex omits many portions of Scripture vital to Christian doctrine. Vaticanus omits Genesis 1:1 through Genesis 46:28; Psalms 106 through 138; Matthew 16:2,3; Romans 16:24; the Pauline Pastoral Epistles; Revelation; and everything in Hebrews after 9:14.[42] Sounds like a reliable witness wouldn't you say?!

It seems suspicious indeed that a manuscript possessed by the Roman Catholic Church omits the portion of the book of Hebrews which exposes the "mass" as totally useless. (Please read Hebrews 10:10-12.) The "mass" and the false doctrine of "Purgatory" go hand-in-hand to form a perpetual money making machine for Rome. Without one or the other, the Roman Catholic Church would go broke!

Vaticanus also omits portions of Scripture telling of the creation (Genesis), the prophetic details of the crucifixion (Psalms 22), and, of course, the portion which prophesies of the destruction of Babylon (Rome), the great whore of Revelation Chapter 17.

Vaticanus, though attractive physically, is found to be of very poor literary quality. Dr. Martin declares, "'B' exhibits numerous places where the scribe has written the same word or phrase twice in succession."[43]

---

42 Ruckman, Peter, *Christian's Handbook on Manuscript Evidence* (Pensacola Bible Press, Pensacola, 1964), p. 70.

43 Fuller, David, *Which Bible?* (Grand Rapids International Publications, Grand Rapids, 1971, Second Edition), p. 272.

–

Dr. J. Smythe states, "From one end to the other, the whole manuscript has been traveled over by the pen of some...scribe of about the tenth century."[44]

So we see that Vaticanus has been corrected, altered, and corrupted throughout its entirety. It is of the poorest quality. If it ever could have been considered a trustworthy text originally, the mass of corrections and scribal changes obviously render its testimony highly suspicious and questionable. It is **not a reliable witness** of the true text of Scripture and can safely be rejected by anyone seeking to reproduce that text.

The corrupt and unreliable nature of these two manuscripts is best summed up by one who thoroughly examined them, John W. Burgon:

> "The impurity of the text exhibited by these codices is not a question of opinion but fact....In the Gospels alone, Codex B (Vatican) leaves out words or whole clauses no less than 1,491 times. It bears traces of careless transcriptions on every page. Codex Sinaiticus abounds with errors of the eye and pen to an extent not indeed unparalleled, but happily rather unusual in documents of first-rate importance. On many occasions 10, 20, 30, 40 words are dropped through very carelessness. Letters and words, even whole sentences, are frequently written twice over, or begun and immediately cancelled; while that gross blunder whereby a clause is omitted because it happens to end in the same words as the clause preceding, occurs no less than 115 times in the New Testament."[45]

---

44 Smythe, Paterson, *How We Got Our Bible,* (James and Pott Co., New York), p. 22.

45 Fuller, David, *True or False?,* (Grand Rapids International Publications, Grand Rapids, 1973), p. 77.

Frederick Scrivener catalogs the multitude of omitted words and clauses in Vaticanus as follows; 330 omission in Matthew, 365 from Mark, 439 from Luke, 357 from John, 384 from Acts and 681 from the Epistles.[46]

If we are to be thorough and discriminatory in our evaluation of the true New Testament text, then we must not , **we cannot**, overlook these facts.

How did these manuscripts come into being? How did it happen that they should be beautiful to the eye, yet within contain such vile and devastating corruptions? It seems that these uncial manuscripts along with the papyrus manuscripts included in this category all resulted from a revision of the true or Universal Text. This revision was enacted in Egypt (remember our study of Egypt) by Egyptian scribes!

Prior to documenting this statement, we will need to identify several of the uncial and papyrus manuscripts which will be referred to in the documentation. These are uncial manuscripts A, B, C, D, and Aleph. Also included are the Chester Beatty Papyri (designated as p45, p46, p47) and the Bodmer Papyri (designated as p66 and p75).

THE LOCAL MESS

It seems that the text type found in these manuscripts was a local text peculiar to Alexandria, Egypt (remember our study of Alexandria), of which Eusebius made fifty copies to fulfill a request by Emperor Constantine. Unfortunately, Eusebius turned to the education center in Egypt and got a "scholarly revision" instead of turning to Antioch for the pure text which was universally accepted by the true Christians.

---

46 Scrivener, Frederick Henry Ambrose, *A Plain Introduction to the Criticism of the New Testament*, (London, 1894), Vol. I, p. 120.

—

Why would Eusebius choose Alexandria over Antioch? Primarily because he was a great admirer of Origen, an Egyptian scholar. Origen, though once exalted by modern-day Christianity as a trustworthy authority, has since been found to have been a heretic who interpreted the Bible in the light of Greek philosophy. He propagated the heresy that Jesus Christ was a "created" God.[47] This is a false doctrine propagated by the Jehovah's Witnesses of our day, who strangely enough get their teaching from the corrupt Alexandrian Text's rendition of John 1:1-5 and John 3:13 a corruption which Origen is responsible for due to his altering of the Universal Text to read in agreement with his personal heresy!

These are not prejudicial statements made in an effort to vilify a good man. All we need to do is listen to Origen himself when he said, "The Scriptures are of little use to those who understand them as they are written."[48]

This explains Bishop Marsh's statement,

> "Whenever therefore grammatical interpretation produced a sense which in Origen's opinion was irrational or impossible, in other words was irrational or impossible according to the philosophy which Origen had learned at Alexandria, he then departs from the literal."[49]

---

47 *New Standard Encyclopedia,* (Standard Educational Corporation, 1977), Volume O, p. 154

48 Fuller, David, *Which Bible?* (Grand Rapids International Publications, Grand Rapids, 1970, First Edition), p. 103.

49 Ibid., p. 71.

Dr. Adam Clarke claims also that Origen was the first person to introduce the false teaching of the existence of "Purgatory."[50]

TOTAL CORRUPTION

Where did this "Local Text," from which all new Bible translations since 1881 are rendered, originate? Let us see what evidence scholars have unearthed in a their effort to discover its source.

Kurt Aland: "proposes that the text of P75 and B represent a revision of a **local text** of Egypt which was enforced as the dominant text in that particular ecclesiastical province."[51] (Emphasis mine)

Professor Hodges assures us,

"Already scholars are willing to concede a common ancestry for p75 and B. We can postulate here that this common ancestor and p66 meet even further back in the stream of transmission...It is quite possible, then, that all three manuscripts go back ultimately to a single parent manuscript in which this amendation was originally made."[52]

Dean Burgon remarks,

"As for the origin of these two curiosities, it can perforce only be divined from their contents, that they exhibit fabricated texts is demonstrable. No amount of honest copying--preserved for any number of centuries--could by possibility have resulted in two such documents. Separated from one another in actual

---

50 Ibid., p. 130.

51 Ibid., p. 13.

52 Ibid., pp. 14,15.

—

date by 50, perhaps by 100 years, they must needs have branched all from a common corrupt ancestor, and straightway become exposed to fresh depraving influence."[53]

Dr. Edward Hills concludes,

"The best way to explain this situation is to suppose that it represents an intentional neglect of the Traditional Text on the part of those ancient Alexandrian scribes who kept revising the text of Papyrus 75 until finally they created the B text."[54]

He also states Aland's opinion: "Aland thinks it possible that the Chester Beatty Papyri also came from this same place."[55]

That meticulous lawyer and former Supreme Court Justice, Philip Mauro, has aptly determined,

"It should be observed, before we proceed with this question, that the agreeing testimony (where they do agree) of the Vatican and Sinaitic manuscripts cannot be properly regarded as having the force of two independent witnesses; for there are sufficient evidences both internal and external to warrant the conclusion that these two Codices are very closely related, that they are, in fact, copies of the same original, itself a very corrupt transcript of the New Testament."[56]

---

53 Burgon, John, *The Revision Revised* (Conservative Classics, Paradise, 1883), p. 318.

54 Hills, Edward, *Believing Bible Study* (The Christian Research Press, Des Moines, 1967), p. 166.

55 Ibid., p. 48.

56 Fuller, David, *True or False?* (Grand Rapids International Publications, Grand Rapids, 1973), p. 82.

He also states,

> "It is admitted on all hands that the Text used as the basis of the Authorized Version correctly represents a Text known to have been widely (if not everywhere) in use as early as the second century (for the Peschito and Old Latin Versions, corroborated by patristic quotations afford ample proof of that). On the other hand, it is now known that the two Codices we are discussing represent anything but copies of a bad original, made worse in the copying."[57]

It also seems generally agreed that this Local Text was used for a basis of the fifty Bibles which Eusebius supplied to Constantine.

The noted Greek scholar A. T. Robertson states,

> "Constantine himself ordered fifty Greek Bibles from Eusebius, Bishop of Caesarea, for the Churches of Constantinople. It is quite possible that Aleph and B are two of these fifty, though the actual copying was probably done in Egypt or by Egyptian scribes."[58]

Gregory adds,

> "This manuscript (Vaticanus) is supposed, as we have seen, to have come from the same place as the Sinaitic Manuscript. I have said that these two show connections with each other and that they would suit very well as a pair of the

---

57 Ibid., p. 88.

58 Clarke, Donald, *Bible Version Manual* (B.T.M. Publications, Millersburg, 1975), p. 37.

fifty manuscripts written at Caesarea for Constantine the Great."[59]

To which Burgon and Miller testify, "Constantine applied to Eusebius for fifty handsome copies, amongst which it is not impossible that the manuscripts B and Aleph were to be actually found."[60]

Dr. David Fuller finalizes,

"Age alone cannot prove that a manuscript is correct. B and Aleph probably owe their preservation to the fact that they were written on vellum, whereas most other documents of that period were written on papyrus. Many students, including Tischendorf and Hort, have thought them to be two of the fifty copies which Eusebius had prepared under the order of Constantine for use in the churches of Constantinople. They are no doubt beautiful manuscripts, but their texts show scribal carelessness. B exhibits numerous places where the scribe has written the same word or phrases twice in succession. Aleph shows the marks of ten different correctors down through the centuries. Burgon's excoriation of Westcott and Hort's method cannot be considered too strong in the light of the facts concerning the character of these two manuscripts."[61]

Who could be responsible for the corruption of the universally accepted text of the New Testament?

Wilkenson reports,

---

59 Ibid., p. 37.

60 Ibid., p. 37.

61 Fuller, David, *Which Bible?,* (Grand Rapids International Publications, Grand Rapids, 1971, Second Edition), p. 272.

"Beginning shortly after the death of the apostle John, four names stand out in prominence whose teaching contributed both to the victorious heresy and to the final issuing of manuscripts of a corrupt New Testament. These names are: 1. Justin Martyr; 2. Tatian; 3. Clement of Alexandria; and 4. Origen."[62]

The local Alexandrian text fell into disuse about 500 AD while the original Universal Text was spreading true Christianity throughout Europe.

Hoskier reports this in his statement,

"Those who accept the Westcott and Hort text are basing their accusations of untruth as to the Gospellists upon an Egyptian revision current 200 to 450 A.D. and abandoned between 500 to 1881, merely revised in our day and stamped as genuine."[63]

So we see that once a pure copy of the Universal Text had been carried down into Egypt, it was recopied. During the process of this recopying, it was revised by men who **did not** revere it as truly the Word of God. This text was examined by the critical eye of Greek philosophy and Egyptian morals. These men saw nothing wrong with putting the Book in subjection to their opinion instead of their opinion being in subjection to the Book. This process produced a text which was local to the educational center of Alexandria, Egypt. This text went no farther than southern Italy, where the Roman Church found its unstable character perfect for overthrowing the true Word of God, which was being used universally by the true Christians.

---

62 Wilkenson, Benjamin, *Our Authorized Bible Vindicated*, (Takoma, 1930), p. 16.

63 Fuller, David, *Which Bible?*, (Grand Rapids International Publications, Grand Rapids, 1970, First Edition), p. 74.

–

At this point, I believe it will be helpful to study the ruthless Roman Catholic Church to more clearly understand her part in all new translations of the Bible since 1881.

Chapter 7

The Enemy

"It is necessary to salvation that every man should submit to the Pope" (Boniface VIII, Unum Sanctum, 1303).

"For by grace are ye saved through faith; and that not of yourselves: it is the gift of God: Not of works, lest any man should boast" (Ephesians 2:8,9).

HERE lie two totally contradictory statements. They cannot **both** be correct. The one which you accept will depend on which authority you believe. If you believe the Roman Catholic pope to be infallible, then the first is for you. If you accept only the Bible as your final authority, then you can't help but thank God for the second. Which of these two statements you accept will also determine where you will spend your eternity following death. Therefore, we see that the stand you take on which of these statements you accept as correct is **the most important decision you will ever make!**

The Roman Catholic Church has long been antagonistic to the doctrine of salvation by grace. Her opposition is easy to understand. For if salvation is by grace, then who needs "mass"? If salvation is by grace, who needs to fear "Purgatory"? If Jesus Christ is the sole (and **soul**) mediator between us and God, who needs the Roman Catholic pope? The Catholic teaching that salvation comes only through submission to their pope gives the Roman Catholic Church tremendous leverage over entire nations as well as individuals. If their pope cannot

intimidate individuals into obeying him, how can he force a nation to
obey him? And without that, the power of the Roman Catholic Church
evaporates!

God's true Bible is the arch-enemy of the Roman Catholic
Church, because it teaches that salvation is through faith in the **finished
work** of Jesus Christ alone. This frees the common man from the
oppression of the Roman Catholic Church or **any religion** that tries to
claim it has control over who goes to Heaven and who doesn't. Rome
can only rule over an ignorant, fear-filled people. The true Bible turns
"unlearned and ignorant" men into gospel preachers and casts out "all
fear." Again, the threat that the perfect Bible poses to the Roman
Catholic system is obvious. For this reason, Rome must find some way
to supplant God's true Gospel with her false gospel, "another gospel,"
as Paul put it in Galatians 1:6-9. The only way to do this is to eliminate
man's faith in the Word of God.

To do this, Rome gladly accepted the corrupted Local Text of
Alexandria, Egypt, and further revised it to suit her own needs. Some
scholars call this revision the "Western" text. This, of course, makes it
part of the already corrupted text, and it therefore still contains the
Local Text readings. This text suited the Roman Catholic Church well,
since it attacked the doctrines of the Bible.

Rome is wise. To attack salvation by grace directly would
expose her plot to all. So instead she used subtlety. The Roman
Catholic Church does not mind at all that the Local Text strips Jesus
Christ of His deity, separating the Divine titles "Lord" and "Christ"
from His human name "Jesus." Therefore we find that Luke 23:42
refers to "Jesus" instead of "Lord" in modern versions. The Local Text
also removes the testimony to Christ's deity and the salvation by faith
of the Ethiopian eunuch in Acts 8:37, positions that the Roman Catholic
Church has no problem with. Furthermore, it eliminates the Trinity in
1 John 5:7. Remember, the Roman Catholic Church's desire is that
"Mary must increase. Jesus must decrease."

You may ask, "Would not a weakening of the position of Jesus Christ weaken the Roman Catholic Church's reason for even existing?" The answer is "No." The Roman Catholic Church does not even claim to represent the gospel of Jesus Christ. Romanist Karl Adam admits this when he arrogantly states: "We Catholics acknowledge readily, without any shame--nay with pride--that Catholicism cannot be identified simply and wholly with primitive Christianity, nor even with the Gospel of Christ."[64] Therefore, Roman Catholicism cannot be considered a biblical religion. It stands separate from the Bible, Jesus Christ and His Gospel.

The watering down of Jesus' divine position in Scripture suits the Roman Catholic Church's plans well. The vacancy left by the diminishing of Christ's exalted position would be easily filled by Mary and other "saints," along with a chain of ritualism so rigid that no practitioner would have time to really "think" about the true Gospel. Instead, he would trust in ritualism and superstition. This, the Roman Catholic "Plan of Salvation," is actually **damnation in disguise.**

INVASION!

During the first three centuries the true Gospel was fast spreading all over Europe. This was enhanced by the existence of the Old Latin translation of the Universal Text of Antioch into the "vulgar" or "common" language. This Bible became known as the "Vulgate" since it was used so commonly all over Europe. It was loved by European Christians and jealously guarded by them.

Having the common people possess a copy of the word of God in their common language was a great obstacle to Roman Catholic supremacy in Europe (and anywhere for that matter.) In hopes of overthrowing the Old Latin Vulgate, Rome enlisted the help of a loyal

---

64 Karl, Adam, The Spirit of Catholicism, (MacMillan, New York, 1928), p. 2.

subject by the name of Jerome. Around 380 AD, at the bidding of his church, he quickly translated the corrupt Local Text of Alexandria into Latin. This version included the Apocryphal books, fourteen books which no Bible-believing Christian accepts as authentic. To insure its success over the Old Latin, the Roman Catholic Church gave it the name "Vulgate," meaning "common," even though this was an obvious misnomer since **no Bible** can be called "common" when it is in fact new and cannot be found **commonly** in the hands of the people. But Jerome's attempt to replace the Old Latin Vulgate foundered on the shores of true Christianity. There was one problem which the Roman Catholic Church had not anticipated, the same problem which the businessmen publishing new versions today cannot seem to avoid. The common people recognized the true Word of God because the Holy Spirit bore witness to it! They refused to accept Rome's counterfeit just as they still do today in rejecting other versions!

It is true that many versions have been sold in the past and are being sold now. Yet this is primarily due to the media "blitz" with which **every** new bible has been introduced since 1881. Every new bible is introduced as "easier to read," "more accurate," or "truer to the originals." Christian bookstores then push the new version on anyone looking to purchase a new Bible. Many bookstores have even reduced the number of King James Bibles that they stock just so they can force a customer to accept an inferior version rather than wait for an ordered King James to arrive.

This is very similar to the tactic used by Satan in Genesis chapter 3. Notice his first recorded words. Do you believe that Satan just walked up to Eve and asked, "Yea, hath God said?" No! In Genesis 3:1 we are picking up in the middle of a conversation, possibly one of many. Satan paved the way for his attack on God's Word by a little "softening up" publicity. Christians today do not realize that they "need a better translation" until they are told so a few times by the Bible salesman. Suddenly, they "realize their need" for a translation which is "closer to the originals" and "easier to understand." (Most of these Christians have never even read the Bible they have.)

After getting Eve to doubt **God's version** of the Truth, Satan offered his own with the assurance that it would make her and her husband "more godly."

An unsuspecting Christian enters a Bible bookstore to buy a King James Bible and is immediately assailed by the salesman for desiring such an "archaic" version. He is then shown all the "benefits" of some new translation. Ignorant of the truth and innocently trusting the salesman he chooses one of those suggested to him. The next thing he knows he has eaten the forbidden fruit and God's blessing is gone from his life. To get God's blessing back, obviously, he needs the next "thoroughly reliable" translation.

This is not an overstatement. An example of the "Bible business" is revealed by Dr. Edward Hills. He speaks in reference to the committee of the American Standard Version , which was originally known as the American Revised Version, promising not to publish their translation at the same time as the English Revised Version. He points out,

> "They promised not to publish their own revised edition of the Bible until 14 years after the publication of the English Revised Version (R.V.), and in exchange for this concession were given the privilege of publishing in an appendix to this version a list of the readings which they favored but which the British revisers declined to adopt."[65]

It was obvious to these "contenders for the faith" that two new Bibles hitting the market at the same time just would not be conducive to good profits. If the American translators really believed that the "common man" needed their translation to clearly understand God's will for their lives, they wouldn't have been willing to keep it out of their hands for **fourteen days**, let alone **fourteen years!** (They

---

65 Hills, Edward, *The King James Version Defended,* (The Christian Research Press, Des Moines, 1956), p. 226.

apparently couldn't have cared less. They ended up waiting **21 years!**)
These men were obviously "led by the spirit," but I am not entirely sure
it was "Holy." It is a sad thing when men make merchandise of the
Word of God.

The name "Vulgate" on the flyleaf of Jerome's unreliable Latin
translation did little to help sales. The Old Latin Bible, or "Italic" as it
is sometimes called, was held fast by all true European Christians who
upheld the authority of the Bible over the authority of Rome or
education. Rome was going to have to take drastic actions if she was
going to replace God's Bible with her own private translation.

Dr. Wilkenson informs us in reference to the Old Latin,

"Not only were such translations in existence long before
the Vulgate was adopted by the Papacy, and well established,
but the people for centuries refused to supplant their old Latin
Bibles by the Vulgate."[66]

He records Jacobus' words, "The old Latin versions were used
longest by the western Christians who would not bow to the authority
of Rome--e.g., the Donatists; the Irish in Ireland, Britain, and the
Continent; the Albigenses: etc."

Dr. Wilkenson also records the words from the "Forum" of June
1887,

"The old Italic version, into rude Low Latin of the second
century, held its own as long as Latin continued to be the
language of the people. The critical version of Jerome never
displaced it, and only replaced it when the Latin ceased to be a
living language, and became the language of the learned. The

---

66 Wilkenson, Benjamin, *Our Authorized Bible Vindicated*, (Takoma Park, 1930), p. 27.

Gothic version of Ulfilas, in the same way, held its own until the tongues in which it was written ceased to exist."[67]

So we see that the Vulgate of Jerome was unwanted and unused by the true Christians of Europe **for over nine hundred years.** This rejection caused the Roman Church much grief. There was only one remedy to the situation: physically eliminate the other "old," "archaic" Latin Bible. If it was necessary to also violently eliminate the people who used this faithful translation, then she would have to do it. The Roman Catholic Church has certainly never been bashful about shedding innocent blood in order to achieve her sinister goals.

What happened in the case of the Old Latin Vulgate and the inferior Latin Vulgate of Jerome is very similar to what has taken place in the case of the King James Bible and modern translations. Rome translated its version when there was no need or call for it. Therefore, the common people ignored it. Rome had to force it on European Christians through persecution and murder. Modern bible publishers have done the very same thing. They produce a "bible" that no one needs or wants. Then they force it on people through underhanded tactics at Christian bookstores. When they find anyone who stands against their plan, they murder him with charges of "cult" and "trouble maker." But the **real victim** is the poor common Christian who ends up with a weak, watered-down "bible" in his hand.

THE PLOT

The Roman Catholic Church has long been known for her persecution of true New Testament Christians. In recent years pope John Paul has admitted to this. Beginning about 600 AD., this merciless organization hounded these Christ-honoring, Bible-loving people. The Roman Catholic pope Gregory I went so far as to systematically destroy

---

67 Ibid., p. 27.

and alter historical records pertaining to these Christians. Concerning one group, the Waldenses (or Waldensians), Dr. Gilly reports,

> "It is a singular thing, that the destruction or rapine, which has been so fatal to Waldensian documents, would have pursued them even to the place of security, to which all, that remained, were consigned by Morland, in 1658, the library of the University of Cambridge. The most ancient of these relics were ticketed in seven packets, distinguished by letters of the alphabet, from A to G. The whole of these were missing when I made inquiry for them in 1823."[68]

Gilly also enlightens us with this report of the actions of Rome:

> "The agents of the Papacy have done their utmost to calumniate their character, to destroy the records of their noble past and to leave no trace of the cruel persecution they underwent. They went even further - they made use of words written against ancient heresies to strike out the name of heretics and fill the blank space by inserting the name of the Waldenses. Just as if, in a book written to record the lawless deeds of some bandit, like Jesse James, his name should be stricken out and the name of Abraham Lincoln substituted. The Jesuit Getser in a book written against the heretics of the twelfth and thirteenth centuries, put the name Waldenses at the point where he struck out the name of these heretics."[69]

We find that Rome's wicked persecutions of the Waldenses culminated in a devastating massacre of their number in the valley of Piedmont in Italy in 1655.[70] The Waldenses were a passive, peace

---

68 Ibid., p. 34.

69 Ibid., pp. 32, 33.

70 Ibid., p. 36.

loving people who rejected violence and never formed any standing army for their own defense. They believed in the liberty of the conscience and religious independence. They accepted the Scriptures as their absolute authority and rejected the claims of the Roman Catholic Church. They believed it was the duty of each individual Christian to carry the Gospel to others.

In spite of their nonthreatening nature, the Roman Catholic Church demanded that they renounce their faith in Jesus Christ and convert to catholicism. They refused. Roman Catholic pope Innocent III (now there's a misnomer!) sent a force of 18,000 papal troops to destroy their towns and villages. On April 17, 1655, the merciless Catholic troops attacked and destroyed entire communities. They showed no mercy on men, women or children as they brutally murdered the defenseless villagers. They crucified, burned, hanged and mutilated their helpless victims. Scores were tortured in horrible ways before meeting death. Entire families were wiped out.[71]

Yet the Waldenses persevered for two hundred more years and in 1848 were finally granted full citizenship and allowed to live and worship in peace. Truth had prevailed over godless Roman Catholic brutality.[72]

COUNTERATTACK

A major blow to the authority of Rome came in 1517 when a young Catholic priest by the name of Martin Luther nailed his historic 95 theses on the church door in Wittenberg. Martin had witnessed the abuses of the Roman Catholic Church firsthand. He had protested against them from within to no avail. Finally he made his grievances

---

71 Military History (Cowles Enthusiast Media, June 1997), p.16.

72 New Standard Encyclopedia, (Standard Educational Corporation, 1977), Vol. W, p. 18.

public by writing all 95 of them down and dramatically nailing them to the front door of the church at Wittenberg. It was a moment that was to alter history. That nail drove deep into the hearts of truly born-again Christians who had for centuries been laboring under the tyranny of the Roman Catholic system. The people flocked to this brave, new leader. From this, Protestantism was born and Lutheranism was established. But even more important, the fires of the Reformation were kindled.

The tide of the Reformation soon came sweeping across all of Europe until it washed the very shores of England. The already weakened authority of Rome was devastated by the onslaught of truth. Two-thirds of Europe was swallowed up in what can probably be referred to as the greatest spiritual awakening of all time. The Reformation was vital to the then future translation of the King James Bible. England, too, had been shackled by the tyranny of Rome. It was the removal of Rome's superstitious bonds that created the spirit in England of the supremacy of the Scripture which was prevalent at the time of the translation of the King James Bible. This would not have been the case had Luther not sparked the Reformation.

The most vital and immovable weapon in Luther's arsenal came in the form of his German translation of the New Testament of 1522. This translation ignored the corrupt Local Text and instead put the pure words of the Universal Text, as found in the Greek text of Desiderius Erasmus, back into the hands of Bible-starved Christians. The Reformation ran wild across the continent, fueled by this faithful translation. Rome at this point was totally helpless to stop it. The Roman papacy needed something with which to fight this dreaded scourge of Truth. It turned in desperation to two different sources.

In 1545 the Roman Catholic Church formed the Council of Trent. The Council of Trent systematically denied the teachings of the Reformation and the Bible. The Council decreed that "tradition" was of equal authority with the Bible. It further decreed that justification was not by faith alone in the shed blood of Jesus Christ. In fact, it stated that anyone believing in this vital Bible doctrine was cursed. The Council's exact words were

> "If anyone saith that justifying faith is nothing else but confidence in the divine mercy which remits sins for Christ's sake or that this confidence alone is that whereby we are justified, **let him be anathema**."[73] (Emphasis mine).

We now see that the Roman Catholic Church is guilty of officially cursing Jesus Christ! Would God use this church to preserve His Words? Would He use this church to spread His Gospel?

The Council of Trent was viewed by the Protestants as somewhat of a "paper tiger." It certainly did not hold any authority over them. Rome's barn door appeared securely locked, but the horse was triumphantly roaming all over the countryside! Yet there was to be an enemy much more feared than the boisterous Council of Trent-the Jesuits!

THE DIABOLICAL JESUITS

The Society of Jesus, whose members are known as "Jesuits," was founded in 1534 by a Spaniard by the name of Ignatius Loyola. Loyola was born don Inigo Lopez de Racalde, in the castle of Loyola in the province of Guipuzcoa in 1491. As a youth he was known to be treacherous, brutal and vindictive. He was referred to as an unruly and conceited soldier. Loyola was wounded at the siege of Pampeluna in 1521. Crippled by a broken leg and plagued by a limp the rest of his life he could no longer serve in a military manner. To replace his life of physical conquests he turned to "spiritual" conquests.[74]

---

73 Council of Trent, Session VI, Cannon 1545.

74. Paris, Edmond, *The Secret History of the Jesuits*, (The Protestant Truth Society, London, 1975), p. 17.

Loyola formed an elite force of men who were extremely loyal to the Roman Catholic pope. The goal of these men was to undermine Protestantism and "heresy" throughout the world and bring all of mankind into subjection to their pope. Their training would require fourteen years of testing and trials designed to leave them with no will at all. They were to learn to be obedient. Loyola taught that their only desire should be to serve their pope.

The head of the Jesuits is called the "Black Pope" and holds the title of General, just as in the military. That they were to be unquestionably loyal to this man and their church is reflected in Loyola's own words, "Let us be convinced that all is well and right when the superior commands it," also, "...even if God gave you an animal without sense for master, you will not hesitate to obey him, as master and guide, because God ordained it to be so." He further elaborates, "We must see black as white, if the Church says so."[75]

THE DEVIL'S PLAINCLOTHESMEN

Their objective in view, all that needed to be decided was how to reach it. What would be the method used by the Jesuits to achieve their goals? Would it be military might? Would it be acts of daring? Would it be a violent revolution to install a Roman sympathizer as ruler over England? No, these actions were assigned to other branches of the Catholic Church and would all have their day of usefulness later.

The Jesuits were to be the Vatican's "plainclothesmen." They were founded to be a secret society that was to slip in behind the scenes and capture the positions of Protestant leadership. The Jesuits knew that to capture the positions of leadership of any particular country or organization is to conquer the entire body. They would become the **teachers** of the next generation of Protestant leaders and instill them

75 Ibid., p. 28.

with Catholic dogma. These future leaders would then take their place as teachers of Protestantism and be open to the Romanizing of the Church of England.

Edmund Paris, the noted French author and a leading authority on the Roman Catholic Church, has written many books exposing the true spirit and goals of the Vatican. He points out, "Politics are their main field of action, as all the efforts of these 'directors' concentrate on one aim: the submission of the world to the papacy, and to attain this the 'heads' must be conquered first."[76]

Of course, any Protestant would be wary of a Roman Catholic priest standing in front of a classroom teaching him. Therefore, the Jesuit priests were not required to dress in the traditional garb of Roman Catholic priests. In fact, their dress was a major part of their disguise. They presented themselves to the world in a variety of manners. They passed themselves off in a number of ways. Paris asserts that this is still true today.

"It is the same today: the 33,000 official members of the Society operate all over the world in the capacity of her personnel, officers of a truly secret army containing in its ranks heads of political parties, high ranking officials, generals, magistrates, physicians, faculty professors, etc., all of them striving to bring about, in their own sphere, 'Opus Dei,' God's work, in reality the plans of the papacy."[77]

They have often been known to feign membership in the religious persuasion which they wish to destroy. Having done this, they would seek positions of leadership where they could slowly influence younger, weaker members to a mind set that was more passive and trusting if not down right respectful of the Roman Catholic Church.

---

76 Ibid., p. 26.

77 Ibid., p. 32.

They would manipulate their converts to manifest all of the destructive force at their hands to weaken and tear down their sworn enemy, "Protestantism." Paris again reports just such an event which took place in Scandinavia in the late 16th century "In 1574 Father Nicolai and other Jesuits were brought to the recently established school of technology where they became fervent Roman proselytizers, while officially assuming Lutheranism."[78]

Dr. Desanctis points out,

> "Despite all the persecution they (the Jesuits) have met with, they have not abandoned England, where there are a greater number of Jesuits than in Italy; there are Jesuits in all classes of society; in Parliament; among the English clergy; among the Protestant laity, even in the higher stations. I could not comprehend how a Jesuit could be a Protestant priest, or how a Protestant priest could be a Jesuit; but my Confessor silenced my scruples by telling me, omnia munda mundis, and that St. Paul became a Jew that he might save the Jews; it is no wonder therefore, if a Jesuit should feign himself a Protestant, for the conversion of Protestants."[79]

HOLY MURDER

As we have seen, murder is certainly not above the "means" which might be considered necessary to be employed by the Jesuits to reach the Catholic Church's desired "end." And punishment for such diabolical crimes need not be feared by the society's members. The General of the Jesuits will forgive any sins which are committed by the

---

78 Ibid, p. 44.

79 Wilkenson, Benjamin, *Our Authorized Bible Vindicated* (Takoma Park, 1930), p. 122.

members of this Satanic order. In reference to the Jesuit General, it is
stated,

> "He also absolves the irregularity issuing from bigamy,
> injuries done to others, murder, assassination...as long as these
> wicked deeds were not publickly known and thus cause of a
> scandal."[80]

That the Jesuit priests have such liberties as murder is reflected
in the following lengthy quote from Paris' book *The Secret History of
the Jesuits*:

> "Amongst the most criminal jesuitic maxims, there is one
> which roused public indignation to the highest point and
> deserves to be examined; it is: 'A monk or priest is allowed to
> kill those who are ready to slander him or his community."

> "So the order gives itself the right to eliminate its
> adversaries and even those of its members who, having come
> out of it, are too talkative. This pearl is found in the Theology of
> Father L'Amy.

> "There is another case where this principle finds its
> application. For this same Jesuit was cynical enough to write: 'If
> a Father, yielding to temptation, abuses a woman and she
> publicizes what has happened, and because of it, dishonours
> him, this same Father can kill her to avoid disgrace'!"[81]

In 1572 the Jesuits, with the help of Prince Henry III, were
responsible for the St. Bartholomew's Day Massacre. At this infamous
event, which took place on August 15, 1572, the Jesuits murdered the

---

80 Paris, Edmond, *The Secret History of the Jesuits* ,(The Protestant Truth Society,
London, 1975), p. 31.

81 Ibid., p. 67.

—

Huguenot (Protestant) leaders gathered in Paris for the wedding of Princess Margaret, a Roman Catholic, and Henry of Navarre, a Huguenot. The murders inspired Roman Catholics to slaughter thousands of Huguenot men, women, and children. Henry of Navarre was not killed but was forced to renounce Protestantism, although his renunciation was insincere, and he remained a Protestant until 1593. The number of victims in this Jesuit conspiracy is estimated to be at least 10,000.[82] In 1589, when Henry III was no longer useful to the Roman Catholic Church, he was assassinated by a monk by the name of Jacques Clement.[83] Clement was called an "angel" by the Jesuit priest, Camelet.[84] Another Jesuit priest by the name of Guigard, who was eventually hanged, taught his students that Clement did nothing wrong. In fact, he voiced his regrets that Henry III had not been murdered earlier at the St. Bartholomew's Day Massacre. He instructed them with lessons such as this:

> "Jacques Clement has done a meritorious act inspired by the Holy Spirit. If we can make war against the king, then let us do it; if we cannot make war against him, then let us put him to death...we made a big mistake at St. Bartholomew; we should have bled the royal vein."[85]

The Jesuits' murderous ways were not yet completed in the history of French Protestants! When Henry III was murdered, Henry of Navarre, a Huguenot, came to power. A hope for Catholic rebellion never materialized, and Henry IV was allowed to reign. In 1592, an

---

82 *New Standard Encyclopedia*, (Standard Educational Corporation, 1977), Vol. S, p. 35.

83 Ibid., Vol. H, p. 141.

84 Paris, Edmond, *The Secret History of the Jesuits*, (The Protestant Truth Society, London, 1975), p. 48.

85 Ibid., p. 48.

attempt to assassinate the Protestant king was made by a man named Barriere. Barriere admitted that he had been instructed to do so by one Father Varade, **a Jesuit priest.** [86]

In 1594 another attempt was made by Jean Chatel who had been taught by Jesuit teachers and had confessed to the Jesuits what he was about to do.[87] It was at this time that Father Guigard, the Jesuit teacher previously mentioned, was seized and hanged for his connection with this plot.[88]

In 1598 King Henry IV issued the Edict of Nantes, granting religious freedom to the Huguenots. They were allowed full civil rights and the right to hold public worship services in towns where they had congregations. This was the last straw! Henry IV had to be eliminated! This time the Jesuits would allow for more careful planning. Edmund Paris details an account of the assassination of King Henry IV:

> "On the 16th of May, 1610, on the eve of his campaign against Austria, he was murdered by Ravaillac who confessed having been inspired by the writing of Fathers Mariana and Suarez. These two sanctioned the murders of heretic 'tyrants' or those insufficiently devoted to the Papacy's interests. The duke of Epernon, who made the king read a letter while the assassin was lying in wait, was a notorious friend of the Jesuits, and Michelet proved that they knew of this attempt. In fact, Ravaillac had confessed to the Jesuit Father d'Aubigny just before and, when the judges interrogated the priest, he merely

---

86 Ibid., p. 48.

87 Ibid., p. 49.

88 Ibid., p. 49.

replied that God had given him the gift to forget immediately what he heard in the confessional."[89]

THIS is the spirit of our enemy! **THIS** is the ruthlessness of the Roman Catholic Church against those who will not bow their knee to Rome! Would God use this church to preserve His Word?

Wherever there is a conspiracy against God's people or God's Word, there seems always to be the shadow of a Jesuit priest near. Often they present themselves as being seemingly innocent of the proceedings around them when, in fact, they are the driving force behind such plots against God's work.

It is often said that you can tell a lot about a man by taking a close look at his enemies. If a man is disliked by Communists, then that shows that he is a non-Communist and considered dangerous to their cause. If a man is disliked by the Roman Catholic Church, then this shows that he is not useful in spreading the Roman Catholic dogma.

This same thing is true of the Bible. What did the Jesuits, the sworn enemy of truth, think of King James I for commissioning the translation of the Authorized Version?

THE GUNPOWDER PLOT

King James I of England had already been ruling in Scotland as King James VI for several years when he ascended the British throne in 1603. One of England's greatest monarchs, he wasted no time in providing for the physical and spiritual welfare of his subjects. Their most pressing spiritual need was for a translation of the Bible into English that could be used by **the common man** rather than being the exclusive property of the Anglican Church. Thus in 1604, just one short

89 Ibid., p. 49.

year after taking the British throne, he commissioned the fifty-four translators that were to produce what the world has come to know as "The King James Bible." Their work was complete in 1611.

The Roman Catholic Church realized the danger she faced from a populus with access to the Holy Scripture. To clearly show the hatred of the Roman Catholic Church against King James for initiating a translation which would not use the corrupt Latin Vulgate or the Jesuit Bible of 1582 as its basis, we must quote from Gustavus Paine's book *The Men Behind the King James Version*. The account recorded took place in 1605-1606.

"The story is too involved to give in detail here, but on October 26, the Lord Chamberlain, Monteagle, received an unsigned letter begging him to stay away from Parliament on the day it opened. He took the letter to Robert Cecil, who on November 1 showed it to the King at a midnight meeting. The King shrewdly surmised a good deal of what it meant.

"Monday, November 4, an agent of the royal party found in a cellar beneath the House of Lords a man named Guy Fawkes, disguised as a servant, beside piles of faggots, billets of wood, and masses of coal. The agent went away. Shortly Monteagle and one other came and talked, but gave no heed to Fawkes, who was still on guard until they were about to go. He told them he was a servant of Thomas Percy, a well-known papist. Still later, at midnight, soldiers found Fawkes booted and spurred and with a lantern outside the cellar door. He had taken few pains to conceal his actions. They dragged him into an alley, searched him, and found on him a tinderbox and a length of slow match. In a fury now, they moved the faggots, billets and coal and came upon barrel after barrel of powder, thirty-six barrels in all. Fawkes then confessed that he meant to blow up the House of Lords and the King.

—

"On November 6, Percy, with others, rushed into an inn at Dunchurch, Warwickshire, with the news that the court was aware of their plan. By the 8th the whole attempt had clearly failed. When Parliament met a week after the stated day, the King, calm, gracious, and splendid told what had happened and then adjourned the meeting. At first Fawkes refused to name any except Percy who, with others, was killed in the course of a chase. In time he gave the names of all, who would have blown up the House of Lords 'at a clap.'

"Guy Fawkes was baptized at St. Michael le Belfrey, York, April 16, 1570, son of Edward Fawkes, a proctor and advocate in the church courts of York. The father died and the mother married a Papist. In 1603 Guy Fawkes went to Madrid to urge that Philip III invade England. Thus he was a confirmed traitor, though egged on and used by more astute plotters.

"Some of these men had been involved in the rising of the Earl of Esses. A number were former members of the Church of England. Most of them had some land and wealth. They were all highly disturbed beings, throwbacks, who meant to subvert the state and get rid of King James. Church and state, they were sure, must be at one, with fealty to the Pope.

"For nearly a year, the plotters had been digging a tunnel from a distance, but had found the wall under the House of Lords nine feet thick. They had then got access to the cellar by renting a building. They had planned to kill the King, seize his children, stir up an open revolt with the aid from Spaniards in Flanders, put Princess Elizabeth on the throne, and marry her to a Papist. Though all but one, Sir Everard Digby, pleaded not guilty, the court, such as it was, condemned them all to death. That same week they were all hanged, four in St. Paul's churchyard where John Overall, the translator, could have looked on and four in the yard of the old palace.

"Three months later came the trial of Henry Garnet, a Jesuit, thought to be head of the Jesuits in England. Brought up a Protestant, he knew of the plot but had shrunk in horror from it, though he left the chosen victims to their fate. The court condemned him also to die.

"All this concerned the men at work on the Bible. At Garnet's hanging, May 3, in St. Paul's churchyard, John Overall, Dean of St. Paul's took time off from his translating to be present. Very gravely and Christianly he and the Dean of Winchester urged upon Garnet, 'a true and lively faith to God-ward,' a free and plain statement to the world of his offense; and if any further treason lay in his knowledge, he was begged to unburden his conscience and show a sorrow and destination of it. Garnet, firm in his beliefs, desired them not to trouble him. So after the men assigned to the gruesome duty had hanged, drawn, and quartered the victim Dean Overall returned to St. Paul's and his Bible task."[90]

Thus, the "Gunpowder Plot" failed. As usual, where there was treachery there was a Jesuit.

Did the failure of this diabolical plan stop the Jesuits? Of course not. Garnet had allowed this drastic plan to be carried out **too soon**. He had forgotten the Jesuit strategy to move very slowly, act a little at a time, "surtout, pas trop de zele" (above all, not too much zeal).

A NEW PLAN

Let it be remembered, **Jesuits do not give up**. Since their plan to blow up Parliament didn't work, they would simply have to bide their time. They would once again resort to undercover activities as

90 Paine, Gustavus, *The Men Behind the King James Version,* (Baker Book House, Grand Rapids, 1959), pp. 88-90.

they had so many times before. Their task would be a difficult one, yet for the unfaltering Jesuits, not impossible. They would have to discredit the Reformation. They would have to dislodge the Universal Greek Text from the firm position it held in the minds and hearts of English scholarship. They would have to "wean" Protestantism back into the fold of Rome. To do this they would use the same plan as they had in similar situations: **captivate the minds of scholarship.**

Men have long been worshipers of education. If an educator makes a claim, the "common" people will usually accept it, because they have been convinced that anyone with so much education could not be wrong.

In this manner evolution has been accepted as a fact by the average American because **educators** claim that it is true. The fact that they can produce no evidence to substantiate their theory is incidental. **Education** says it is so! Therefore, it must be so.

The task of the Jesuits was to entice Protestant scholarship back to the fold of Rome. They knew that they could not wean the leaders of Protestantism off of the Bible and back into Rome as long as these stubborn "heretics" clung to the pure text of the Reformers. Their Bible would have to be replaced with one which contained the pro-Roman Catholic readings of Jerome's Vulgate and the Jesuit English translation of 1582. In order to get Protestants to see the "value" of the Roman Catholic text it would be necessary to "educate" the Protestant scholars to believe that their Reformation Text was unreliable and that their Authorized Version was "not scholarly." Thus programmed, the egotistical scholars would spontaneously attack their own Bible and believe that they were helping God. From that point, on they would voluntarily do all of Rome's dirty work while the papists sat back and laughed up their sleeves.

The most important objective of the Roman Catholic Church would be to replace the great King James Bible as the final authority of Protestantism with that of the Roman Catholic Church.

The Authorized Version had become a mightier foe than Rome had anticipated, as Dr. McClure points out:

> "The printing of the English Bible has proved to be by far the mightiest barrier ever reared to repel the advance of Popery, and to damage all the resources of the Papacy. Originally intended for the five or six millions who dwelt within the narrow limits of the British Islands, it at once formed and fixed their language, till then unsettled; and has since gone with that language to the isles and shores of every sea."

THE DREADED HAPPENING

Today the Roman Catholic Church is being assailed from without and within. Bible believers refuse to trust the Great Whore of Revelation 17 and resist all attempts at Ecumenicism, (until the "Promise Keepers" showed up that is!), meanwhile liberal-minded papists are rebelling against her conservative policies. The Roman Catholic Church is busy dealing with those who favor abortion, homosexual rights and the ordination of women into the priesthood. But **none** of these attacks have caused it as much damage as the publication of the Bible in English.

With the publication of the King James Bible the event that the Roman Catholic Church had always dreaded had come to pass. The Word of God was translated from God's true Universal Text into the clearest form of the common language, English. Protestants had long refuted and neutralized Roman Catholicism by the phrase, "The Bible says so." The Roman Catholic Church had been built on about 10% twisted Scripture and 90% pagan superstition. Where men were ignorant, the Roman Church could rule by playing on their fears. But, when the "unlearned and ignorant" people received Christ as personal Saviour and clung faithfully to the King James Bible, they were not only immovable but could easily refute any heresy, be it Catholic or otherwise. This could be allowed to continue.

It would be up to the ever faithful Jesuits to destroy Protestantism's confidence and loyalty to the King James Bible and replace it with one of their own choosing.

AIDING THE ENEMY

The job of the Jesuits would be aided by the natural process of time. Every major religious persuasion follows a natural pattern which is nearly impossible to avoid a process that leads from seeing the glory of God to experiencing His judgement. A religious movement begins in the form of a **revival** not a week-long "revival meeting," but a spiritual awakening which leads its followers away from the world system and into Bible literalism. The Reformation is a good example of this. During the Reformation people drew nearer to the Bible, believed it literally, and the end result was a revival which swept across Europe and drew people out of the Roman Catholic system and ended with the establishment of Lutheranism.

The step following "revival" is **education**. The infant Reformation had nowhere to send its converts to learn the Bible correctly. There was nowhere for its future clergy to learn the doctrines as taught by Protestantism. It certainly could not allow them to return to the Roman school of philosophy for their education. So this second step requires the founding of institutions of higher learning through which to train its own preachers and teachers.

Of course, in this there is an inherent weakness. For if the positions of teaching can be captured, then those taught can be easily led astray. This is exactly what the Jesuits did in England and what is being done across America in "Bible" colleges that criticize the King James Bible.[91]

---

91 Bob Jones University has long taken an outward stand against Roman Catholicism. Is it not **strange** then that Bob Jones IV should attend **Notre Dame University** of all

The third step that any movement takes in its unstoppable descent toward destruction is to seek to develop **culture**. Once a movement has established itself, it forms its own culture. This process takes from 50 to 100 years. After this period of time, the movement has proved to the world that it is not a "fly by night" outfit but a force to be reckoned with. Emphasis is put on beautiful buildings and stately college grounds. The value of the fine arts is promoted. Ministers are restrained from using any incorrect grammar and the gap between "clergy" and "laity" begins to widen. This was true of Lutheranism, as it is true today of Fundamentalism.

Fifty years ago, a Fundamentalist preacher was considered an uneducated backwoods "hick" with no education who was able to preach nothing more than "hellfire and damnation." Today, the world has awakened to the fact that Fundamentalism is a powerful force. Fundamental churches are found to be the largest and fastest growing in the country. Television and magazines are producing special stories concerning the Fundamental movement. The election of Ronald Reagan as President of the United States in 1980 showed the amount of influence that Fundamentalism could wield. Fundamentalism has proved that it is here to stay and is a force to be reckoned with.

This acceptance produces a kind of "home-grown" arrogance. This is not a derogatory comment, but is simply the truth. When the preachers of the Reformation graduated from basements and dungeons to the pulpits of the largest, fastest growing churches in Europe, they realized that they had fought their way to a great victory. As they saw their colleges grow and multiply, they prided themselves in the job they had done. But the newfound ease of life began to make subtle changes in them. They found themselves beginning to appreciate the "finer" things of life. A pastor who had been satisfied in the early days of the

places? Can you imagine? Will Bob Jones University someday be run by a **graduate** of the premier Roman Catholic school in the country; Jesuit trained, and are we to be so naive as to believe that his Catholic education will have no effect on how he would direct that institution?

–

Reformation with a basement and one candle for light to preach by, twenty-five years later found himself in a fine, clean, functional building. As his congregation grew and space was needed, the church built bigger buildings, but the new buildings passed from mere functional simplicity to a "touch of elegance." Simple lights became chandeliers and in time the chandeliers became more ornate. Church ceilings became higher. The pews grew more comfortable. The windows saw the use of stained glass, a Roman Catholic custom. The pastor found social acceptance in the community. Each succeeding building was "bigger and better" with more elaborate masonry. Leading universities taught preachers and people to "appreciate" the arts and sciences. Christians soon had a culture which was separate from, but parallel to, that of the world. This left the door open for the next and final step, **apostasy**.

These "preachers" now became the "clergy." They were "God's anointed" and demanded the authority that such a title eluded to. Their separated lives and biblical education led to a proud spirit of Phariseeism. Their colleges expanded from just training ministers to covering a wider spectrum of occupations. Basic Bible courses were supplemented by a study of "the arts." Man became more addicted to education and culture. But worst of all, these "Bible believers" thought that they were immune to the adverse effects of culture. Certainly **others** had fallen prey to apostasy. But **they** were never "Bible believers" like **we** are. They felt a false assurance that their earlier establishment on the Bible and its doctrines would innoculate them from the effects of apostasy.

Revival is from God. **Education** is necessary for the training of God's ministers, but **culture** is a product that appeals to the flesh. Once the flesh is allowed to offer its preferences, **apostasy** sets in. Standards become a little more lax. College professors are hired according to their **academic abilities** first and the **spiritual convictions** second. Statements like "We must have the best" and "I want to be first-class" are used to comfort the fears of anyone who feels that the churches and schools seem a little too worldly. Of course, a school administrator might comfort himself by thinking, "The average Christian doesn't understand our minute changes. They aren't as educated like we are."

Then suddenly there appears a Christian with an open Bible, who points out Scripture which may condemn the new-found "culture" of a church or school. The school amazingly finds itself in the same position as the Roman Catholic Church, refuted by an ignorant Christian who simply believes the Bible. Now the question to be answered is, "Which is to be our **final authority**, the school or the Bible?" Time after time, education has found that it has come too far to turn back. "We are!" came the answer from Oxford, Cambridge, and Westminster in England. "We are!" came the answer from Harvard, Princeton, and Yale in America. "We are!" came the answer from Mercer, Biola, Wake Forest and Carson-Newman of the Southern Baptists. "We are!" came the answer from Bob Jones University, Tennessee Temple, Baptist Bible College and others of the Fundamentalists. **Education has conceived culture and given birth to apostasy!**

RIPE FOR CONQUEST

Due to centuries of covert work by the Jesuits, England in the early 1800's was ripe for apostasy. The Reformation had come a long way since Luther nailed his theses on the door at Wittenberg. It had traversed Europe with the truth, leaving in its wake churches and schools that represented the pure text of Scripture. The educational foundation had been laid, upon which culture was to be built. Gone were the attempts to blow up Parliament. Gone was the fear of ending up like Tyndale for believing "the Book." Gone was the reign of terror inflicted by "bloody" Mary. The churches built around the Authorized Version were rich and prosperous. The colleges, from their meager beginnings, had become great universities, pressing on with higher education. There were a few "common" people who still feared Rome, but the "educators" knew that their fears were "unfounded." They knew they were safe in the arms of the Church of England. Unfortunately, this complacency left England ripe for a transfer of authority from the Bible to education, and Rome was willing to supply that education. They felt sure that the absolute reign of the Authorized Version would soon end.

"OPERATION UNDERMINE"

Over the years the Authorized Version had withstood countless individual attacks by its critics. But it would now be subjected to a **systematic campaign** to exalt several deceptive authorities to a position equal to it. These perverted "authorities" would then join forces to portray the Authorized Version as weak, unreliable, inaccurate, outmoded, and generally untrustworthy. Once the Authorized Version had been successfully dethroned, **education** would be free to exalt whatever authority it desired. The Roman Catholic Church, of course, would be close at hand to see to it that the authority which was to be exalted would be in agreement with its own corrupt Latin Vulgate.

The authorities to be exalted as equal to the Authorized Version came from several different quarters, but all with the same intent replace the Universal Text of the Authorized Version with the Local Text of Alexandria, Egypt.

SCIENCE "FALSELY SO-CALLED"

One of the authorities which was used to discredit the Authorized Version was the so-called "science" textual criticism.

Textual criticism is known as a "science." Because it is classified as a science, it is accepted by the educated mind as a credible authority. It is a process which looks at the Bible as it would look at the uninspired writings of any secular writer. This one fact alone means that any **supernatural** power of God to preserve His word is ignored in favor of the naturalistic method of evaluating the "chance" of God's Word being preserved. Textual criticism allows God to "inspire" His originals, but **seeks to replace God as the active agent in preserving His word.**

Dr. Frederick Henry Ambrose Scrivener states this very plainly:

> "The design of the science of TEXTUAL CRITICISM, as applied to the Greek New Testament, will now be readily understood. By collecting and comparing and weighing the variations of the text to which we have access, it aims at bringing back that text, so far as it may be, to the condition in which it stood in the sacred autographs; at removing all spurious additions, if such be found in our present printed copies; at restoring whatsoever may have been lost or corrupted or accidentally changed in the lapse of eighteen hundred years."[92]

Earlier we established that the Bible was a **spiritual** book, that God was active in its conception, and that it would be reasonable to assume that God could be just as active in its preservation. **He doesn't need textual criticism.** Some may counter that the very canon of Scripture had to be decided by men. But **that was done once** in history and has been a closed issue for fifteen hundred years. But textual criticism **never** arrives at a fixed answer but is constantly making alterations and conjectures concerning the text. This theory of scholars being able to produce the original text has been exercised unnumerable times since the invention of textual criticism, and yet **those very scholars** will be the **first** to admit that their finished work is by no means to be accepted as a **final** authority!

---

92 Scrivener, F. H. A., *A Plain Introduction To The Criticism Of The New Testament*, (Cambridge, 1894) Vol I. p.5.

–

One might ask at this point if textual criticism could not be the method which God used to preserve His words? The answer is unequivocally, "No." Here are the reasons why:

Textual critics look at the Bible today through the same eyes as did the Egyptian scribes who perverted the Universal Text as they constructed the Local Text centuries ago. Those well-educated scribes thought that **the Bible was subject to them** instead of **them being subject to the Bible**. This outlook allowed them to eliminate the power of God from their minds and make whatever changes they deemed necessary to reach a conclusion which seemed logical to them. In their minds they were the Holy Spirit!

Today textual critics do the very same thing, in that, before they ever start their work, they are convinced that God cannot preserve His word without their assistance. Scholars today believe that God inspired **words** but preserved **thoughts**. Therefore, they are free to toy with the **words** to their liking. The Bible is subject to them. **They** are not subject to the Bible.

Another reason why textual criticism could not be the method God used to preserve His word is that textual criticism is an invention of Rome. God is certainly not going to use such a blood-thirsty, power hungry organization to be the custodian of His Holy Book.

As to the conception of this enemy of God's authority (textual criticism), the Catholic Encyclopedia states,

"A French priest, Richard Simon (1638-1712), was the first who subjected the general questions concerning the Bible to a treatment which was at once comprehensive in scope and scientific in method. Simon is the forerunner of modern Biblical criticism...The use of internal evidence by which Simon arrived at it entitles him to be called the father of Biblical criticism."[93]

The same source also mentions the Catholic scholar Jean Astruc and his part in undermining confidence in God's ability to preserve His words:

> "In 1753 Jean Astruc, a French Catholic physician of considerable note, published a little book, <u>Conjectures sur les memoires originaux dont il parait que Moise s'est servi pour composer le livre de la Genese</u>, in which he conjectured, from the alternating use of two names of God in the Hebrew Genesis, that Moses had incorporated therein two pre-existing documents, one of which employed Elohim and the other Jehovah. The idea attracted little attention till it was taken up by a German scholar, who, however, claims to have made the discovery independently. This was Johann Gottfried Eichhorn...Eichhorn greatly developed Astruc's hypothesis."[94]

Here we find the Mosaic authorship of the Pentateuch brought into question. This hypothesis, that Moses did no more than combine several existing documents written by several authors who were identified by their unique titles for God, became known as "Astruc's Clue" (more like "Astruc's Fairytale"). But such a wild theory was all that was needed as a starting point for those Bible-rejecting minds who were "gunning" for the Bible. It only gets worse, for we see that the Catholic Encyclopedia further speaks of yet another Roman Catholic infidel and his attack on Scripture:

> "Yet, it was a Catholic priest of Scottish origin, Alexander Geddes (1737-1802), who broached a theory of the

---

93 Wilkenson, Benjamin, *Our Authorized Bible Vindicated*, (Takoma Park, 1930), p. 104.

94 Ibid., p. 104.

origin of the Five Books (to which he attached Joshua) exceeding in boldness either Simon's or Eichhorn's. This was the well-known 'Fragment' hypothesis, which reduced the Pentateuch to a collection of fragmentary sections partly of Mosaic origin, but put together in the reign of Solomon. Geddes' opinion was introduced into Germany in 1805 by Vater."[95]

Dr. Benjamin Wilkenson records how the naturalistic, unsaved Roman Catholic scholars judged in favor of the perverted Egyptian manuscripts:

"Some of the earliest critics in the field of collecting variant readings of the New Testament Greek were Mill and Bengel. We have Dr. Kenrich, Catholic Bishop of Philadelphia in 1849, as authority that they and others had examined these manuscripts recently exalted as superior, such as the Vaticanus, Alexandrinus, Beza, and Ephraem, and had pronounced in favor of the Vulgate, the Catholic Bible."[96]

Stop and think! Naturalistic as opposed to spiritual. Unsaved as opposed to saved. Roman Catholic as opposed to Biblical. These men conceived and developed theories which attacked the reliability of Scripture and judged in favor of the perverted Egyptian manuscripts. Rome had **invented** a "science" and then provided that "science" with an entire inventory of "experts," all conveniently parroting the same Bible-destroying message.

Are these men and methods worthy of our confidence? Would a perfect and righteous God use such a hodgepodge of infidelity to preserve His hallowed words? Some may say that textual criticism is

95 Ibid., pp. 104-105.

96 Ibid., p. 105

good if carried on by good, godly Christian men. (Then so is bartending!) This cannot be true. The "mass" is a Roman Catholic invention contrived to prevent people from knowing the truth. Would the mass be "good" if performed by good, Bible-believing scholars? Of course not! Elisha took poison and made it fit to eat (2 Kings 4:38-41). We cannot! Neither can we take a method instigated by the Roman Catholic Church in order to overthrow the Bible and filled with the poison of Romanism and **miraculously** make it fit to use! Textual criticism is a "science" ("falsely so-called," 1 Timothy 6:20) whose authority we cannot accept in place of the Bible.

THE GREEK GAME

Another authority by which to criticize and downgrade the absolute authority of the Authorized Version is to put an unreasonable emphases on "the Greek" rather than the English words of our Bible. This is done for several reasons:

1. The common Christian does not know Greek. Therefore, he is **immediately** put at the mercy of the speaker for a "correct" interpretation of what the Bible "really" says.

2. It is a wonder boost to the ego of a vain preacher to be able to say, "The original Greek says..." to add authority to whatever theory he wishes to foist on his helpless listeners.

3. A lazy preacher need not even open his Bible and study. He can simply look up a word in a Greek dictionary and expound on **any choice he wants to** as long as it wasn't the same as that of the King James translators.

The sad part of this is that the armor of "the Greek says" is just about impenetrable for the common Christian who may not like or agree with the changes made by some self-proclaimed scholar but who is unable to refute them. They are left with the helpless and

–

embarrassing conclusion of having to say, "But he's had **years** of study in the Greek. How can I say he's wrong?" Of course, the "mental-midget" preacher loves to exalt his ability by ever telling his poor hearers of how arduously he studies "the original Greek."

The **fact** of the matter is that it is **not difficult at all** to "correct" the Bible with the Greek. Please keep in mind that I believe the Bible is **perfect** and cannot be "corrected" in any way. I only use the term "correct" because that is the term most bandied about by the Bible's critics. In fact, in my seminars **defending** the King James Bible, I use "The Greek Game" to teach attendees how to "correct" the Bible **in just one half-hour**. Again, please understand. I **don't** believe the Bible can be "corrected," because I believe it is infallible. But I teach my students how it's done in just a half-hour so they will not be so impressed with some large-headed pseudo-scholar who does it and claims the right to do so because of "years of study in the original languages" The sad thing is that what I do in light-hearted humor,[97] Bible colleges across the nation do with a sincerity and intensity that thoroughly corrupts the pliable mind of a zealous young student.

Upon beginning his class, the unsuspecting student is first taught that he must not accept a word as it is found in the Authorized Version. (The only rule to "The Greek Game" is: **"The King James Bible is always wrong."**) When studying any passage in the King James Bible he is told to consult the Greek or Hebrew words to see if there is another way the word could have been translated. The student, with the purest of motives, proceeds to a lexicon or a Greek or Hebrew dictionary and discovers to his horror that the translators of the Authorized Version have translated the word improperly! In truth, the exact opposite has happened. The lexicon and/or dictionary has defined the word improperly! The poor, naive, well-meaning student does not

---

97 See this author's work entitled, *The Answer Book*, Question #47 for a thorough study of how "The Greek Game" is used by Bible correctors to fool and intimidate their listeners.

know it, but he has been "headed off at the pass" by a wickedly wise, Jesuit-inspired teacher. He stands before his classmates and presents **his guess** at what the Bible should actually say, based on his feeble interpretation of "the original Greek." It doesn't take long for his ego to swell with the **power** this gives him. If the day comes somewhere down life's road that the fallacy of this procedure is pointed out to him he quickly realizes that he will have to admit to **years** of misleading his congregation. His human nature will not allow this, so he become a rabid critic of **anyone** who claims that the Bible really is perfect.

What this poor student doesn't know is that years before he ever turned the first page of his lexicon, Roman Catholics had provided the pages he would turn! Let me explain. If the student can be taught to doubt the accuracy of the translation of any given word in the Bible, then he will turn to a lexicon or dictionary to find the "true" meaning. He does not realize it, but in doing this, he removes the Bible from its position as **final authority** and bestows that honor upon an **uninspired** lexicon or dictionary. All this leaves for Satan to do is to provide that student with a lexicon or dictionary which reads the way he (Satan) wants it to! This is a subtle and dangerous precedent. Most often, it is taught in complete, innocent sincerity.

This is much like the phrase used to explain the Communists' takeover of many countries which were once thriving with many missionaries: "The missionaries taught us to read, but the Communists gave us the books." (The Communists do not argue about the proper translation of Marx.)

Many unsuspecting colleges teach their students to accept the lexicon or dictionary as an authority **above the Bible**, but the lexicons and dictionaries are provided by the infidels.

John R. Rice points out the result of such "authority switching" while discussing Isaiah 7:14 in the Revised Standard Version:

—

"The most active opposition to the Revised Standard Version has been about changing the translation of Isaiah 7:14 from, 'Behold, a virgin shall conceive,' to "Behold, a young woman shall conceive and bear a son.' Dr. Luther Weigle, chairman of the translators, said that in the Hebrew English lexicon the word 'alma' means simply 'young woman,' not necessarily 'virgin' and he said that the word for 'virgin' in the Hebrew is 'bethulah.' He did not tell you, however, that the lexicon he uses was prepared by unbelieving critics.

"Gesenius, the German orientalist and biblical critic, is described in the Encyclopedia Britannica in these words:

'To Gesenius, who was an exceptionally popular teacher, belongs in a large measure the credit of having freed Semitic philosophy from theological and religious prepossession, and of inaugurating the strictly scientific (and comparative) method.

'His chief work, Hebraisches u. Chaldaisches Handworterbuch (1810-1812), has passed through several editions (Eng. ed.: Francis Brown, S.R. Driver and Charles A. Brigs, A Hebrew and English Lexicon of the Old Testament, 1907).

'Gesenius, a notorious liberal, specialized in changing the theological terminology of the Bible into that of liberals. Brown, Driver, and Briggs, translators of the lexicon in English were, all three of them, radical liberals, and two of them were tried in the Presbyterian church for outrageous infidelity.'"[98]

Benjamin Wilkenson reports that two of the infamous Roman Catholic scholars previously mentioned also entered into the practice

---

98 Rice, John, *Our God-Breathed Book--The Bible,* (Sword of the Lord Publishers, Murfreesboro, 1969), p. 387.

of providing definitive works. "Simon and Eichhorn were co-authors of a Hebrew Dictionary."[99]

Such infidelic works are accepted because they are produced by "great scholars." They are then used by good, godly men who do not realize the price of bowing to unbelieving scholarship.

GRIESBACH

Another important step in subtly attacking the authority of the Authorized Version is to exalt the unreliable manuscripts of the Local Text of Egypt as being superior to those of the Universal Text of Antioch. This will be commented on later. Let it suffice for now to reveal the man who laid the groundwork for just such a move. His name was J.J. Griesbach (1745-1812).

In order to enhance the image of the inferior Local Text manuscripts, Griesbach divided all Bible witnesses into three groups or "families." One was called the "Constantinopolitan" family, which is our Universal Text. The other two were known as "Western" and "Alexandrian."

As can be expected, Griesbach was **not** a Bible believer. In fact, he harbored an almost hostile attitude toward Scripture, which is revealed by his statement: "The New Testament abounds in more glosses, additions, and interpolations purposely introduced than any other book."[100] No Bible-believing, Bible-loving Christian should hand his sacred Book over to such a man for critical appraisal. His

---

99 Wilkenson, Benjamin, *Our Authorized Bible Vindicated,* (Takoma Park, 1930), p. 105.

100 Hills, Edward, *The King James Version Defended,* (The Christian Research Press, Des Moines, 1956), p. 65.

–

conclusion can easily be predicted. He will deduce that there is no perfect Bible on earth.

Griesbach was also antagonistic to any verse which taught the fundamental doctrines of the Christian faith. Whenever possible, he devised means to cast doubt on such passages. He said,

> "the most suspicious reading of all, is the one that yields a sense favorable to the nourishment of piety (especially monastic piety). When there are many variant readings in one place, that reading which more than the others manifestly favors the dogmas of the orthodox is deservedly regarded as suspicious."[101]

It is strange indeed that Dr. Griesbach should expect orthodox Christians to manipulate the Book which they truly believe to be from God, in order to teach Christianity more fervently. He never mentioned any apprehension that **heretics** might delete and alter doctrinal passages. (Sounds a great deal like former First Lady Hellery Clinton's "Great Right Wing Conspiracy" theory.) What kind of "scholarship" is it that naturally suspects born-again Christians of an act bordering on sacrilege, but never doubts the integrity of infidels? Is this God's method? **No!** It is simply part of a calculated plan to destroy the Bible as man's guidebook.

Whatever it was that possessed Griesbach to suspect Christians of such criminal acts also possessed two of his followers. Hills explains:

> "Westcott and Hort professed to 'venerate' the name of Griesbach above that of every other textual critic of the New Testament. Like Griesbach they believed that the orthodox Christian scribes had altered the New Testament manuscripts in the interest of orthodoxy. Hence like Griesbach, they ruled out

---

101 Ibid., p. 65.

in advance any possibility of the providential preservation of the New Testament text through the usage of believers. But at the same time they were very zealous to deny that heretics had made any intentional changes in the New Testament text. 'It will not be out of place,' they wrote, 'to add here a distinct expression of our belief that even among the numerous unquestionably spurious readings of the New Testament, there are no signs of deliberate falsification of the text for dogmatic purposes.' The effect of this one-sided theory was to condemn the text found in the majority of the New Testament manuscripts and exonerate that of B and Aleph."[102]

Thus the Local Text, supported by the Roman Catholic Church and her hand-picked "scholars" in her self-invented "science" of Textual Criticism, became an authority **equal to or higher than** the Universal Text of the Authorized Version in spite of the many doctrinal changes. After all, Griesbach, Westcott, and Hort had already established that heretics **never** falsify Scripture--only Christians do! Thus, only the "good guys" are bad and unworthy of our trust and only the "bad guys" are good and can be trusted not to corrupt Scripture (Isaiah 5:20, 21).

As the infidelity of men such as this is accepted as authoritative, Christians begin to look at their Bible with more and more skepticism. They begin to wonder if a word or passage was "really in the originals." The Bible's authority is questioned and its reliability is doubted. What more could Satan want?

Are these self-exalted scholars to be blamed for their failure to accept the Bible as infallible, or have they been unsuspecting dupes of a plan much bigger and far more serious than they could have ever suspected? Let us see.

102 Ibid., p. 66.

THE PUPPETEER

One man who became greatly responsible for the fall of English scholarship to a sympathetic acceptance of Roman Catholic ideas was **Cardinal Wiseman** (1802-1865). Wiseman was the prime mover in installing the Roman Catholic Church back on the shores of England. He was born and raised in England. He went to Rome to study under Cardinal Mai, the editor of the Vatican Manuscript.

Like any Roman Catholic, Wiseman had a desire to see England return to the fold of Rome. There were two major obstacles to this. One was the supremacy which the Authorized Version held in the English church Where the Authorized Version prevails, Rome cannot. Something would have to be done about the loyalty that English Christians ascribed to the King James Bible.

The second hindrance to Roman supremacy was the strict biblical influence that the Evangelicals held in the Church of England. Wiseman would be a key player in the destruction of these anti-Roman enemies in the Church of England.

THE PUPPETS

While Wiseman was in Rome, he was visited by several Neo-Protestants. He was instrumental in "weaning" these men back into subjection to the Roman pope. One of his visitors was **William Gladstone** (1809-1898), who was later to become prime minister of England. He was a man known for his change from being a conservative to a liberal.

Another of Wiseman's visitors was Anglican **Archbishop Trench**, who returned to England to promote a revision of the Authorized Version and even joined the Revision Committee of 1871. Wiseman's subversion was showing fruit!

Still another was **John Henry Newman**. Newman was the brilliant English churchman who was a leader of Oxford University and the English clergy. He was ordained a priest in the Church of England in 1824 and in less than ten years was going to assert himself as a powerful force for the Roman Catholic Church. He was to become one Rome's greatest assets in its battle to Romanize the Church of England.

One of Newman's close friends was **Richard Hurrell Froude**. Froude, Wilkenson tells us, was the son of a High Churchman, "who loathed Protestantism, denounced the Evangelicals, and brought up his sons to do the same."[103]

These two, Newman and Froude, joined affinity with **John Keble**. Keble, like Froude, was of High Church background. He was strongly anti-Protestant and anti-Evangelical.[104] These men were determined to do all that was within their power to influence the Church of England into the fold of Rome.

Newman and Froude visited Wiseman in Rome in 1833. Having been taken in by the beautiful architecture of Rome's cathedrals and the solemn grandeur of its high masses, the two Oxford professors enquired of Wiseman as to what terms the Roman Catholic Church would require to accept the Church of England back into Rome's fold. Wiseman's reply was cold and clear: The Church of England must accept the Council of Trent in its entirety. At this, Newman left Rome stating, "I have a work to do in England," a work indeed, in which he, Froude, Keble, and **Edward Pusey** joined forces to swing England back to Rome and to remove their primary adversary, the hated King James Bible.

---

103 Wilkenson, Benjamin, *Our Authorized Bible Vindicated*, (Takoma Park, 1930), p. 127.

104 Ibid., p. 127.

THE OXFORD MOVEMENT

The "work" Newman referred to became known as **"The Oxford Movement"** both Newman and Wiseman date its beginning from their July 14, 1833, meeting. Newman and Froude's meeting with then Monsignor Wiseman was kept secret. In fact, years later many of their followers stated that they never would have joined them had they known about their secret pact with Rome.

Rev. William Palmer was an earlier cohort of Newman's but left the movement when he recognized its bent toward the Great Whore. He later wrote:

> "... Newman had been anxious to ascertain the terms upon which they could be admitted to Communion by the Roman Church, *supposing that some dispensation might be granted which would enable them to communicate with Rome without violation of conscience*...if I had supposed him willing to forsake the Church of England, I should have said that I could in that case have had no communion with him."[105] (Emphasis his)

Thus we see that from its very inception, Newman's conspiratorial movement was to be shrouded in secrecy. This was absolutely necessary to their desired goals of reuniting the churches of Rome and England. We will see that this fear of being exposed guided many of their actions.

Newman, brilliant man that he was, provided the strong intellectual leadership needed to draw in the inquisitive. Pusey was the moralist, and Keble spoke through the delicate words of the poet and captivated the hearts and minds of many an unsuspecting young scholar. Any unsuspecting young student who lacked a strong stand on

---

105 Walsh, Walter, *The Secret History of The Oxford Movement*, (London, 1897), p.264.

Bible principles would be easy prey for these apostates. And there were **many!**

Before any progress could be made, secrecy had to be assured by Newman and his cohorts. Therefore, Newman began to subtly teach the Roman Catholic doctrine of "Reservation" in teaching, which he presented to his hearers as the "Disciplina Arcani" or "secret teachings." This insidious doctrine was combined with what he termed "Economy" of teaching. Basically both were used to excuse Newman and friends from **telling the truth of their Romish intents**. In this manner they could gently steer their adherents toward Rome with their subtle statements while never admitting-yea while even **denying**-that was their desired goal.

Newman pointed out that the church at Alexandria[106] used this mode of teaching to keep secret any offensive teaching. He quoted Clement of Alexandria as stating that a minister is to tell the truth, "*...except when careful treatment is necessary* and then, as a physician for the good of his patients, *he will* LIE, or rather utter a LIE, as the Sophists say...Nothing, however, but his neighbour's good will lead him to do this."[107] (Emphasis his)

Thus, since Newman felt that the best thing for the Church of England was that it return to Rome, he considered himself **doing a good work** if he lied about his intentions if the truth would turn people away from his desired goal (**Shades of Bill Clinton!**) Therefore, Newman and company began the practice of teaching the accepted doctrines of the Church of England from their pulpits but then clandestinely promoted their Romish doctrines in private to those they could trust not to betray them.

---

106 Anyone who has studied the Bible's view of Alexandria knows that it is certainly **not** the place to turn for examples of correct doctrine.

107 Walsh, Walter, *The Secret History of The Oxford Movement*, (London, 1897), p.2.

–

After the Oxford Movement was thwarted in 1845, its hellish vision spawned numerous secret societies which shared the common goal of Romanizing the Church of England. "The Society of the Holy Cross," "The Order of Corporate Reunion," "The Confraternity of the Blessed Sacrament," "The Guild of All Souls," "The Secret Order of the Holy Redeemer," "The Brotherhood of the Holy Cross" and "The Order of St. John the Divine" are just a few of the later secret organizations whose goal was the submission of all to Rome. Their membership rolls, meetings and constitutions were all closely guarded secrets. In fact, they sound all too much like "The Knights of Columbus," "The Masonic Order" and the multitude of **secret societies** thriving in our midst today. I wonder what **their** secret goals are?

Newman and his cohorts did not overlook the power of the printed page in their endeavors. Two of the key avenues used to disseminate their doctrines were a paper entitled *Essays and Reviews* and a series of **anonymous** individual tracts under the title "Tracts for Our Times," which attempted to redefine the Church of England's "Thirty-Nine Articles" as not being the anti-Roman Catholic statement that they indeed were. The tracts became such well known agents in propagating their teachings that the Oxford Movement soon became known also as the "Tractarian Movement" and its adherents called "Tractarians". Yet even the authorship and source of these tracts was to be kept a closely guarded secret. One of the leaders, Rev. William Palmer, admitted, "There was, indeed, much misapprehension abroad as to our motives, *without the danger of giving publicity to our proceedings, which,* in the then state of the public mind on Church matters, *might have led to dangerous results.*"[108] (Emphasis his)

Newman himself acknowledged his fear of exposure when he wrote to his friend Mr. J. W. Bowden, " We are just setting up here

---

108 Ibid, p.4.

Societies for the Defence (sic) of the Church. *We do not like our names known*, but we hope the plan will succeed."[109] (Emphasis his)

The sole desire of the Oxford Movement was to gently nudge the Church of England into accepting the Roman Catholic Council of Trent as authoritative and to surrender its autonomy to the Roman Church. Newman, Pusey, Froude and company knew that this goal dare never be found out. Lies, mis-information and dis-information were the order of the day and **absolutely necessary** to their success. In the name of the diabolical doctrine of "Reserve," they would do everything within their power to hide their true intentions and mislead their critics. They would delicately follow the Jesuit mandate, "above all, not too much zeal" in their clandestine attempt to turn the heat up a degree at a time on their Church of England "frog,"

Both Newman and Froude confided to friends in their private correspondence that they needed to keep their true goal from public view in order to succeed. Newman wrote to Rev. S. Rickards:

"I must just touch upon the notice of the Lord's Supper. *In confidence to a friend*, I can only admit it was imprudent, for I do think that we have most of us dreadfully low notions of the Blessed Sacrament. *I expect to be called a Papist when my opinions are known*. But (please God) I shall lead on a little way,..."[110] (Emphasis his)

Years later, in a work entitled *Apologia Pro Sua Vitay* Newman admitted that he believed "There is some kind or other of verbal misleading, which is not sin."[111]

---

109 Ibid, p.4.

110 Ibid, p.6.

111 Ibid. p.25.

Hurrell Froude also admitted in private that his actions since returning from his secret visit with Wiseman were less than above board. "Since I have been at home, I have been doing what I can to *proselytise* (sic) *in an underhand way.*" [112] (Emphasis His)

Rev. William George Ward, whose bombastic manner later became the catalyst that brought down the Movement, was very bold in expounding the need for **lying** in order to keep the Tractarians' Romish goals a secret. His son explains:

> "In discussing the doctrine of equivocation, as to how far it is lawful on occasion, he maintained, as against those who admit the lawfulness of words literally true but misleading, that the more straightforward principle is that occasionally when duties conflict, *another duty may be more imperative than the duty of truthfulness.* But he expressed it thus: 'Make yourself clear that you are *justified in deception,* and THEN LIE LIKE A TROOPER.'"[113] (Emphasis his)

Froude had been raised with a loathing for all things Protestant. He viewed any influence that the Reformation might have on the Church of England as negative and promoted the Roman Catholic Church in a far more positive light than the Church of England accepted.[114] Froude shared a strange trait with many of his fellow

---

112 Ibid, p.6.

113 Ibid. p.16. Had he been born one hundred years **later**, Rev. Ward would have qualified to be one of President Clinton's speech writers ...Forget it. He could have been President!

114 R. W. Church records that Froude answered the question ("What is the Church?") the same as other Anglicans but added two contrary points "(1) that there were great and to most people unsuspected faults and shortcomings in the English Church, for some of which the Reformation was gravely responsible; (2) that the Roman Church was more right than we had been taught to think in many parts both of principle and practice, and that our quarrel with it on these points arose from our own ignorance and prejudices."

Tractarians in that, though he was a young man, he was sickly and feeble a state that led to his early death in 1836 at the age of only thirty-three.[115]

Following Froude's death, his friends errantly published selections from his journals and letters. His violate hatred for the Reformers finally came to public light and the reaction was adverse to the Oxford Movement. Church reports, "Sermons and newspapers drew attention to Froude's extravagances with horror and disgust."[116] Of Froude's venomous condemnations of the Reformers and his blatant Romanism Mr. Church further informs us, "Undoubtedly, they warned off many who had so far gone along with the movement, and who now drew back."[117] In fact, even Church, whose feeble defenses of Froude fail as an attempt to vindicate him, had to admit in the end, "But when all is said, it still remains true that Froude was often intemperate and unjust."[118]

The battle lines were drawn. Newman, Froude, Pusey and company set themselves against their enemies the Evangelicals, the Reformers and the Methodists and **anyone** who tended to be **biblical** rather than Roman Catholic. Their obstacles were the Privy Council,

---

Church, R. W, *The Oxford Movement 1833 - 1845*, (Macmillan & Co., London, 1891), p. 46.

115 Church relates that in addition to Froude's feeble constitution, other "Movers & Shakers " of the Movement shared poor health. Of Charles Marriot he tells us, "His health was weak."; of Isaac Williams he says, " He suffered for the greatest part of his life from a distressing and disabling chronic asthma..." and of Tractarian Hugh James Rose he informs us, "But his action in the movement was impeded by his failure in health, and cut short by his early death."
      Ibid., pp. 74, 68, 87.

116 Ibid., p. 37.

117 Ibid., p. 38.

118 Ibid., p. 39.

Heads of Houses and The Convocation, the governing bodies of Oxford and the Church of England. Their hope was to use their broad and powerful influence on Oxford's student body as a method of steering the Church of England back to Rome.

While Newman led the movement's intellectual front, Prof. Edward Pusey reached out to the High Churchmen. His was the goal of bestowing on all whom he could the mystical tenants of Romanism. It was his desire (as it was Froude's) to see monasteries re-established on English soil. Dr. Pusey was as dedicated to secrecy and deceit as were his fellow Romanists. Early in the movement they lent themselves to verbal and written statements against popery while clandestinely promoting what they inferred to be "true" catholicism. Their anti-**papal** smokescreen deceived many into thinking they were also anti-**catholic**. Pusey admitted this to a confidant when he wrote,

"I know not that the Popish controversy may not just be the very best way of handling Ultra-Protestantism, *i.e.,* neglecting it, not advancing against, but setting Catholic views against Roman Catholicism and *so disposing of Ultra-Protestantism by a side wind, and teaching people Catholicism, without their suspecting,* while they are only bent on demolishing Romanism. I suspect we might thus have people with us, instead of against us, and that *they might find themselves Catholic before they are aware.*"[119] (Emphasis his)

Pusey used his influence among his young, impressionable students to steer them into forbidden and even depraved Roman Catholic practices such as self-flagellation, the act of whipping oneself as an atonement for sins. The whip used for such acts was known as a "Discipline." Pusey wrote a friend traveling on the continent to see if he could purchase one for him and information as to the proper (and safe) usage of it. Walsh reveals Pusey's request:

---

119 Walsh, Walter, *The Secret History of The Oxford Movement*, (London, 1897), p.10.

"I see in a spiritual writer that even for such, corporal severities are not to be neglected, but so many of the are unsafe. *I suspect the 'Discipline' to be one of the safest,* and with internal humiliation *the best.* Could you procure and send me one by B.? What was described was of a very sacred character; *5 cords, each with 5 knots,* in memory of the wounds of our Lord. I should be glad also to know whether there were any cases in which it is unsafe, e.g., in a nervous person."[120] (Emphasis his)

Sounds like a customer as a Sado-Masochist shop! Dr. Pusey used and advised the use of other forms of "mild torture" as well. He even records that he wore the "Hair Shirt." This was a garment of corse hair worn next to the skin to cause discomfort to the wearer again, designed to cause suffering that was supposed to make the victim holier. Pusey's only complaint concerning the hair shirt was that it didn't hurt him enough, so he wanted to whip himself!

"I am a great coward about inflicting pain upon myself, partly, I hope, from a derangement of my nervous system. Hair Cloth I know not how to make pain: it is only symbolical, except when worn to an extent which seemed to wear me out. *I have it on again, by God's mercy.* I would try to get some sharper sort. Lying hard I like best, unless it is such to take away sleep, and that seems too unfit for my duties...Praying with my arms in the form of a cross, seemed to distract me, and act upon my head, from this same miserable nervousness. *I think I should like to be bid to use the Discipline.* I cannot smite upon my breast much because the pressure on my lungs seemed bad."[121] (Emphasis his)

---

120 Ibid., p. 36.

121 Ibid., p. 36, 37.

Contrary to the will and teaching of the Church of England, Pusey sought the establishment of convents for the training of "Sisters of Mercy" over which he held authority and even recommended the whipping of these innocent young woman by their Superior. His recommendation was "For mortifications; the Discipline for about a quarter of a hour a day."[122]

Such vile doctrine combined with the **absolute authority** of a Superior begs for abuse and never goes unsatisfied. We can hear the testimony of just such a crime against a helpless young girl of misguided devotion in the girl's own words:

"One day I was coming from Nones at 2:45 P.M. This 'Mother' commanded me to stay where I was, and not to return to work, and then said:---'You have the Devil in you, and I am going to beat him out.' All left the sacristy but myself, the Mother Superior, and one Nun, who was ordered to be present at the casting out of the devil. I was commanded first to strip. I saw *"the Discipline,"* with its seven lashes of knotted whipcord her hand...I should mention at certain times *it was the rule to Discipline oneself*...Then I began to undress; but when I came to my vest, shame again overcame me. 'Take that thing off,' said the Mother Superior. I replied, I cannot, reverend Mother; it's too tight.' The Nun who was present was told to help me get it off. A deep feeling of shame came over me at being half-nude. The Mother then ordered the Nun to say the *'Miserere'*, and while it was recited *she lashed me several times with all her strength.* I was determined not to utter a sound, but at last I could not restrain a smothered groan, whereat she gave me one last and cruel lash, and then ceased. Even three weeks after she had 'Disciplined' me, I had a very sore back, and it hurt me greatly to lie on it (our beds were straw put into sacks). There

---

122 Ibid., p. 39. This scurrilous practice is still followed in countries shackled by the bonds of Romanism and behind the closed doors of convents and monasteries. But regardless of this demoniac teaching, **torture is not the road to holiness!**

was a looking-glass in the room I now occupied (Nuns do not usually have them), and I looked to see if my back was marked, as it was so sore. Never shall I forget the shock it gave me. I turned quickly away, for *my back was black, blue, and green all over.*"[123] (Emphasis hers)

It is horrible, demoniac practices like this that **the Bible holds at bay!** Such actions are not accepted in societies ruled by Scripture. But remove the Bible and replace it with religion and excess and cruelty literally become **a way of life**. If **you** are not a **Bible reader** and a **Bible promoter** you are helping such heathen practices take root in our society!

Edward Pusey became one of the prime movers of the Oxford Movement to such an extent that the label "Puseyite" was added to those used to describe adherents to its tenets.

It is easy to see why such men as Newman, Froude and Pusey would see Protestants, Evangelicals and Methodists as obstacles to their vile scheme. So it is no wonder that they uplifted tradition and superstition and hated the high standing in which **preaching** was held by their opponents. Their desire was to diminish the place of Scripture in the services of the Church of England and replace it with a sacredolical reverence for High Church and the sacraments. So here they were. Members of the Church of England who were **in fact** Roman Catholic in spirit and agents of that organization, who were dedicated to herding the English church back into the fold of Rome. They shared a universal hatred for all things Protestant and biblical. Flushed with the liberties granted them by the silence of the Bishops of the Church of England they over extended themselves in two crucial actions that brought all the wrath of Convocation down on them and **literally** drove them to the church they truly loved, Rome.

---

123 Sister Mary Agnes, O. S. B., *Nunnery Life in the Church of England*, pp.97-99.

One vehicle of their undoing was Tract #90 written by Newman and published in late 1841. In it he desperately, and unsuccessfully, tried to convince his readers that the Thirty-nine Articles were not at all intended to be anti-Roman Catholic. He twisted and reinterpreted (Something today we would call "Revisionist History") the Articles in slobbering attempt to overwhelm the anti-Roman sentiments of the English church. It did not work and drew blistering criticism from the now fully awakened governing bodies of both the Church as well as the university. The Theological Faculty of the University censured the tract.

The year 1842 began with a fully aroused university seeking to purge itself of the Roman collaborators within it. A Tractarian, Isaac Williams, was turned down for the Poetry Professorship. Followers of the movement were slowly but methodically purged from places of rank and authority. Roman Catholics, no matter what they called themselves, were not going to be allowed free rein in Oxford.

In early 1843, Dr. Pusey, in an attempt to stem the tide that was fast rising against them, preached a sermon in which he nearly deified the "Holy Eucharist." Rather than securing a victory for the fast fading Tractarians, he "shot himself in the foot." He was brought up on charges of heresy, condemned and forbidden to preach at the university for two years. That year also saw the end of the Oxford Review, a mouthpiece of the movement.

Then 1844 saw an audacious, last-ditch effort by **W. G. Ward** to re-establish the forward momentum that the movement had been enjoying in its former years. He published *Ideal of a Christian Church, considered in Comparison with Existing Practice.* Here was a man who hated the doctrine of Justification by Faith. He now demanded complete and outright submission to Rome. He was called before the Board of the Heads of Houses, where his book was openly condemned, and had his degree revoked.

As 1845 began, the Oxford Movement was in a shambles. Some were outwardly leaving the Church of England for the church of Rome while others, shocked into sensibility by the exposure of the Romanist plot, fled the movement. And now there were rumblings of judgement yet to come against the movement's chief perpetrator, John Henry Newman. There was only one escape for Newman, escape to Rome! Wilkenson records Newman's betrayal:

> "Public sentiment was again aroused to intensity in 1845 when Ward, an outstanding Tractarian, published his book which taught the most offensive Roman views, Mariolatry, and mental reservation in subscribing to the Thirty-nine Articles. When Oxford degraded him from his university rights, he went over in September to the Church of Rome. It became very evident that Newman soon would follow. On the night of October 8 Father Dominic, of the Italian Passionists, arrived at Newman's quarters in a down pouring rain. After being received, he was standing before the fire drying his wet garments. He turned around to see Newman prostrate at his feet, begging his blessing, and asking him to hear his confession. Thus the author of *Lead Kindly Light* passed over to Rome, and within one year 150 clergymen and eminent laymen also had joined the Catholic Church."[124]

Where was Wiseman through all of this? He was naturally close at hand. In 1836, three years following Newman and Froude's visit, he had moved to Ireland to supervise the Oxford Movement through his paper, the Dublin Review. Wiseman was described as "...a textual critic of the first rank, and assisted by the information seemingly passed on to him from the **Jesuits**, he was able to furnish the facts well calculated to combat confidence in the **Protestant Bible**."[125](Emphasis mine.)

---

124 Wilkenson, Benjamin, *Our Authorized Bible Vindicated* (Takoma Park, 1930), pp. 135, 136.

125 Ibid., p. 135.

–

Ironically, the purging of the Oxford Movement did not secure the fidelity of the Church of England. They had already allowed the leaven in the church. The Bible had already been diminished in stature and ritualism exalted in its place. By 1852 it was said that there were **more Jesuits in England than in all of Italy!** And where were they? Walsh records:

"...there are Jesuits in all classes of society; in Parliament; *among the English clergy*; among Protestant laity, and even in higher stations. I could not comprehend how a Jesuit could be a Protestant priest, or how a Protestant priest could be a Jesuit; but my confessor silenced my scruples by telling me, *omnia munda mundis*, and that St. Paul became as a Jew that he might save the Jews; it was no wonder, therefore, if a Jesuit should feign himself a Protestant, for the conversion of Protestants.

"The English clergy were formerly too much attached to their Articles of Faith to be shaken from them...so the Jesuits of England tried another plan. This was to demonstrate from history and ecclesiastical antiquity the legitimacy of the uses of the English Church, whence, through the exertions of **the Jesuits concealed among its clergy**, might arise a studious attention to Christian antiquity. This was designed to occupy the clergy in long, laborious, and abstruse investigation, and to **alienate them from their Bibles**"[126] (Emphasis mine)

R. W. Church reports that the Tractarians were gone but not forgotten as they had been replaced with a new generation dedicated to the destruction of the Word of God. "But a younger set of men brought,

126 Walsh, Walter, *The Secret History of The Oxford Movement*, (London, 1897), p.33.

mainly from Rugby and Arnold's teaching, a **new kind of Liberalism**."[127] (Emphasis mine)

This Liberalism infested the higher levels of education until it succeeded in its cry for a "revision" of the King James Bible. A revision that was the first in a long line of versions that **coincidentally** use the Roman Catholic manuscript Vaticanus as their primary authority. Our we to believe this all happened by accident?

So we see that by 1870 England had graduated from "**revival**" to "**education**," and her "**education**" had developed into her own unique "**culture**." Culture is of the flesh and **no one** knows how to deal with the flesh better than Rome. So from there, the Roman Catholic Church was more than willing to supply the "**apostasy**."

AGENTS OF APOSTASY

One of the things we must come to realize is that **apostasy doesn't just "happen" by accident**. Nor is it a gradual process that results from slowly drifting from the truth. The apostasy that swept the Church of England did not happen spontaneously. It was **intentionally inserted** into the stream of the church by powers that had a desired end in mind. Newman, Froude, Pusey, Keble, none were "well meaning but misguided" men. They were **agents of apostasy** who were intentionally carrying out a predetermined plan to change the course of the English church and send it back to Rome which has happened. They were placed in high and influential positions from which they could mold **the next generation** of English churchmen. Although they did not achieve their goal of returning the Church of England to the fold of Rome **personally**, they did succeed it tainting their innocent students with

---

127 Church, R. W., *The Oxford Movement 1833 - 1845*, (Macmillan & Co., London), 1891, p. 338.

enough Roman poison that they obeyed their masters and brought the church in line with Rome's desires.

How did this happen? As I've already stated it did not happen by accident. It was planned and carried out with cunning and forethought. So is it impossible to stop? Maybe. But it certainly isn't impossible to **fight**. First we have to identify exactly how apostasy was inserted into the English church so we know what to watch for and how to react to it.

1. EXALTING MEN - It cannot be denied that there are some men who stand out and above their peers. To pretend that we are all the same would be both dishonest and counter-productive. These men naturally tend to help and influence those around them, preferably for the good. But the sad truth is that **good men don't always stay good!** 2 Chronicles 14 and 15 tell of the great and good king Asa and his dedication and dependence on the Lord. He did that which was right in the eyes of the Lord. He cast out idols and images and trusted God in battle against armies greater than his. He further entered into a renewed covenant with God and directed Judah to turn to Him. This great man ruled in God's will for **thirty-five years**. Yet in his thirty-sixth year, Baasha, the king of Israel came against him and he **forsook God**. He was a **good man who didn't stay good.**

What Christian - what Bible college student - can't look back to some "great man" who has helped them in some way at an hour of need or to better know the Lord? We can all remember someone who was there at a crucial point in our lives someone we feel more than a casual loyalty to for his selfless help.

There can be no doubt that John Henry Newman, John Keble and Edward Pusey had all helped weak brethren in a multitude of ways. But **good men don't always stay good**.

Our problem is that when our mentor - our close compatriot - takes a turn in the **wrong direction**, we don't want to acknowledge it.

We can't stand to think that someone who has meant so much to us could go bad. Even worse we can't stand the thought of being alienated from him, or (worse yet) having to take a stand against him.

Please understand history is full of **good men** who **never** went bad. It isn't predestinated. But there are also those who started out **good** and went **bad** later in life. Benedict Arnold was a **hero** before he was a traitor. Jack Kevorkian tried to save lives before he turned to ending them. And need I mention Judas? Just because someone **was** great, just because we may feel we are indebted to him, **doesn't guarantee that he will remain straight**. And we have to accept this and **cut ourselves off from him** when we see it. No one says we have to hate him. We can even sadly feel our indebtedness to him. But we cannot turn our heads when we see him saying or doing things that **we know** are wrong!

2. CHANGING TERMINOLOGY - One of the tactics used by Newman and company was to **redefine** terms that were plainly understood as having a different meaning than was originally intended. The Thirty-nine Articles, written in condemnation of the Roman Catholic Church, were **reinterpreted by the Tractarians** as being anti-**Roman** but not anti-**catholic.**

We see this very thing taking place in our own society as power hungry, oppression-minded Liberals seek to **redefine** the **plain truth** of our Constitution. "Cruel and unusual punishment," which was directed against **torture,** is now claimed by the deceitful News Industry to mean "capital punishment". Even though the framers of the Constitution **practiced capital punishment!** The same is done with the Second Amendment and the woman's "right" to murder her unborn baby.

When someone takes **a plain truth** and smoothly turns it around to mean just the opposite of what it says, it is time to take **a giant step back.** This is exactly what the authors of the New King James Version did with 2 Timothy 3:3. Here Paul warns us against people who are "Without natural affection." Who are these people? Well think!

–

Homosexuals are "without natural affection." Environmentalists are "without natural affection." Animal-rightists are "without natural affection." Child molesters are "without natural affection." Yet the authors of the New King James Version have removed "without natural affection" from the passage and altered the verse to read "Unloving,"[128] So the perverts of our society get soft treatment from this and other modern versions. But wait! Not only do they get exempted from scriptural condemnation, but they can now use **the very same verse** to bash their critics for being "unloving."

When someone begins to slyly redefine terms so that they mean the opposite of what they say, **get away from him!** I don't care what he's ever done for you or how "great" you think he is. You may not even be able to argue against their presentation, but you just know something is wrong. Just get away. You owe no one an explanation.

3. "BREAKING DOWN THE WALLS" - The Promise Keepers, non-denominationalists and other ecumenicalists like to cry that we need to "break down the walls" that keep us from enjoying fellowship with each other. Where did this cry come from? (Besides **Hell**, I mean.) Walter Walsh clearly identifies the source as he quotes a letter sent to the Bishops of the Church of England in 1867 by The Society of the Holy Cross, one of many pro-Roman societies that sprang up in the wake of the Oxford Movement:

> "We are mindful of efforts made in former time by English and foreign Bishops and theologians *to effect*, by mutual explanations on either side, *a reconciliation between the Roman and Anglican Communions.* And, considering the intimate and visible union which existed between the Church of England and the rest of Western Christendom, we earnestly entreat your

---

128 The corrupt New American Standard Version "Amens!" this with "Unloving," while its sinister cohort the New International Version reads "Without love." Good News For Modern Man whines, "Unkind," and the Living Bible says, "Hard headed." **Trash!** All of them!

lordships seriously to consider the best means of renewing like endeavours; and to adopt such measures as may, under the guidance if God's Holy Spirit, be effectual in REMOVING THE BARRIERS which now divide the Western Branch of the Catholic Church."[129]

So we see that when someone tries mingle people of different faiths together he runs into "barriers" which hamper his insidious desires. What are some of these "walls" that need broken down?

A. Doctrine - One of the cries of interdenominationalists is that "doctrine divides." **That's right!** Doctrine is **supposed to divide**. "Salvation by Grace," "Eternal Security" and a few others will divide a group of Christians faster than "Attention K-Mart shoppers." Those who wish to introduce apostasy into fundamental churches realize the need to "get everyone together" and they know they can't do it if doctrine is upheld. So when you see someone **de-emphasizing** Bible doctrine, you know you have someone who is trying to destroy your Bible purity.

B. Standards - Standards against worldly music and dress, against worldly practices and ways are designed to keep apostasy out of our lives and help us to live more holy than those who are without Christ. Standards in themselves do not automatically make us holy. They simply help keep us from getting into situations where we might be prone to compromise our purity for fun or convenience.

In this area we can learn a lesson from the Amish. We all know about the Amish. Those folks who dress in long dark clothing, ride around in horse-drawn buggies, and don't believe in electricity or rubber tires. I studied the Amish once and was amazed to find out that they **do not have a conviction against electricity or rubber tires!** Rather, they **exclude** them from their lives as **barriers** to the world.

129 Walsh, Walter, *The Secret History of The Oxford Movement*, (London, 1897), pp..324, 325.

–

They realize that "you've got to stop the world somewhere" and have chosen to stop it with the exclusion of these modern conveniences. They simply understand that with electricity will come some other invasion of the world into their midst, so they've chosen to stop the world there with a **barrier**.

By no means am I advocating that we get rid of our cars and electricity and wear long dark clothing and go around in horse-drawn buggies.[130] But we do need to establish some **inconvenient** barriers to keep our flesh from getting too caught up in the things of the world.

C. The King James Bible - Apostates and Romanists are greatly hampered in their efforts by the purity and power of the King James Bible. Congregations where this divine Book is upheld seem almost impenetrable to them. Before they can institute their vile desires on a congregation or denomination they must first remove the King James Bible from its place of preeminence. We have seen how this is done by subverting the faith of believers with "scholarship" and new versions.

WHERE WE STAND

Today in colleges and churches across America and around the world, truly good, godly men who love the Lord Jesus and sincerely desire to serve Him are unsuspectingly propagating the Roman Catholic "science" of textual criticism. In some cases this is done with "malice afore-thought," but most are simply parroting what they were taught by agents of apostasy a generation ago. The result of this is that Christian soldiers who go out to fight Rome do so from a terribly inferior position. Either they go out with a perfect Bible which they have been

---

130 Some of the brethren actually do advocate this. They call themselves "Plain People" and like to think of themselves as being closer to God than others. I call them the "Proud People" because they are **so proud of their "humility."**

taught to doubt, or else an unreliable translation of the Rome-supported Local Text, which is worthy of all suspicion.

Christian education in America has come to the place of either having to swallow its pride, admit it has been wrong, and return to the true Bible; or else make another more vehement attack on the Authorized Bible and it proponents in hopes of finally silencing it and its supporters in the hope of hiding its mistake. Christians, be advised! The Revised Version did not ring the death knell for the King James Bible. It rang the death knell for England!

Most of the translations before and after 1881 which were going to replace the Authorized Version lie silently in the "grave" right now. Those which do not shall soon join their ranks in the halls of the "improved," "thoroughly reliable," "truly accurate," and "starters of a new tradition" dead. They have failed to start one revival. They have failed to induce Christians back to reading their Bibles and have only succeeded in casting doubt on the true Word of God. The question is, Can we repair the damage already done and proceed from here? The answer is **YES**!

Chapter 8

Westcott and Hort

BROOKE Foss **Westcott** (1825-1903) and **Fenton John Anthony Hort** (1828-1892) have been highly controversial figures in the history of the English Bible. Their theories have been pivotal in swaying scholarship away from the tried and true Universal Text of Antioch and into the web of Alexandrian higher criticism. Their accomplishments have been both lauded and cajoled.

On one side, their supporters have heralded them as great men of God who have greatly advanced the search for the original Greek text. Most Christian colleges still trumpet praise for them and teach their theories as faithfully as a public school teacher espouses evolution.

On the other side, their opponents have leveled charges of heresy, infidelity, apostasy, and many others errors, claiming that they are guilty of wreaking great damage on the true text of Scripture. There are a faithful few Bible schools who are brave enough to break with tradition and expose the fallacies of their works. But these are condemned by the deceived as being "unscholarly." (Thank God!)

I have no desire to "sling mud" nor a desire to hide facts. But I believe it is essential at this time that we examine what we know about these men and their theories concerning the text of the Bible. We must investigate just what they believed in order to understand how they arrived at the conclusions that they did.

I long sought for copies of the books about their lives. These are *The Life and Letters of Brooke Foss Westcott* by his son Arthur, and *The Life and Letters of Fenton John Anthony Hort*, written by his son. After literally months of trying, I was able to acquire copies of them both for study. Most of the material in this chapter will be directly from these sources so as to prevent it from being secondhand.

We cannot blindly accept the finding of **any** scholar without investigating what his beliefs are concerning the Bible and its doctrines. As we have seen, scholarship alone makes for an inadequate and dangerous authority, therefore, we are forced to scrutinize these men's beliefs, their actions and their values.

A MONUMENTAL SWITCH

More than two hundred years after its publication in 1611, the King James Bible was still the pre-eminent Bible used by Christians in England and around the world. There had been weak attempts made to replace it, but each endeavor had failed miserably. The agents of apostasy dove into the fray and began their work of casting doubt on its reliability. The Oxford Movement was successful in damaging the integrity of the Church of England beyond repair. So by the mid-nineteenth century the forces of the Roman Catholic Church had so saturated the Church of England that they were successful in finally getting Convocation to call for a "revision" of the Authorized Version. The revisors began their work in 1871 and published their New Testament in 1881 and the Old in 1884. It was known as the Revised Version.

When they were seated, the revisers were commissioned to "correct" what they perceived as errors in the Authorized Version. (There **are no errors** in the Authorized Version to "correct.") They were carefully instructed to maintain the Textus Receptus as the Greek text underlying their work. They were not authorized to change to a different Greek text for their work. Yet by the time their work was completed they had completely discarded the Universal Text in favor of the inferior Local Text of Alexandria, Egypt. How was it done? Through chicanery, intimidation and outright dishonesty.

Brooke Foss Westcott and F. J. A. Hort, members of the revision committee, were responsible for this underhanded action. Bit by bit they secretly, unsuspectingly introduced their own **unpublished** rendition of Alexandria's corruption of Scripture into the revision committee. By patient guidance they achieved the greatest feat in textual criticism. They managed to supplant the Universal Text of the Authorized Version with the Local Text of Egypt and the Roman Catholic Church **without authority** to do so and **against** the wishes of the Convocation.

Neither Westcott nor Hort was a Bible believer and both were known to have resented the pre-eminence given to the Authorized Version and its underlying Greek text. They had been deceived into believing that the Roman Catholic manuscripts Vaticanus and Aleph were better because they were "older." They believed this even though Hort admitted that the or Universal Text was **equal** in antiquity to the old Egyptian manuscripts.

"The fundamental Text of the late extant Greek manuscripts generally is beyond all question identical with the dominant or Graeco-Syrian Text of the second half of the Fourth Century."[131]

VICIOUS PREJUDICE

---

131 Burgon, John, *The Revision Revised*, (Conservative Classics, Paradise, 1883), p. 257.

In spite of the fact that **they knew** the readings of the Universal Text were found to be as old or older than the Egyptian text, Westcott and Hort still sought to dislodge it from its place of high standing in biblical history. Hort occasionally let his emotions show.

> "I had no idea till the last few weeks of the importance of text, having read so little Greek Testament, and dragged on with the villainous Textus Receptus...Think of the vile Textus Receptus leaning entirely on late MSS; it is a blessing there are such early ones."[132]

Rather than submit to the will of Convocation, Westcott and Hort **manufactured** their own Greek text based primarily on a handful of uncial manuscripts of the Local Text of Alexandria, Egypt. It has been stated earlier that these perverted manuscripts do not even agree among themselves. Therefore, their attraction to the two Oxford scholars was their opposing view to that of the Universal Text and not any **pretended** textual purity. The ironic thing is that Westcott and Hort knew that these Egyptian manuscripts did not agree among themselves when they formed their text! Burgon exposed Dr. Hort's confession to this fact:

> "Even Hort had occasion to notice an instance of the concordia discourse. Commenting on the four places in Mark's gospel (14:30, 68, 72, a, b) where the cock's crowing is mentioned, said, 'The confusion of attestation introduced by these several cross currents of change is so great that of the seven principal manuscripts, Aleph, A, B, C, D, L, no two have the same text in all four places.'"[133]

---

132 Hort, Arthur Fenton, *Life and Letters of Fenton John Anthony Hort*, (New York, 1896), Volume I, p. 211.

133 Fuller, David, *True or False?*, (Grand Rapids International Publications, Grand Rapids, 1973), p. 261

So we see that these men were no more prompted by pure motives than John Henry Newman was when he began the Oxford Movement. Quite apparently Westcott and Hort had "a great work to do England" as well. And it was one that was every bit as insidious as that of Newman and his cohorts.

A SHOCKING REVELATION

That these men should lend their influence to a family of manuscripts which have a history of attacking and diluting the major doctrines of the Bible should not come as a surprise to anyone who has investigated the doctrinal positions of either man. They were not what we would call **straight** doctrinally. They were, in fact, nothing more than a couple of lost Episcopalians who had no more respect for the Bible than any other lost religious person. In fact, neither man believed that the Bible should be treated any differently than the writings of the lost historians and philosophers! That is by no means the position taken by anyone who **loves** the Bible and upholds it as God perfect Word.

Hort wrote,

> "For ourselves, we dare not introduce considerations which could not reasonably be applied to other ancient texts, supposing them to have documentary attestation of equal amount, variety and antiquity."[134]

He also states,

> "In the New Testament, **as in almost all prose writings which have been much copied**, corruptions by interpolation are

---

134 Hills, Edward, *Believing Bible Study,* (The Christian Research Press, Des Moines, 1967), p. 122.

many times more numerous than corruptions by omission." [135] (Emphasis mine.)

We must consider these things for a moment. Would God use men who do not believe that His Book is any different than Shakespeare, Plato, or Dickens? It is a fundamental belief that the Bible is different from all other writings. Why did these men not believe so? But beyond that, why would **anyone who claims** to believe and love the Bible give any credence to the opinions such men had concerning Scripture?

BLATANT DISBELIEF

The skepticism of Westcott and Hort does, in fact, go even deeper than this. They openly discounted some of the bedrock doctrines of Christianity. Yet somehow they have managed to become famous for being able to deny scriptural truth and still be upheld by fundamental Christianity as credible biblical authorities! Both Westcott and Hort failed to accept the basic Bible doctrines which we hold so dear and vital to our fundamental faith. That **anyone** calling himself a "Fundamentalist" would accept their finding as authoritative is a shame to that individual.

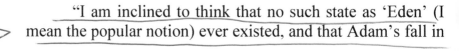

Of their many failing we find that F. J. A. Hort **didn't believe in creation** and openly denied the reality of Eden:

"I am inclined to think that no such state as 'Eden' (I mean the popular notion) ever existed, and that Adam's fall in

---

135 Fuller, David, *True or False?,* (Grand Rapids International Publications, Grand Rapids, 1973), p. 240.

–

no degree differed from the fall of each of his descendants, as Coleridge justly argues."[136]

Think about this. Here we have a man who is upheld by Fundamentalists and fundamental colleges as a reliable authority in the area of biblical manuscripts and yet he defied one of the most basic Bible doctrines, creation. With a stand like, that do you think that some of the very colleges that exalt him would dare even let him speak on their campuses if he were alive today?

Earlier we studied the Oxford Movement and its Romanizing influence on the Church of England. Loyal Anglican churchmen turned away from and denounced the Tractarians. Not Hort. **He agreed with them!** In a letter to Rev. Rowland Williams, dated October 21, 1858, Hort writes,

> "Further I agree with them [authors of Essays and Reviews] in condemning many leading specific doctrines of the popular theology...Evangelicals seem to me perverted rather than untrue. There are, I fear, still more serious differences between us on the subject of authority, and especially the authority of the Bible."[137]

You will remember that is was the more biblical Evangelicals who withstood the Romanizers of the Oxford Movement. They put too much stock in the Bible for Newman and the rest. They minimized the importance of tradition and totally mistrusted Rome obvious positions that were unacceptable to Newman, Pusey and the others and apparently unacceptable to Fenton John Anthony Hort as well!

---

136 Hort, Arthur Fenton, *Life and Letters of Fenton John Anthony Hort*, (New York, 1896), Vol. I, p. 78.

137 Ibid., p. 400.

If that were not enough, Hort didn't even accept the Bible as **infallible**. When asked to join the Revision Committee, he stated, "If you make a decided conviction of the absolute infallibility of the N.T. practically a sine qua non for co-operation, I fear I could not join you."

He also stated:

> "As I was writing the last words a note came from Westcott. He too mentions having had fears, which he now pronounces 'groundless,' on the strength of our last conversation, in which he discovered that I did 'recognize' 'Providence' in biblical writings. Most strongly I recognize it; but I am not prepared to say that it necessarily involves absolute infallibility. So I still await judgment."

And he further commented to a colleague: "But I am not able to go as far as you in asserting the absolute infallibility of a canonical writing."[138]

No college or university that calls itself "Christian" could possibly exalt such an infidel as an authority who can be trusted! He simply **did not believe the Bible** was perfect. He ranks with Carl Sagan and Harry Emerson Fosdick, not John Burgon or Robert Dick Wilson. Again, we would **never** allow anyone who believed as this in one of our pulpits. So why should we allow him in our classrooms?

STRANGE BEDFELLOWS

Although he had mean things to say about the evangelicals of his day, Hort had great admiration for a famous enemy of Christianity...**Charles Darwin!** To his colleague B.F. Westcott, he wrote excitedly:

---

138 Ibid., pp. 420-422.

—

"...Have you ever read Darwin? How I should like to talk with you about it! In spite of difficulties, **I am inclined to think it unanswerable**. In any case it is a treat to read such a book." (Emphasis mine.)

Further establishing his adherence to the theory of evolution, he confided to his friend John Ellerton,

"But the book which has most engaged me is Darwin. Whatever may be thought of it, it is a book that one is proud to be contemporary with...My feeling is strong that the theory is unanswerable. If so, it opens up a new period."[139]

Let me ask you, would **you** say that you were "proud" to be contemporary with Charles Darwin and his faulty theory? Fenton John Anthony Hort was. He even went so far as to admit that he believed the theory of evolution to be "unanswerable".

Dr. Hort was also an adherent of the teachings of Samuel Taylor Coleridge. His son writes: "In undergraduate days, if not before, he came under the spell of Coleridge."[140]

Coleridge was the college drop-out whose drug addiction is an historical fact. "The opium habit, begun earlier to deaden the pain of rheumatism, grew stronger. After vainly trying in Malta and Italy to break away from opium, Coleridge came back to England in 1806."[141] This opium habit was said to have greatly hampered his creativity. His famous poems amount to only about twenty pages of text.

---

139 Ibid., pp. 414-416.

140 Ibid., p. 42.

141 *New Standard Encyclopedia,* (Standard Educational Corporation, 1977), p. 450.

Apparently Coleridge's opium had some effect on his view of man's relationship to God. For one of his most famous works was *Aids to Reflection*. "Its chief aim is to harmonize formal Christianity with Coleridge's variety of transcendental philosophy. He also did much to introduce Immanual Kant and other German philosophers to English readers."[142]

Coleridge was not a man whose sway would be welcomed by any Bible-believing college. Yet, Coleridge had a great influence on the two scholars from Cambridge. And these two errant professors have had an adverse effect on Christianity through those very same colleges.

FORSAKING COLOSSIANS 2:8

In addition to the poetry of a drug addict, Hort was also a lover of Greek philosophy. In writing to Mr. A. MacMillian, he stated:

> "You seem to make (Greek) philosophy worthless for those who have received the Christian revelation. To me, though in a hazy way, it seems full of precious truth of which I find nothing, and should be very much astonished and perplexed to find anything in revelation."[143]

I don't think I've ever heard a Bible believer ever describe Greek philosophy as being "full of precious truth"! But then, if you were **lost** you might see some value in it.

Thus, we see that Hort was more an admirer of **philosophy** than **Scripture**. He placed high regard in drug addicted poets but thought that soul winners were "perverted." Dr. Hort could not possibly be

---

142 Ibid., pp. 450-451.

143 Hort, Arthur Fenton, *Life and Letters of Fenton John Anthony Hort,* (New York, 1896), Vol. I, p. 449.

–

accepted as a credible witness in resolving the question of which family of Bible manuscripts we should trust.

LOST IN THE FOREST

In some cases Hort seemed to wander in the woods. In others he can only be described as being utterly "lost in the forest." Take, for example, his views on fundamental Bible truths. Truths that are fundamental to the Christian faith and anyone who holds the Bible dear to them.

HORT'S "DEVIL"

Concerning the existence of a personal devil, Hort wrote:

"The discussion which immediately precedes these four lines naturally leads to another enigma most intimately connected with that of everlasting penalties, namely that of the personality of the devil. It was Coleridge who some three years ago first raised any doubts in my mind on the subject--doubts which have never yet been at all set at rest, one way or the other. You yourself are very cautious in your language.

"Now if there be a devil, he cannot merely bear a corrupted and marred image of God; he must be wholly evil, his name evil, his every energy and act evil. Would it not be a violation of the divine attributes for the Word to be actively the support of such a nature as that?"[144]

HORT'S "HELL"

144 Ibid., p. 121.

Dr. Hort also shrunk from the belief in a literal, eternal "hell." He stated,

> "I think Maurice's letter to me sufficiently showed that we have no sure knowledge respecting the duration of future punishment, and that the word 'eternal' has a far higher meaning than the merely material one of excessively long duration; extinction always grates against my mind as something impossible."[145]

> "Certainly in my case it proceeds from no personal dread; when I have been living most godlessly, I have never been able to frighten myself with visions of a distant future, even while I 'held' the doctrine."[146]

I have often heard the defenders of Westcott and Hort claim that any "strange doctrines" that they held, they held in their youth, and that in later years they had got straightened out. Yet here we have a **plain admission** from Hort himself that he actually **had** believed in a literal hell in earlier days and then disavowed it in later years. It seems the two Cambridge doctors got **father from truth** as the years went by, not closer.

HORT'S "PURGATORY"

Although the idea of a literal devil and a literal hell found no place in Hort's educated mind, he was a very real believer in the fictitious Roman Catholic doctrine of "purgatory." To Rev. John Ellerton he wrote in 1854:

---

145 Ibid., p. 149.

146 Ibid., p. 122.

–

"I agree with you in thinking it a pity that Maurice verbally repudiates purgatory, but I fully and unwaveringly agree with him in the three cardinal points of the controversy: (1) that eternity is independent of duration; (2) that the power of repentance is not limited to this life; (3) that it is not revealed whether or not all will ultimately repent. The modern denial of the second has, I suppose, had more to do with the despiritualizing of theology than almost anything that could be named."[147]

Here we once again find Hort cruising the waters of the Oxford Movement. F. D. Maurice was another "fellow traveler" with the Roman Catholic Tractarians. Yet Hort strangely finds himself aligned with him. Even though Maurice had been forced to repudiate the Roman Catholic doctrine (which was a **disappointment** to Hort), he still believed that there was a chance for repentance **after death** a misguided point to which Hort readily agreed.

But this isn't the only time that Hort's latent Roman Catholicism showed through. He also advised a young student:

"The idea of purgation, of cleansing as by fire, seems to me inseparable from what the Bible teaches us of the Divine chastisements; and, though little is directly said respecting the future state, it seems to me incredible that the Divine chastisements should in this respect change their character when this visible life is ended.

"I do not hold it contradictory to the Article to think that the condemned doctrine has not been wholly injurious,

---

147 Ibid., p. 275.

inasmuch as it has kept alive some sort of belief in a great and important truth."[148]

Thus, we see that Dr. Hort's opinions were certainly not inhibited by orthodoxy. Yet his wayward ways do not end here. For as his own writings display, Dr. Hort fell short in several other fundamental areas.

HORT'S "ATONEMENT"

Fenton John Anthony Hort was by no means a man of a **few** heresies. He seemed to want to make sure that he contradicted Scripture on **every** major issue. It is no wonder then that we find that he also had a misconception concerning the blood atonement made by Jesus Christ for the sins of all mankind.

"The fact is, I do not see how God's justice can be satisfied without every man's suffering in his own person the full penalty for his sins."[149]

What soul winner hasn't had some lost man tell him the very same thing?! **Hort talks like a lost man.** I wonder why?

But denying the Blood Atonement wasn't enough for Dr. Hort. He made it clear that **he considered the teachings of Christ's atonement as heresy!**

"Certainly nothing can be more unscriptural than the modern limiting of Christ's bearing our sins and sufferings to

---

148 Ibid., Vol. II, pp. 336, 337.

149 Ibid., Vol. I, p. 120.

—

His death; but indeed that is only one aspect of an almost universal heresy."[150]

Therefore, if you believe in that Jesus' blood paid for the sins of all mankind, Dr. Hort thinks you're a heretic. So we now see that Dr. Hort has managed to do the same thing that the Roman Catholic Church did at the Council of Trent. He has condemned Peter, James, John, Paul, all the New Testament Christians **and Jesus Christ** as **heretics!** So where do **you** line up on this issue? With Hort and the rest of the Roman Catholics? Or with Jesus Christ and His followers?

The fact is that Hort not only denied the blood atonement of Jesus Christ but he believed that Satan was more worthy of accepting Christ's payment for sins than God.

"I confess I have no repugnance to the primitive doctrine of a ransom paid to Satan, though neither am I prepared to give full assent to it. But I can see no other possible form in which the doctrine of a ransom is at all tenable; anything is better than the notion of a ransom paid to the Father."[151]

HORT'S "BAPTISM"

Dr. Hort also believed in the Roman Catholic teaching of "baptismal regeneration", a wayward doctrine that the Church of England was never able to overcome. Yet Hort put more stock in the Roman Catholic doctrine baptism than the "evangelical" teaching of baptism being performed only on those who had already trusted Jesus Christ as their personal Saviour. He stated:

---

150 Ibid., p. 430.

151 Ibid., p. 428.

"...at the same time in language stating that we maintain 'Baptismal Regeneration' as the most important of doctrines...**the pure 'Romish' view seems to me nearer, and more likely to lead to, the truth than the Evangelical.**"[152] (Emphasis mine)

He also states that, "Baptism assures us that we are children of God, members of Christ and His body, and heirs of the heavenly kingdom."[153]

Anyone trusting his baptism to get him to Heaven is on his way to Hell. More than one "baptized-catechized" church member has ended up there because of this heresy. In fact, Hort's heretical view of baptism probably cost his own son his eternal soul, assuring his eldest son Arthur that his infant baptism **was** his salvation:

"You were not only born into the world of men. You were also born of Christian parents in a Christian land. While yet an infant you were claimed for God by being made in Baptism an unconscious member of His Church, the great Divine Society which has lived on unceasingly from the Apostles' time till now. You have been surrounded by Christian influences; taught to lift up your eyes to the Father in heaven as your own Father; to feel yourself in a wonderful sense a member or part of Christ, united to Him by strange invisible bonds; to know that you have as your birthright a share in the kingdom of heaven."[154]

HORT'S TWISTED BELIEF

152 Ibid., p. 76.

153 Ibid., Vol. II, p. 81.

154 Ibid., p. 273.

Along with Hort's unregenerated misconceptions of basic Bible truths, there were his quirkish and sometimes quackish personal beliefs. One such example is **his hatred for democracy** in general and America in particular, as he asserts in a letter to Rev. Westcott dated April 28, 1865:

> "...I dare not prophesy about America, but I cannot say that I see much as yet to soften my deep hatred of democracy in all its forms."[155]

In fact, Hort's hope, during the years of the American Civil War was that the South would win. This desire was fostered by the hope that such a victory would destroy both countries and eliminate America's threat to England's domination of the world. His own words betray this in a letter which he wrote to Rev. John Ellerton in September 1862:

> "I care more for England and for Europe than for America, how much more than for all the **niggers** in the world! And I contend that the highest morality requires me to do so. Some thirty years ago Niebuhr wrote to this effect: 'Whatever people may say to the contrary, the American empire is standing menace to the whole civilization of Europe and sooner or later one or the other must perish.' Every year has, I think, brought fresh proof of the entire truth of these words. American doctrine (only too well echoed from Europe itself, though felt to be at variance with the institutions of Europe) destroys the root of everything vitally precious which man has by painful growth been learning from the earliest times till now, and tends only to reduce us to the gorilla state. The American empire seems to me mainly an embodiment of American doctrine, its leading principle being lawless force. Surely, if ever Babylon or Rome were rightly cursed it cannot be wrong to desire and pray from

---

155 Ibid., p. 34.

the bottom of one's heart that the American Union may be shivered to pieces.

"I do not for a moment forget what slavery is, or the frightful effects which Olmsted has shown it to be producing on white society in the South; but I hate it much more for its influence on the whites than on the **niggers** themselves. The refusal of education to them is abominable; how far they are capable of being ennobled by it is not clear. As yet everywhere (not in slavery only) they have surely shown themselves only as an **immeasurably inferior race, just human and no more**, their religion frothy and sensuous, their highest virtues, those of a good Newfoundland dog."[156] (Emphasis mine)

Along with the vicious hatred he bore for America Hort also had no respect for prominent Americans, be they politicians or preachers. Concerning President Abraham Lincoln he wrote: "I cannot see that he has shown any special virtues or statesmanlike capacities."[157] Of course, Lincoln's statesmanship preserved the Union from certain destruction. Anyone with the hatred for America and its freedoms that Hort had would obviously hate Lincoln also.

But Abraham Lincoln wasn't the only target of Hort's ire. This so-called "man of God" had no use for American preachers either. Of the great preacher D.L. Moody he had to say:

"Think of my going with Gray yesterday afternoon to hear 'Moody and Sankey' at the Haymarket. I am very glad to have been, but should not care to go again. All was much as I expected, except that the music was inferior, and altogether Sankey did not leave a favourable impression. Moody had great sincerity, earnestness, and good sense, with some American

---

156 Ibid., Vol. I, pp. 458, 459.

157 Ibid., p. 458.

humour which he mostly keeps under restraint, but in matter is quite conventional and commonplace. Much the most remarkable thing is the congregation or rather audience."[158]

How many lost sinners have made similar statements about a preacher after they had rejected Christ as their personal Saviour. I do not know if Hort ever had another opportunity to hear the true Gospel of the Grace of God, but you can be sure that he heard it that night. Think of the difference it could have made in his life if he had humbly walked the aisle that night and trusted Christ. He may have become a Bible believer and then used his genius **upholding** the Word of God rather than attacking it. You can be sure that he has often thought again about this meeting...**in Hell**.

Some defenders may try to claim that Hort's distaste for America was nothing more than a dose of "English patriotism." But patriotism may not be its source as much as the tainting of his thinking by a touch of **Communism** was. These facts are brought out in his continued correspondence with Rev. John Ellerton, circa 1850:

> "I have pretty well made up my mind to devote my three or four years up here to the study of this subject of Communism."[159]

> "I can only say that it was through the region of pure politics that I myself approach Communism."[160]

---

158 Ibid., Vol. II, p. 207.

159 Ibid., Vol. I, p. 130.

160 Ibid., p. 138.

"To be without responsibility, to be in no degree our 'brother's keeper,' would be the heaviest curse imaginable."[161]

"Surely every man is meant to be God's steward of every blessing and 'talent' (power, wealth, influence, station, birth, etc., etc.) which He gives him, for the benefit of his neighbours."[162]

If anything can be said about Hort, it is that he was ahead of his time. Here he was preaching Communism **a half century** before Lenin or Trotsky had ever been heard of! Fenton John Anthony Hort **the first Bolshevik!**

Disbelief that the Bible was infallible, misconceptions on major Bible doctrines, espousal of the Roman Catholic doctrine of purgatory, delving into Communism; even **these** were not the limit of Hort's spiritual degradation. He also had an acute interest in the occult. (**Why** should that surprise us?) Hort explored the supernatural along with his good friend Brooke Foss Westcott and others in what was called the "Ghostly Guild" (more on this later).

Hort candidly admits his occultism:

"Westcott, Gorham, C.B., Scott, Benson, Bradshaw, Luard, etc., and I have started a society for the investigation of ghosts and all supernatural appearances and effects, being all disposed to believe that such things really exist, and ought to be discriminated from hoaxes and mere subjective delusions; we shall be happy to obtain any good accounts well authenticated with names. Westcott is drawing up a schedule of questions.

---

161 Ibid., p. 140.

162 Ibid., p. 139.

–

Cope calls us the 'Cock and Bull Club;' our own temporary name is the 'Ghostly Guild.'"[163]

What was it that so influenced this man's thinking? Greek philosophy? Spirits? Or was there another influence? It is possible that the learned doctor was influenced by more than mere philosophy, as we see in his description of a hotel in the Alps where he often vacationed:

"Pontresina, Hotel Krone; homely, but very clean and comfortable;...beer excellent."[164]

It is not an amazing thing that any one man could hold to so many unscriptural and ungodly beliefs. Hollywood, the News Industry and secular universities are **filled** with men that equal or even surpass Hort's spiritual degradation. What is amazing is that such a man could be exalted by Bible-believing preachers and college professors to a point of authority higher than the King James Bible! Dr. Hort was a truly great Greek scholar, yet a great intellect does not make one an authority over the Bible when he himself does not even claim to believe it! Albert Einstein was a man of great intellect, but he rejected Scripture, and so where he speaks on the subject of Scripture, he is not to be accepted as authoritative. Possessing a great mind or great ability does not guarantee that a person will be a great spiritual leader. Dr. Hort was a scholar, but his scholarship alone is no reason to accept his perverted theories concerning Bible truth.

If fundamental pastors of today enlisted the services of an evangelist and found that this evangelist had beliefs paralleling those of Fenton John Anthony Hort, I believe that the pastor would cancel the meeting. Strangely enough, when a pastor discovers such to be true about Dr. Hort, he ignores his infidelity and excuses him as "a great

---

163 Ibid., p. 211.

164 Ibid., p. 377.

Greek scholar" and presents his Authorized Version to him to be maliciously dissected and then discarded. Then Dr. Hort sets himself down in the seat of authority which the Bible once held. Here again I must assert that most often this is done with childlike faith on the part of the pastor, due to the education he received while in seminary. But the seminary is not really guilty either, for it has simply and unsuspectingly accepted the authority of two men raised under the influence of a campaign by the Jesuits to re-Romanize England. Wilkenson reports that Hort had been influenced by these Roman Catholic forces: "Dr. Hort tells us that the writings of Simon had a large share in the movement to discredit the Textus Receptus class of MSS and Bibles."[165]

PROBLEMS WITH WESTCOTT

Unfortunately for the "new Bible" supporters, Dr. Westcott's credentials are even **more anti-biblical** than those of Hort. Brooke Foss Westcott was no more a Christian than Hort. And he held that man's disdain for all things biblical.

Just like Hort, Westcott did not believe in Creation. In fact, he did not think that Genesis 1-3 should be taken literally. He also thought that "Moses" and "David" were poetic characters whom Jesus Christ referred to by name only because the common people accepted them as authentic. Westcott states:

> "No one now, I suppose, holds that the first three chapters of Genesis, for example, give a literal history--I could never understand how anyone reading them with open eyes could think they did--yet they disclose to us a Gospel. So it is probably elsewhere. Are we not going through a trial in regard to the use of popular language on literary subjects like that

165 Wilkenson, Benjamin, *Our Authorized Bible Vindicated*, (Takoma Park, 1930), p. 104.

through which we went, not without sad losses in regard to the use of popular language on physical subjects? If you feel now that it was, to speak humanly, necessary that the Lord should speak of the 'sun rising,' it was no less necessary that he would use the names 'Moses' and 'David' as His contemporaries used them. There was no critical question at issue. (Poetry is, I think, a thousand times more true than History; this is a private parenthesis for myself alone.)"[166]

He also said "David" is not a chronological but a spiritual person.[167] How many **Bible believers** would stand with Westcott against the teaching of creation in Genesis chapters 1-3? How many **Bible believers** would "Amen!" Westcott if he stood behind their pulpit and declared that Moses and David were figments of the corporate Jewish mind rather than real, historic individuals? **None!** That the first three chapters of Genesis are all allegory has been believed by liberals and modernists for years. Do today's fundamentalists realize that those modernists' beliefs were nurtured in the heart of this Bible critic? So why would any "Bible" college uphold this man as an authority in biblical matters?

Of course, there is even more to Westcott's biblical infidelity. He was also a doubter of the biblical account of miracles:

"I never read an account of a miracle but I seem instinctively to feel its improbability, and discover somewhat of evidence in the account of it."[168]

166 Westcott, Arthur, *Life and Letters of Brooke Foss Westcott,* (New York, 1903). Volume II, p. 69.

167 Ibid., p. 147.

168 Ibid., Vol. I, p. 52.

If a famous fundamental preacher of our day were to make this statement, he would be called apostate. What then of Westcott?

Furthermore, Westcott believed that the second coming of Jesus Christ was not a physical coming but a spiritual coming. He made this plain when he wrote:

"As far as I can remember, I said very shortly what I hold to be the 'Lord's coming' in my little book on the Historic Faith. I hold very strongly that the Fall of Jerusalem was the coming which first fulfilled the Lord's words; and, as there have been other comings, I cannot doubt that He is 'coming' to us now."[169]

WESTCOTT'S "HEAVEN"

Wait! Christ's physical return to earth is not the last fundamental truth of Scripture to be denied by Bishop Westcott, for he believed Heaven to be a **state of mind** and **not a literal place**. Note the following quotations from Bishop Westcott:

"No doubt the language of the Rubric is unguarded, but it saves us from the error of connecting the Presence of Christ's glorified humanity with place; 'heaven is a state and not a place.'"[170]

"Yet the unseen is the largest part of life. Heaven lies about us now in infancy alone; and by swift, silent pauses for thought, for recollection, for aspiration, we cannot only keep

---

169 Ibid., Vol. II, p. 308.

170 Ibid., p. 49.

–

fresh the influence of that diviner atmosphere, but breathe it more habitually."[171]

These are beautifully poetic words. But we are talking about **Heaven!** We are not talking about **poetry!** Yet it is true the only hope that Westcott had in his mind was that of finding his "heaven" here on earth.

> "We may reasonably hope, by patient, resolute, faithful, united endeavour to find heaven about us here, the glory of our earthly life."[172]

WESTCOTT'S "NEWMANISM"

Any wise English churchman who claimed to love and believe the Bible knew that John Henry Newman was a man to be shunned and avoided. But Dr. Westcott found an attraction to this agent of apostasy. Westcott was deeply devoted to the Roman Catholic defector who took 150 Church of England clergymen with him when he made his escape to Rome. Those of his disciples who did not make the physical change to Rome, made the spiritual change to Romanism, though many, like Westcott, never admitted it.

In writing to his future wife in 1852, Westcott said:

> "Today I have again taken up 'Tracts for the Times' and Dr. Newman. Don't tell me that he will do me harm. At least today he will, has done me good, and had you been here I should have asked you to read his solemn words to me. My purchase

---

171 Ibid., p. 253.

172 Ibid., p. 394.

has already amply repaid me. I think I shall choose a volume for one of my Christmas companions."[173]

This was written **after** Newman had defected to Rome! Westcott found spiritual salve in the words of a Roman Catholic defector, an infidel. He found solace in the words of a man who could not accept the Bible as authoritative as Wilkenson explains,

> "By voice and pen, the teaching of Newman changed in the minds of many their attitude toward the Bible. Stanley shows us that the allegorizing of German theology, under whose influence Newman and the leaders of the movement were, was Origen's method of allegorizing. Newman contended that God never intended the Bible to teach doctrines."

Westcott also resented criticism of the Essays and Reviews. Upon hearing the Bishop of Manchester deride the apostate authors of these heretical essays, Westcott wrote, "But his language about the Essays and Reviews roused my indignation beyond expression."[174]

These are the convictions of a man greatly responsible for the destruction of Christian faith in the Greek Text of the Authorized Version. Place Mr. Westcott next to any present fundamental preacher or educator, and he would be judged a **modernist, liberal and heretic**. In spite of his outstanding ability in Greek, a man of his convictions would not be welcome on the campus of any **truly** Christian college in America. This is not an overstatement, nor is it malicious. The Christian colleges of today hold very high standards and simply would not settle for a man of such apostate convictions, no matter how great his ability to teach a given subject. So what does that tell you about a "Christian" college that **does** exalt Westcott as a reliable biblical authority?

---

173 Ibid., Vol. I, p. 223.

174 Ibid., p. 279.

WESTCOTT'S DEFENDERS

It is truly amazing that a man who believed things completely contrary to the convictions of today's fundamental preachers and educators could be exalted and defended by them. Of course, I believe this is done primarily because our fundamental brethren know little of what either Dr. Westcott or Dr. Hort really believed and taught. If they did, they would repudiate the teachings of both of these men and ban their books from the campus.

Unfortunately, ignorance is not always the case. You can imagine the embarrassment that a university would feel if it had been upholding Westcott for decades and then suddenly found out the truth. It would take an immense amount of **humility** to stand up and admit that it had been wrong and now planned to right that wrong. It would be much more convenient to simply **shoot the messenger** who delivered the truth and continue on as it had been.

WESTCOTT'S SOCIALISM

But even this does not completely describe Brooke Foss Westcott, the man. This man was a devout socialist and post-millennialist. Socialism and post-millennialism go hand in hand. Post-millennialism is the belief that we shall bring in the millennial reign of Christ ourselves, without Christ's help through social change. Socialism is usually the means of establishing that thousand-year reign of peace. The arch-typical socialist organization today is the United Nations. This world-wide monster seeks to establish a "millennium" of its own without any need for Christ. It desires a "peace" while rejecting the "Prince of Peace" (Isaiah 57:21).

A post-millennialist would see a spiritual "coming" of Christ in any great event which drew the world closer to his idea of peace. It is also easy to see why he would believe that a "heaven" was attainable here on earth; Westcott's statement "We may reasonably hope, by patient, resolute, faithful, united endeavour, to find heaven about us here, the glory of our earthly life." clearly displays his post-millennial beliefs.

These are only two small glimmers of the socialistic light which burned in Westcott's breast. If they were all of the evidence available, it would make for a weak case indeed. They are not!

Dr. Westcott was also a devout pacifist. His pacifist nature showed up early in his life. He was known as a "shy, nervous, thoughtful boy" while attending school. His hobbies were as follows:

"He used his leisure chiefly in sketching, arranging his collections of ferns, butterflies, and moths, and in reading books of natural history or poetry."[175]

He developed an interest in social reform early on. He was known about his school for talking about things "which very few schoolboys talk about - points of theology, problems of morality, and the ethics of politics."[176]

His son Arthur describes him with these words:

"As a boy my father took keen interest in the Chartist movement[177], and the effect then produced upon his youthful imagination by the popular presentation of the sufferings of the masses never faded. His diary shows how he deserted his meals to be present at various stirring scenes, and in particular to listen

---

175 Ibid., p. 13.

176 Ibid., p. 6.

177 The Chartist movement was a campaign for social reform in England from 1838-1848.

to the oratory of 'the great agitator,' presumably Feargus O'Connor himself. He would often in later years speak of these early impressions, which served in no small degree to keep alive his intense hatred of every form of injustice and oppression. He even later disapproved of his father's fishing excursions, because his sympathies were so entirely on the side of the fish. On one occasion, being then a little boy, he was carrying a fish-basket, when his father put a live fish into it, and late in life he used to declare that he would still feel the struggles of that fish against his back."[178]

This one paragraph reveals the temperament which would characterize Westcott for the rest of his life. Had he been alive today, we would no doubt find him picketing for nuclear disarmament, fighting for "animal rights," and chaining himself to some tree in hopes of preventing some poor logger from making a living.

He was ever in favor of any action that would establish socialism, at any cost, as he himself stated in speaking of the French Revolution:

"The French Revolution has been a great object of interest. I confess to a strong sympathy with the republicans. Their leaders at least have been distinguished by great zeal and sincerity. Lamartine, who I fancy you know by name, quite wins my admiration."[179]

WESTCOTT'S POETICAL INFLUENCES

---

178 Westcott, Arthur, *Life and Letters of Brooke Foss Westcott,* (New York, 1903). Vol. I, p. 7.

179 Ibid., p. 135.

Westcott was ever a lover of poetry and was deeply influenced by its message. This explains his admiration of Alphonse de Lamartine. Lamartine was a French poet whose writings helped influence the French people into revolution. Ironically, but I am sure not coincidentally, Lamartine had studied under the Jesuits. He is a fool who thinks a poet's pen is not a mighty weapon!

Westcott's romantic attitude explains why he would make the earlier statement that "Poetry is, I think, a thousand times more true than history." It also explains his susceptibility to the subtle Romanizing influence of the poet Keble. Westcott had a fondness for poetry and an unusual fondness for Keble's poetry. No poet is mentioned more often in his writings than Keble.

Westcott writes concerning Keble,

"But I intend reading some Keble, which has been a great delight to me during the whole week, and perhaps that will now be better than filling you with all my dark, dark, dark gloominess."[180]

It seems Keble's poetry inspired Westcott to see that the Church of England needed to make a change:

"I have been reading Keble for the day, and though I do not recollect noticing the hymn particularly before, it now seems to me one of the most beautiful; and especially does it apply to those feelings which I have so often described to you: that general sorrow and despair which we feel when we look at the state of things around us and try to picture the results which soon must burst upon our Church and country."[181]

---

180 Ibid., p. 60.

181 Ibid., p. 73.

–

Westcott found time to quote Keble to express his feelings.

"On these look long and well,
Cleansing thy sight by prayer and faith,
And thou shalt know what secret spell
Preserves them in their living death.

"That hymn of Keble's contains very, very much. You have read it again and again now, I am sure, and understand it."[182]

WESTCOTT'S ROMANISM

That Keble nurtured in Westcott a passive attitude toward Christianity's archenemy, Rome is evident by Westcott's reaction to a sermon condemning Popery:

"As for Mr. Oldham's meetings, I think they are not good in their tendency, and nothing can be so bad as making them the vehicle of controversy. What an exquisitely beautiful verse is that of Keble's, 'And yearns not her parental heart,' etc. We seem now to have lost all sense of pity in bitterness and ill-feeling. Should not our arm against Rome be prayer and not speeches; the efforts of our inmost heart, and not the display of secular reason?"[183]

It has been often stated that "You are what you read." Westcott's constant exposure to pro-Roman influences set a pattern for his thinking, even though he may not have been aware of it. Westcott even refused to abandon Keble as his writings became more obviously popish.

---

182 Ibid., p. 77.

183 Ibid., p. 77.

"Keble has lately published some sermons in which, as well as in a preface on 'the position of Churchmen,' I am afraid he will offend many. I can in some measure sympathize with him."[184]

Remembering the hatred Westcott had for what he considered "injustice and oppression," and his submission to the programming poetry of Keble, we find him slipping farther away from a truly biblical stand after hearing another advocate of Rome, Maurice.

"See Maurice's new lectures, with a preface on development written apparently with marvelous candour and fairness, and free from all controversial bitterness. He makes a remark which I have often written and said, that the danger of our Church is from atheism, not Romanism. What a striking picture is that he quotes from Newman of the present aspect of the Roman Church - as despised, rejected, persecuted in public opinion."[185]

It is **blasphemous** to steal the words of Isaiah the Prophet in his prophetic description of Jesus Christ found in Chapter 53 and apply them to **the Great Whore** of Revelation 17! To feel sympathy for such a murderous organization is unconscionable.

This constant barrage of Romanizing influences caused Westcott to incorporate many Roman Catholic practices into his thinking. In February 1849 he decided to investigate two favorite subjects of the Romanizers: "Inspiration - Apostolical Succession. May I inquire on all these topics with simple sincerity, seeking only the truth!"[186]

---

184 Ibid., p. 93.

185 Ibid., p. 43.

186 Ibid., p. 110.

—

The result of the first study led to Westcott's believing the Bible to be absolutely true, but he refused to call it infallible.

> "My dear Hort - I am glad to have seen both your note and Lightfoot's - glad too that we have had such an opportunity of openly speaking. For I too must disclaim setting forth infallibility in the front of my convictions. All I hold is, that the more I learn, the more I am convinced that fresh doubts come from my own ignorance, and that at present I find the presumption in favor of the absolute truth - I reject the word infallibility - of Holy Scripture overwhelming."[187]

Our good Bishop has now lost the conviction that Scripture is "infallible." We are never told the result of his study of the Roman Catholic teaching of "Apostolic Succession," but the thought is chilling.

WESTCOTT'S ICONISM

Westcott's drift toward Rome naturally led him to see value in the same things as did the Roman Catholics. He had an affinity for statues, since his poetic spirit had the ability to read a great deal into that which he saw. He explains:

> "Our Cathedral buildings at Peterborough are far from rich in works of sculpture, but among the works which we have there are two which have always seemed to me to be of the deepest interest. The one is a statue of a Benedictine monk, which occupies a niche in the gateway built by Godfrey of Croyland about 1308; the other is an effigy of an unknown abbot of considerably earlier date, carved upon the slab which once covered his grave, and which now lies in the south aisle of the

187 Ibid., p. 110.

choir. They are widely different in character and significance. The statue of the monk, which Flaxman took as an illustration of his lectures on sculpture, is one of the noblest of medieval figures. The effigy of the abbot has no artistic merit whatever. But both alike are studies from life; and together they seem to me to bring very vividly before us the vital power of early monasticism in England."[188]

Here we find Westcott not only extolling the attributes of statuary but making a statement on monasticism that seems to long for the forbidden Roman Catholic perversion of life. The man was a Roman Catholic at heart whether he **ever** openly joined the Roman church.

The plan of the Jesuit is to introduce the ways of Rome into the minds of Protestants slowly and familiarize them with the "High Church" atmosphere then little by little allow these Roman ideas to intertwine themselves with the worship service. Dr. Wylie aptly describes how this pattern showed in the Tractarians:

> "Tract 90, where the doctrine of reserves is broached, bears strong marks of a Jesuit origin. Could we know all the secret instructions given to the leaders in the Puseyite movement, the mental reservations prescribed to them, we might well be astonished. 'Go gently,' we think we hear the great Roothan say to them. 'Remember the motto of our dear son, the cidevant Bishop Autun, "surtout, pas trop de zele"'(above all, not too much zeal). Bring into view, little by little, the authority of the church. If you can succeed in rendering it equal to that of the Bible, you have done much. Change the table of the Lord into an altar; elevate that altar a few inches above the level of the floor; gradually turn around to it when you read the Liturgy; place lighted tapers upon it; teach the people the virtues of stained glass, and cause them to feel the majesty of Gothic

---

188 Ibid., p. 318.

—

basilisques. Introduce first the dogmas, beginning with that of baptismal regeneration; next the ceremonies and sacraments, as penance and the confessional; and lastly, the images of the Virgin and the saints'."[189]

This trend was quite apparent in the mind of Bishop Westcott as he reveals to us in this statement concerning baptism regeneration:

"I do not say that baptism is absolutely necessary, though from the words of Scripture I can see no exception, but I do not think we have no right to exclaim against the idea of the commencement of a spiritual life, conditionally from baptism, any more than we have to deny the commencement of a moral life from birth."[190]

And again his Roman desires for stained glass, which is beautiful, but can be spiritually deadly:

"Dear Mr. Perrott--I had sketched out a plan in my mind for the windows in the chancel at Somersham which I should have been glad to carry out, but now, as you know, my connection with the parish has practically ceased, and in a few weeks will formally cease. My wish was to have a figure of John the Baptist opposite that of the Virgin, to represent the Old Dispensation, and to have the work executed by Heaton and Butler, who executed the window for Mr. Mason."[191]

189 Wilkenson, Benjamin, *Our Authorized Bible Vindicated* (Takoma Park, 1930), pp. 143,144.

190 Westcott, Arthur, *Life and Letters of Brooke Foss Westcott* (New York, 1903), Vol. II, p. 160.

191 Ibid., p. 439.

WESTCOTT'S PURGATORY

"Birds of a feather...go to Hell together!" That is what can be said of Westcott and Hort. For just as Hort had an active belief in the Romish doctrine of Purgatory, his soulmate Westcott was also an advocate of this hellish lie. In fact, Westcott's Romanistic leanings eventually led him into allowing the practice of "prayers for the dead." In writing to a clergyman in August of 1900 concerning this Roman Catholic practice which had found its way into an Anglican church, **he stated**:

> "I considered very carefully, in conference with some other bishops of large knowledge and experience, the attitude of our church with regard to prayers for the dead. We agreed unanimously that we are, as things are now, forbidden to pray for the dead apart from the whole church *in our public services*. No restriction is placed upon private devotions."[192] (Emphasis his)

Notice that the Bishop advised against prayers for the dead in "public service," but he **did not even attempt** to discourage the practice in "private devotions"! Would one of today's fundamental preachers who have such high regard for the Westcott and Hort Greek Text respond in the same manner? Would we hear one of our Bible-believing brethren confront the matter with, "Well, we don't practice prayers for the dead here in our services, but if you want to do it in your private devotions, it's okay." **NEVER!** We are to hate the garment "spotted by the flesh" (Jude 23). Dr. Westcott's garment is spotted to the point of resembling a leopard's skin! Are we to expect an unbiased rendering of the Greek Text by a man whose convictions would rival Jerome's in loyalty to Roman teaching? I trow not!

---

192 Ibid., Vol. II, p. 349.

—

But to allow prayers for the dead would be futile if there were only Heaven and Hell. The "dead" in Heaven would need no prayers, and the "dead" in Hell would be beyond hope. Seems there would have to be **a place** where the dead went so that prayers for them could do them some good.

Benjamin Wilkenson provides the missing link in Westcott's chain of Romanism when commenting on the Revised Version translation of John 14:2:

> "King James: 'In my Father's house are many mansions.'

> "Revised: 'In my Father's house are many abiding places.' (margin)

> "In the following quotation from the Expositor, the writer points out that, by the marginal reading of the Revised, Dr. Westcott and the Committee referred, not to a final future state, but to intermediate stations in the future before the final one.

> "Dr. Westcott in his Commentary of St. John's Gospel gives the following explanation of the words. 'In my Father's house are many mansions. The rendering comes from the Vulgate mansiones, which were resting places, and especially the stations on a great road, where travelers found refreshment. This appears to be the true meaning of the Greek word here; so that the contrasted notions of repose and progress are combined in this vision of the future.'

> "'For thirty years now,' said Dr. Samuel Cox, in 1886, 'I have been preaching what is called the larger hope, through good and ill report.

> "The larger hope meant a probation after this life, such a time of purifying, by fire or otherwise, after death as would insure another opportunity of salvation to all men. Dr. Cox, like

others, rejoices that the changes in the Revised Version sustain this doctrine. 'Had the new version been in our hands, I should not have felt any special gravity in the assertion,' he said. Doctors Westcott and Hort, both Revisers, believed this larger hope." (This Roman Catholic translation also appears in the NASV).[193]

Considering the Romanistic ideals which Dr. Westcott possessed, it is no surprise that his close friend and companion, Dr. Hort, would compare him to, of all people, the Roman Catholic defector John Newman!

"It is hard to resist a vague feeling that Westcott's going to Peterborough will be the beginning of a great movement in the church, less conspicuous but not less powerful, than that which proceeded from Newman."[194]

It is also not surprising that Westcott would call the Jesuit-inspired Oxford Movement "the Oxford **Revival**"! He said,

"The Oxford Revival in the middle of the century, quickened anew that sense of corporate life. But the evangelical movement touched only a part of human interest."[195]

Imagine! A movement designed to usher the Church of England back into the Roman Catholic Church is called a "revival" by this man. It is at this point that we actually have to wonder if Westcott wasn't one

---

193 Wilkenson, Benjamin, *Our Authorized Bible Vindicated,* (Takoma Park, 1930), p. 157.

194 Ibid., p. 157.

195 Westcott, Arthur, *Life and Letters of Brooke Foss Westcott*, (New York, 1903), Vol. II, p. 251.

of those Jesuits that so permeated England at this time; as Walsh has
told us;

> "...there are Jesuits in all classes of society; in Parliament;
> ***among the English clergy***; among Protestant laity, and even in
> higher stations. I could not comprehend how a Jesuit could be a
> Protestant priest, or how a Protestant priest could be a Jesuit; but
> my confessor silenced my scruples by telling me, *omnia munda
> mundis*, and that St. Paul became as a Jew that he might save the
> Jews; it was no wonder, therefore, **if a Jesuit should feign
> himself a Protestant, for the conversion of Protestants.**

> "The English clergy were formerly too much attached to
> their Articles of Faith to be shaken from them...so the Jesuits of
> England tried another plan. This was to demonstrate from
> history and ecclesiastical antiquity the legitimacy of the uses of
> the English Church, whence, through the exertions of **the
> Jesuits concealed among its clergy**, might arise a studious
> attention to Christian antiquity. This was designed to occupy the
> clergy in long, laborious, and abstruse investigation, and to
> **alienate them from their Bibles.**"[196] (Emphasis mine)

The fact of the matter is simple. If Westcott **wasn't** a Jesuit, he
couldn't have done more for the Roman Catholic Church if he was!

WESTCOTT'S MARIOLATRY

Another heretical doctrine dear to Roman Catholics is the
adoration of Mary. Here also Dr. Westcott did not let the Roman
Catholic Church down, as he reveals in a letter to his fiancee Sarah
Louisa Whittard.

---

196 Walsh, Walter, *The Secret History of The Oxford Movement*, (London, 1897), p.33.

"After leaving the monastery, we shaped our course to a little oratory which we discovered on the summit of a neighboring hill...Fortunately we found the door open. It is very small, with one kneeling-place, and behind a screen was a 'Pieta' the size of life (i.e., a Virgin and dead Christ)...Had I been alone, I could have knelt there for hours."[197]

Westcott's affection for Mary is also indicated by his son, Arthur, in describing his father's reaction to the painting "The Sistine Madonna."

"It is smaller than I expected, and the colouring is less rich, but in expression it is perfect. The face of the virgin is unspeakably beautiful. I looked till the lip seemed to tremble with intensity of feeling--of feeling simply, for it would be impossible to say whether it be awe or joy or hope--humanity shrinking before the divine, or swelling with its conscious possession. It is enough that there is deep, intensely deep, emotion such as the mother of the Lord may have had."[198]

The intensity of Westcott's admiration for Christ's mother is best revealed by his desire to change his fiancee's name to "Mary"; as Arthur explains

"My mother, whose name was Sarah Louisa Whittard, was the eldest of three sisters. She afterwards, at the time of her confirmation at my father's request, took the name of Mary in addition."[199]

---

197 Westcott, Arthur, *Life and Letters of Brooke Foss Westcott,* (New York, 1903), Vol. I, p. 81.

198 Ibid., p. 183.

199 Ibid., p. 8.

The above examples illustrate Dr. Westcott's strong Roman Catholic allegiance. Again I must say that I do not believe that a man who lived today with the convictions we have just studied, would be welcome in a fundamental pulpit anywhere in America, be his name Bishop Westcott or Hort or Schuler or any other.

WESTCOTT'S COMMUNAL LIVING

Few of Bishop Westcott's twentieth century supporters know the true thoughts and intents of his heart. If they did, they would know that **he was an advocate of communal living!**

Let the record speak for itself. His son Arthur stated in his book *Life and Letters of Brooke Foss Westcott*:

> "In later years of his Harrow residence (approximately 1868) my father was very full of the idea of a 'Coenobium.' [Arthur's footnote for the word "Coenobium" states simply, "community life."] Every form of luxury was to him abhorrent, and he viewed with alarm the increasing tendency amongst all classes of society to encourage extravagant display and wasteful self-indulgence. His own extreme simplicity of life is well-known to all his friends. He looked to the family and not the individual for the exhibition of the simple life. His views upon this subject are accessible to all who care to study them. I only wish to put it on record that he was very much in earnest in this matter and felt that he had not done all he might have for its furtherance."[200]

On the idea of the Coenobium, Bishop Westcott's socialism bordered very close to communism, as we see by his own description of what a Coenobium was to be.

---

200 Ibid., pp. 263, 264.

"It would consist primarily of an **association of families**, bound together by **common principles of life, of work, of devotion**, subject during the time of voluntary co-operation to central control, and united by definite obligations. **Such a corporate life would be best realized under the conditions of collegiate union** with the hall and schools and chapel, **with a common income**, though not common property, and **an organized government**; but the sense of fellowship and the power of sympathy, though they would be largely developed by these, would yet remain vigorous whenever and in whatever form combination in the furtherance of the general ends was possible. Indeed, complete isolation from the mass of society would defeat the very objects of the institution. These objects--the conquest of luxury, the disciplining of intellectual labor, the consecration of every fragment of life by religious exercises--would be expressed in a threefold obligation; an obligation to poverty, an obligation to study, and obligation to devotion."[201] (Emphasis mine.)

Little did the esteemed professor realize that the college students of a hundred years later would be more than happy to turn his dream into a reality!

Arthur viewed the establishment of the Coenobium with much fear and trembling. Westcott's children were assured of its future reality quite often:

"My own recollections of the Coenobium are very vivid. Whenever we children showed signs of greediness or other selfishness, we were assured that such things would be unheard of in the Coenobium. There the greedy would have no second portions of desirable puddings. We should not there be allowed a choice of meats, but should be constrained to take which was

---

201 Ibid., p. 264.

–

judged to be best for us. We viewed the establishment of the Coenobium with gloomy apprehension, not quite sure whether it was within the bounds of practical politics or not. I was myself inclined to believe that it really was coming and that we, with the Bensons (maybe) and Horts and a few other families, would find ourselves living in a community life. I remember confiding to a younger brother that I had overheard some conversation which convinced me that the Coenobium was an event of the immediate future, and that a site had been selected for it in Northamptonshire; I even pointed out Peterborough on the map."[202]

Westcott's fascination with communal living was not a passing fancy. In a letter to his old college friend Dr. E.W. Benson, dated November 24, 1868, Dr. Westcott states his regrets that the Coenobium had not yet been established, and wonders if he wouldn't have done better to have pursued the matter further.

"My dear Benson--alas! I feel most deeply that I ought not to speak one word about the Coenobium. One seems to be entangled in the affairs of life. The work must be for those who have a fresh life to give. Yet sometimes I think that I have been faithless to call which might have grown distinct if I had listened."[203]

Two years later he was still promoting the idea through articles in a periodical entitled Contemporary, as he explains in another letter to Benson dated March 21, 1870:

"...the paper on the Coenobium will appear, I think, in the next number of the 'Contemporary.' It was a trial to me not to

---

202 Ibid., pp. 264, 265.

203 Ibid., p. 265.

send it to you and Lightfoot and Wordsworth for criticism, but on the whole I thought it best to venture for myself, and speak simply what I feel. If anything is to come of the idea it will be handled variously, and something is gained even by incompleteness. On the true reconciliation of classes I have said a few words which are, I hope, intelligible."[204]

Two years after he'd made it young Arthur's naive-sounding 1868 prediction of the establishing of such a Coenobium in Peterborough seemed almost prophetic. It must be noted that this letter puts to rest that lame defense that Westcott and Hort's defenders are forever making about the "foolish ideas of youth." In 1870, **one year before he sat on the Revision Committee**, Westcott was still pursuing his communistic "heaven."

In December 1868, Dr. Westcott became Examining Chaplain in the Diocese of Peterborough. (Scary thought!) Just prior to the move, he wrote Benson, "The Coenobium comes at least one step nearer."[205]

Apparently Westcott was hoping that he would be able to use this position to impose his socialistic nightmare on his unsuspecting parishioners. Young Arthur's fears seemed somewhat realized:

> "The move to Peterborough was a great venture of faith on my father's part. He had a large family to educate, and yet he exchanged the comparative opulence of a Harrow house master for the precarious income attached to a canonry in an impoverished Chapter. Our manner of life was already adapted to the idea of the Coenobium in its strict simplicity, so the only

---

204 Ibid., pp. 265, 266.

205 Ibid., p. 267.

–

luxury that could be abolished was meat for breakfast, which however, was retained as a Sunday treat."[206]

Thus we see a side of Dr. Westcott which is not too publicized by his worshipers, yet it was there nonetheless. In addition to his desire to see the Authorized Version replaced, the Church of England Romanized, and a college Coenobium established, he had one other great driving force; the fanciful abolition of war.

WESTCOTT'S PEACE MOVEMENT

World peace is a noble cause and no true Christian loves war. A Bible believer takes the premillennial view and realizes that war is caused by the sinful nature of mankind. (James 4:1). He understands that this will all be changed at Christ's return (Philippians 3:21). Therefore, a Bible-believer realizes that he **is not** going to be able to abolish war.

A Bible rejecter, who has chosen the post-millennial viewpoint, cannot allow himself to believe that mankind is bad. He must find a way to show that man is basically good. All men must be brothers in his eyes. "Brothers," he assumes, will just naturally work toward peace. This is the view of every world leader today. This is the view of every New Ager. This was the view of Brooke Foss Westcott.

Westcott, a post-millennial socialist, had this to say concerning the "brotherhood" of man in regard to instituting "peace on earth":

"Christianity rests upon the central fact that the Word became flesh. This fact establishes not only a brotherhood of men, but also a brotherhood of nations; for history has shown that nations are an element in the fulfillment of the Divine

---

206 Ibid., p. 305

counsel, by which humanity advances toward its appointed end."[207]

What should these "brothers" do to help establish "peace on earth"? According to Westcott, it's simple, "We can at once recognize the part which the Christian society is called upon to take with regard to three great measures which tend to peace— meditation, arbitration, and (ultimately) disarmament--and at least silently work for them."[208]

"Combine action, in any ways possible, for the bringing about of a simultaneous reduction of the armaments."[209]

Once again the Cambridge professor is ahead of his time. "Disarmament" has been the cry of liberal, pro-Communist college students for two decades. Every liberty-hating news journalist shares Westcott's hope. Strange it is that as the "peace" movement of the 1960's was led by a "minister" with the exact same philosophy about world peace! And there **has never been a case** where disarmament **ever prevented a war**.

But like all lost "do-gooder" politicians, Westcott wasn't going to allow **facts** to taint the rosy view he had of his ideal. He wanted an "arbitration board" made up of the "Christian society" to decide international policy concerning disarmament quotas. He first envisioned England and the United States submitting to this idea, assuming then that the rest of the world would be forced to follow. The participation of the United States is absolutely necessary to any "one-worlder" peace movement. The old "League of Nations" died an early death because a wise Congress refused to allow the United States to join. By 1945 the famous socialist Franklin Delano Roosevelt had better luck conning the

207 Ibid., Vol. II, p. 22.

208 Ibid., pp. 22, 23.

209 Ibid., p. 18.

U. S. into the "United Nations," and "world peace" has been purchased ever since by the blood, money and freedoms of the citizens of the United States of America. Brooke Foss Westcott would have been proud! He prophesied:

> "The United States and England are already bound so closely together by their common language and common descent, that an Arbitration Treaty which shall exclude the thought of war--a civil war[210]— between them seems to be within measurable distance. When once the general principle of arbitration has been adopted by two great nations, it cannot but be that the example will be followed, and then, at last, however remote the vision may seem, disarmament will be a natural consequent of the acceptance of a rational and legal method of settling national disputes."[211]

Westcott even felt that world peace would be worth an "Ecumenical Movement."

> "Other cognate subjects were touched upon--the proposed Permanent Treaty of Arbitration between the United States and Great Britain, the significance of war as extreme outcome of that spirit of selfish competition which follows from the acceptance of a material standard of well being, the desirability of seeking cooperation with the movement on the part of the Roman and Greek Churches--but it seemed best to

---

210 Westcott's use of the term **"civil** war" to describe any future war that might occur between the United States and England shows that he never really considered England's claim on the U. S. to be broken by the 1776 War for Independence. He did not recognize or respect the independence of the United States of America. This man is **not** our friend!

211 Westcott, Arthur, *Life and Letters of Brooke Foss Westcott,* (New York, 1903), Vol. II., p. 23.

confine immediate action to a single point on which there was complete agreement."[212]

Westcott would feel comfortable with Bill Clinton, Ted Turner and Desmond Tutu in his blind socialistic drive to dominate the people of the world with what he called "peace." He viewed that goal as being of the utmost importance.

"The proposal to work for the simultaneous reduction of European armament is definite, and deals with an urgent peril. Such a disarmament would secure the lasting and honourable peace which the leaders of Europe have shown lately, once and again, that they sincerely desire. We are all sensible of the difficulties by which the question of disarmament is beset, but we cannot admit that they are insuperable."[213]

All this was to be done, of course, in **the name of Christ**. Like all totalitarian socialists, Westcott felt that he was simply trying to bring to pass Luke 2:14 as he misinterpreted it. He truly considered himself a man with whom God was "pleased," as that verse had been mistranslated in the Revised Version. Like all confused "holy men" who have ever murdered **in the name of God**, Westcott used Jesus Christ as his excuse for his socialist desires.

"The question of international relations has not hitherto been considered in the light of the Incarnation, and till this has been done, I do not see that we can look for the establishment of that peace which was heralded at the Nativity."[214]

212 Ibid., p. 19.

213 Ibid., p. 19.

214 Ibid., p. 23.

WESTCOTT'S FAITH

In Brooke Foss Westcott we have a man who doubted the miracles which Christ performed, as he admitted when he stated, "I never read an account of a miracle, but I seem instinctively to feel its improbability, and discover some what of evidence in the account of it."[215] What would you do with a preacher who told you he **doubted** the miracles that the Bible records Jesus Christ as performing? Invite him to preach in your church? Enjoy "good fellowship" with him? Or get as far away from him as you could?

Yet even though Westcott had trouble believing in the miracles of Jesus Christ, he **didn't doubt that a Roman Catholic priest could perform them**, as he reveals when he explains what he saw in France at the "Our Lady of La Salette" shrine.

> "A written narrative can convey no notion of the effect of such a recital. The eager energy of the father, the modest thankfulness of the daughter, the quick glances of the spectators from one to the other, the calm satisfaction of the priest, the comments of look and nod, combined to form a scene which appeared hardly to belong to the nineteenth century. An age of faith was restored before our sight in its ancient guise. We talked about the cures to a young layman who had throughout showed us singular courtesy. When we remarked upon the peculiar circumstances[216] by which they were attended, his own comment was: 'Sans croire, comment l'expliquer?' (translated:

---

215 Ibid., p. 52.

216 Westcott never reveals what these "peculiar circumstances" were, but thoughts of some of the "healings" of charlatans like Benny Hinn come to mind. And the fending off of any doubts with the lame, "Without believing how can it be explained?" is the same con-job that skeptics of today's side-show evangelists have met with. Yet Westcott says **nothing** is wrong with any of this! He **never** doubts a Catholic priest...**only Jesus Christ!**

'Without believing how can it be explained?') And in this lay the real significance and power of the place."[217]

What wisdom! Westcott was so wise that **he knew** that Jesus Christ couldn't be trusted to perform a miracle. **He knew** that Jesus Christ might be a fraud who used phony miracles to deceive his onlookers. But a Roman Catholic priest...lie?...deceive? **Never!** (I would not follow this man **across the street,** let alone believe what he had to say about Bible manuscripts!)

WESTCOTT'S TREPIDATION

So here is this man who could read and exalt the Jesuit-inspired poet Keble, but when it came to reading anything that presented Rome in a negative light, such as *Fox's Book of Holy Martyrs*, he wasn't interested. Here in the land where "Bloody Mary's" reign of terror brought death to thousands-where he daily could pass places where Christ's martyrs shed their blood for their Saviour-where the records of those terrible deaths were still close at hand, Brooke Foss Westcott could not find any interest in himself to learn the truth of the Roman Catholic blood-bath. Of *Fox's Book of Holy Martyrs* he said, "I never read any of Fox's book."[218]

Westcott liked to think so highly of his longing for world peace that he couldn't engage of conflict or hostility of any kind. He "humbly" claimed, "I cannot myself reconcile the spirit of controversy and that of Christian faith."[219] He had better never have read Matthew

217 Westcott, Arthur, *Life and Letters of Brooke Foss Westcott,* (New York, 1903), Vol. I, p. 254.

218 Ibid., p. 135.

219 Ibid., p. 77.

–

Chapter 23 or he would have had more to doubt about Jesus Christ than His ability to perform miracles!

Since Westcott saw all controversy as "un-Christian," he refused to answer John Burgon's arguments concerning the Local Text of Alexandria which Westcott helped exalt. He simply said, "I cannot read Mr. Burgon yet. A glance at one or two sentences leads me to think that his violence answers himself."[220]

It is a sad thing that Westcott's prejudice closed his mind to Burgon's comments. Burgon was harsh, but Burgon was correct. Time has since proven that.[221] It is **a dangerous spirit** which ignores a man's **facts** just because of a "holier than thou" attitude which teaches that "anyone who is right must be gentlemanly." Had more people in the late 1800's looked past Burgon's harsh comments and examined his

---

220 Ibid., p. 404.

Burgon was known for his caustic appraisal of the unbiblical work of Westcott and Hort. He railed on their flimsy conjectures with comments that they were just so much "moonshine."

It seems that God **has always** had a "rude'n'crude" prophet along the pathway of history that would terrify His adversaries with his "violence." The Apostle Paul admitted to being rude. (2 Cor. 11:6). Peter was no wallflower. Luther was scathing in his attacks on the Roman Catholic pope. Zwingli went so far as to draw the sword. Wesley, long black robe or not, delivered blistering condemnations of his hearers. Peter Cartwright would physically take a man in hand. J. Frank Norris was so violent that to this day **many of the Brethren** have hopefully consigned him to Hell. Peter S. Ruckman is one of the latest in this line of unpopular "prophets." His language is often loudly condemned by his critics in hopes that no one will **hear what he's saying** in defense of the Bible's infallibility.

This is not to say that we must **all** be boisterous. Nor does it imply that such language **always guarantees** that the speaker is "led of God." What **it does mean** is that we need to at least stop and listen to what such a person is saying lest we inadvertently overlook **truth** simply because we don't like the package it is wrapped in.

221 The 26th edition of *Nestle's Novum Testamentum-Graece* reinserted **hundreds** of manuscript readings that Burgon had defended as authentic but which had been removed by the Bible skeptics Westcott and Hort in their Greek New Testament.

facts, Christianity would be richer today and Westcott and Hort would have been selling used carriages where they belonged.

We have in Brooke Foss Westcott a man who believed in communal living; a man who believed that the second coming of Christ was not physical; a man to whom "Heaven" was a state of mind, prayers for the dead were permissible in private devotions, and Christ had come to bring peace through international disarmament. He believed in purgatory and admiration for Mary, and he thought the Bible was no more inspired than Shakespeare. **This is the man who walked into the Revision Committee and sat in judgment of our Bible.** He thought he saw room for improvement in the Authorized Version and offered a pro-Roman Catholic Greek text with which to "correct" it. The ironic thing is that Bible-believing Christian educators and preachers (who would never agree with his theology) have for years exalted his opinion of "the Greek" as nearly infallible. These facts alone should be reason enough to condemn Westcott and Hort, their Greek Text, and the manuscripts which they used to arrive at such a text. Just as a world watched in awe as President Bill Clinton's vile immorality became public, **while Liberals still supported him because he said what they wanted to hear**, the infidelity of Westcott and Hort has, over the years, been exposed **for all to see**, but "Bible scholars" still support them. No why do you suppose that is?

But let us look at Westcott and Hort's actions concerning the molesting of the pure words of the King James Bible in favor of Rome. They could never find it in themselves to even give the Textus Receptus a break. They seemed almost to be bent on eradicating the King James Bible from existence. Driven by an unnatural hatred for this Book, they had no qualms about using anything within their power to overthrow it and to place in its stead a representative of the corrupt Alexandrian text.

BROOKE FOSS WESTCOTT...LOST!

–

Saddest of all, we have in Brooke Foss Westcott a man who neither believed in salvation by grace nor ever experienced it. There is no record in his *Life and Letters* that he ever accepted Christ as his personal Saviour. In a letter to his then future wife, he stated how strongly (and how **wrongly**) he trusted his salvation to his baptism rather than Christ's blood:

"My dearest Mary--I quite forget whether we have ever talked upon the subject alluded to in my last note--Baptismal Regeneration--but I think we have, for it is one of the few points on which I have clear views, and which is, I am sure, more misunderstood and misrepresented than any other. Do not we see that God generally employs means? I will not say exclusively, that He has appointed an outward Church as the receptacle of His promises, and outward rites for admission into it, and thus for being placed in a relation with Him by which we may receive His further grace; for till we are so connected by admission into His outward Church, we have no right to think that he will convey to us the benefits of His spiritual Church, when we have neglected the primary means which He provides. It does not, of course, follow that the outward and spiritual churches are co-extensive, that **all who have been placed in relation with God by Baptism, and so made heirs of heaven** conditionally, will avail themselves of that relation to fulfill those conditions--and here lies the ambiguity: because a child is born again into the Church of God, as he has been born into the world before, people seem to conclude that he must discharge all the duties of his new station, which in temporal matters we know he does not. By birth he may, if he will, truly live here; **by baptism he may if he will, truly live forever.** I do not say that Baptism is absolutely necessary, though from the word of the Scripture **I can see no exception**, but I do not think we have a right to exclaim against the idea of the commencement of a spiritual life, conditionally from Baptism, any more than we have to deny the commencement of a moral life from birth."[222] (Emphasis mine)

Here, the "Piper," whom all of the faculties of the major Christian colleges blindly follow, reveals that he **looked to water for his salvation** rather than to the death, burial and resurrection of Jesus Christ. A blind leader of the blind!

As has already been established, both Drs. Westcott and Hort were hostile to the true Greek text of the King James Bible. Dr. Westcott may have been unconsciously influenced into a pro-Roman Catholic attitude or he may have had "malice afore thought." It must also be pointed out that earlier Dr. Hort had been a student of Dr. Westcott's, as Arthur Westcott points out: "Another of Westcott's private pupils was F.J.A. Hort."[223]

The meticulous care with which he taught his pupils is noted by Dr. Whewell, Master of Trinity at the time, "The pains he bestows upon his pupils here (private pupils) is unparalleled, and his teaching is judicious as well as careful."[224]

The common desire of these two Cambridge scholars was to eliminate the authority of the Universal Greek Text of the King James Bible. Scholars had long sought to do this but were baffled by the obvious evidence testifying that the Universal Text was indeed the true text of the Bible and therefore a preservation of the original autographs. These scholars, subtly influenced by Rome, knew that their duty was to overthrow this pure, Protestant, Christ-honoring text and replace it with the Local Text of Alexandria, Egypt, but the overwhelming evidence

---

222 Westcott, Arthur, *Life and Letters of Brooke Foss Westcott,* (New York, 1903). Vol. I, p. 160.

223 Ibid., p. 108.

224 Ibid., p. 108.

–

was always weighted in God's favor. No one, even the Roman Catholic Church, could find a way to explain why 95% of all extant manuscripts belonged to the Universal Text. "Textual criticism" was at a standstill until this roadblock could be circumvented.

HORT'S FICTION

It was the genius of Fenton John Anthony Hort which rode to the rescue of the forlorn Roman Catholic text. As scholars had waited eagerly for a champion who would free them from the bonds of **truth,** Fenton John Anthony Hort rode to their rescue. Amazingly, this man used the same method to overthrow the authority of the Universal Text that Charles Darwin had used to overthrow the fact of creation. He used a **THEORY**!

Hort's theory was that the "originals" agreed with the Local Text, and that this Local Text was "edited" by the Syrian church at Antioch in the 4th Century to produce what we now know as the Universal Text. According to Hort, this text was then **forced** upon the people by a church council.[225]

Just as was true for Darwin's theory, Hort's vaporous musings were opposed by common sense, all available facts, and the nature of God. But just as Darwin did, Hort collected minute scraps of evidence, then twisted and magnified his evidence, and theorized that he was right. Just like Darwin's, his theory was manufactured in his head, and was **independent** of historical facts and evidence. But just like Darwin's, his theory was overwhelmingly accepted by the overeducated men of his day who were looking for a way to overthrow God's

---

225 Anyone who has studied the Roman Catholic Church's **800-year-long** attempt to force Jerome's corrupt "Vulgate" on a resistant populous will see through this feeble argument like a window. You can't **force** people to use a particular Bible. Rome changed her tactics and instead compared the **implied** inferiority of the King James Bible to what she offered from Alexandria and people have lined up to get it!

authority. The theory of evolution was music to the ears of scientists, biologists, and college professors who resented the thought of creation. The sound of "God did it; that settles it" just naturally mustered all of the animosity and rebellion that is resident in the human flesh (Romans 7:18). When Darwin issued his theory to the world, the world was happy to believe the lie.

The same thing was true of Christian scholarship. Scholars had long resented the thought that God could or would preserve His words without their help. Like the lost scientists, they begrudgingly had to acknowledge that the evidence and facts of history testified in favor of the Authorized Version. The issuing of Hort's theory, with the backing of Dr. Westcott, was heralded as the "liberation" of textual criticism. Dr. Alfred Martin explains the delight of liberals when they first learned of Hort's theory:

"Men who had long denied the infallibility of the Bible--and there are many such in the Church of England and in the independent churches—eagerly acclaimed a theory which they thought to be in harmony with their position.

"At precisely the time when liberalism[226] was carrying the field in the English churches the theory of Westcott and Hort received wide acclaim. These are not isolated facts. Recent contributions of the subject--that is, in the present century--following mainly the Westcott-Hort principles have been made largely by men who deny the inspiration of the Bible."[227]

---

226 Like Hezekiah who begat Manassah, the worst king Judah ever had-the movement that had died in 1845 had not passed away before it brought forth liberalism the "Manassah" which has devastated the entire world with its idolatry.

227 Fuller, David, *Which Bible?*, (Grand Rapids International Publications, Grand Rapids, 1971, Second Edition), pp. 265, 266.

—

As with Darwin's theory, men with different viewpoints using Hort's theory arrived at different conclusions. Hort was aware of this as Dr. Martin records, "Hort freely admits this and concedes that 'in dealing with this kind of evidence equally competent as to the same variations'."[228]

Of course, the fact that there were inconsistent conclusions resulting from Hort's data did not hamper his followers. They were not interested in establishing the **correct** conclusion. They were interested in abolishing the old one, i.e., that the King James Bible is the Word and the words of God.

A textual critic is not like a man driving an automobile to a destination which only he knows. He is more like a little child standing behind the wheel who doesn't particularly care where he goes, just as long as **he** is doing the driving. Dr. Martin exposed this tendency: "Their principal method, an extreme reliance upon the internal evidence of readings, is fallacious and dangerous, because it makes the mind of the critic the arbiter of the text of the Word of God."[229]

The feeling of power to be the judge of God's Word, coupled with the old nature which exists in the flesh of all men-**even in Christian scholars**-becomes overwhelming to the mind. As Paul stated in Romans 7:18,

For I know that in me (that is, in my flesh), dwelleth no good thing; for to will is present with me, but how to perform that which is good I find not.

Jeremiah concluded in Chapter 17, verse 9,

---

228 Ibid., p. 268.

229 Ibid., p. 270.

The heart is deceitful above all things, and desperately wicked; who can know it?

Even a saved man has bad flesh. Give this flesh the authority to change God's Word and he will soon plant himself on God's throne. As it has been said, "Put a beggar on horseback, and he will ride off at a gallop." Hort had helped all of scholarship onto their mounts and they were now wildly riding in all directions. Where were they going? Who cared! At least **they** were doing the "driving."

SCHOLARLY PREJUDICE

Another similarity between Hort's theory and Darwin's theory is that both are still held in high esteem long after they have been disproved. Darwin's theory has long ago suffered irreparable damage by historical evidence, the word of God, and of course common sense. Yet, scientists have doggedly upheld it as reliable. This is not done because they feel that Darwin's theory will ever lead them to the truth, but because Darwin's theory leads them away from the authority they so detest, the Bible.

Hort's theory has been just as ill-handled by the truth as Dr. Kurt Aland points out:

> "We still live in the world of Westcott and Hort with our conception of different recensions and text-types, although this conception has lost its raison d'etre, or, it needs at least to be newly and convincingly demonstrated. For the increase of the documentary evidence and the entirely new areas of research which were opened to us on the discovery of the papyri, mean the end of Westcott and Hort's conception."[230]

---

230 Fuller, David, *True or False?* (Grand Rapids International Publications, Grand Rapids, 1973), p. 231.

—

Aland used even stronger language when he stated, "The age of Westcott and Hort ...is definitely over!"[231]

Dr. Jacob Geerlings, who has extensively studied the manuscript evidence of the New Testament, states concerning the Universal Text:

> "Its origins as well as those of other so-called text-types probably go back to the autographs. It is now abundantly clear that the Eastern Church never officially adopted or recognized a received or authorized text and only by a long process of slow evolution did the Greek text of the New Testament undergo the various changes that we can dimly see in the few extant uncial codices identified with the Byzantine [i.e. Majority] text."

Dr. David Otis Fuller concludes,

> "Thus the view popularized by Westcott and Hort before the turn-of-the-century, that the Majority Text issued from an authoritative ecclesiastical revision of the Greek text, is widely abandoned as no longer tenable."[232]

As previously quoted, Dr. Martin has asserted, "The trend of scholars in more recent years has been away from the original Westcott-Hort position."[233]

In spite of new evidence, historical facts, and God's continued blessing of the Authorized Version, Christian scholars still exalt Hort's fiction as though it were the truth. This is not done because they feel

---

231 Nestle, Eberhard, *Novum Testamentum Graece*, Deutsche Bibelstiftung, Stuttgart, 1979, 26th Edition, p.43*.

232 Fuller, David, *Which Bible?* (Grand Rapids International Publications, Grand Rapids, 1971, First Edition), p. 16.

233 Ibid., p. 16.

that Hort's theory will eventually lead them to the true Word of God. These men **don't believe** God has a perfect Bible. Any honest "Christian" scholar today who upholds Hort's outmoded theory will be glad to tell you that there is no perfect translation of "the Bible" in English today. He will acknowledge each new translation as "a step in the right direction," but even the newest translation is not without errors. This attitude is due to the fact that man's human nature resents the idea that God could preserve His words without the help of "good, godly Christians." It also springs from **the natural resistence of men to be in subjection to God**. The supporters of Westcott and Hort possess a loyalty which borders on cultic, as Dr. Martin again has faithfully pointed out:

> "The theory was hailed by many when it came forth as practically final, certainly definitive. It has been considered by some the acme in textual criticism of the New Testament. Some of the followers of Westcott and Hort have been almost **unreasoning in their devotion** to the theory; and many people, even today, who have no idea what the Westcott-Hort theory is, or at best only a vague notion, accept the labors of those two scholars without question. During the past seventy years **it has often been considered textual heresy to deviate from their position** or to intimate that, sincere as they undoubtedly were, they may have been mistaken."[234] (Emphasis mine)

This slavish loyalty is very evident in scholarship today. Just dare suggest that Westcott and Hort may have been wrong and you will be subject to a tirade that would wilt a flower. Such cultic devotion was even observed in 1891 by Hort's friend Professor Armitage Robinson, who stated that a **"kind of cult"** had sprung up around the venerated old scholar.[235]

---

234 Ibid., Second Edition, p. 254.

235 Hort, Arthur, *Life and Letters of Fenton John Anthony Hort,* (New York, 1986), Vol. II, p. 368.

—

To criticize either Dr. Westcott or Dr. Hort is almost sacrilegious in the eyes of worshiping scholarship. We can almost hear Dr. Westcott's own words, "I cannot myself reconcile the spirit of controversy and that of Christian faith." This he used as a defense against the "fanatics" who thought that the Bible was perfect and who would dare challenge his tainted findings. Once accepted, **pride** makes the decaying process almost irreversible. As any parent who has questioned his guilty son or daughter knows, being caught "red-handed" is not nearly as difficult for the child to take as is admitting that he or she has been wrong. <u>Scholars may have the damning evidence before them, but their **pride** will never allow them to admit they're wrong.</u>

FREEDOM. THEN SLAVERY

Less than one hundred years prior to the translation of the King James Bible, England had broken free of the oppressive yoke of Rome. Just barely two hundred years after the Authorized Version was published, England once again started down the road back to Rome in the wake of the Oxford Movement. So for a brief "parenthesis" in its history, England was free of Roman influence. This was just long enough to translate and propagate a perfect Bible.

As we have seen, by the latter half of the Nineteenth Century, England had again, bit-by-bit, fallen to Roman influence. The Romanizing effects of the Oxford Movement, the corrupt tracts of Newman, Pusey, and other pro-Romanists, the decisions by the Privy Council in favor of the anti-scriptural position of the <u>Essays and Reviews</u> had wrought their desired effect. In 1845 Newman made a formal break with the Church of England to join the Roman Catholic Church. His decision influenced over 150 Church of England clergymen to do the same. In 1850, the aggressive Roman Catholic Cardinal Wiseman who had done so much to lead Newman to Rome, and had directed the Oxford Movement via his paper, <u>The Dublin Review</u>, had been commissioned by the pope to formally re-establish the Roman Catholic Church on the shores of England. Rome was back! And would be heard from again.

Through the exaltation of scholarship, England had come from the Bible-honoring, Rome-rejecting position of the Reformation to the ritualistic, pro-Roman attitude which mistrusts and condemns the Bible. English divinity students had heard their Bible maligned with such regularity that they had come to believe that it needed to be updated. As this generation matured and became the prime movers of the Church of England, they unconsciously followed the programming they had received while in college. They were puppets without strings and couldn't prevent their own folly and the downfall of England.

England was ripe for revision!

THE TRAP IS SET

Having had doubts about the reliability of the Authorized Version firmly planted in their brains in seminary and led by "progressives" (some of which were doubtless the Jesuits in disguise that we have previously mentioned), in 1870 the Convocation of the Church of England commissioned a revision of the Authorized Version. A gleam of hope shone in the eye of every Roman Catholic in England and the Continent. An eager anticipation filled every Jesuit-inspired Protestant scholar in England. Although it was meant to correct a few supposed "errors" in the Authorized Version, the textual critics of the day assured themselves that they would never again have to submit to the divine authority of the Universal Text. Secret plans were made to clandestinely take over the Revision Committee so that the Authorized Version could be disposed of once and for all.

In November 1870, Westcott testified of just such a spirit in a letter to Dr. Benson: "In a few minutes I go with Lightfoot to

–

Westminster. More will come of these meetings, I think, than simply a revised version."[236]

The Convocation had instructed the Revision Committee to review the English Bible and to make as few changes as possible. They were instructed **not** to deal with the underlying Greek text of the Authorized Version. They were instructed to do as follows:

1. To introduce as few alterations as possible into the text of the King James Bible, and

2. to limit...the expression of any alterations to the language of the Authorized Version.[237]

Westcott and Hort had other plans. They wanted to see an overthrow of the Textus Receptus entirely and to replace it with a variant of the Local Text of Egypt. They had edited the corrupt Vatican and Sinaitic manuscripts of the Local Text and had produced their own Greek text. Wisely they had never published it. Thus, its existence was unknown to the world. Westcott and Hort did not have to worry about the investigative eyes of their contemporary scholars, such as Dean John Burgon. Had their Greek text been made public prior to the revision, it would have been exposed as corrupt and unfit for translation into English. Drs. Westcott and Hort were definitely "wise as serpents," but unfortunately they were equally as harmful.

SCHOLARLY DECEIT

Since the Committee had been instructed not to deal with matters of the Greek text, and since the Westcott and Hort text had not been published, it was necessary for the two Cambridge Catholics to get it

---

236 Westcott, Arthur, *Life and Letter of Brooke Foss Westcott,* (New York, 1903), p. 367.

237 Clarke, Donald, *Bible Version Manual*, (B.T.M. Publications, Millersburg, 1975), p. 39.

into the hands-and hearts-of the Revision Committee in some manner that would not cause alarm. Therefore, they submitted it little by little to the Committee. Even this was done in secret so that those who were faithful to the true text of Scripture would not be aware until too late.

In order to establish their own Greek text as authoritive, they met together in secret and first planned the strategy prior to the first meeting of the Committee. Their old friend Bishop Lightfoot was even there to help, as Westcott notes in a letter to Hort dated May 1870:

> "Your note came with one from Ellicott this morning...Though I think the Convocation is not competent to initiate such a measure, yet I feel that as 'we three' are together it would be wrong not to 'make the best of it' as Lightfoot says...There is some hope that alternative readings might find a place in the margin."[238]

The next month he wrote to Lightfoot himself: "Ought we not to have a conference before the first meeting for revision? There are many points on which it is important that we should be agreed."[239]

Having predetermined which way the Committee should go, they then secretly submitted their text to its members. Then they stayed close by their sides to see to it that their scheme was carried out. As Dr. Wilkenson informs us,

> "The new Greek Testament upon which Westcott and Hort had been working for twenty years was, portion by portion, secretly committed into the hand of the Revision Committee. Their Greek text was strongly radical and revolutionary. The Revisors followed the guidance of the two Cambridge editors,

238 Westcott, Arthur, *Life and Letters of Brooke Foss Westcott,* (The Macmillan Co., 1903), p. 390.

239 Ibid., p. 391.

> Westcott and Hort, who were constantly at their elbow, and whose radical Greek New Testament, deviating the furthest possible from the Received Text, is to all intents and purposes the Greek New Testament followed by the Revision Committee. This Greek text, in the main, follows the Vatican and Sinaiticus Manuscripts."[240]

These actions reek of Jesuit underhandedness! Although Westcott and Hort were men of scholarship, they were not men of integrity their motives were the destruction of the Authorized Version and its pre-eminent position in England. They didn't desire to replace it with anything that they considered perfect or even "better." They wanted to eliminate the King James Bible and replace it something **that was theirs**.

DEFENDING THE INFIDEL

For the most part, Westcott and Hort found a welcome audience for their abolition of the Universal Text, for the spirit of the revision had been set when the Christ-denying Unitarian preacher Dr. Vance Smith was seated on the Committee. Unitarians do not believe in the truth of the Trinity. It was **plain** that such a man didn't belong on a committee with those who held the doctrine. Protests were made prior to the beginning of the work and voices demanded Smith's omission.

Westcott and Hort, **never known for their allegiance to good doctrine**, resisted the efforts to remove Smith. Dr. Hort shared his feeling concerning Smith's appointment with co-conspirator Lightfoot.

---

240 Fuller, David, *Which Bible?*, (Grand Rapids International Publications, Grand Rapids, 1971, Second Edition), p. 204.

"It is, I think, difficult to measure the weight of acceptance won before the hand for the Revision by the single fact of our welcoming an Unitarian."[241]

Westcott exposed his loyalty to apostasy when he **threatened to quit** if the Convocation were successful in ejecting Smith from the Committee.

"I never felt more clear as to my duty. If the Company accepts the dictation of Convocation, my work must end. I see no escape from the conclusion."[242]

That Smith was a heretic and had no business on the Committee is obvious to any unprejudiced observer. He did not hold the doctrines that Christian view as correct. Wilkenson records Smith's animosity towards the Virgin Birth of Jesus Christ in his comments concerning Isaiah 7:14: "This change **gives room to doubt the virgin birth of Christ**. The meaning of the words of Isaiah may, therefore, be presented thus: 'Behold the young wife is with child.'"[243] (Emphasis mine)

Dr. Smith not only rejected the Virgin Birth but called the belief in Christ's second coming **an error** as Wilkenson once again reveals,

"This idea of the Second Coming ought now to be passed by as a merely temporary incident of early Christian belief. Like many another error, it has answered its transitory purpose in the

---

241 Ibid., p. 206.

242 Westcott, Arthur, *Life and Letters of Brooke Foss Westcott,* (New York, 1903), p. 394.

243 Wilkenson, Benjamin, *Our Authorized Bible Vindicated*, (Takoma Park, 1930), p. 193.

–

providential plan, and may well, at length, be left to rest in peace."[244]

Dr. Smith was nothing more than a rank unbeliever. He had no business doing so much as **taking the offering** in a Bible-believing church, let alone **sitting on a committee to change the Bible!** His doctrine, or lack of it, would be unwelcome in any fundamental church in the country. Yet both Drs. Westcott and Hort **were militant** about having him on the Revision Committee. Why? Because **they too were unbelievers!** They had no more use for the Bible or correct doctrine than did Smith. The Convocation could have just as well seated Nietzsche, Voltaire and Darwin himself on the Revision Committee. There was no difference in what they all believed.

In fact, Dr. Westcott felt that **doctrine was unimportant**. He believed that he as a scholar should decide the text, then theologians could add their remarks afterwards. He stated,

> "I hardly feel with you on the question of discussing anything doctrinally or on doctrine. This seems to me to be wholly out of our province. We have only to determine what is written and how it can be rendered. Theologians may deal with the text and version afterwards."[245]

What did Westcott think of Smith's theological beliefs? "Perhaps we agree in spirit but express ourselves differently. At least we agree in hope."[246]

---

244 Ibid., pp. 197.198.

245 Westcott, Arthur, *Life and Letters of Brooke Foss Westcott,* (The Macmillan Co., 1903), p. 393.

246 Ibid., p. 393.

This last statement may very well hold more truth than Westcott intended. Westcott and Hort were as **hopelessly lost** as was Smith. They are together again, pondering their folly.

It may help here to point out that the Church of England defector to Rome, Dr. John Henry Newman, was also asked to be on the Committee, but he refused.[247] This should reveal the true spirit which the revisors had in their attempt to "bring the Bible up-to-date."

This is not the first revision Newman was asked to sit in on. In 1847, two years after defecting, Cardinal Wiseman, the militant Roman Catholic priest, wrote him from Rome as follows:

> "The Superior of the Franciscans, Father Benigno, in the Trastevere, wishes us out of his own head to engage in an English Authorized Translation of the Bible. He is a learned man and on the Congregation of the Index. What he wished was, that we would take the Protestant translation, correct it by the Vulgate...and get it sanctioned here."[248]

This suggestion is interesting. Could it be that this mysterious Cardinal Wiseman, the man behind the origin of the Romanizing Oxford Movement, was also the originator of the "desire" for a revision of the Authorized Version? Was the revision of 1881 the **actual** product of this earlier proposal? Was this revision the end result of yet another of the Great Puppeteer's productions?

The revision that Wiseman suggested to Newman never took place, we are told. Strangely enough, though, **the desire** of Wiseman to "correct" the Authorized Version with Jerome's corrupt Vulgate is

---

247 Wilkenson, Benjamin, *Our Authorized Bible Vindicated,* (Takoma Park, 1930), p. 147.

248 Ibid., p. 147.

exactly what Protestant scholars did in 1881, 1901, 1952, 1960, 1973, and in every other "new" and "improved" translation since 1611.

MISSION ACCOMPLISHED

Westcott and Hort were so successful at their secret task of subtly guiding the decisions of the Revision Committee that many Committee members did not suspect that they had been used by the Cambridge duo to help destroy the authority of the Authorized Version and give the world yet another Roman Catholic Bible. That meticulous investigator Philip Mauro records:

"In view of all the facts it seems clear that, not until after the Committee had disbanded, and their work had come under the scrutiny of able scholars and faithful men, were they themselves aware that they had seemingly given their official sanction to the substitution of the 'New Greek Text' of Westcott and Hort for the Textus Receptus. The Westcott and Hort text had not yet been published, and hence had never been subject to scrutiny and criticism; nor had the principles upon which it was constructed been investigated. Only after it was too late were the facts realized, even by the Revisors themselves."[249]

Through their subtle guidance Westcott and Hort had led the Revision Committee in a direction one hundred and eighty degrees from what they had been instructed by Convocation. These master deceivers had slowly, methodically introduced **their own personal Greek text** into the Committee and replaced the Textus Receptus with it. Their hypnotic ability had shielded them from discovery and in the end the Church of England had nothing more than a "Protestant translation, corrected it by the Vulgate." It can be safely said that if

---

249 Fuller, David, *True or False?*, (Grand Rapids International Publications, Grand Rapids, 1971, Second Edition), p. 91.

Westcott and Hort were not two Jesuit priests acting on secret orders from the Vatican, then two Jesuit priests acting under such orders could not have done a better job of overthrowing the authority of God's true Bible and establishing the pro-Roman Catholic text of Alexandria, Egypt!

In light of all the evidence of their apostasy it is truly amazing that Westcott and Hort should be so revered by modern conservative scholarship. It is strange indeed that men who believe in the premillennial return of Christ would defend men who did not that men who believe that salvation is by grace through faith could uphold men who not only did not believe in it but sadly did not experience it. It is amazing that men who believe with all their heart that the Bible is the Word of God could be so blind to the infidelity to that Word of these two men.

Revival in America is still possible, but as Jacob told his household in Genesis 35:2, 3 Christian scholarship must **"put away the strange gods"** and **"go up to Bethel**." We need to get back to That Book!

Chapter 9

The

Authorized Version

AFTER an undeserved assault that has lasted for over one hundred years, the criticisms of the King James Bible are usually accepted without any investigation. In this chapter we will be looking at some of the common misrepresentations of the Authorized Version. Many of these misrepresentations are unintentional. Most of the comments against the Authorized Version are, in fact, simply repetitions of what the commentator heard from a pulpit, read in a book, or learned in a classroom.

Before we begin you must realize that there are **two** kinds of critics of the King James Bible. There are those who **know the truth** and for some reason seek to over-throw it for secret reasons. It may be a college professor who feels his job may be in jeopardy if people realize that they **don't need** what he's teaching. It may be an individual whose **great pride** desires to be viewed as an authority equal with the Bible. Or, as we have seen, it may be someone who is **an agent of the Roman Catholic Church** and therefore is trying to destroy the Protestant Bible.

Most such people would be extremely well educated, older and well placed in positions of education and authority so that they can wield as much influence and do as much damage as possible. They may be kind, gracious and loving. But they have a mission and will do what they must to accomplish it. They will endear themselves to fellow Christians and condescend to students in order to entrench themselves in their favor so that their criticisms of the King James Bible will not be challenged. The greatest ally of this group is the simple truth that **people will believe anything they're taught!** Converting these folks to **the truth** is just about impossible because **they already know the truth** and are agents against it.

The other group of critics are those who have been misguided by the above. They can be Christian school or college students. They may be common workers and housewives. Many are pastors who were deceived when in Bible college and refuse to change now due to the cost to their social standing. This crowd is the largest of the two. These folks can be pulled from the snare they are in. But it must be remembered that this is **a heart decision**, not a change of thought, for it is **still** contrary to one's **pride** to admit he are wrong

Unfortunately, both groups have one thing in common: the exaltation of education and the exhilaration experienced by those who surrender to it. Therefore, most of the fervency against the Authorized Version is not so much due to a conscious hatred against the Book as much as it is a show of one's education. This fact, which is a **conscious malice**, is then coupled with the "flesh" or "natural man," which may be an **unconscious malice**, to form a constant antagonism toward the true Word of God.

This "old nature" exists in every person, even Christians. It will not change until the rapture. This nature manifests itself in an innate desire not to submit to the authority of God. Satan realizes this and uses it to his own advantage by giving the flesh ammunition to fight a battle which it naturally wants to fight. The sad result of this spirit of judgment is that the Word of God never really gets a fair trial.

INSPIRATION vs. PRESERVATION

Today it is widely taught and accepted that God wrote the originals perfectly but that there is no perfect translation. This "truth" is taught with evangelistic fervor to Bible college students who then graduate and parrot it to their congregations. Yet **there is no Scripture that teaches any such thing!** This teaching is based on **logic**, man's logic. Christian educators of today say that it is absurd to believe that God could use sinful men to translate His Word perfectly. They say that translations are written by **men** and that their sinful natures taint the work. But such a supposition of a perfect translation is no more absurd than the teaching that God used sinful men to write the Bible perfectly in the originals! If God could overcome a man's sinful nature **to write the originals**, then it only follows that He can also overcome a man's sinful nature **to pen a translation**. Every argument for inerrant, infallible inspiration applies also for inerrant, infallible preservation. **It is the same God!**

If a believer in perfect inspiration says that God overpowered the writers' ability to make a mistake, the believer in perfect preservation can also state that God overpowered the translators' ability to make a mistake. It can also very happily be pointed out that a man who claims that God preserved His Words can at least **produce** what he claims to believe in!

PUT UP or SHUT UP

I personally believe that God has perfectly preserved His Word in the King James (or Authorized) Version. I can at least produce a King James Bible to show what I believe in. Any person who claims that God inspired the original autographs perfectly, cannot produce those original manuscripts to prove it! I do not believe that the King James Bible is a new inspiration. "Inspiration" starts with a blank sheet of paper, a man of God, and God. I am saying that the Authorized

Version is every word of God that was in the original autographs, preserved to this day. "Preservation" starts with God's manuscripts, a man of God, and God. The end result of both is the same: the perfect Word and words of God. It only makes sense.

Many of today's preachers and self-proclaimed scholars slam their fists down on their pulpits in simulated "righteous indignation" while holding a Bible over their heads and loudly proclaim, "This Book doesn't '**CONTAIN**' the word of God, it **IS** the Word of God! Perfect! Infallible! Without admixture of error!" to the delight of the audience. But ask them, while out of their pulpit, if they believe **that the Book in their hand** is truly without error, and they immediately go into a song and dance routine that it's "just a translation **of** the Bible" and say something about "Forever, O LORD, thy word is settled in heaven." Try pressing the issue, and they will question your authority to do so (Matthew 21:23), and if you persist you will be labeled a "Ruckmanite," all for simply believing that this "godly man" really believed what he had said when he was **performing** behind his pulpit!

UNWILLING ALLIES

Earlier we studied the history of the manuscripts of the New Testament and the historical plans and attempts to overthrow God's preservation of His Word. We have seen that the vast majority of manuscripts and of the historical evidence points to the Authorized Version as God's preserved Word. Still, there is an air of antagonism against the Authorized Version. Strange as it may seem, the only things which Roman Catholics, apostates, Protestants, and fundamentalists can agree on is that the King James Bible should be eliminated! This striking truth in itself should be enough to shock born-again Christians into scrutinizing their position to make sure of which side of the fence they stand when we find ourselves aligned with Satan's church against Scripture, we find ourselves in a very dangerous position. This is especially true when we consider what the result would be if these groups were successful in abolishing the King James Bible. The

—

elimination of the Authorized Version finds us **without a Bible**, at which time we find Rome rushing to the rescue with her 1582 Jesuit translation, and the anti-God Local Text of Alexandria. Knowing that no fundamentalist would consciously use a Roman Catholic Bible, the Roman Church has obliged us by changing the cover to read; "Revised Version," "American Standard Version," "Good News for Modern Man," "The Living Bible," "The Amplified Bible," "The Jerusalem Bible," "The Common Bible," "The New International Version," "The New Scofield Reference Bible," "The Contemporary English Version"and many more. The story is true; the names have been changed to protect the guilty.

SOWERS of DISCORD

Long ago Rome realized that there is **not one** of these new Roman Catholic translations which will ever replace God's Authorized Version. Her plan is to get any one of these translations to replace the Authorized Version in any group of Christians. Let the fundamentalists use one of the Revised Standard Version's "twin sons," the New American Standard Version or the New International Version. Convince the young people that they cannot understand the "thee's" and "thou's" in God's Authorized Version and hand them a "Good News for Modern Man" or a "Living Bible." Promote each new translation of the Local Text of Alexandria, Egypt, as "thoroughly reliable" or "more accurate," until the Authorized Version is removed from the hearts of Christians little by little.

How many young "preacher boys" have had their faith in God's **perfect** Word trampled and destroyed while they sat in independent, fundamental Bible colleges where they thought that they were safe? How many found themselves, upon graduation three or four years later, indebted to their "alma mater" for teaching them what the "originals really said" and, in so doing saving them from being drawn into that group of "King James fanatics," that "lunatic fringe," that "cult"? They found themselves leaving college with the confidence(?) that the Book under their arm was **NOT** perfect, and thanking God for the school that had shown them that!

The only person happier than they were was the pope. After all, who wants someone who speaks with authority? (Mark 1:22)

The correlation with the theory of evolution and Bible correctors is unignorable. Most young people believe in creation until **they are taught** that it "isn't true." Most new Christians believe that the Bible is absolutely perfect **until they are taught** that it "isn't." Have our "Bible" colleges become **the enemy** of our children and of our faith?

MANY SHALL COME

It must be remembered at this time that **every** new bible that is published is introduced as being "better" than the Authorized Version. It may also be noted that **every** false prophet is introduced as "better" than Jesus Christ. Mohammed had supposedly come to finish the work which Christ began. Charles Manson claimed that he was Jesus Christ. Sun Nyung Moon claims to have finished the job which Jesus Christ failed to finish. Jim Jones claimed to be Jesus Christ. Even the Beatles claimed to be more popular than Jesus Christ. Notice that Jim Jones did not claim to be Mohammed. Notice that Moon did not claim to be the replacement for Buddha. All false prophets belittle and then attempt to replace Jesus Christ.

BETTER THAN the MODEL T!

Just as all false prophets attack and attempt to replace Jesus Christ, all new bible versions attack and try to replace the King James Bible. Notice that the Good News for Modern Man does not claim to be better than the American Standard Version, but it does claim to be better than the Authorized Version. Notice also that the New International Version does not claim to be better than the American

Standard Version; it claims to be better than the Authorized Version. A **false prophet** can always be recognized, because he attacks the true prophet. A **false bible** can be recognized because it attacks the true Bible. This is an utterly amazing occurrence! Why? Because scholars and Bible publishers have told us for years that the King James Bible is archaic, outdated and no longer relevant for this age. Oh really!

Imagine this scenario for a moment. Next year Chevrolet brings out a brand new car model and advertises it as follows: "This car is **better than the Ford Model T!** It has windows, air conditioning, better tires, more power and a multitude of improvements that make it **better than the Model T.**"

That would be absurd! It wouldn't even be a fair comparison because the **new car** is so mush more advanced than the Model T. Nor would customers flock to their Chevy dealers to see this new model, And if they did, could you imagine the Chevy dealer telling them, Now you want **this** new version of our car rather than an old archaic Ford Model T." It would be insane! Why? Because the Model T is **archaic**. It is **outdated**. It is **no longer relevant** for this age. Why on earth would Chevrolet bring out a new car and then compare it to a car that is almost one hundred-years-old? Why not compare it to Ford's **latest** model?

So, if the King James Bible is so archaic and out of date, **why does EVERY new version compare itself to this "irrelevant" Bible?!** Why wouldn't they present themselves as an improvement over the **most recent translation**? Why compare themselves to a Book that is almost **four hundred years old?!** In fact, are we to believe that the English language is changing **so rapidly** that we need someone to update the Bible **every year**? Sometimes two or three times in the same year? Hogwash! It is hogwash. It is Hollywood. It is Madison Avenue sales techniques being used to supplant the true Word of God with an **inferior** translation of the Egyptian Local Text.[250]

THE SUPER SACK PHILOSOPHY

Let me allegorize for a moment. The claims of the new bibles are strikingly similar to the claims of the famous "Super Sack" grocery bag which swept the country a few years ago before the arrival of plastic grocery bags.

The grocery bag producers wanted to cut their production costs. The "old reliable" double bag was just about indestructible when it came to doing its job, but it was **too costly** to produce. The manufacturers wanted to produce a cheaper bag but feared it would be rejected by the public as inferior. They came up with the idea of producing an **inferior** product but **calling it** "superior."

It has happened to us all. One day, on a trip with our wives to the grocery store, we picked up our groceries and noticed the bag. It wasn't a double bag! "They've made them cheaper," we thought. Then we noticed an official looking statement on the side: "This new Super Sack is made from a new high strength paper. There is **no double bagging needed**."

"Well," we realized, "then it isn't an inferior product after all. It's new and better. That's good to know."

---

250 At the time of this writing, it has come to this author's attention that the Oxford Press is considering a new type setting of the New Scofield Reference Version. When that version was first published **over thirty years ago,** the publishers removed certain words from the King James text to the margin and inserted their own replacement. They are now considering **replacing** the Authorized Version readings **back into the text.** Why would they have to take a "bible" which they have promoted for **over thirty years** as being an **improvement** over the King James and make it read like an **old, archaic** King James Bible in order to get it to sell? Are they admitting the original King James readings are superior to the ones they inserted thirty years ago?

—

We had "bought the pitch." In our trusting, childlike manner, we **believed** that the "Super Sack" was better than the "old reliable" double bag, just because someone **told** us that it was.

"This new Super Sack...**no double bagging needed**."

How many times have these words echoed through my head as I heard a horrifying, tearing sound! I watched as the cans rolled across the grocery store parking lot. I watched the flour break open in the back seat of the car. After finally getting the survivors into the car, we headed for home.

"This new Super Sack...**no double bagging needed**."

We hear that sound! We watch broken eggs as they pour their contents out into the driveway. The cereal has broken open, and now the neighbor's dog picks up our last package of hamburger. We make a wild dash for the house, leaving a trail of canned goods, broken jelly jars, and spilled milk in our wake. We arrive at the back door holding **nothing more** than a large piece of brown paper with words on the side reading: "This Super Sack is made from a new high strength paper. There is **no double bagging needed**."

At times like that, standing there, surveying the damage, I can hardly frame the proper words with which to "thank" the manufacturers for "blessing" me with this wonderful, new, improved "Super Sack."

THE "SUPER SACK" VERSION

This same "Super Sack" philosophy has existed in the field of Bible translations for years. Every new translation published appears first with a giant "public relations campaign" directed at the Christian community. This campaign is designed to **tell** the Christians that they "**need**" this new translation, because the Christians **do not know it**.

How are they going to get suckers...er...I mean...customers to buy a new version if they **don't know** that they need it? So they begin an advertising campaign designed to "inform" Christians of their "need" for this new "Super Sack Version." Of course, they're not going to have many takers if the reluctant common Christian is **satisfied with his King James Bible** so they have to con the poor sap into thinking his **perfect Bible** is outdated and useless. He needs their "improved" version.

This is **not an overstatement**. It is proven true by the Preface to the New American Standard Version of 1963. The last paragraph in the Preface begins with this statement:

"It is enthusiastically anticipated that **the general public will** be grateful to **learn** of the availability, value, and **need** of the New American Standard Version." (Emphasis mine)

Here we see that the Lockman Foundation has **admitted** translating a bible that the general public **doesn't know that it needs!** It is intended for the general public to realize that they "need" this Bible when they read the advertisements. This is just like a laundry detergent. This is just like a motor oil. This is just like **any** inferior item that is foisted on the general public as "improved".

THE SALES PITCH

Let us look into the way in which this "Bible advertising" works.

We read a few Christian periodicals and observe that a new translation has been published. It is, of course, compared to the Authorized Version. The "mistakes" of the Authorized Version are revealed to show us the "need" for a new translation. We are made to feel insecure with our King James Bible because of all of its weaknesses. It is no longer relevant to or society. It is wrought with errors. It isn't in today's English. (Thank God!)

—

Next, this new translation is unveiled with exclamations of "thoroughly reliable," "true to the Original Greek," and "starting a new tradition." We read but are skeptical.

We proceed to the "Bible" bookstore to look over this new translation. The salesman there assures us that of **all** the "Bibles" we could want, we don't want an old, archaic King James Bible.[251]

After having the "sales pitch" from the man behind the counter, we leave carrying a grocery bag (Super Sack) full of "new," "modern," "easy to read" translations in which we are assured that "all of the fundamentals can be found." On the way home, we decide to try out these "more accurate," "Christ-exalting" translations.

THE BIG LET DOWN

On our way home we meet a Jehovah's Witness. In the ensuing discussion we try to convince him that **Jesus Christ was not a created God**. He shows us John 1:18 in his "New World Translation." It reads that Christ was the "only begotten God." We snicker. "That's just **your** version," we say, reaching for a New International Version. To our amazement it also reads "only begotten God"!

Being fully embarrassed, we change the subject to **the Trinity**. "1 John 5:7!" we exclaim. Now we've got him! We turn to 1 John 5:7 in the "Good News for Modern Man." "There are three witnesses," is all that it says.

---

251 Try it yourself. Go to the average Christian bookstore and tell a salesman that you want to buy a King James Bible. He will begin a sales pitch as to why you **don't** want one. He will try to get you to buy **anything** but an Authorized Version. Why? His store would make as much profit from selling a King James Bible as any modern version.

Now go and tell another bookstore salesman you want to buy an NIV. He **will not** try to talk you into any other new version. You're **not** buying a King James Bible and that's good enough for him.

Our Jehovah's Witness asks, "So, what does **that** teach?" We stammer, "Wait a minute," as we reach for a New American Standard Version. "And it is the Spirit who bears witness, because the Spirit is truth."

"So how is the Trinity taught from **that** verse?" he demands.

With our face glowing red and phrases like "thoroughly reliable" and "faithful to the originals" spinning through our head, we desperately grab a New King James Version.

"For there are three that bear record in heaven, the Father, the Word, and the Holy Spirit; and these three are one." (1 John 5:7).

"There it is! There it is!" we exclaim, "See there, the Trinity!"

"Read the footnote on it," he states calmly. "Out loud!"

With growing apprehension we look to the **only footnote** New King James Version translators allowed, *"The words from 'in heaven' (v. 7) through 'on earth' (v. 8) are from the Latin Bible, although three Greek mss. from the 15th Century and later also contain them."*

"You see," says our adversary, "it doesn't belong there."

Thankfully he hasn't got any more time to talk, and he leaves.

We tear our "Super Sack" slightly as we pick it back up and head for home, not quite understanding what has taken place. In our mind we hear the bible bookstore salesman saying, "But I can find the fundamentals in these new versions."

DEVASTATING REVELATIONS

In an attempt to boost our own morale, **we try to lead a man to Christ**. We tell him the simplicity of conversion. We relate to him how easy it was for the Ethiopian eunuch to be saved. We open a Revised Standard Version to show it to him. We read Acts 8:36 and then the next verse, **verse 38!**

"Wait just a second; I seem to have skipped over a verse," we say apologetically.

We read verse 36, then carefully run our finger across the line to the next verse, verse 38! **There is no verse 37!** The eunuch in **this** "bible" never believed on the Lord Jesus Christ!

"Excuse me," we apologize. "I seem to have picked up the wrong bible." We lay down the Revised Standard Version. That's right! We remember someone telling us that the Revised Standard Version was translated by **liberal** scholars. We now see where their liberalism has tainted the text. We pick up the New American Standard Version. We have heard that **it** was translated by **conservative** scholars. Yeah! That's what we need! A bible translated by **conservative** scholars. They're our friends. They'll help us!

We read again. This time we arrive at verse 37. It says, "See footnote."

"No thank you!" we say to ourselves.

Having lost his train of thought, our lost friend walks off, shaking his head and wondering why Christians don't know their Bibles better than they do.

Next, of all things, we run into **an infidel** before we can reach the safety of our home.

"Jesus Christ was **not** God in the flesh," he states.

"Oh yes He was!" we retort confidently, happy to have the opportunity to redeem ourselves for the bad showing earlier. "Look at 1 Timothy 3:16 "we challenge.

We pick the Living Bible.

"But the answer lies in Christ, who came to earth as a **man**...."

"There's no 'God' in that verse," he declares.

The statement of the salesmen comes to mind again, "But I can find the fundamentals in these."

"**Where?**" we ask ourselves returning to the Revised Standard Version.

"**He** was manifested in the flesh...."

"Where is God?" demands our infidel. We wonder the same thing!

"**He** appeared in human form," says the Good News for Modern Man.

"**He** who was revealed in the flesh," states the New American Standard Version.

"Where is God?" demands our infidel with finality.

"I don't know. I really don't know," we reply with our heads down in sorrow.

But now, while we are weak and wounded, the devil pounces. A skeptic confronts us with the confident statement, "There's no such place as 'Calvary.'"

Well now **surely** we will win this confrontation. **Everybody** knows about "Calvary." So **why** is he smiling so gleefully as we open our New International Version to Luke 23:33, the **only** verse where the word "Calvary" appears?

"When they came to **the place called the Skull**, there they crucified him, along with the criminals-one on his right, the other on his left."

"See?" exclaims our skeptical adversary with joy. "You believe in a fictitious god who 'died' in a nonexistent place. Good bye!"

We are **devilstated** (sic)! Here we stand with an entire "Super Sack" (we hear a tearing sound) of "new, improved" versions and we have lost **every encounter** with the enemy. Wounded and dejected, we drag ourselves home. Words cannot describe our "gratitude" to the Lockman Foundation and all the rest of those "godly, conservative scholars" who gave us these "accurate, reliable, true to the original" translations. As we reach the back door we hear a horrifying, tearing sound!

After cleaning up the mess on the back porch, confused and discouraged, we take a glance through that "old, archaic" King James Bible that the bible salesman assured us that we didn't want anymore. **And there we see it!**

Luke 23:33 "And when they were come to the place, which is called **Calvary**, there they crucified him, and the malefactors, one on the right hand, and the other on the left."

It **is** in the Bible! There **is** a place called "Calvary"!

But wait! What about the rest?

I John 5:7 "For there are three that bear record in heaven, the Father, the Word, and the Holy Ghost: and these three are one." **And no footnote!**

Acts 8:37 "And Philip said, If thou believest with all thine heart, thou mayest. And he answered and said, I believe that Jesus Christ is the Son of God."

1 Tim 3:16 "And without controversy great is the mystery of godliness: God was manifest in the flesh, justified in the Spirit, seen of angels, preached unto the Gentiles, believed on in the world, received up into glory."

They're there! They're ALL there! "Thank You God, for the King James Bible! Thank You for Your perfect Word!"

The next morning the garbage man finds a garbage bag full of brand new, unused "bibles" covered by a large, torn piece of brown paper with the words on the side saying: "This new Super Sack is made from a new high strength paper. There is **no double bagging needed**."

No, thank you, we will stick with our "old, archaic" King James 1611.

This story has been an allegory, but the philosophy it describes is very true.

COMMON COMPLAINTS

We shall now look at some of the common complaints made about the Authorized Version. These complaints and charges are seldom made in sincerity but rather "made up as they go along" in a desperate attempt to get Christians to abandon their King James Bibles.

All new versions are defended by the argument, "But I can still find the fundamentals in this new version." But remember being able to "find the fundamentals" in a version is not enough. This was the claim of the corrupt Revised Version! As Wilkenson points out, "There are many who claim that the changes in the Revised Version did not affect any doctrine."

The problem with this statement is that even if the major doctrines can be found in these new Roman Catholic bibles, these doctrines always appear in a watered down form.

Yes, the Blood Atonement can be taught in spite of the removal of the word "blood" from Colossians 1:14 in new versions. The doctrine of the Blood Atonement is found in other passages. The danger is this. Where the Authorized Version teaches a given doctrine in maybe **thirty** different places, the New American Standard Version may teach the same doctrine in only **twenty**. The New International Version may only teach this doctrine in **fifteen** passages. The next "new and improved" version may teach it only **three** or **four**, until it is reduced to only one passage. How then can we teach a new convert this "major" doctrine from only one passage?

All of the doctrines which today's fundamentalists claim to be able to "find" in these new translations have been taught to these same fundamentalists **through the use of a King James Bible**. How will the next generation of Christians learn pure doctrine from a watered down bible? How can we even call something a "major" doctrine which is taught only in one or two verses?

Remember, Satan is not worried at all about what people think of Jesus if he can just keep us from being able to prove that He was virgin-born, shed His blood for our sins, rose from the dead, or is coming back physically. Without Scripture to prove the above, Jesus was just a man.

The new bibles have no Blood in them, no Lord, no second coming, nor other vital doctrines. In other words, the **new bibles have all of the convictions of B.F. Westcott.**

An example of a major Bible doctrine that is lost with modern translations is the doctrine of the Bodily Ascension of Jesus Christ into Heaven. This major doctrine is only found in **three places** in Scripture:

1. - Acts 1:9 - "And when he had spoken these things, while they beheld, **he was taken up**; and a cloud received him out of their sight."

2. - Luke 24:51 - "And it came to pass, while he blessed them, he was parted from them, **and carried up into heaven.**"

3. - Mark 16:19 - "So then after the Lord had spoken unto them, **he was received up into heaven,** and sat on the right hand of God."

There it is. 1-2-3, a major Bible doctrine is **plainly** confirmed in the King James Bible.

But what happens when we try to affirm this precious truth in a "thoroughly reliable, modern" New American Standard Version? Let's see.

1. - Acts 1:9 - "And after He had said these things, **He was lifted up** while they were looking on, and a cloud received Him out of their sight."

In Acts 1:9 we find that this great Bible truth is there. So far. So good.

2. - Luke 24:51 - "And it came about that while He was blessing them, He parted from them."

Whoa! Wait a minute! Something's missing. What? Simply "and carried up into heaven." Simply the **bodily ascension of Jesus Christ!**

The "thoroughly reliable" NASV is now down by **one!**

3. - Mark 16:19 - "So then, when the Lord Jesus had spoken to them, He was received up into heaven, and 'SAT DOWN AT THE RIGHT HAND OF GOD'"

There it is! At least it's in a **second** time! But wait! Before your celebration goes too far, back up and read the **footnote** for verse 9.

"Some of the oldest manuscripts do not contain vs. 9-20"

Uh oh! We got "torpedoed" by another footnote!

So how did this **major** doctrine fare in the King James Bible? It was found in the text, unquestioned **all three times**.

How did the "thoroughly reliable" New American Standard Version do on preserving this doctrine in these three crucial passages?

1. Acts 1:9. **In the text.**

2. Luke 24:51. **Not there!**

3. Mark 16:19. There, but **its authenticity is called into question** by an earlier footnote, (not to mention that a spurious, alternate ending for the book is offered).

That means that the Bodily Ascension of Jesus Christ can only be taught **clearly** from **one verse** in the NASV. And we say, "You can't establish a major Bible doctrine with just a single verse." James White did not dare to address this in his book when he kept saying, "But the doctrine can be found elsewhere in Scripture." It is **not found** elsewhere in the **NASV,** yet it can be clearly and confidently taught from the **perfect, inerrant** King James Bible!

"Thank You God, for the King James Bible! Thank You for Your perfect Word!"

THE SCHOLAR SCAM

Many Christian educators (especially scholars) claim that they have the authority to make changes in the Bible because the scholarship of today is greater than that of the days of King James. To hear them talk, you would think that the King James translators were a bunch of incompetent, bumbling old men who "lucked out" by getting to sit in on the premier scholarly plumb of the century **several** centuries!

How can they say such a thing? How can men who claim to believe that the Bible teaches that everything will get **worse and worse with time** then claim that **education** is the exception? We see the signs of apostasy all around us. They are evident in world economic systems. They are evident in educational systems. They are evident in the apostasy of religious groups which were formerly loyal to the Bible. They are evident in the worldly leanings of many, once separated, Christian colleges. Are we to believe that **the entire world system** has deteriorated but that somehow **"scholarship"** has avoided this "downhill progress?" That is far from being realistic.

Scholar for scholar, the men on the King James translating committee were **far greater men of God** than Westcott, Hort, or any other new translator. They were not only educated in a powerful, anti-Roman atmosphere, but they looked at the manuscripts which they handled as representative of the Holy Word of God. They state this very thing in their Dedicatory to King James:

"So that if, on the one side, we shall be traduced by Popish persons at home or abroad, who therefore will malign us, because we are poor instruments to make **God's holy Truth** to be yet more and more known unto the people, whom they desire still to keep in ignorance and darkness; or if, on the other side, we shall be maligned by self-conceited brethren, who run their own ways, and give liking unto nothing, but what is framed by themselves, and hammered on their anvil...."(Emphasis mine)

As can be seen, they considered themselves "unworthy instruments," for these were humble men.

It must also be noted that these men were almost prophetic in foreseeing their future antagonists. They knew they would criticized by **two groups**.

1. Popish persons - The Roman Catholic Church has long hated the King James Bible. It is her supreme goal to eliminate it and replace it with her own self-serving version of Alexandria.

2. Self-conceited brethren - This is the very crowd with which we have so much trouble today: Men, legitimately educated, who hold an **over-inflated view** of their importance. And they are not about to submit to "a mere book"!

Now compare the words of the King James translators to the pride of the anonymous Lockman Foundation who cursed the world with the New American Standard Version:

"The producers of this translation were imbued with the conviction that interest in the American Standard Version should be renewed and increased. Perhaps the most weighty impetus for this undertaking can be attributed to a disturbing awareness that the American Standard Version of 1901 was fast disappearing from the scene. As a generation 'which knew not Joseph' was born, even so a generation unacquainted with this great and important work has come into being. Recognizing a responsibility to posterity, the Lockman Foundation felt an urgency to rescue this noble achievement from an inevitable demise, to reserve it as a heritage for coming generations, and to do so in such a form as the demands of passing time dictate. It is enthusiastically anticipated that the general public will be grateful to learn of the availability, value and need of the New American Standard Bible. It is released with the strong confidence that those who seek a knowledge of the Scriptures will find herein a source of genuine satisfaction for a clear and accurate rendering of divinely-revealed truth."[252]

The mysterious Lockman Foundation seems to believe that it has done us a great service. It seems almost comical to imagine the fright the these astute men must have felt when they realized that the old American Standard Version was passing off the scene. There it was, "the Word of God," **and no one was buying it!** Obviously God was in big trouble. He was about to slip from the "Best Seller" list to that of a "Has Been." He needed their help!

Most amazing is that these men seem to feel that we "ignorant" members of the general public should be **grateful** to them for their "clear and accurate" translation. Of course we are grateful. We are just as grateful to the Lockman Foundation as we are to the manufacturers of the "Super Sack." Their products seem to be equal in quality.

GENUINE SCHOLARSHIP

As stated earlier, the translation of the King James Bible was achieved during a "Parenthesis of Purity" in English history. It was produced during that brief period following the overthrow of Roman authority and prior to the apostasy of the Church of England. Also, it was translated in the era when the still young English language was at

---

3. Lockman Foundation, New American Standard New Testament Preface, (Gospel Light Publications, Glendale, 1971), p. VI.

its height of purity. Dr. McClure succeeds in aptly describing this esteemed company of translators:

"As to the capability of those men, we say again, that, by the good providence of God, their work was undertaken in a fortunate time. Not only had **the English language, that singular compound, then ripened to its full perfection**, but the study of Greek and of the Oriental tongues and/or rabbinical lore had then been carried to a greater extent in England than ever before or since.

"This particular field of learning has never been so highly cultivated among English divines as it was at that day. To evidence this fact, so far as necessary limits will admit, it will be requisite to sketch the characters and scholarship of those men, who have made all coming ages their debtors. When this pleasing task is done, it is confidently expected that the reader of these pages will yield to the conviction, that **all of the colleges of Great Britain and America, even in this proud day of boasting, could not bring together the same number of divines equally qualified by learning and piety for the great undertaking**. Few indeed are the living names worthy to be enrolled with those mighty men. It would be **impossible to convene out of any one Christian denomination, or out of all, a body of translators on whom the whole Christian community would bestow such a confidence as is reposed upon that illustrious company**, or who would prove themselves as deserving of such confidence. Very many self-styled 'improved versions' of the Bible, or of parts of it, have been paraded before the world, but **the religious public has doomed them all**, without exception, to utter neglect."[253] (Emphasis mine)

---

253 McClure, Alexander, *Translators Revived*, (Maranatha Publications, Worthington), pp. 63,64.

As Dr. McClure has already stated, to fully appreciate the depth of true scholarship present at the translation of the King James Bible, it is necessary to investigate the character of the individuals on the translating committee. His excellent book *Translators Revived* will be the primary source of the following brief biographical comments. You are urged to secure your own copy and read the entire work.

Lancelot Andrews

Dr. Lancelot Andrews, a member of the Westminster Company, is known for his linguistic ability.

> "Once a year, at Easter, he used to pass a month with his parents. During this vacation, he would find a master, from whom he learned some language to which he was a stranger. In this way after a few years, he acquired most of the modern languages of Europe."[254]

And how do you spend **your** vacation? I'm sure that you use the time to learn an entirely new language! I know of men who spend **years** trying to learn a language and Dr. Andrews used to do it in a month. How many of today's "scholars" could do this?

> "He was not a man of 'head knowledge' only. He was a man of great practical preaching ability and an ardent opponent of Rome. His conspicuous talents soon gained him powerful patrons. Henry, Earl of Huntington, took him into the north of England, where he was the means of converting many Papists by his preaching and disputations."[255]

---

254 Ibid., p. 78.

255 Ibid., p. 79.

"As a preacher, Bishop Andrews was right famous in his day. He was called the 'star of preachers.'"[256]

Here we see that this man of great intellect was also a fervent preacher. He didn't spend his days locked in his ivory tower admiring the degree hanging on his office wall. He actually engaged in public preaching and defense of the Word of God.

Dr. Andrews was also known as a great man of prayer.

"Many hours he spent each day in private and family devotions; and there were some who used to desire that 'they might end their days in Bishop Andrews' chapel.' He was one in whom was proved the truth of Luther's saying, that 'to have prayed well, is to have studied well.'"[257]

Do any of today's scholars even **have** a prayer life?

But we also see that, although Dr. Andrews education was **in** his head it hadn't gone **to** his head. For in addition to being a mighty preacher and prayer warrior, he was not "above" the people around him.

"This worthy diocesan was much 'given to hospitality,' and especially to literary strangers. So bountiful was his cheer, that it used to be said, 'My Lord of Winchester keeps Christmas all year 'round.'"[258]

This man actually sounds like someone you could enjoy fellowshipping with! And a **scholar** to boot! But these attributes,

---

256 Ibid., p. 85.

257 Ibid., p. 86.

258 Ibid., p. 87.

though admirable, do not qualify a man to sit down and translate the Bible. Lastly we will review his ability as a translator of the Word of God.

> "But we are chiefly concerned to know what were his qualifications as a translator of the Bible. He ever bore the character of a 'right godly man,' and a 'prodigious student.' One competent judge speaks of him as 'that great gulf of learning'! It was also said, that 'the world wanted learning to know how learned this man was.' A brave, old chronicler remarks, that such was his skill in all languages, especially the Oriental, that had he been present at the confusion of tongues at Babel, he might have served as the Interpreter-General! In his funeral sermon by Dr. Buckridge, Bishop of Rochester, it is said that Dr. Andrews was conversant with fifteen languages."[259]

John Overall

Lancelot Andrews was not alone in his outstanding qualities as both a translator and a defender of the faith. Dr. John Overall was another of the King James translators. He, too, was known for his opposition to the scriptural perversions of Rome. Dr. Overall was present at the hanging of the Jesuit Henry Garnet, mastermind of "the Gunpowder Plot."

In spite of his opposition to Rome, he had an interest in **individual souls** and urged Garnet to make "a true and lively faith to Godward."[260]

Garnet died unrepentant.

---

259 Ibid., p. 87.

260 Paine, Gustavus, *The Men Behind the KJV*, (Baker Book House, Grand Rapids, 1959), p. 90.

—

Dr. Overall was vital to the translation because of his knowledge of quotations of the early church fathers. Without a man with such knowledge, it might have been impossible to verify the authenticity of passages such as 1 John 5:7. This verse has a multitude of evidence among church fathers, though its manuscript evidence suffers from the attacks of Alexandria's philosophers.

This disputed verse is known among textual circles as the "Johannine Comma." Dr. Edward Hills records some of the evidence in its favor:

"The first undisputed citations of the Johannine Comma occur in the writings of two fourth century Spanish bishops, Pricillian, who in 385 was beheaded by the emperor Maimus in the charge of sorcery and heresy, and Idacious Clarus, Priscillian's principal adversary and accuser. In the Fifth Century the Johannine Comma was quoted by several orthodox African writers to defend the doctrine of the Trinity against the gainsaying of the Vandals, who ruled North Africa from 439 to 534 and were fanatically attached to the Arian heresy. About the same time it was cited by Cassiodorus (480-570) in Italy. The Comma is also found in r, an old Latin manuscript of the fifth or sixth century, and in the Speculum, a treatise which contains an old Latin text. It was not included in Jerome's original edition of the Latin Vulgate, but around the year 800 it was taken into the text of the Vulgate from the old Latin manuscripts. It was found in the great mass of the later Vulgate manuscripts and in the Clementine edition of the Vulgate, the official Bible of the Roman Catholic Church."[261]

---

261 Hills, Edward, *Believing Bible Study*, (The Christian Research Press, Des Moines, 1967), p. 190.

It was also cited by Cyprian in 225 A.D.[262]

This is one hundred and seventy-five years before Eusebius penned the Vatican manuscript.

We can see then that Dr. Overall's contribution to the translation would be of the utmost importance. No "modern" translation has so candidly investigated the evidence of the church fathers.

Hadrian Saravia #3

Dr. Hadrian Saravia, another learned translator, was as evangelistic as he was scholarly. McClure reports:

> "He was sent by Queen Elizabeth's council as a sort of missionary to the islands of Guernsey and Jersey, where he was one of the first Protestant ministers; knowing, as he says of himself, in a letter, 'which were the beginnings, and by what means and occasions the preaching of God's Word was planted there.' He labored there in a two-fold capacity, doing the work of an evangelist, and conducting a newly established school, called Elizabeth College."[263]

He too, as any truly dedicated soldier for Christ, was a constant foe of Rome. In 1611 he published a treatise on Papal primacy against the Jesuit Gretser.

He is also said to have been "educated in all kinds of literature in his younger days, especially several languages."[264]

---

262 Ruckman, Peter, *Manuscript Evidence*, (Pensacola Bible Press, Pensacola, 1970), p. 128.

263 McClure, Alexander, *Translators Revived*, (Maranatha Publications, Worthington), pp. 93,94.

264 Ibid., p. 95.

John Laifield #4

Dr. John Laifield was another man of unique talents which lent to his extraordinary value as a translator. Of him it is said: "That being skilled in architecture, his judgment was much relied on for the fabric of the tabernacle and temple."[265]

The seating of Dr. Laifield seems to indicate an amazing insight on the behalf of the translators which drove them to be certain that they examined their assignment from all angles.

Robert Tighe #5

Dr. Robert Tighe was known as "an excellent textuary and profound linguist."[266]

William Bedwell #6

Dr. William Bedwell was "an eminent Oriental scholar." His epitaph mentions that he was "for the Eastern tongues, as learned a man as most lived in these modern times."

"He published in quarto an edition of the epistles of St. John in Arabic, with a Latin version, printed at the press of Raphelengius, at Antwerp, in 1612. He also left many Arabic manuscripts to the University of Cambridge, with numerous notes upon them, and a font of types of printing them. His fame for Arabic learning was so great, that when Erpenius, a most renowned Orientalist, resided in England in 1606, he was much indebted to Bedwell for direction in his studies. To Bedwell, rather than to Erpenius, who commonly enjoys it, belongs the honor of being the first who considerably promoted and revived

---

265 Ibid., p. 97.

266 Ibid., p. 98.

the study of the Arabic language and literature in Europe. He was also tutor to another Orientalist of renown, Dr. Pococke."[267]

"Some modern scholars have fancied, that we have an advantage in our times over the translators of King James' day, by reason of the greater attention which is supposed to be paid at present to what are called the 'cognate' and 'Shemitic' languages, and especially the Arabic by which much light is thought to be reflected upon Hebrew words and phrases. It is evident, however, that Mr. Bedwell and others, among his fellow-laborers, were thoroughly conversant in this part of the broad field of sacred criticism."[268]

An Arabic translation of John's epistles **with** a Latin version included is no small work But this was not Dr. Bedwell's only accomplishments. In addition to his work on the Authorized Version, Dr. Bedwell left several other contributions to his age:

"Dr. Bedwell also commenced a Persian dictionary, which is among Archbishop Laid's manuscripts, still preserved in the Bodelian Library at Oxford. In 1615 he published his book, *A Discovery of the Impostures of Mahomet and of the Koran*. To this was annexed his Arabian Trudgeman.

"Dr. Bedwell had a fondness for mathematical studies. He invented a ruler for geometrical purposes, like that we call Gunther's Scale, which went by the 'Bedwell's Ruler'.

"After Bedwell's death, the voluminous manuscripts of his lexicon were loaned to the University of Cambridge to aid

---

267 Ibid., p. 100.

268 Ibid., pp. 100, 101.

the compilation of Dr. Castell's colossal work, the Lexicon Heptaglotton."[269]

A Persian dictionary? A geometric rule for mathematics? His own personal lexicon? Dr. Bedwell certainly occupied himself with more than a cheap computer Bible program and his cell phone! In comparison to the depth of Bedwell's scholarship, the intellect of today's Bible correctors is "a shallow dive." And the stature of today's overinflated "wanna be" scholars who can do no more than parrot what they read in a book **pales** in the shadow of the monumental intellect of this single translator.

Edward Lively #7

Dr. Edward Lively was known as "one of the best linguists in the world...Much dependence was placed on his surpassing skill in Oriental languages."[270]

Lawrence Chaderton # 8

Dr. Lawrence Chaderton was raised a Roman Catholic and encouraged by his family to become a lawyer. He traveled to London, where he was converted to Christ and joined the Puritan Congregation there.[271] It is said that,

> "He made himself familiar with the Latin, Greek, and Hebrew tongues and was thoroughly skilled in them. Moreover he had diligently investigated the numerous writings of the Rabbis, so far as they seemed to promise any aid to the understanding of the Scriptures."[272]

---

269 Ibid., pp. 101, 102.

270 Ibid., p. 103.

271 Ibid., p. 107.

272 Ibid., pp. 108, 109.

Like his fellow translators, Dr. Chaderton's contribution to the cause of Christ was not restricted to the intellectual realm. He was a **powerful preacher** who lived to the age of one hundred and three. Congregations never tired of hearing the scriptural offerings of this great soldier. A preaching engagement in his later years was described as follows:

> "Having addressed his audience for two full hours by the glass, he paused and said, 'I will no longer trespass on your patience.' And now comes the marvel; for the whole congregation cried out with one consent, 'For God's sake, go on!' He accordingly proceeded much longer, to their great satisfaction and delight."[273]

Dr. McClure leaves us to ponder the direction scholarship has taken in these modern times. "For even now people like to hear such preaching as is preaching. But where shall we find men for the work like those who gave us our version of the Bible?"

You must realize that to dedicate oneself to **academic objectives,** one must read literally **volumes** of old, dry literature. He must engage his mind in certain mental disciplines and fill his head with mountains of seemingly mundane facts that would have no value to anyone other than himself. Such dry, sheerly academic studies tend to **deaden one's spiritual perceptions**. This is why most scholars lose sight of the **spiritual side** of the Bible debate and view things only from the cold, hard standpoint of a seasoned educator. It is truly difficult to maintain a robust mind and a fervent heart. That is why Chaderton's intense scholarship and dynamic preaching ability are **not to be taken lightly**. Many men have one or the other. Only a handful in history have every possessed **both!**

---

273 Ibid., p. 115.

And even **more amazing** is that the translation of the King James Bible could have include **so many of them!**

Francis Dillingham #9

Dr. Francis Dillingham was so studied in the original languages that he participated in public debate in Greek.[274]

How many of today's scholars could accomplish such a feat as public debate in Greek?! And if you could find one that could, would he then be able to match Dr. Dillingham's fervent anti-Roman zeal? Read on!

Dr. Dillingham was another soldier for Christ who took aggressive action against the teaching of Rome. He used his great intellect as a weapon against the scourge of Romanism:

> "He collected out of Cardinal Bellarmine's writings, all the concessions made by the acute author in favor of Protestantism. He published a *Manual of Christian Faith*, taken from the Fathers, and a variety of treatises on different points belonging to the Romish controversy."[275]

Where the "spirit" of scholarship reigns there is usually the heady air of condescension to Rome. Amazingly, the scholars that have no problem with confronting and belittling Bible believers will bend over backwards not to say or do anything to offend the Roman Catholic Church. Could this be that since Rome is the "Spiritual Father" of their discipline, **textual criticism**, that they feel an unconscious paternal allegiance to that organization?

Thomas Harrison #10

---

274 Ibid., p. 116.

275 Ibid., p. 112.

Dr. Thomas Harrison, it is recorded, was chosen to assist the King James translation due to his knowledge of Greek and Hebrew. In fact his ability served him well in his duties as Vice-Master of Trinity College in Cambridge.

> "On account of his exquisite skill in the Hebrew and Greek idioms, he was one of the chief examiners in the University of those who sought to be public professors of these languages."[276]

Here is a man who was not **just** a Greek and Hebrew professor. He was the examiner **for** Greek and Hebrew professors! If someone wanted to teach Greek or Hebrew he had to pass Dr. Harrison's scrutiny. This is no "little leaguer."

John Harding #11

Dr. John Harding was an ardent scholar of whom it is said concerning his ability: "At the time of his appointment to aid in the translation of the Bible, he had been **Royal Professor of Hebrew in the University for thirteen years**. His occupancy of that chair, at a time when the study of sacred literature was pursued by thousands with a zeal amounting to a possession, is a fair intimation that Dr. Harding was the man for the post he occupied."[277] (Emphasis mine)

John Reynolds #12

Dr. John Reynolds was another translator who had been raised in the spiritual darkness that is Roman Catholicism. As Chaderton, he too trusted Christ and became a Puritan. The academic and spiritual attributes he possessed that led to his place on the translation committee are recorded as follows:

---

276 Ibid., p. 118.

277 Ibid., p. 120.

"Determined to explore the whole field and make himself master of the subject, he devoted himself to the study of the Scriptures in the original tongues, and read all the Greek and Latin fathers, and all the ancient records of the Church."[278]

Once again. Just as many of his colleagues on the committee, Dr. Reynolds was an ardent and active anti-Papist. His aggressive nature toward the false teachings of his former church are exemplified in the following record:

"About the year 1578, John Hart, a popish zealot, challenged all the learned men in the nation to a public debate. At the solicitation of one of Queen Elizabeth's privy counselors, Mr. Reynolds encountered him. After several combats, the Romish champion owned himself driven from the field.

"At that time, the celebrated Cardinal Bellarmine, the Goliath of the Philistines at Rome, was professor of theology in the English Seminary at that city. As fast as he delivered his popish doctrine, it was taken down in writing, and regularly sent to Dr. Reynolds; who from time to time, publicly confuted it at Oxford. Thus Bellarmine's books were answered, even before they were printed."[279]

Here was yet **another** of King James's noble translators who gave Rome no quarter. He had an aggression again Rome's falsehood that is sadly lacking in the diplomatic air of today's heady scholarship. Furthermore, his skills in Hebrew and Greek made his appointment to the company of translators a wise one.

To someone who was not raised in Romanism, as I was, it is impossible to understand the great personal indignation the Roman

278 Ibid., p. 122.

279 Ibid., pp. 123, 124.

Catholic Church feels when one of her victims leaves it for the Truth. The Roman Catholic Church will do **anything** to minimize and downplay the damage caused by such a defection. One of the ploys she uses is the lie of a "death bed recantation" of Christianity followed by a humble return to the Roman fold. Obviously, the dead saint is in no position to refute Rome's lie. This tactic was attempted with Reynolds. Unfortunately for Rome the good doctor wasn't "dead enough" and received word of the rumor. While on his death bed, it is recorded:

> "The papists started a report, that their famous opposer had recanted his Protestant sentiments. He was much grieved at hearing of the rumor; but too feeble to speak, set his name to the following declaration: 'These are to testify to all the world, that I die in the possession of that faith which I have taught all my life, both in my preachings and in my writings, with an assured hope of my salvation, only by the merits of Christ my Savior.'"[280]

Dr. Reynold's statement, "**...with an assured hope of my salvation, only by the merits of Christ my Savior**." is a wonderfully clear testimony of his salvation by grace through the shed blood of Jesus Christ. It is just such a clear cut testimony of faith in Christ that **is missing** from any of the writings of Westcott and Hort!

Richard Kilby #13

Dr. Richard Kilby was a man worthy of the position of translator. One incident in his life, which occurred shortly after the Authorized Version had been published, suffices not only to reveal his depth, but also the dangers of the self-esteemed "scholars" changing the translation **of even one word** in God's Book.

> "I must here stop my reader, and tell him that this Dr. Kilby was a man so great in learning and wisdom, and so excellent a critic in the Hebrew tongue, that he was made

---

280 Ibid., p. 132.

—

professor of it in this University; and as also so perfect a Grecian, that he was by King James appointed to be one of the translators of the Bible, and that this Doctor and Mr. Sanderson had frequent discourses, and loved as father and son. The Doctor was to ride a journey into Derbyshire, and took Mr. Sanderson to bear him company; and they resting on a Sunday with the Doctor's friend, and going together to that parish church where they were, found the young preacher to have no more discretion than to **waste a great part of the hour** allotted for his sermon in exceptions against the late translation of several words, (not expecting such a hearer as Dr. Kilby) and showed **three reasons** why a particular word should have been otherwise translated. When evening prayer was ended, the preacher was invited to the Doctor's friend's house, where after some other confidence, the Doctor told him, he might have preached more useful doctrine, and not filled his auditor's ears with needless exceptions against the translation; and for that word for which he offered to that poor congregation three reasons why it ought to have been translated as he and others **had considered all of them, and found thirteen more considerable reasons why it was translated as now** printed."[281] (Emphasis mine)

In addition to an example of Dr. Kilby's qualifications as a translator there is a very interesting side note to this account. Today's "wanna be" Bible scholars are **all too often** heard to weary their listeners with boring statements such as "A better translation is..." and "The King James translators should have translated it...." It must be remembered by the reader when they hear such futile charges that the alternate translation that they offer had probably **already been considered** by the King James translators **and rejected** for far more weighty reasons...**by men far more qualified than the speaker!**

---

281 Ibid., p. 139.

"Correcting" the Bible is not a show of one's **intellect.** It is a show of one's **ignorance!**

Miles Smith #14

Dr. Miles Smith was another of the translators of the King James Bible. He is the man responsible for writing the preface to the King James Bible. This preface is no longer printed in present copies of the Book.

Dr. Smith had a great wealth of knowledge concerning the Greek and Latin fathers, and was being expert in Chaldee, Syriac, and Arabic. "Hebrew he had at his finger's end."[282]

Henry Saville #15

Dr. Henry Saville was known for his Greek and mathematical learning. He was so well known for his education, skill with languages, and knowledge of the Word, that he became Greek and mathematical tutor to Queen Elizabeth during the reign of her father Henry VIII.[283]

Now wait! Don't read over that statement so fast. This man was recognized as such a learned man that he was the one-**the only one-**chosen to tutor the future Queen of England. Is the academic stature of the King James translators finally starting to dawn on you? Can you yet see the abject shallowness of **the best** that scholarship has to offer today? (It must gall men like James White to realize the great gap between them and **real** intellect!)

Furthermore, Dr. McClure tells us, "He is chiefly known, however, by being the first to edit the complete works of John Chrysostom, the most famous of the Greek Fathers."[284]

---

282 Ibid., p. 143.

283 Ibid., p. 165.

284 Ibid., p. 166.

We could go on and on concerning the tremendous scholarship of the King James translators, but we have not the space here. Dr. McClure's book *Translators Revived* is recommended for an in-depth study of the lives of these men.

It should be noted that these men were qualified in the readings of the church fathers which prevented them from being "bound" to the manuscripts which many times causes earlier readings to be overlooked. This is vastly better than the methods used by modern translators.

It should also be recognized that these men did not live in "ivory towers." They were men who were just as renowned for their **preaching ability** as they were for their esteemed education. It is a lesson in humility to see men of such great spiritual stature call themselves "poor instruments to make God's Holy Truth to be yet more and more known."

"REVISED" SCHOLARSHIP

When the ship of apostasy, by the name of the "HMS Oxford Movement," sailed through the waters of educational England, it left irreparable devastation in its wake. Although the perpetrators themselves had been thwarted, English scholarship had been "snake bit." It only took a few years for the serpent's poison to seep through the entire educational system of England and the throngs of death followed. Never again would there be an anti-Roman element to English scholarship. Never again would God's Textus Receptus receive the pre-eminence it deserved. English scholarship had abandoned God. But worse yet **He had abandon it!**

It is essential that you have a taste of "modern" scholarship so that you can compare what we have today to those outstanding men of the King James translations committee Therefore we shall now briefly examine a few of the translators of the Revised Standard Version. The reasons that we shall examine these revisors are as follows:

First, it is due to the secrecy surrounding translations such as the New American Standard Version and the New International Version. The Lockman Foundation has elected to remain anonymous.[285] This is, of course, the safest method, as it prevents investigative eyes from discovering truths such as those we shall see concerning the Revised Standard Version translators.

The translating committee of the New International Version is also nameless. We are assured of their "scholarship" although words without proof ring of a snake oil salesman in the days of the Old West. Of course, it must be admitted, they are both in the "selling business." And both offer a product that their customers **don't know they need** until the fast-talking salesman tells them they do.

Secondly, we have chosen to examine the Revised Standard Version translators because they are of the exact same conviction concerning biblical manuscripts as Brooke Foss Westcott, Fenton John Anthony Hort, Eberhard Nestle, the Lockman Foundation, the New Scofield Board of Editors, and the majority of unsuspecting college professors and preachers across America today. Namely, they believed the Vatican and Sinaitic manuscripts of the Egyptian Local Text are superior to the God-preserved Universal Text. The story is always the same, only the players change.

Thirdly, due to this mistaken preference for Roman Catholic manuscripts, **every** Bible translation since 1881 is **linked directly to**

---

285 At the time the first edition of this book was written, this was true. Over the ensuing years it has proved impossible for the Lockman Foundation to remain a secret organization. (Secret? Did I say "secret" organization? Like those following the Oxford Movement who continued its Romanizing work?) A letter requesting the names of the translators was rebuffed at the time of the writing of the first edition. Since the "damage has been done" the names of the translators is now public. There names are listed in Appendix A in the back of this book.

the Revised Version and has had nothing to do with the Authorized Version. All new translations follow the same manuscript family as the Revised Version. This family is the Local Text of Alexandria, Egypt and has no relationship whatsoever to the Authorized Version. It is the text which Satan has altered and promotes as a replacement for God's Universal Text. This "Apostate Succession" has led from the Revised Standard Version of 1881 to the American Standard Version of 1901,[286] then to the Revised Standard Version of 1952. All modern translations after this are linked to the Revised Standard Version.

Don't expect any "Laifields," "Bedwells" or "Chadertons" in the following list. Think more in the vein of "Westcott," "Hort," "Pusey," "Newman" and "Nestle"... or maybe, Carl Sagan.

Edgar Goodspeed

Edgar Goodspeed was on the Revised Standard Version committee. Goodspeed **did not believe in the deity of Jesus Christ**. He looked at Jesus Christ as a social reformer who gave His life as a martyr for a "cause." Goodspeed said,

> "Jesus' youth was probably one of the dawning and increasing dissatisfaction with the prevalent form of the Jewish religion in Nazareth and in his own home. HE DID NOT IN THOSE EARLY YEARS SEE WHAT HE COULD DO ABOUT IT, but he must have felt a growing sense that there was something deeply wrong about it, which should be corrected."[287]

The apostate Dr. Goodspeed continues,

---

286 The American Standard Version of 1901 was originally marketed as the **American** Revised Version--an American creation growing from the **English** Revised Version of 1881.

287 Rockwood, Perry F., God's Inspired Preserved Bible, (Peoples Gospel Hour, Halifax, 1979), pp. 17, 18.

"He faced the question of his next step in his work. He had no mind to die obscured in some corner of Galilee, to no purpose. A bolder plan was now taking shape in his mind. He would present himself to Jerusalem...publicly offer them their Messianic destiny, AND TAKE THE CONSEQUENCES. And he would do this in ways that would make his death something that would never be forgotten, but would carry the message to the end of time. Yet how could this be done?"[288]

Goodspeed makes the Incarnate Son of God sound like some ancient version of David Koresh. Jesus wasn't a revolutionary! He was the Son of God! He wasn't a martyr! He was the Supreme sacrifice for the sins of all mankind!

Goodspeed also, like Westcott, seemed to think it necessary to explain away Christ's miracles. Here we see what he thought took place at the feeding of the five thousand:

"He took the five loaves and two fishes and looked up to heaven and blessed the loaves, and broke them in pieces, and gave them to the disciples to pass to the people. He also divided the two fishes among them all. And they all ate, and had enough. JESUS' SIMPLE EXAMPLE OF SHARING ALL he and his disciples had with their guests must have MOVED THOSE GALILEANS as it moves us still. THEY COULD NOT DO LESS THAN HE HAD DONE. THEY FOLLOWED HIS EXAMPLE. He simply showed the way, and they gladly took it."[289]

---

288 Ibid., pp. 18, 19.

289 Ibid., p. 18.

Goodspeed called Genesis the product of an "Oriental story teller at his best."[290]

Again, where is this any different than Hort's statement, "I am inclined to think that no such state as 'Eden' (I mean the popular notion) ever existed, and that Adam's fall in no degree differed from the fall of each of his descendants, as Coleridge justly argues."[291]

Where does it differ from Westcott who said,

"No one now, I suppose, holds that the first three chapters of Genesis, for example, give a literal history--I could never understand how anyone reading them with open eyes could think they did--yet they disclose to us a Gospel. So it is probably elsewhere. Are we not going through a trial in regard to the use of popular language on literary subjects like that through which we went, not without sad losses in regard to the use of popular language on physical subjects? If you feel now that it was, to speak humanly, necessary that the Lord should speak of the 'sun rising,' it was no less necessary that he would use the names 'Moses' and 'David' as His contemporaries used them. There was no critical question at issue. (Poetry is, I think, a thousand times more true than History; this is a private parenthesis for myself alone.)"[292]

You can plainly see that all of these Bible correctors believe the same things concerning Scripture. They **truly are** "poor instruments to make God's Holy Truth to be yet more and more known." They are

---

290 Ibid., p. 18.

291 Hort, Arthur Fenton, *Life and Letters of Fenton John Anthony Hort*, (New York, 1896), Vol. I, p. 78.

292 Westcott, Arthur, *Life and Letters of Brooke Foss Westcott*, (New York, 1903). Vol. II, p. 69.

"Agents of Apostasy" and their work is good for a cold New England night and wood burning stove.

Julius Brewer

Julius Brewer, another revisor, stated, "The dates and figures found in the first five books of the Bible turn out to be altogether unreliable."[293]

Henry Cadbury

Henry Cadbury, another member of the revision committee, believed that **Jesus Christ was a just man who was subject to story telling**. "He was given to overstatements, in his case, not a personal idiosyncrasy, but a characteristic of the Oriental world."[294]

He also **doubted the deity of Christ**. "A psychology of God, if that is what Jesus was, is not available."[295]

Cadbury, like Westcott, was a socialist, and he attempted to fit Jesus Christ into the same mold. "His [Jesus'] gospel was in brief, a social gospel."[296]

Anyone who believes the Bible knows that Jesus did **not** preach a social gospel. Every socialist, every preacher of "Liberation Theology" would like to claim that he did. But it simply isn't true. So why would anyone let a man who believed such a falsehood translate the Bible?

---

293 Rockwood, Perry F., *God's Inspired Preserved Bible*, (Peoples Gospel Hour, Halifax, 1979), p. 19.

294 Ibid., p. 20.

295 Ibid., p. 20.

296 Ibid., p. 20.

Walter Bowie

Walter Bowie was another revisor who believed that the Old Testament was **legend** rather than **fact**. In reference to Abraham he says, "The story of Abraham comes down from the ancient times; and how much of it is fact and how much of it is legend, no one can positively tell."[297]

In speaking of Jacob wrestling with the Angel, he says, "The man of whom these words were written (Genesis 32:31) belongs to a time so long ago that it is uncertain whether it records history or legend."[298]

Furthermore, Bowie did not believe in the miracle of the burning bush. Here is how he believed it happened:

> "One day he (Moses) had a vision. In the shimmering heat of the desert, beneath the blaze of that Eastern sun, he saw a bush that **seemed to be on fire**, and the bush was not consumed."[299] (Emphasis mine)

Clarence Craig

Clarence Craig was one of the revisors who went so far as to **deny the bodily resurrection of Christ**. By his own admission he states,

> "It is to be remembered that there were no eyewitnesses of the resurrection of Jesus. No canonical gospel PRESUMED to describe Jesus emerging from the tomb. The mere fact that a tomb was found empty was CAPABLE OF MANY EXPLANATIONS. THE VERY LAST ONE THAT WOULD

---

297 Ibid., p. 21.

298 Ibid., p. 21.

299 Ibid., p. 21.

BE CREDIBLE TO A MODERN MAN WOULD BE THE EXPLANATION OF A PHYSICAL RESURRECTION OF THE BODY."[300]

Would you allow such an **infidel** to take his scalpel to your Bible? If you would, you deserve what you end up with!

Craig also held Westcott's view that **Christ's second coming was a spiritual coming**, not physical.

"In other words, the coming of Christ is to THE HEARTS of those who love him. IT IS NOT HOPE FOR SOME FUTURE TIME, but a present reality of faith."[301]

Strangely enough, Craig is found to agree with the position of the present day "godly Christian scholars" who believe that **God is not able to preserve His Word**. He declares,

"If God once wrote His revelation in an inerrant book, He certainly failed to provide any means by which this could be passed on without contamination through human fallibility...The true Christian position is that the Bible CONTAINS the record of revelations."[302]

Frederick Grant

Frederick Grant was in agreement with Westcott and Hort's belief in **prayers for the dead**. His shameless Roman Catholicism is revealed when he states,

300 Ibid., p. 22.

301 Ibid., p. 22.

302 Ibid., p. 22.

"It would seem that modern thought...demands that if prayer be real or effective at all, it shall not cease when those who have gone before advance, as by a bend in the road beyond our sight...must we cease to pray for them? The answer is CEASE NOT TO PRAY, for they are living still, in this world or the other, and still have need of prayers."[303]

Willard Sperry

Anyone who has studied the Bible knows that the four Gospels are often split into two groups by scholars. Matthew, Mark and Luke are placed together and John is left to stand alone. This segregation is due to the immense testimony to the deity of Christ that is found in John. Scholars like to single it out for "special hatred." Willard Sperry was one such man. Sperry shows his dislike for the gospel of John in the following statement.

"Some of these sayings, it is true, come from the Fourth Gospel (John), AND WE DO NOT PRESS THAT GOSPEL FOR TOO GREAT VERBAL ACCURACY IN ITS RECORD OF THE SAYINGS OF JESUS."[304]

Notice the veiled animosity Sperry holds for John's Gospel. But his vehement hatred is really no different than that of any modern day Bible corrector. **They both have the same spirit!**

William Irwin

William Irwin believed that the Jewish prophets inflated the position of God in the Bible. He lamely claims,

"The prophets were forced by the disasters that befell to do some hard, painful thinking. THEY WERE FORCED BY

---

303 Ibid., p. 22.

304 Ibid., p. 22.

THE HISTORY OF THEIR OWN TIMES TO REVISE THEIR
MESSAGES AGAIN AND AGAIN IN ORDER TO KEEP UP
WITH THE PROGRESS OF THE AGE. THE ASSYRIANS
AND THE BABYLONIANS FORCED THEM TO REVISE
THEIR CONCEPTION OF YAHWEH FROM TIME TO TIME
UNTIL THEY FINALLY MADE HIM GOD OF THE
UNIVERSE."[305]

Fleming James

Fleming James was yet another Bible revisor who was as much
an infidel as any secular college professor in America today. He said
concerning Moses' authorship of the first five books of the Bible,

"The idea (of Mosaic authorship) has been shown by
scholars to be untenable on many grounds. The view that now
prevails is that through these five books, there were FOUR
DIFFERENT STRANDS OF NARRATIVE WHICH HAVE
BEEN PIECED TOGETHER to make the present story...Two
are older and more reliable as history, two proceed from later
time and are so coloured by later ideas that they can hardly be
called history at all."[306]

This almost coincides with Fenton John Anthony Hort's belief
concerning the synoptic gospels, Matthew, Mark, and Luke.

"I quite agree that it is most essential to study each
Synoptist by himself as a single whole. Only I should add that
such a study soon leads one to the fact of their having all largely

---

305 Ibid., p. 23.

306 Ibid., p. 23.

used at least one common source, and that fact becomes an additional element in their criticism."[307]

We also find that James doubted the miracle of Israel's Red Sea crossing.

"What really happened at the Red Sea WE CAN NO LONGER KNOW; but scholars are pretty well agreed that the narrative goes back to some striking and pretentious event which impressed both Moses and the people with the belief that YAHWEH had intervened to save them. THE SAME MAY BE SAID OF THE ACCOUNT OF THE PLAGUES."[308]

Concerning Elijah's action in 2 Kings 1:10, he said, "The narrative of calling down fire from heaven upon soldiers sent to arrest him is PLAINLY LEGENDARY."[309]

Millar Burrows

Millar Burrows finalizes the true convictions of these apostate revisors in his statement, "We cannot take the Bible as a whole and in every part as stating with divine authority what we must believe and do."[310]

Earlier we studied the perverted beliefs of Drs. Westcott and Hort. We can see how all of these men fit together so well and were able to completely reject God's text in favor of Rome's. Many may make a defense for new translations in claiming that these men are

307 Hort, Arthur Fenton, *Life and Letters of Fenton John Anthony Hort* (New York, 1896), Vol. I, p. 423.

308 Rockwood, Perry F., *God's Inspired Preserved Bible*, (Peoples Gospel Hour, Halifax, 1979), p. 23.

309 Ibid., p. 23.

310 Ibid., p. 24.

"liberal" scholars, while today's modern translations such as the New American Standard Version and the New International Version are translated by "conservative" scholars. This claim is an empty one, though, because concerning which manuscripts are to be judged as "best, most reliable, etc....," "conservative" scholars of the day agree wholeheartedly with the conviction of the "liberal" revisors of the 1881 and 1952 revision committees. They **both** believe that the Roman Catholic text found in Vaticanus, Sinaiticus, etc., is better than the Universal Text of the Authorized Version. "Conservative" scholars also agree with their liberal counterparts in their conviction that God could not preserve His words through history.

We see then that the men of the King James Bible were men of great education, education which was tempered by true spirituality and biblical convictions. They were used by God as instruments in His plan for the preservation of His words. They were not "inspired" to write a new revelation. They were empowered by the Holy Spirit to preserve that which had already been written. This is what God had promised in Psalms 12:7.

MODERN SCHOLARSHIP

In the summer of 1995 I was invited to participate in a nationally broadcast televised debate concerning the claims of perfection for the King James Bible. The participants consisted of three King James proponents versus five Bible critics and the host, John Ancherberg. We recorded eight half-hour television programs for broadcast on The John Ancherberg Show. Thus I was able to meet several of today's leading scholars, some who have worked on some of the modern translations and some who are nothing more than by-standing critics. Here is what I observed.

 Dan Wallace

Dr. Wallace is truly an eminent scholar. He a professor of textual criticism at Dallas Theological Seminary. He is also very hostile to the position of infallibility of Scripture although he may take the standard dodge of hiding behind a belief in a perfect **but lost** original. Dr. Wallace at one point could do no more than discard the King James Bible because of what he claimed was an unclear rendition of Titus 2:12. He stated that the King James rendition, which he quoted as, "Looking for that blessed hope, and the glorious appearing of our great God and of our Saviour Jesus Christ." seems to imply that "God" and "Jesus Christ" were two distinct entities.

To be honest, I thought to myself that his observation was correct. But something didn't sound quite right, so **I opened my Bible**, which I had with me, to the verse in question and read it, "Looking for that blessed hope, and the glorious appearing of **the** great God and of our Saviour Jesus Christ."

If you look carefully you will notice that the first "our" quoted by Dr. Wallace wasn't in the verse. He had replaced the word "the" with the word "our," which would lend credence to his argument. But the verse as rendered by the scholars of the King James translation committee in no way alludes to there being a difference between "God" and "Jesus Christ." He was duly embarrassed and defeated.

Do I think he was trying to be deceitful? It has to be considered that he may have been but I personally think he simply didn't know the Bible well enough to quote the verse correctly. If he **did** know his Bible, he could not possibly have had such a shallow argument. He would have noticed that the book of Titus is one of the strongest for identifying "Jesus Christ" as "God." If Dr. Wallace had been a student of **the Bible** rather than of textual criticism he would have known that Titus 1:3 refers to "...God our Saviour;" and then in the very next verse records "...the Lord Jesus Christ our Saviour." Then again in chapter 2:10 Titus says, "...God our Saviour..." and then in Dr. Wallace's text says, "...our Saviour Jesus Christ." Titus finishes his obvious statement on the deity of Jesus Christ in 3:4 with, "...God our Saviour..." and then in verse six, "...Jesus Christ our Saviour". Now either Titus is telling us that "God" and "Jesus Christ" are one in the same or we have **two** "Saviours"!

What should be noted here is the **sad lack of simple Bible knowledge** that is possessed by one of today's leading biblical "scholars." Thus, a knowledge of the **insignificant** field of textual criticism does not make a man a **Bible** scholar!

James White

James White is on of Bible criticism's newest heroes. If you desire fame and a pat on the head by scholarship, just write a book attacking the King James Bible. White has proved this with his book, *The King James Only Controversy*. His book is decidedly misleading. In it he claims that the Jerome's Roman Catholic Latin translation "became known" as the "Vulgate."[311] This isn't true. The **Old Latin** Bible "became known" as the "Vulgate" ("common"). By the time Roman Catholic Church had Jerome translate the corrupt Alexandrian text into Latin in 380 AD, the **Old Latin** was already being well used by believers and had **assumed the name** "Vulgate" because of this **common** usage. Then the Roman Catholic Church issued Jerome's work and **officially named it** "The Vulgate." This was in hopes of overthrowing the hold that the **true** Vulgate had over biblical Christianity. Now, James White and company get **real upset** and whimper about "mean-spiritedness" when we Bible believers call them "liars." But I simply have a hard time believing that a man of White education **didn't already know this when he wrote his misleading comment!** Now **what would that make him?**

In his book White takes the standard, soggy, worn-out arguments against the King James Bible and tries one more time to make them sound believable. But he is forced to close an eye to the very practices

---

311 White, James R., *The King James Only Controversy*, (Bethany House Publishers, Minneapolis, 1995), p. 13.

he criticizes the King James translators for when they are implemented by his friends on the modern version committees. He, like his ilk, believes **only orthodox Christians** ever altered Scripture and that there was **never** any conspiracy **to corrupt** the Bible.[312]

One of his most fraudulent and transparently dishonest criticisms of Bible believers is his condemnation of the bombastic style of Dr. Peter Ruckman. Oh, to be assured, Ruckman's style is indefensibly caustic. Yet White is forced to be both **deaf and dumb** to **the very same style** when exercised by one of his Bible-rejecting friends, Bob Ross. In an endnote to chapter 5 of his book he states, "We note especially the fine ongoing work of men such as Bob Ross, Doug Kutilek and Gary Hudson."[313] (!)

White uses many charts and "facts and figures" in an attempt the belittle the Authorized Version and uphold modern translations in his book. Then, seemingly overcome by a momentary wave of honesty, he admits, "...for one can always make the data appear to support your perspective by manipulating the *way* it is presented."[314] (Emphasis his)

Basically, James White appears to be desperate for any Bible corrector with "Dr." in front of his name to notice him. He is willing to be their spokesman if they will just recognize him as one of them. Shucks, Jim, that's not hard. They'd replace **you** with **me** tomorrow if

---

312 White quite literally "wears out" the term, "expansion of piety" in his book in an attempt to convince his readers that ancient Bible believers made a regular practice of wilfully altering a **text that they held sacred** while he further tries to portray all Bible correctors as idyllically innocent seekers of truth who mean no harm **no matter how corrupt** their work turns out. (For **a few** examples of the former see pages 43 - 46 and 159. For the latter see his anemic defense of his friends on pages 155, 208, and 216, 217 in his *The King James Only Controversy*. Both occur time after time throughout his work.

313 White, James R., *The King James Only Controversy*, (Bethany House Publishers, Minneapolis, 1995), p. 121.

314 Ibid., pp. 195, 196.

I decided to recant my faith in God's Word and further enforce their arguments against the Bible and its supporters. I just don't plan on selling out the truth for a pat on the head by **anyone,** especially men who do the devil's work for him.

Bob Ross

I wasn't going to include Bob Ross in this section but White's praise encouraged me to do so. Since James White welcomes a man of Ross' "quality" into his ranks, I thought it only fair to reveal some facts about a man who makes Peter Ruckman seem to be the picture of civility.

Bob Ross lives in Pasadena, Texas, and has made his money printing the worthy works of Charles Haddon Spurgeon through his company Pilgrim Publications. In fact, Ross even sells statuettes of Spurgeon (500 units @ $89.95 a piece. You do the math.) and is on record as saying. "All hail the power of Spurgeon's name. Let angels prostrate fall."[315] Charles Spurgeon was one of the great preachers of the Nineteenth Century, but I believe he would have not reacted positively to Ross' comment.

Both Ruckman and Ross vilify anyone who opposes them. The difference is that at least Ruckman has something of historical **facts** backing up his position. Ross seems only motivated by a bitter hatred for all he opposes. Ross sends literal volumes of harassing letters, comics, and altered photocopies to anyone on his hit list [316](read that, "Bible believer") in many cases possibly broaching copyright laws. Ross calls Ruckman "Possel" and refers to "Posselcola" (Pensacola) and anyone who believes the King James Bible as a "posselite." He rails on Jack Hyles, Wally Beebe, Gail Riplinger, Curtis Hutson,

---

315 See Ross' recorded comments in the video, <u>A Predestinated Failure</u>, available through the Bible Baptist Bookstore, P.O. Box 1735, Pensacola, FL, 32534. Or call 850-477-8812.

316 I have a two-inch-thick folder of **just the stuff I kept** in case it would needed for any legal matters in the future. There isn't a rational argument in any of it.

Shelton Smith, Jack Chick me and anyone else he can level his shotgun of venom at. While adversaries of Ruckman may be delighted by such antics, it can hardly be described as "Christian" and is worthy of the well-worn "mean-spirited" label used so often by Bible correctors to paint Bible believers. Ross approaches his victims with the same gleam in his eye as a Roman Catholic inquisitor with a handful of matches and five gallons of gasoline. He's already decided he's going to burn you at the stake. Now all he needs is to twist your words enough to justify it.

Ross has even been forced to **fabricate** a charge against Bible believers. For some reason, known only to his own disturbed way of thinking, he decided that anyone who believed the King James Bible somehow **didn't** believe in the eternal Sonship of Jesus Christ. He even felt compelled to make more money by writing on book on the subject. I know of **no one**, in or out of the King James camp, who has publicly denied the eternal Sonship of Jesus Christ. Yet you need only read his rantings to know that Ross is the "foolish man" of Proverbs 29:9. There is no winning an argument with him for there is nothing **rational** in his thought patterns to cause him to understand his error. He simply rants and raves, and when corrected, twists the response and rants and raves some more. He will answer your correspondence by twisting your words to say something that they didn't say and then pop up with an unrelated statement like, "What I want to know is why are your wasting time reading this letter? You should be out winning souls!"[317] And with such a charge he smugly seems to conclude, "Well I won **that** argument!"

The answer to Ross' problem is found in Proverbs 19:29. But our society no longer handles fools this way so we are forced to endure the verbal pyrotechnics of man who thinks that hitting you in the fist with his face is somehow a great tactical victory on his part. Anyone **with an objective mind** would admit that Ross' rantings hint of mental instability. And **this** is the man that James White refers to as doing a

---

317 Personal correspondence from the madman himself. Dated January 25, 1996.

"fine ongoing work"! It is such a double standard that does such damage to the argument of the Bible correctors.

Don Wilkins

Dr. Don Wilkins was the representative from the New American Standard Version committee. He was not a translator of that version but is on the committee attempting to resurrect this obscure version and resell it to an overly advertisement-oriented public. Wilkins was there in lieu of the head of the NASV's translation committee, Dr. Frank Logsdon. There were two insurmountable reasons why Dr. Logsdon could not attend the debate. The first is that he had already passed on and therefore was predisposed. But the second is that he wouldn't have come to defend the NASV **if he had been alive** for he had repudiated all connection with the wayward translation years earlier! Before his death Dr. Logsdon made a public repudiation of his involvement with the inferior NASV when he stated,

> "I must under God renounce every attachment to the *New American Standard Version*. I'm afraid I'm in trouble with the Lord...
>
> The deletions are absolutely frightening...there are so many... Are we so naive that we do not suspect Satanic deception in all of this?
>
> Upon investigation, I wrote my dear friend, Mr. Lockman, explaining that I was forced to renounce all attachment with the NASV. The product is grievous to my heart and helps to complicate matters in these already troublous times...I don't want anything to do with it.
>
> I believe the Spirit of God led the translators of the *Authorized Version*."[318]

His defection has caused irreparable damage to the modern version cause. It is a major embarrassment to have one of your best

---

318 Riplinger, GA, *New Age Bible Versions*, (AV Publications, Munroe Falls, 1993), opening pages.

leave the ranks and join Bible believers in their criticism of a modern translation. **All** modern translators would do well to join the late Dr. Logsdon in repudiating **all** modern versions and taking up the worthy cause of God's perfect Bible, the King James Authorized Version!

Dr. Wilkins seemed a cordial enough person. His problems arose more from interference by **God** than from any of his critics in the debate. At one point, when the host (John Ancherberg) asked the question, "Did men die, go insane or lose their voices while working on the New American Standard Version?", Dr. Wilkins **began** to respond but suddenly had his voice trail off. Near panic he croaked, "I've lost my voice!" Taping was stopped, Wilkins drank some water, regained his composure and had the question asked again with the cameras rolling. This time he answers, half in jest, half in contempt, "No, John. As you can see. **I** haven't lost **my** voice." A chorus of chuckles can be heard in the background as the entire panel stifled their laughter at the arrogant response.

Later, while we were sitting there, a large lens assembly fell off a camera located just behind Wilkins and crashed to the floor, sending him on what looked like a "Rapture Drill." I have often wondered why the Lord had such an interest in Dr. Wilkins' testimony against His Book that day and if Wilkins ever got the message.

Arthur Farstad

Dr. Farstad was the head of the New King James Version committee. Unlike the others on his side of the dais, Dr. Farstad takes a stand much closer to the King James Bible in that he rejects the supposed supremacy of the modern Nestle's *Novum Testamentum-Graece* and supports the Majority Text of the King James Bible. This caused some anxious moments for "his" side when he abandoned attacks of the King James Bible advocates present and turned to criticize the handling of the last twelve verses of Mark by the NASV and the NIV.

My personal observation and determination concerning Dr. Farstad is that he is a humble man who truly loves the Lord Jesus Christ. I believe that he truly thought he was "helping" Bible believers when he headed the New King James translation. He simply lacked understanding of the militant jealousy that Bible believers have for their Bible. Following the debate he came over to me and stated in apologetic embarrassment, "I'm sorry I couldn't help you more. But...ah..." the understood remainder of the sentence being, "But I have to work with these men." Then he turned and walked away.

Farstad displays evidence of having much more love and reverence for the Scripture than his contemporaries. In his writings he is much more jealous for God concerning inerrancy. In his book *The New King James Version in the Great Tradition*, although he promotes the version whose translation he was chiefly responsible for, he does not exhibit the animosity or vehemence that a James White, Jack Lewis or most Bible correctors display. He gives well thought out arguments **in favor** of Mark 16:9-20 and John 7:53-8:11. He is a great defender of the Greek text of the King James Bible, though not a proponent of the Book itself which is sad. It is unfortunate that he was associated with the New King James Version, which is **by no means** equal to, let alone **better** than, the King James Bible.

Dr. Farstad's greatest testimony of the value of the New King James Version came during our round table discussion on the John Ancherberg Show when he admitted that he didn't even think it was worth using for his personal devotions. During this broadcast, the Editor-in-Chief of the New King James Version admitted that he preferred to use **the Latin** in his daily devotions rather than the very translation that he had helped to create! Are **you** going to use a "bible" that its chief editor rejects?

Kenneth Barker

Dr. Kenneth Barker was the head of the New International Version committee. Dr. Barker was probably the most belligerent of the opponents of God's Word that day. His attitude was mean and aggressive. Fine, as long as the facts back him up, which they didn't. In fact, Dr. Barker's "saviour" that day wasn't Jesus Christ. It was John Ancherberg. Ancherberg had envisioned the King James Bible supporters "going down in flames" on nationwide television. He produced eight programs in hopes of putting the King James issue to rest once and for all, while hawking his own NIV study bible during the commercial breaks. It didn't take long for Ancherberg to see that his "glory boys" were failing miserably **so miserably** that he himself had to interject comments and steer conversations away from the embarrassingly indefensible position of his Bible rejecting "Dream Team."

At one point I "nailed" Barker with the inexcusable and unprofessional practice of **incorrectly** translating the Greek word "Hebros" (Hebrew) as "Aramaic" in **every reference** that dealt with it as a language. There is **no authority** for this travesty of translation which serves only to undergird the Roman Catholic claim that Jesus spoke Aramaic rather than Greek or Hebrew and thus renders His statement in Matthew 16:18 an affirmation of the Roman Catholic claim that Jesus founded His church on **Peter** rather than Himself. In Greek the word for "Peter" and the word for "rock" are **two different words**. But in Aramaic they are the same. Roman Catholicism is desperate to prove that Aramaic was the language of Jesus Christ. Dr. Barker and his cohorts served their Roman Catholic masters well in inventing a meaning for "Hebros" which simply does not exist. When I confronted Barker with this inexcusable rendering he was speechless. Before the embarrassment of this infidelity to the Greek text that they hold so dear could sink into the minds of viewers, John Ancherberg interrupted and steered ths conversation away from the subject. But Barker's greatest gaff was yet to come!

Bible believers make a great deal of the biblical statement on the **inspiration** of Scripture found in Psalm 12:6., ""The words of the LORD are pure words: as silver tried in a furnace of earth, purified seven times."

They also are quick to point out the **Divine promise** of **preservation** found in verse 7, "Thou shalt keep them, O LORD, thou shalt preserve them from this generation forever."

The reader can only imagine the untold damage this promise does to those who try to convince Christianity that "There's no **perfect** Bible anywhere." You can also imagine the great obstacle this verse must have presented to Barker & co. as they endeavored to circumvent this promise and usurp the King James Bible. It should be noted at this point that the Hebrew of Psalm 12:7 is in the **third person plural**, i.e. "they, them." There is **no manuscript in existence** that reads in the **first person plural**, "us, we." Yet, with **the facts of the original Hebrew staring them in the face**, "Barker's Boobs" produced the **fictitious** rendering of, "O LORD, you will keep **us** safe and protect **us** from such people forever."

Once again I confronted Barker with this glaring example of translational incompetence accomplished by his team of "competent scholars." This time he reacted before Ancherberg could ride to his rescue. With a look of hatred beaming from his learned face he stated, "I believe verse seven is referring to 'the poor' of verse five, **not** 'the words' of verse six." Then he leaned forward and in unrepentant defiance said, "I'd **never** translate it **that** [like the King James] way!"

Now please understand. Dr. Barker is free to interpret Psalm 12:7 any way he pleases. But he is **not** free to invent a phony translation to back up his prejudice. There isn't even **one manuscript** that supports or even pretends to support Barker's lame claim. These men are **supposed** to be professional enough to lay their personal prejudice aside (their personal prejudice against the King James Bible) and do work objectively. Obviously Barker and his crew of "semi-learned men" lack whatever it takes to do that.

I am reminded by this unprofessional action of the vehemence with which preachers castigate Dr. Peter Ruckman for saying, "You can correct the Greek with the English." What Dr. Ruckman is claiming is not that you can correct **the original** with the English, but the **Greek texts that we possess** with the English. And there is not **an honest** proponent of **any Greek text** (Nestle, United Bible Society, **or** the Textus Receptus) that would accept a word-for-word translation of their favored text into English as "perfect." Therefore, the King James English, which doesn't even slavishly follow the Textus Receptus, represents what the **original** would read like if we had it here today. Therefore, it can shed light on the minute or major errors of the extant texts that we possess.

Yet here is the renowned Dr. Barker, who with no Hebrew authority whatsoever to support his **personal beliefs,** apparently believes that **he** can **correct the Hebrew** with **his** English. So please, where is the outcry of indignation so frequently leveled at Ruckman? To assault Ruckman and **not** Barker is kin to the shameless prejudice shown by the environmentalists when they bemoan an (American) *Exxon Valdez* oil spill and yet are strangely (and hypocritically) silent when a non-American (Saddam Hussein) **deliberately** pours millions more gallons of raw crude into the Persian Gulf. Could it be that critics harbor their own share of prejudice?

Jack Lewis

As a rule I have chosen not to call people by name in my books and then call them names. Yet at this point **I am forced** to say that Jack Lewis is both a **deceiver** and a **liar**. I will clearly prove my point. In 1981 Baker Book House published a book by Lewis entitled *The English Bible From KJV to NIV A History and Evaluation*. Such a title would immediately lead the reader to believe that this author has a multitude of Bible versions (11 to be exact) and then gives the reader his **objective** conclusion of which are good and which are bad. **That** is where Lewis is a deceiver. You need go **no farther than the table of contents** to see this. His chapter "evaluating" the New English Bible is imply titled, "The New English Bible." The chapter concerning the NIV is similarly entitled, "The New International Version." Thus he **objectively** addresses the various translations in his book. So **what** do you suppose the chapter "evaluating" the King James Bible is called?

Well, if you thought it would be "The King James Version," **you were deceived**! It's called "Doctrinal Problems in the King James Version." Thus, **before you even get past the table of contents** you can see that Lewis is **prejudiced** against the King James Bible. In fact, Lewis doesn't even ascribe "doctrinal problems" to the chapter evaluating the Jehovah's Witness' version! It is simply called "The New World Translation of the Holy Scriptures." He has more grace with heretics than with Bible believers!

What **are** the "doctrinal problems" Lewis "stumbled upon" while "objectively evaluating" the King James Bible? He gives none. Yet he blows smoke about his dislike for the King James Bible and then defends his choice of the title for this chapter by saying, "'Doctrine' means 'teaching,' and any failure to present the Word of God accurately, completely, and clearly in a translation is a doctrinal problem."(!)[319] I could **believe** that Lewis used such a loose and flimsy definition of "doctrinal problems" **if** he had entitled the other chapters **"The Doctrinal Problems in** The New International Version," "**The Doctrinal Problems in** The New American Standard Version" and so on for only a **deceiver** would attempt to **pretend** that the King James Bible has doctrinal problems and then further **pretend** to be blind to the **clear "doctrinal problems"** of the other modern versions. But Lewis doesn't do this because Jack Lewis is a **deceiver**.

But is he a "liar"? Yes. On page 55 of his book he has a paragraph full of words in the King James Bible that he claims have "passed completely out of use." These are the infamous "archaic" words we hear so much about. In this list Lewis **deceivingly** includes, "talitha cumi." This is not **archaic**! It's **Aramaic**! It is nothing more than a transliteration of the Aramaic words used in the passage. Once again, Lewis attempts deception. But his crowning work is found in the same list, where he states that "sanctum sanctorum" are "words in the KJV which have passed completely out of use,." "Sanctum sanctorum"

---

319 Lewis, Jack P., *The English Bible From KJV to NIV, A History and Evaluation,* (Baker Book House, Grand Rapids, 1981), p.61.

appears nowhere in the King James Bible! Lewis is a liar. And yet men like James White will refer to him as an authority to justify the elimination of the King James Bible.

Personally I am not offended by Lewis' attempts at deception and his outright lie. I welcome them. I am always pleased to see my adversary[320] forced to actions that are plainly dishonest and insincere. For if they **really believed they were right,** they would never do so. Thank you, Jack! Thank you, James!

Kurt Aland

Kurt Aland is probably the leading authority on Bible manuscripts alive today. He resides in his native Germany, where he is the head of the Institute for New Testament Textual Research in Münster, Westphalia. For years he was the co-editor of the *Nestles Novum Testamentum-Graece* until the death of Erwin Nestle, Eberhard's son, in 1972, when he became the controlling force for the text. He also works with the United Bible Society on the board of editors for it's *Greek New Testament*.

Aland's writing is clear and forceful. He shoulders his way into any situation and presents himself as a force to be reckoned with. It is no mere coincidence that he managed to get himself onto the editing board of **both** of the leading critical Greek texts used today. I personally enjoy the glimpses I have caught of his personality when reading his works. His work is informative yet overweight in scholarly claptrap. Unfortunately, he comes down on the wrong side of the fence on the issue of which Greek text is the right one. He is joined-at-the-

---

320 I don't consider Bible correctors to be my personal "enemies" (Ross tries to make himself that though) since they seek to destroy **the Bible** rather than **me** personally. I consider them my "adversaries" because I have chosen to confront and withstand their attacks on God's perfect Bible and refute their arguments while presenting a few of my own. I am not sure they feel the same way. I was once smacked in the face by a Bible correctors after **he chose to start an argument** and then lost it. For all the derogatory things Bible correctors say about us Bible believers I do not know of this type of thing happening in reverse. So **who** is **really** "mean-spirited" and "hateful"?

brain with Dan Wallace and company in their almost vicious prejudice against the Textus Receptus. Aland cannot mention that text without always taking a shot at it. Add this to the fact that there is no public record of his having taken Christ as Saviour and it muddies his finding to the point of being unreliable as an authority in textual matters. A brief review of his book *The Text of The New Testament* reveals the blindness that hangs over him like a veil. A veil that will not be removed until he trusts Christ and turns away from the corrupting philosophy of Alexandria.

What is the saddest thing about Aland is that his work reveals that he has **the facts** right in front of him yet cannot interpret them correctly due to his incorrect philosophical position and the threat to his somewhat robust ego.

Aland freely admits that the scribes in Alexandria **altered manuscripts** yet doesn't seem the least upset about it. He states:

> "It was assumed that in the early period there were several recensions of the text...or that at the beginning of the fourth century scholars at Alexandria and elsewhere took as many good manuscripts as were available and applied their philosophical methods to compile a new uniform text (this was the view of our fathers, and is still that of many textual critics today as well)."[321]

Aland even admits that Alexandrian scholars treated the text of the New Testament so loosely that they produced a distinctly "freer" text than that which they started with.

> "Quite possibly Bishop Demetrius had manuscripts prepared for his newly recognized diocese (now under the direction of his newly appointed chorepiscopoi) and its church

---

321 Aland, Kurt, *The Text of The New Testament*, (William B Eerdmans, Grand Rapids, 1989), p. 50.

in a scriptorium related to the Cathchetical School (which probably existed despite the lack of any documentary evidence). Designating particular manuscripts (which probably were imported from other provinces of the broader church) to be master exemplars[322] would have created a special 'Alexandrian' text. But this hypothesis, however intrinsically possible, does not square with the evidence of the manuscripts up to the third/fourth century. Thus p45, p46, p66, and a whole group of other manuscripts offer a 'free' text, i.e. **a text dealing with the original text in a relatively free manner** with no suggestion of a program of standardization (or were these manuscripts also imported from elsewhere?)."[323] (Emphasis mine)

It is first to be noted that Aland has great faith in a scriptorium which he has no proof ever existed. Next we need to note his admission that the manuscripts coming out of Alexandria are considered to contain a text that is "freer" in style that the originals. In other words, Alexandrian scholars took casual liberties in altering the text of the exemplars they used to produce a unique (call it "Local") text.

Aland further admits to this when he states, "The more loosely organized a diosece, or the greater the differences between its constituent churches, the more likely different text types would coexist **(as in early Egypt)**."[324]

How can Dr. Aland admit such slack handling of the Word of God and yet uphold Alexandria as **the source** for the correct New

---

322 Concerning the "elemplars" Aland refers to an "exemplar" is any manuscript from which a copy is made. It is considered the "parent" and the copy is its "child" or "offspring." Textual criticism basically seeks to follow the trail of copies back to their exemplars in a vain hope of discovering the original text.

323 Aland, Kurt, *The Text of The New Testament*, (William B Eerdmans, Grand Rapids, 1989), p. 59.

324 Ibid., pp. 55, 56.

Testament text? No one can be this **ignorantly** blind. It can only be willful.

But Aland isn't finished arguing our case for us. He further admits that Christianity was concentrated in the East (Antioch), not the West (Alexandria).

> "The overall impression is that the concentration of Christianity was in the East. Churches become fewer in number as we go westward. Large areas of the West were still untouched by Christianity. Even around A.D. 325 the scene was still largely unchanged. Asia Minor continued to be the heartland of the church."[325]

There are two things that are amazing about this admission. First, **the Church** (the body of born-again believers, **not** the Roman Catholic organization) is the **custodian of Scripture**, not scholarship. The dearth of churches in the West disqualifies it from being a feasible location for God to use to preserve His Bible.

Secondly, Aland admits this scarcity of churches right up into the fourth century which is the time of the creation of the famous uncials of Egypt: Aleph, A, B, and C. These manuscripts were the product of professional scholars editing the original text to the tune of their personal philosophies rather than the loving reproductions of the originals which stem from the multitude of churches existing in Antioch at the time. It is estimated that there were as many as 100,000 Christians in Antioch by the end of the first century alone.

While busy highjacking the text of Scripture in 1871 Westcott and Hort all but **begged** their fellow revisors to believe that there had been a recension of Scripture performed in Antioch in the fourth century. They pointed out how the text of Antioch seems to literally explode into existence around this time with very few witnesses from the first three centuries. They claim that this is proof that the Byzantine

---

325 Ibid., p. 53.

text was "created" in Antioch about this time. This leaves Bible believers with the embarrassing position of defending a text which consists of a multitude of late witnesses while being sparse in the early centuries. How can we explain this? **We don't have to!** The reason for this is expertly presented by none other than Dr. Aland.

> "Asia Minor and Greece, the centers of early Christianity, undoubtedly exercised a substantive if not critical influence on the development of the New Testament text, but it is impossible to demonstrate because the climate in these regions has been unfavorable to the preservation of any papyri from the early period."[326]

These are the desperate pleas of a frantic Bible-believer trying to defend his favored text. These are the authoritative declarations of our oppositions great voice! But Dr. Aland is not finished providing us with his expert assistance.

Aland clearly explains that this lack of early witnesses is due to the **destruction** of the Byzantine text's early witnesses during the Diocletianic persecution of the churches of Asia Minor.

> "But the period of persecution which lasted almost ten years in the West and **much longer** in the East was characterized by the systematic destruction of church buildings (and church centers), and **any manuscripts that were found in them were publicly burned**. Church officials were further required to surrender for public burning all holy books in their possession or custody. Although clergy who submitted to the demands of the state were branded as traitors and defectors from the faith, their number was by no means small. The result was

---

326 Ibid., p. 67.

a widespread scarcity of New Testament manuscripts which became all the more acute when the persecution ceased."[327]

Aland unwittingly explains why there is such an absence of early witnesses for the Byzantine (Textus Receptus) text prior to the fourth century. And what of the explosion of witnesses beginning with that same period? Dr. Aland continues:

"For when Christianity could again engage freely in missionary activity there was a tremendous growth in both the size of the existing churches and the number of new churches. There also followed a sudden demand for large numbers of New Testament manuscripts in all provinces of the empire."[328]

Following the end of the Diocletianic persecutions, the churches in Antioch and the surrounding areas immediately began generate copies of their remaining manuscripts to fill the void. Thus we find large numbers of manuscripts appearing around this time. It wasn't the result of an orchestrated recension. It was the normal recovery process of an unstoppable church.

But in this single report, Aland's blind prejudice prevents him from seeing what is right in front of his face! The question screams to be asked, "If the churches in Asia Minor were curtailed and destroyed by Emperor Diocletian's Bill Clinton-like tactics, why wasn't the veritably unmolested text of Egypt hungrily embraced and copied by the remaining churches?" The question is all too clear from the actions of our historic fathers. They didn't adopt the text on Alexandria, Egypt, in place of that of Antioch because they recognized that it had been corrupted by Egyptian philosophy. While **education** accepted the Alexandria text (and still does!), the Church the **custodian of Scripture,** rejected it and always has! If they had thought the

327 Ibid., p. 65.

328 Ibid., p. 65.

Alexandrian text to be a reproduction of the **original text,** they would have scooped it up, reproduced it fanatically, and today it would predominate the number of extant manuscripts instead of numbering in the mere handfuls. But the church rejected the corrupt text of Alexandria and when she saw the opportunity to reproduce and promote the text, she jumped at the fortuitous event and reproduced the **correct text** in huge volumes. In doing so she proved the wisdom of God in assigning the text **to her** for safe keeping rather than to the whim of a bunch of Egyptian scholars whether in the **fourth** century or the **twentieth**.

Aland's blindness prevents him either from **seeing** this or from **admitting** it. But that should not came as a surprise to anyone who took note of the **great omission** in his book. For in over three hundred and thirty pages, Aland **never once** refers to "Divine inspiration," "Divine preservation" or even "**God**"! He, like White, Wallace and the rest of the **educational establishment,** does not view the Bible as Divinely inspired or preserved. They do not see or even look for God's handiwork in its transmission across the ocean of time. Again, this is the great gulf between us and them. They are carnally minded professionals who cannot countenance the supernatural in the preservation of a Book that is received as supernatural by most of its users. They, like Westcott & Hort, treat the Bible as any other literary work albeit one with a large field of ancient witnesses and an even larger following. What more could we expect of men who think such things as:

> "1 Peter and 2 Peter, for example, were clearly written by two different authors for completely different occasions and were brought together only by a much later church tradition."[329]

I can understand the lack of faith that White, Wallace, Lewis, Aland and their cohorts suffer from. They do not view the Bible as we

---

329 Ibid., p. 49.

---

do. They do not guard it jealously as we do. Why? It is simple. We are the Church. We are an extension of the group the God established two thousand years ago to protect and preserve His Book. **They** are the people we are protecting it from!

While Aland's manner isn't as boring as a Wallace's "cracker-dust" personally or as slobberingly "Me too!-ish" as James White's he still does not qualify as being someone we should turn to when looking for a Book that we believe **God** wrote and that **God** promised to preserve.

THE KING JAMES APOCRYPHA

Another one of the assaults on the Authorized Version is that the early editions contained the Apocrypha between the Old and New Testaments. In defense, we shall list the seven reasons why the Apocrypha was **NOT** considered inspired by the Authorized Version translators. The reasons for not admitting the Apocryphal books into the Canon, or list, of inspired Scriptures are briefly as follows:

1. Not one of them is in the Hebrew language, which was alone used by the inspired historians and poets of the Old Testament.

2. Not one of the writers lays any claim to inspiration.

3. These books were never acknowledged as sacred Scriptures by the Jewish church and, therefore, never sanctioned by our Lord.

4. They were not allowed among the sacred books, during the first four centuries of the Christian church.

5. They contain fabulous statements, and statements which contradict not only the canonical Scriptures, but themselves; as when, in the two books of Maccabees, Antiochus Epiphanes is made to die three different deaths in as many places.[330]

6. It includes doctrines at variance with the Bible, such as prayers for the dead and sinless perfection.

7. It teaches immoral practices, such as lying, suicide, assassination, and magical incantation.

For these and other reasons the Apocryphal books, which are all in Greek except one (which is extant only in Latin), are valuable only as "ancient documents, illustrative of the manners, language, opinions, and history of the East."[331]

We see then that the King James translators did not accept the books of the Apocrypha as having been inspired by God and would not accord them a place within the text of Scripture. It is also to be noted that this same Apocrypha is found in separate books distributed **within the text** of the Old Testament in Vaticanus, Siniaticus and the other Egyptian manuscripts that modern translators favor.

---

330 In 1 Maccabees 6:1-16, Antiochus Epiphanes (Antiochus IV) is reported to die in bed in Persia due to a broken spirit caused by distressing reports of military failures. He is supposedly surrounded by friends. In 2 Maccabees 1:14-17 he dies a second time. Again he is in Persia, but this time is in the temple of the goddess Nanea for his wedding. Enemies hidden in the ceiling above reportedly hurl stones down on him, crushing him to death and then dismember his body. Then in 2 Maccabees 9:1-29 poor Antiochus IV dies yet one more time. This time he is on the road to Jerusalem to do battle with Israel. Since he is picking on God's chosen people, God curses him with sickness and he falls from his chariot. Then, since even dismemberment hadn't been able to stop him before, God has his skin rot off and worms eat his body. Apparently this time he gets the hint and is not heard from again. It is to be noted that in this last account Antiochus is reported to have repented and become a Jew and written a letter of peace to the Jews while he still had fingers left!

331 Rockwood, Perry F., *God's Inspired Preserved Bible*, (Peoples Gospel Hour, Halifax, 1979), pp. 185,186.

THE GREEK GAME IN ACTION

Still another complaint against God's Authorized Version is the manner in which certain Greek words have been translated. Today's "God-honoring" scholars "love the Lord and His Bible" but are quick to point out and attack any seeming inconsistency in translation in the Authorized Version. Even the most infinitesimal Greek article is attacked under the guise of seeking to give a more "grammatically correct" translation. This is the claim consistently made by translating groups such as the anonymous Lockman Foundation.

This is all very noble sounding. It puts into one's mind a picture of these "hardworking scholars" slaving away to remove all of the "mistakes" from the Authorized Version so that we can finally have the pure "Word of God." This is the farthest thing from the truth. The truth is that the new "bibles" are translated by men who first desire to eliminate the detested Authorized Version and second, though never admitting it, to make money in the "Bible business." Sad as that is to think, it is true.

The problem with their hyper-critical examination of the Authorized Version is that the same scrutiny is never applied to their own work.

There is another, more innocent group that uses this tactic when approaching Scripture. While some "correct" the Bible with the Greek due to an over-enlarged ego, there are some who approach the Bible in this flawed manner because it is the only method they know of to "teach" the Bible. Their "Bible" college taught them very little Bible but instead assured them that the King James Bible was so thoroughly flawed that they could freely offer their own rendering for anything the King James translators had done. I have often said that **"Greek** study is not **Bible** study." You can study "the Greek" without even having a Bible in the same room. So how can you possibly be studying the **Bible**? If this group can forsake its errant teaching and approach the

Bible as truly infallible it will open an entire field of true, rewarding **Bible** study.

THE GREEK GAME IN REVERSE

Dr. Peter S. Ruckman, who is known for being very Burgonian in his comments, is nonetheless an outstanding authority in manuscript readings. In several of his works, he has done no more than to examine the new translations under the same unyielding eye with which the modern translators examine the Authorized Version.

Before examining any of his findings and the evidence of the critical apparatus of Nestle's 23rd edition,[332] it must first be remembered that the present day translations and translators act under the premise that the Nestle's *Novum Testamentum-Graece* is the closest Greek text to the original. Nestle's text is basically Westcott and Hort's text, which is in turn primarily Vaticanus and Sinaiticus, as Dr. Wilkenson has recorded.

"It was of necessity that Westcott and Hort should take this position. Their own Greek New Testament upon which they had been working for twenty years was founded on Codex B and Codex (Aleph), as the following quotations show:

"If Westcott and Hort have failed, it is an overestimate of the Vatican Codex, to which (like Lachman and Tregelles) they assign the supremacy, while Tischendorf may have given too much weight to the Sinaitic Codex."[333]

---

332 The New American Standard Version is Nestle's 23rd edition translated into English. That Greek text has presently reached its 27th edition. Although there have been numerous text changes, the **manuscript evidence** for the readings mentioned has not changed.

333 Wilkenson, Benjamin, Our Authorized Bible Vindicated, (Takoma Park, 1930), p. 172.

All modern translators give B and Aleph unbalanced superiority, assuming them to be more accurate because they assume that they are older. They willfully overlook the fact that the Universal Text has manuscripts just as old, plus the backing of the church fathers. They also seem not to realize that Egypt is **not** the location for the pure text-old manuscripts maybe, but not pure readings.

Modern translators build their arguments for changing the Authorized Version readings around two very loose rules:

1. The oldest reading is best.

2. The majority reading is best.

This sounds very good except for one small problem. What happens when the oldest reading conflicts with the majority? The answer is, "Do what you want as long as you **do not** agree with the Authorized Version." This is not an overstatement, but it describes the animosity which modern scholarship has for the text of the Authorized Version.

Following will be examples of translations in which modern translators break all their own rules of translating in order to eliminate the readings of the Universal Text of the King James Bible. The readings to be examined are those which have been pointed out by Dr. Ruckman. We shall compare his references to the footnotes in the critical apparatus of Nestle's 23rd Edition of his *Novum Testamentum-Graece*, unless he states such evidence already. The English translation to be examined will be the New American Standard Version, since it is the one which is assumed by most fundamentalists to be sound.

First, the verse to be discussed will be quoted from the Authorized Version, then it will be quoted from the New American Standard Version. The word, words, or passage in question will be italicized.

Mark 1:2

AV: "As it is written in the prophets, Behold I send my messenger before thy face, which shall prepare thy way before thee."

NASV: "As it is written in *Isaiah the prophet*, Behold, I will send my messenger before your face, who will prepare your way."

Here the New American Standard Version sticks with the premise of using what its translators feel is the "oldest" reading. The phrase "Isaiah the prophet" appears in the Hesychian (Local Text) family represented primarily by B, C, and Aleph.

The problem arises when you do more than **read** the remainder of verse two and then verse three. The Old Testament quotation in verse 2 is **not** from Isaiah! It is quoted from **Malachi 3:1**. Verse 3 is from Isaiah (Isaiah 40:3). Malachi plus Isaiah does not equal "Isaiah the prophet"; it equals "the prophets."

The correct reading, "the prophets," which is found in the King James Bible, is found in W along with the Textus Receptus (Universal Text), which is represented by E, F, G, and H in the gospels. It is also found in the majority of witnesses. Also it was cited in 202 A.D., 150 years before Vaticanus or Sinaiticus.

Immediately we run into the problem of the "oldest" versus the "majority." It happens though that neither of these two groups is to be judged just because of what they represent. The deciding factor is; "Which group reads with the Universal Text?" That group is the correct group and it is the King James that does that.

In sticking with the Local Text of Egypt, the Lockman Foundation has managed to print a Bible with a **mistake** in it! It is obvious that the reading "Isaiah the prophet" is wrong, because Isaiah never said what is quoted in verse two. (Check other modern translations here and see how they have approached the passage.)

Why would anyone try to hide the quotation of Malachi? Dr. Ruckman explains, "You see, the quotation from Malachi was a reference to Jehovah God the Father! If anyone were to find this reference, they would see that 'thy' and 'thee' of Mark 1:1,2 is the 'me' of Malachi 3:1!"[334] Thus, the deity of Christ is **hidden** in the New American Standard Version even though it claims to "confirm" the Lordship of Jesus Christ. Unfortunately for the egos of the nameless Lockman Foundation, the Lordship of Jesus Christ was "confirmed" in the wilderness in Matthew chapter four, and God did not have to wait over 1900 years for them to "confirm" it for Him!

Luke 24:51

AV: "And it came to pass while he blessed them, he was parted from them *and carried up to heaven.*"

NASV: "And it came about that while He was blessing them, He parted from them."

Here we see a portion of Scripture where both the "oldest" and "majority" texts read in favor of the Authorized Version. The inconsistent Lockman Foundation has omitted the phrase "and carried up into heaven" (kai ephereto eis ton houranan) which is in; P75, a papyrus manuscript of the second century, as well as manuscripts; B, C, E, F, G, H, L, S, T, V, Y, Z, Delta, Theta, Psi, Omega, most other witnesses, and every Latin copy.

---

334 Ruckman, Peter, Satan's Masterpiece!, (Pensacola Bible Press, Pensacola, 1974), p. 38.

—

On what "weighty" evidence does the Lockman Foundation remove the bodily ascension of Jesus Christ? On the weight of **one** copy of Aleph and **one** copy of D, plus cursive manuscript number 52 and a 5th century palimpsest.

As stated before the only rule which is consistently kept by supposed "godly Christian scholars" is the practice of attacking the Authorized Version reading because it upholds the deity of Christ. Manuscript evidence is really not the issue.

It might be advisable for us to look at Acts 1:1,2.

The former treatise have I made, O Theophilus, of all that Jesus began both to do and teach.

Until the day in which he was taken up, after that he through the Holy Ghost had given commandments unto the apostles whom he had chosen.

You will notice that Luke claims that his "former treatise" (the gospel of Luke) ended with a record of Jesus being "taken up." But in the New American Standard Version's translation of Luke's gospel, Jesus Christ does **not** ascend, but He is left standing flat-footed on the Mount of Olives. Thus, we see that if the gospelist Luke could examine both a King James Bible and a New American Standard Version, he would quickly expose the New American Standard Version as a fraudulent adulteration of his "former treatise."

In other words, "If the King James Bible is good enough for the disciple Luke, then it's good enough for me!"

Luke 24:52

AV: *"And they worshipped him,* and returned to Jerusalem with great joy."

NASV: "And they returned to Jerusalem with great joy."

In the case of "And they worshipped him" (proskunesantes auton), the New American Standard Version translators actually lose a witness from their roster, for in Luke 24:52 the manuscript evidence is identical to that of Luke 24:51, except that this time even Aleph joins the innumerable mass of witnesses in favor of the King James translators' scholarship. This leaves D to stand alone against several thousands of manuscripts which uphold the deity of Christ.

With evidence like this, it seems somewhat hypocritical to hear "good, godly men" deride Erasmus for using only five manuscripts which represented the oldest and the majority, to collate his text, a text which upholds our Saviour. Here we see that the Lockman Foundation's corrupters use a **minority of the minority** to attack two major doctrines of the Bible, the bodily ascension and the deity of Christ.

The argument may be forwarded that "I can still find these doctrines in the New American Standard Version." Yes you can, but not in as many places as in the Authorized Version. There is **no** Bible which upholds Christ's deity as clearly as the Authorized King James Version.

2 Timothy 2:15

AV: "Study to shew thyself approved unto God, a workman that needeth not to be ashamed, *rightly dividing* the word of truth."

NASV: "Be diligent to present yourself approved to God as a workman who need not to be ashamed, handling accurately the word of truth."

The critics of the Authorized Version often complain that the scholars of the translation of 1611 have translated a Greek word with an English word which supposedly does not correspond with the correct meaning. This makes the modern translators seem very sincere in that they present themselves as if they would never do such a thing. Here in 2 Timothy 2:15 we find them guilty of that very thing for which they assail the King James translators.

The Greek word the King James translators translate "rightly dividing" (orthotomeo) means just that. The Analytical Greek Lexicon (Zondervan 1970) has it as "to cut straight." There is no Greek evidence for the two words "handling accurately." The Greek word for "handle" (pselapho) is found in 1 John 1:1. The Greek word for "accurate" (doloo) does not appear in the Bible. These two words together in no way resemble the Greek word used in 2 Timothy 2:15 and correctly translated "rightly dividing" by the King James translators. As Dr. Ruckman points out, "The Greek word for 'rightly dividing' is found in all four families of manuscripts, all cursives and uncials, of any century."[335] It might be good to note here that Nestle's Greek text does not even allow for an alternate reading!

The question which naturally comes to mind is "Why would anyone want 2 Timothy 2:15 to read 'handling accurately?'" The answer is found in the preface to the New American Standard Version in which the NASV is called a translation of "linguistic accuracy."[336] In other words the Lockman Foundation says, "Be diligent to present yourself approved to God as a workman who does not need to be ashamed, handling accurately the word of truth." The Lockman Foundation then says that **it** has handled God's Word accurately! To pat oneself on the back so often and so obviously must make for tired arms.

Next let's look at a word change which is designed to keep the Roman Catholic Church "in business."

---

335 Ibid., p. 55.

336 Lockman Foundation, New American Standard New Testament Preface, (Gospel Light Publications, Glendale, 1971), p. I.

James 5:16

AV: "Confess your *faults* one to another, and pray one for another, that ye may be healed. The effectual fervent prayer of a righteous man availeth much."

NASV: "Therefore, confess your sins to one another, and pray for one another, so that you may be healed. The effective prayer of a righteous man can accomplish much."

Confession of sins to a Catholic priest has been a teaching of the Roman Catholic Church for centuries. Here the NASV upholds the practice by devising a translation that will make it look scriptural.

The Greek word translated "faults" in the King James Bible (paraptomata) is found in manuscripts E, F, G, H, S, V, Y, and Omega, plus the rest of the Receptus family and the greater number of all remaining witnesses. Nestle's text inserts "sins" (tax amartias) with **no** manuscript authority. The misguided men of the Lockman Foundation accept it with no evidence, no resistance and no questions. Perhaps there are more Jesuits lurking in the shadows than we think! Anyone accepting an alternate reading with no evidence **cannot** be credited with acting ethically or scholarly.

One last passage shall suffice:

John 9:35

AV: "Jesus heard that they had cast him out; and when he had found him, he said unto him, Dost thou believe on the Son of *God*?"

NASV: "Jesus heard that they had put him out; and finding him, He said, 'Do you believe in the Son of Man?'"

Here once again the "conservative scholars" of the New American Standard Version and other "bibles" have attempted to water down the deity of Christ.

The word for "God" (theou) is found in manuscripts E, F, G, H, S, V, Y, Omega, Theta, the majority of the remaining minuscules, most of the remaining witnesses, plus the entire Latin tradition.

The Greek word "man" (anthropouo) is upheld by one Twelth Century Greek scholar!

It is strange indeed that the Lockman Foundation is quick to strip Jesus Christ's Godship away from Him. Here, the "conservative" scholars of the secret Lockman Foundation are in complete agreement with the "liberal" scholars of the Revised Standard Version. These are strange bedfellows! I am certainly glad that the translators of the Christ-exalting Authorized Version never "slept" in this bed.

This is, of course, **not** a "God-honoring" translation. I know that the deity of Christ "can be found" in other places in the New American Standard Version, but it now "can be found" in one less place than in the Authorized Version.

Would John, in penning the gospel that is intended to exalt Jesus Christ as God, use the term "Son of Man"? Dr. Ruckman explains:

> "One of the great critical dictums for correcting the A.V. 1611 Greek manuscripts is that 'one should always choose language and expressions most characteristic of the author.' Well, what in the world would possess a man who was acquainted with John's style (in the Gospels), to suddenly write 'Son of Man' where Jesus is dealing with a sinner on matters of doctrinal belief? Is this characteristic of John? It isn't in any 20 passages, anywhere, in the Gospel of John! 'The Son of God' is the correct reading, and the ASV, RSV, and all the new

'Bibles' are greatly in error, 'not knowing the Scriptures, nor the power of God.'"[337]

The Apostle John **never** called Jesus Christ the "Son of Man" anywhere in his gospel when dealing with a doctrinal belief. Furthermore, the context of the book defines the correct translation in that the multitude cried for Jesus Christ's crucifixion in John 19:7 because "he made himself the Son of God." (Greek: huion theos heauton epoinsen). This statement so struck the already frantic Pilate that "he was more afraid" (John 19:8), at which time he hurried back to where Jesus Christ was waiting and asked, "Whence art thou?" Pilate realized that there was something supernatural about Jesus Christ. It is too bad the elusive Lockman Foundation has never come to such a realization.

We have looked at only a few passages where modern translators have made unwarranted changes in God's Word. The result is a change in doctrine. It is evident, then, that no matter what Bible salesmen may say about being able to "find" the fundamentals in any of the new translations, they are still weaker on doctrine than the God-honoring Authorized Version. I repeat, **every** new "bible" is doctrinally weaker than the King James Authorized Version. Why then should any school or preacher use a "bible" in which he must "search" to prove doctrines which are more clearly evident in the King James Bible? If we honor Jesus Christ, then we should just naturally choose and use the Bible which honors Him the most. In case after case, the Christ-honoring Bible is found to be the King James Bible.

MORE THAN DOCTRINE

We have looked at some **doctrinal problems** with the New American Standard Version, which are also evident in most other new

---

337 Ruckman, Peter, *Manuscript Evidence*, (Pensacola Bible Press, Pensacola, 1970), p. 108.

—

translations. Yet the Bible is **more than a doctrinal textbook**. It is our **power to preach**! Without the Bible preachers around the world are emasculated and have nothing to authorize their sermons but their own prejudice. Therefore, we shall now visit a few passages that **do not** deal directly with any of the great doctrines of the Bible but are still discredited and watered down in modern translations. I'm sure you will find them informative, humorous and **sad**.

The problem faced by modern bible translators is a great one. They desire to replace the King James Bible **with anything**. Therefore, they need to "make a case" that you "need" a new translation. They usually can produce about a half-a-dozen passages in the Authorized Version which, presented with sufficient prejudice, can succeed in planting doubt in the mind of their audience. The problem is, six, or ten, or fifty such contorted verses **do not justify a completely new translation!** Therefore, once they begin their work they are forced to make **unnecessary**, **uncalled for** and even **foolish** changes in an effort to justify the need for what they are doing. Through this comparison you will discover that "improving," "clarifying" and "accuracy" have **nothing** to do with the goals of modern bible translators. In fact, you will discover that there is only **one rule modern bible translators follow**, "The King James Bible is always wrong."

Several versions will be consulted and several verses examined. You won't need any knowledge of "the Greek" or Hebrew to recognize the foolishness of men who claim that you can trust your Bible to their judgement. The abbreviations used are; TEV- Today's English Version (also known as "Good News For Modern Man"), Living - Living Bible; Amp - Amplified Version; NEB - New English Bible; NKJV - New King James Version; NASV - New American Standard Version and NIV - New International Version. Obviously "The Bible" represents **the Bible**, the King James Bible. Only the pertinent portion of the verse will be examined and the word/s in question will be in bold face type. Not every version will be compared in every case.

I Samuel 13:1

The Bible: "Saul reigned **one year**; and when he had reigned **two years** over Israel,"

TEV: The verse is omitted.

Living: "By this time Saul had reigned for **one year**. In the **second year** of his reign."

Amp: "Saul was [*forty*] **years old** when he began to reign; and when he had reigned **two years** over Israel."

NEB: "Saul was **fifty years old** when he became king, and he reigned over Israel **twenty-two years**."

NKJV: "Saul reigned **one year**; and when he had reigned **two years** over Israel,"

NASV: "Saul was **forty years old** when he began to reign, and he reigned **thirty years** over Israel."

NIV: "Saul was **thirty years old** when he became king, and he reigned over Israel **forty-two years**."

In 1 Samuel 13:1 we find that the translators of modern versions feel that your spiritual growth is threatened by the King James rendering. So they all change it...**in a different way**. (Remember! The rule of Bible translation is "The King James Bible is always wrong.") If you like a good laugh, you have to compare the NEB, NASV and the NIV. The NEB claims Saul began to reign at age **50** and reigned for **22** years. The NASV claims he was **40** and reigned for **32** years. While the NIV disagrees with both and says he was **30** years old and reigned **42** years. Will somebody please make up their mind?! Oh, that's right. They did..."The King James Bible is always wrong."

If you will check Acts 13:21 in **any** of these three versions, you will find that **all three** state that Saul reigned for **40** years. Thus we have in any one of these three versions the "bible" that every drunk and infidel has been talking about for years. You have a "bible" that **has a contradiction in it!**

Luke 14:5

The Bible: "And answered them, saying, Which of you shall have and **ass** or an ox fallen into a pit..."

TEV: "If any one of you had a **son** or an ox..."

Living: "If your **cow** falls into a pit..."

Amp: "...Which of you, having a **son** or a donkey or an ox..."

NEB: "...If one of you has a **donkey** or an ox..."

NKJV: "...Which of you, having a **donkey** or an ox..."

NASV: "...Which of you shall have a **son** or an ox..."

NIV: "...If one of you has a **son** or an ox..."

Whenever I read Luke 14:5 in most modern versions, I am led to wonder if there are severe family problems in the homes of most modern translators. Where the Lord Jesus Christ uses a common idiom (check Luke 13:15) about "an ass or an ox," the modern translators decided they would replace "ass" with "son" except, of course, for the translator of the Living Bible who, we hope, learns the difference between a "cow" and an "ox"...**before** milking time!

Luke 23:33

The Bible: "And when they were come to the place, which is called **Calvary**..."

TEV: "When they came to the place called 'The Skull'..."

Living: ...at a place called 'The Skull'..."

Amp: "And when they came to the place which is called **The Skull** [**Calvary**, from the Latin; Golgotha, the Hebrew equivalent]..."

NEB: "...when they reached the place called The Skull..."

NKJV: "And when they had come to the place called **Calvary**..."

NASV: "And when they came to the place which is called **The Skull**..."

NIV: "When they came to the place which is called **the Skull**..."

Do you..."believe in a hill called Mount Calvary..."? If you do, you got it from **the King James Bible**. The name "Calvary" appears only **once** in Scripture, **and not at all** in most modern translations. Have you ever sung a hymn about "Calvary"? Do you attend a church with "Calvary" in its name? Have you ever said, "Thank God for Calvary!"? If so, you should thank the translators of the King James Bible and deeply resent its removal from modern translations. If you're going to use such a translation, you need to rip every hymn out of your church hymnal with the word "Calvary" in it and banish the word from your glossary, for **according to modern translators**, such a place **never existed**.[338] (What do you think the **Latin**-speaking Romans called it?) If you're going to keep using the word "Calvary," then you need to throw out your modern translation and banish **it** from your home and use the **perfect** Word of the God, The King James Bible.

Isaiah 14:12

The Bible: "How art thou fallen from heaven, **O Lucifer**..."
TEV: "King of Babylon, bright and **morning star**,..."
Living: "...**O Lucifer**, son of the morning..."
Amp: "How are you fallen from heaven, **O light-bringer and day-star**, son of the morning..."
NEB: "How you have fallen from heaven, **bright morning star**..."
NKJV: "How are you fallen from heaven, **O Lucifer**..."
NASV: "How you have fallen from heaven, **O star of the morning,** son of the dawn!..."
NIV: "How you have fallen from heaven, **O morning star**,..."

Just as the word "Calvary" appears only once in Scripture, so does Satan's name: "Lucifer." Lucifer was not a name invented by the

---

338 Not even Dr. Kenneth Barker, the Executive Director of the Committee for Bible Translation, the producer of the NIV, or James White, the defender of modern versions, dared to address this in their writings.

King James translators but was used as early as 1380 by John Wycliffe in his translation. Yet here almost every modern translation covers Satan's tracks for him and changes "Lucifer" to some form of "morning star." Who is called the "morning star" in Scripture? In Revelation 22:16 none other than **Jesus Christ Himself** lays claim to the title when He states, "...I am the root and offspring of David, and the bright and morning star." If that is so, the TEV, Amplified Version, NEB, NASV and NIV not only claim in Isaiah that Jesus Christ is "fallen from heaven," but according to verse 15, they **damn** Him to "hell," "Sheol," the grave" and "the pit." Who are these men who would consign the eternal Son of God the Hell?! I will greatly enjoy the day they stand naked before Him and then we will see Who damns whom!

2 Timothy 3:3

The Bible: "Without natural affection,..."
TEV: "they will be **unkind**..."
Living: "They will be **hardheaded**..."
Amp: "[They will be] **without natural (human) affection**..."
NEB: "...**no natural affection**..."
NKJV: "**unloving**..."
NASV: "**unloving**..."
NIV: "**without love**..."

The Bible is more than simply a doctrine textbook doomed to use in a college classroom. It is the very power and authority by which we preach not just the Gospel but **against** the many sins of mankind. Thus, a preacher of righteousness can take his King James Bible, turn to 2 Timothy, and preach against the sins of homosexuality, lesbianism, animal rights, environmentalism and any number of examples of the unnatural affection prevalent in our society today. Yet he **is stripped** of this power and authority by the modern translations. He can't accurately preach from a TEV, Living Bible, NKJV, NASV or NIV. In fact, these versions have not only stripped him of his power to preach, but they have perverted the text (the Greek allows only "without natural affection") so that it can now be pointed at the **Bible believer** for being "unkind," "hardheaded" and "unloving." This is much like Senator John McCain (Cain?!) accusing Christians of being hateful during his bid for the presidency and ignoring the hatred spewed by homosexuals for the Christians. He, like moderns translators, turned the tables on Christianity and "called evil good and good evil."

Galatians 5:12

The Bible: "I would they were even **cut off** which trouble you."

TEV: "...let them go on and **castrate themselves!**"

Living: "...**cut themselves off from you** and leave you alone!"

Amp: "I wish those who unsettle and confuse you would [go all the way and] **cut themselves off!**"

NEB: "As for these agitators, they had better go the whole way and **make eunuchs of themselves!**"

NKJV: "I could wish that those who trouble you would even **cut themselves off!**"

NASV: "Would that those who are troubling you would **mutilate themselves.**"

NIV: "As for these agitators, I wish they would go the whole way and **emasculate themselves!**"

The various renditions of the modern versions (**definitely** earning the label **"perversion"** here) would be funny if it was not the Word of God that we were dealing with. Would you equate the TEV's rendering as being "good news" for modern man? Would you prefer the NEB to be used by your church for matters of church discipline? Do you realize that in the NASV we finally have a Bible that **teaches** the practices of body piercing and branding being practiced by the wayward teens of our nation? Do you really want to make the claim that the Holy Spirit directed Paul to say what the NIV says? And, in light of these others, are you willing to trust just what is meant by "cut

—

themselves off" in the Amplified and NKJV? If so, good luck to you. I wouldn't touch these perversions with a bloody knife!

Yet in the various reading above we may see an ominous and far more frightening truth than first appears. The Bible says that a "good tree" brings forth "good fruit" and an "evil tree" brings forth "evil fruit." Stop and think for a moments (if you can do that without a remote in your hand). How is it that the nation (America) that has **more Bibles** in its native languages than any other nation on earth can produce such perversions as a man who could have sex with a another man and then kill him and eat him (Jeffrey Daumer)? How can it be that we have children shooting each other in our schools? How is that we can have a mother strap her children into a car and drive it into a lake? How can a woman give birth to a baby and then throw it into a dumpster? These aren't acts of **sin**. They are acts of **perversion**! I submit that the **perverted acts** we read and hear about daily are **the fruit** of the **perverted versions** that have been sown across this country since the publication of the American Standard Version in 1901. Sow corn and you reap corn. Sow **perversions** and you reap **perverts**!

Judges 1:14

The Bible: "And it came to pass, when she came to him, that she moved him to ask of her father a field: and she lighted from off her ass; and Caleb said unto her, What wilt thou?"

NEB: "As she sat on the ass, **she broke wind**, and Caleb said, 'What did you mean by that?'"

Isn't that a gas!? Even **I** know what she meant by **that!** Can you believe that **anyone** could possibly **honestly** come up with that rendering? It becomes especially humorous if you first read the mission statement of the NEB translators. In this they claim that it was their desire to achieve "...clarity, dignity and in many cases true poetry..." Well, I must admit that their rendition of Judges 1:14 is **clear**! It does seem to fall a bit short on **dignity**, though. But it's as close to **true**

poetry as you can get! What's **doubly** sad is that that is in the NEB **twice!** You'll find this literary atrocity repeated in Joshua 15:17.

I don't know what you're going to have to answer for at the Judgement Seat of Christ. I will have plenty. But aren't you glad that...**you don't have to answer to having done that to the Word of God?!**

Psalm 23

There will be no comparison here. Instead, just a challenge. One of the lame complaints that Bible correctors make against Bible believers is "This Bible issue is causing great division in the cause of Christ." Then they look at **us** like **we** are the cause of the division. They smugly claim **they** are interested in **unity** but **we** are preventing that by all this "division" we cause over the King James Bible.

Here's the challenge. Get a group of people and about eight to ten different translations. Have the group stand together and read Psalm 23 from **all of the versions at once**. I do this all the time when teaching at a King James Bible conference. It sounds worse than all those discourteous reporters all trying to ask the President a question at the same time. Immediately after doing so I ask the congregation, "What one word describes what you just heard?" "Confusion!" comes the reply. "Well, this is what the advocates of using multiple versions want in your churches. But "God is not the author of confusion." Thus, God **cannot be** the **author** of the multiple version controversy." Then, to clean out their ears, we all read Psalm 23 in unison again. But this time from only the King James Bible. The difference is amazing. "That's what we call 'unity.' That's what we'd have in all of our churches if we King James Bible believers had **our** way and everybody just used a King James Bible."

WHAT ABOUT THE NEW SCOFIELD VERSION?

The New Scofield Reference Bible is unfortunately a **double lie**. In fact, this deceitful version lies to its readers **twice** on the title page. On that page it claims to be an "Authorized King James Version." Yet on almost every page a King James word has been removed from the text and placed in the margin preceded by "KJV." This happens **on the average** of three times per page! No one can make three changes per page and **pretend** that he is printing a King James Bible!

The title page also claims to be a "Scofield" Reference Bible. This is also a lie. Why? Because in the footnote found under 1 Corinthians 11:23, the "**New** Scofield Version" states that the Lord's supper is a "**sacrament**." The standard teaching of the Roman Catholic Church is that a "sacrament" is something that "bestows saving grace." Yet when you check the same verse in the **old** Scofield reference Bible...**there is no such note!** This is a **Roman Catholic** note, not a **Scofield** note.

Again, in Acts 8:12 there is another footnote that claims that baptism is a "sacrament." Again the closet Roman Catholics on the **New** Scofield board of editors have spoken. Yet when you check the **old** Scofield for a footnote in Acts 8:12, you find that **there is no note**. This is a **Roman Catholic** note, not a **Scofield** note.

Yet the worse is yet to come! In the footnote found under 1 Chronicles 11:11 the reader will find this, "God gave us a Bible free from error **in the original manuscripts**. In its preservation through many generations of recopying, He providentially kept it from **serious error**, although **He permitted a few scribal mistakes**." (Emphasis mine) Here we have the **New** Scofield board of editors claiming not only that the Bible has mistakes in it but that **God put them there!** Check the **old** Scofield. No such note exists. It is not a Scofield note and the New Scofield Reference Version **is not** a Scofield Bible.

Most people that get a New Scofield Version are tricked into it. They either buy one because they **think** that it a King James Bible or some loved one buys it for them because they **think** that they're buying a King James Bible.

Thus we see that the New Scofield Reference Version lies to you **twice** before you get past the title page. Now if it lies to you twice on the title page what do you think it is going to do in its text?

VIRTUE, NOT FANFARE

Finally, it must be remembered that the Authorized Version is the only Bible ever released without fanfare.

The Revised Version, the American Standard Version, the Revised Standard Version, the New American Standard Version, the Living Bible, the Good News for Modern Man, the New International Version, the New King James Version, and all other new translations have been published with a great advertising "blitz." They have all attempted to replace the Authorized Version in the study, in the pulpit, in memorization, and in the hearts of believers. They have all failed. Those which have not failed are destined to fail, except for one.

THE COUNTERFEITS

To explain the last statement, let us look at a few facts. For every truth which God has, Satan has many counterfeits and then one ultimate counterfeit. Look at the following example:

God's Truth	Satan's Counterfeits	Satan's Ultimate Counterfeit
One God	Many "gods"	Satan is "god" of this world
One Christ	Many "anti-christs"	The Anti-christ
One Church	Many false churches	One ultimate church, Rome
One Bible (AV)	Many "bibles" (NASV, NIV, etc.)	One ultimate false "bible"

—

We see from the above example that there is **one true God**. Satan has many false "gods" for people in this world to worship. Then Satan himself is the ultimate "false god."

We further see that there is **one true Christ**. Satan has many spirits of anti-christ. During the tribulation there will be a manifestation of "the Anti-christ."

God has **one true church** made up of born-again believers. Satan has many congregations serving him on this earth today. During the tribulation the ultimate Satanic church located in Rome (Babylon the Great) will again be in power.

God has preserved His Words in **one true Bible**. Satan has many "bibles." I believe it seems certain that some day in the future he will have one ultimate Satanic "bible." It will probably be called a "New Authorized Version."[339]

Notice that in the examples above, the "many" counterfeits seem to run in conjunction with the Church Age. But Satan's **ultimate** counterfeit is always manifested during the Great Tribulation when the Holy Spirit has ceased to deal with mankind. I believe that there is a time when Satan will have an anti-bible exalted as the true Word of God just as surely as he will have an Anti-christ exalted as the Son of God. It seems likely that this will not take place until the great Tribulation. Until then, God will be exalted, Jesus Christ will be exalted, Christ's church will be exalted, and the Authorized Version will be exalted. Whose side does that put today's Bible critics on?

---

339 As mentioned earlier, I have for years speculated that the "bible" of the Anti-christ would be called the "New Authorized Version." In the July 19, 1999 issue of The New American there was a review of a new translation entitled *The Third Millenium Bible* by one Father James Thornton. The review includes a picture of the cover of this new version. Beneath the name, *Third Millenium Bible* are the words *New Authorized Version of the Holy Bible* Could this be the "bible" of the Anti-christ?

THE ASV "BUST"

In spite of the publicity campaigns to sell "Bibles," they all fail. The American Standard Version is a prime example. It was heralded as a replacement for the King James when it was published in 1901. Twenty-three years later it went broke and sold its copyright to the National Council of Churches. Was God's hand on this "Bible"? If so, **why** wasn't it accepted and used by Christianity even **more** than the Authorized Version? Was Satan able to overcome God's will? If God's hand was not on the American Standard Version, why would the Lockman Foundation try to "resurrect" it in the form of the New American Standard Version? Here's what they said in the Preface of their newest failure:

> "The producers of this translation were imbued with the conviction that interest in the American Standard Version should be renewed and increased.

> "Perhaps the most weighty impetus for this undertaking can be attributed to a disturbing awareness that the American Standard Version of 1901 was fast disappearing from the scene."[340]

If God wouldn't use the American Standard Version, **why** would the Lockman Foundation want to? If God's blessing was **on** the American Standard Version, and it died in twenty-three years without even a minor revival, **how** has the Authorized Version lasted nearly four hundred years in spite of all of the "better translations" which God has supposedly been "blessing"?

Of course, there is no answer for these questions, unless it is admitted that **God's** Bible is the Authorized Version and that He will preserve it whether the Christian educators and bookstore operators

---

340 Lockman Foundation, New American Standard New Testament Preface, (Gospel Light Publications, Glendale, 1971), p. IV, V.

accept it or not. God will continue to use this English version of the Universal Text and will continue to ignore the English versions of the Local Text, no matter who the fundamentalist is that recommends them and no matter what size college may use them. Advertisement will not help.

THE NIV SCAM

Much has been made in recent years of the NIV **supposedly** surpassing of the King James Bible in total sales. This sales figure is a sham. It is **artificially inflated** by large quantify purchases of modernist evangelical organizations in order to make it look like the NIV is passing the King James in popularity. The fact is that **in individual purchases** the King James Bible is **still** more popular than **any** modern perversion.

A survey conducted by the Barna Group Ltd. among adults 18 years or older in the 48 continental states of the United States found the following to be true:

1. 80% named **the Bible** as the most influential book in human history

2. 58% believe the Bible is totally accurate in all it teaches

3. 91% of all households own at least one Bible

4. The **typical** household owns three Bibles

5. Among Bible readers, the average amount of time spent reading the Bible during the week is 52 minutes

6. 22% say they have read the entire Bible

7. The King James Bible is **more likely to be read** than is the NIV during the week by a 5:1ratio!

Chapter 10

The "King" of the King James Bible

THE "King James" of the King James Bible was James Charles Stuart (or Stewart). He was born in Edinburgh Castle on June 19, 1566.[341] He was baptized into the Roman Catholic Church against his will at the bidding of his mother Mary, Queen of Scots. He acceded to the throne of Scotland while still an infant on July 24, 1567, when Mary was forced to abdicate. His father Henry Lord Darnley was murdered in February 1567. It is believed that Mary may have had a hand in his death. Being yet an infant, James was rescued from the Roman church and raised under staunch Presbyterian guidance. This action was never forgiven by the Roman Catholic Church; therefore, he was subject to plots and counter-plots designed to overthrow him and reestablish Roman Catholic rule four such plots coming in rapid succession between 1600 and 1605. Violence surrounded the young king. While only 19 years old, James witnessed the death

---

341 Most (but not all) of the information in this segment comes from the excellent work of Stephen A. Coston, Sr., *King James the VI of Scotland & the I of England, Unjustly Accused?* Some is general information and simply included in the text. Other items of particular interest are duly footnoted. The reader is **strongly** urged to secure a copy of Mr. Coston's work and read it.

of several friends in a plot designed to murder the Earl of Mar and bring control of the monarchy under Roman Catholic domination.[342] The young king knew then that intrigue would follow him all the days of his life and never forgot that his life could end by doing no more than walking around the next corner or sleeping unguarded in his bedroom. It is most likely for this reason that he hated violence and war.[343]

The good king was blessed with many virtues. His mind was keen and sharp. Olga S. Opfell tells us,

"Among those justifiably attributed refinements was his reputation as a paragon of learning, crammed with Greek and Latin and other tongues. In spite of his physical disabilities , his mind was first rate. Already at the age of seven he 'was able extempore...to read a chapter of the Bible out of Latin into French and next out of French into English as well as few men could have added anything to his translation.' In due time he became known as the most educated sovereign in Europe."[344]

James' love for higher learning was so profound that he often quipped that if he were ever to be a prisoner, he desired to be incarcerated in the great library at Oxford University.[345]

---

342 Ralston, David, *The Real King James, The British Solomon,* (Tabernacle Baptist Press, Louisville, 1986), p. 3.

343 Opfell, Olga S., *The King James Bible Translators*, (McFarland & Co., London, 1982), p. 9.

344 Ibid., p. 1.

345 "If he were a prisoner, James insisted, he would choose it (the library at Oxford) for his prison and be chained with the good authors represented there." Opfell, Olga S., *The King James Bible Translators*,(McFarland & Co., London, 1982), p. 55.

James married Anne, the second daughter of Frederick II, King of Denmark on August 20, 1589. They had eight children;

1. Henry, born February 19, 1594. Died on November 6, 1612, at age 18.

2. Elizabeth, born August 19, 1596. Died on February 13, 1662, at age 65.

3. Margaret, born December 1598. Died in December 1600 at age 2.

4. Charles (who due to the early death of Henry) succeeded his father in 1625 as King Charles I, born November 19, 1600. Murdered in1649 at age 49.

5. Robert, born January 18, 1602. Died May 27, 1602, at age 4 months.

6. A stillborn child born in May 1603.

7. May, born April 8, 1605. Died September 16, 1607, at age 2.

8. Sophia, born June 22, 1606. Died the next day, age one day.

King James VI of Scotland became King James I of England when he acceded that throne on March 24, 1603, and thus united the two countries under a single monarch. He died almost exactly twenty-two years later on March 27, 1625, having ruled well and been loved greatly by his subjects.

James suffered from numerous physical ailments all of his life. He had very weak legs and often had to be supported when he walked. He had limited use of his hands, which required that he have a secretary or chamberlain write for him. He also suffered from gout, arthritis and possibly Porphyra, a debilitating disease also often referred to as "The Royal Disease." These maladies left him weak and quite often bedridden. Thus, James, bedroom became his "office" of sorts with him surrounded by courtiers who waited on and served their king. The king did not sleep well and once awakened had great difficulty regaining his sleep. He would then have a courtier, usually sleeping in the same room as a bodyguard, read to him until he dozed off again. James suffered bouts of pain that sometimes left him delirious.[346] James also suffered from an overlarge tongue, which caused him to drool frequently and slurp loudly when he drank. Basically, **the great king was physically repulsive** [347]...and he knew it. Men with such outwardly repulsive physiques have two options in life. They can be as personally abhorrent as their bodies by being foul-spirited and mean, thus giving them an excuse other than their physical condition for being rejected. Or they can seek to be bigger than their infirmities by a personal kindness that is above the average. James chose the latter.

"JAMES the KIND"

There is ample testimony to the kindness and great intellect of King James. Aside from being fluent in Latin, Greek and French and schooled in Italian and Spanish, the king was also worthy of praise for his kind treatment of others. Bishop Godfrey Goodman described James in the following manner:

> "Here unto you may add the carriage and disposition of King James; truly I did never know any man of so great an appreciation, of so great love and affection. A man so truly just, so free from all cruelty and pride, such a lover of the church, and one who had done so much good for the church."[348]

Sir Henry Wotton wrote of James in 1602:

---

346 Coston Sr., Stephen A., *King James the VI of Scotland & I of England, Unjustly Accused*, (Konigs Wort, St. Peterburg, 1996), p. 36.

347 If these physical deficiencies are to be held against the king then we must also reject the great mind of the also physically handicapped Stephen Hawkins.

348 Coston Sr., Stephen A., *King James the VI of Scotland & I of England, Unjustly Accused*, (Konigs Wort, St. Peterburg, 1996), p. 26.

"There appears a certain natural goodness verging on modesty...among his good qualities none shines more brightly than the chastness of his life, which he has preserved without stain down to the present time, contrary to the example of almost all his ancestors, who disturbed the kingdom with the great number of bastards which they left..."[349]

Sir Roger Wilbraham stated in 1603, "The King is of the sharpest wit and invention...of the sweetest most pleasant and best nature that I ever knew, desiring nor affecting anything but true honor."[350]

F. A. Inderwick reports, "James had a reputation for learning, for piety, for good nature, and for liberality."[351]

Robert Chambers affirms that King James was "a monarch whose character was good..."[352] Still later Chambers tells us that James, "was very much beloved by his people."[353] And again he states that James was "no coward, and at various times in his life he displayed considerable nerve in facing danger."[354]

---

349 Ibid., p. 39.

350 Ibid., p. 40.

351 Coston Sr., Stephen A., *King James the VI of Scotland & I of England, Unjustly Accused*, (Konigs Wort, St. Peterburg, 1996), p. 43.

352 Ibid., p. 308.

353 Ibid., p. 309.

354 Ibid., p. 309.

Hugh Walpole tells us, "He had large, prominent blue eyes, and they stared at the person with whom he talked as though he would read all secrets."[355]

Stephen A. Coston, Sr., shares the praise of Lucy Aikin, which she wrote in 1823. Mrs Aikin states:

> "On his propensity to favoritism...the only excuse for his blind indulgence to the objects of his affection, must be derived from his boundless good-nature; which overflowed upon all who approached him, and rendered it a moral impossibility for him to refuse any request urged with importunity. His profane liberality which sprang from the same source, was the chief if not the sole cause of his constant want of money..."[356]

"JAMES the REMARKABLE"

Although James Stuart lived his whole life hampered by his physical ailments, he was a man of great character. His personal greatness made men admire and praise him naturally, so he did not need to oppress his subjects in order to gain their respect and/or obedience. He was a pillar of morality who not only lived morally himself but promoted such moral living in his friends and family. Although handicapped, he had the heart and soul of a lion.

Once again F. A. Inderwick informs us of James' outstanding good character by telling us:

---

355 Opiell, Olga S., *The King James Bible Translators*, (McFarland & Co., London, 1982), p. 5.

356 Coston Sr., Stephen A., *King James the VI of Scotland & I of England, Unjustly Accused*, (Konigs Wort, St. Peterburg, 1996), p. 298.

"...as to his personal character, it is, I think only justice to say,...he was personally a man of good MORAL character, a quality which was probably much indebted to the strict and careful training he received from his Presbyterian tutors..."[357]

Despite his many physical deformities, James was "a man's man" in that he promoted masculinity and despised the effeminate. Until his untimely death, James' eldest son Henry was destined to take his place on the throne. James was vehement about the need for a sovereign to be pure, manly and moral. Therefore, he authored a work that was to instruct Henry in the proper way a monarch should behave both personally and toward others.[358] It was entitled *Basilicon Doran,* which simply meant "The Kingly Gift." The title was not just a reference to James' gift of the work to his son but a description of how Henry's reign should be a "kingly gift" to his subjects. James charged Henry:

"But especially eschew to be effeminate in your clothes, in perfuming, preining, or such like...and make not a fool of yourself in disguising or wearing long your hair or nails, which are but excrements of nature."[359]

In other writings he advised his son, "Guard against corrupt leide, as book-language, and pen-and-ink horn terms, and last of all, mignard and effeminate ones."[360]

---

357 Ibid., p. 303.

358 After Henry's death the work was issued to Charles as his personal instructions on how to be a good king. Perhaps due to this kingly, and fatherly, advice Charles was known for his personal moral chastity even if he did fall short of his father's advice in other areas.

359 Coston Sr., Stephen A., *King James the VI of Scotland & I of England, Unjustly Accused,* (Konigs Wort, St. Peterburg, 1996), p. 4.

360 Ibid., p. 3.

Of the vices of prosperity he warned:

"Our peace hath bread wealth: and peace and wealth hath brought forth a general sluggishness which makes us wallow in all sorts of idle delights and soft delicacies, the first seeds of subversion of all great monarchies."[361]

James was loth to anything that feminized men or abused women. That is why he was so set against the vile habit of smoking. He wrote a treatise against the habit entitled *A Counterblaste To Tobacco*[362] in which he displayed several of his great attributes, not the least of which was his farsightedness. He sums up the tobacco habit as:

"...loathsome to the eye, hateful to the nose, harmful to the brain, dangerous to the lungs and in the black stinking fumes thereof, nearest resembling that horrible Stygian smoke of that pit which is bottomless...Such is the force of that natural self love as we cannot be content unless we imitate everything that our fellows do, and so prove ourselves capable of everything whereof they are capable; like apes, counterfeiting the manners of others, to our own destruction."[363]

Here the great king reveals how far ahead of his time he was. He recognized the **health** hazard that smoking was when none of his peers did, nor would they **for several hundred years**! But James' "Counterblaste" also served to reveal the high esteem he had for womanhood at a time when a woman was considered more a piece of

---

361 Ibid., p. 303.

362 James wrote numerous works of a spiritual nature. In 1597 he even produced one entitled *Daemonology* which warned against the wiles of the devil. Opfell, Olga S., *The King James Bible Translators*, (McFarland & Co., London, 1982), p. 82.

363 <u>The Gospel Catholic</u>, January 1988, The Conversion Center, Inc., p. 1.

property than a genuine person. Again, concerning smoking, James' stated:

> "The husband shall not be ashamed, to reduce thereby his delicate, wholesome and clear complexioned wife to that extremity that either she must also corrupt her sweet breath therewith, or else resolve to live in a perpetual stinking torment."[364]

And just what did the good king think it was that caused Englishmen to be interested in and then get caught up in such an unclean habit? Robert Chambers enlightens us to James' feelings when he reveals:

> "In the preface to the counter blast, He (James) alleges, as the cause of this vice, the great increase of wealth in England during the Age of Peace, which had rendered men effeminate and compelled them to resort to improper indulgences."[365]

So we see that James was "death" on the effeminate. He felt that it was vital to the survival of a nation that its men be manly and not give themselves to effeminate behavior in either dress or actions. In fact, sexual perverts (read that "homosexuals") and their aberrant behavior were singled out for special venom! In *Basilicon Doran* he advised his heir,

> "There are some horrible crimes that ye are bound in conscience never to forgive: such as witchcraft, willful murder, incest, and sodomy..."[366]

---

364 Ibid., p. 1.

365 Coston Sr., Stephen A., *King James the VI of Scotland & I of England, Unjustly Accused*, (Konigs Wort, St. Peterburg, 1996), p. 3.

366 Ibid., p. 48.

The sad fact of old England was that their kings had not **always** been of the highest moral fiber. Dalliances with women other than their wives were all too common. In fact, some were known for being morally loose while demanding chastity of their wives. But James was a different kind of man from any who had ever occupied that high office, and he was determined that his heirs would preserve his high moral standards for generations to come. Again in *Basilicon Doran* he exhorted his son to:

> "Keep your body clean and unpolluted while you give it to your wife whom to only it belongs for how can you justly crave to be joined to a Virgin if your body be polluted? Why should the one half be clean, and the other defiled? And suppose I know, fornication is thought but a veniall sin by most of the world, yet remember well what I said in my first book regarding conscience, and count every sin and breach of God's law, not according as the vain world esteems of it, but as God judge and maker of the law accounts of the same:"[367]

James went on to advise,

> "Be not ashamed to keep clean your body (which is the temple of the Holy Spirit) notwithstanding all vain allurements to the contrary."[368]

James didn't see the privileges of the throne to include immorality:

> "Think not therefore, that the highness of your dignity diminisheth your faults (much less giveth you a license to sin)

---

367 Ibid., p. 44.

368 Ibid., p. 44.

but by the contrary, your fault shall be aggravated according to the height of your dignity..."[369]

James saw a king as being obligated to his subjects to be pure and honest:

"Make your court and company to be a pattern of godliness and all honest virtues to all the rest of the people...Be careful to prefer the gentlest natured."[370]

"Holiness being the first and most requisite quality of a Christian (as proceeding from true fear and knowledge of God.)."[371]

"...it is not enough to be a good king, by the thralldom of good laws well execute to govern his people if he joins therewith a virtuous life in his own person and in the person of his court and company, by his good example alluring his subjects to the love of virtue, and hatred of vice..."[372]

"And this example in your own life and person...in the government of your court and followers in all godliness and virtue... Having your mind decked and enriched so with all virtuous qualities, that there with ye may worthily rule your people...Have a double care for the ruling of your own servants..."[373]

---

369 Ibid., p. 47.

370 Ibid., p. 53.

371 Ibid., p. 55.

372 Ibid., p. 52.

373 Ibid., p. 53.

The reader can almost here the strains of Solomon in the Proverbs also pleading with his son to be virtuous and upright. Is it any wonder then that James was so frequently compared to his great counterpart from Scripture? David Ralston describes him this way:

> "King James was regarded by those of his own time as 'The British Solomon'. He was wise not only in politics and academics, but in Theology. He was devoutly interested in the Word of God. He made it clear that he wanted the Holy Word of God to be in the hands of people and not chained to pulpits or hoarded in cellars to be read only by Greek scholars."[374]

Were Ralston's comments extreme? Were they exaggerated? No. In fact, if anything, they were understated. While preaching James' funeral sermon, Bishop Williams compared this distinguished monarch to Solomon in no less than eleven different particulars.[375]

We see then that this great lion of a king was loved of his subjects and loved them dearly in return. What other virtues did this historic figure exhibit?

"JAMES the CHRISTIAN"

Yes, this noble monarch was also a devout Christian. That fact is also revealed many times in his own writings. In his instructions to Henry in *Basilicon Doran,* James advised:

> "God gives not kings the style of gods in vain, for on his throne his scepter do the sway...So kings should fear and serve

---

374 Ralston, David, *The Real King James, The British Solomon,* Tabernacle Baptist Press, Louisville, 1986), p. 8.

375 Coston Sr., Stephen A., *King James the VI of Scotland & I of England, Unjustly Accused,* (Konigs Wort, St. Peterburg, 1996), p. 56.

their God again. If they would enjoy a happy reign, observe the statues of your heavenly king; and from his law make all your laws to spring:...and so ye (shall in princely virtues shine). Resembling right your mighty king divine."[376]

It is to be noted that unlike some monarchs (**and** presidents **and** preachers), James did **not** believe a king was answerable to no one. He drove home the point that he, his heir, and all kings were in subjection to their "heavenly king." In fact, James saw a king as being **twice** as obligated to serve the Lord, once as a common Christian and once more as a sovereign: "Therefore (my son) first of all things, learn to know and love that God whom to ye have a double obligation,"[377]

The good king knew, as all great men do, that true wisdom came from God and that a good and wise king should have a close and consistent relationship with Him:

> "Now faith...is the free gift of God (as Paul sayeth). It must be nourished by prayer, which is no thing else but a friendly talking to God. Use oft to pray when ye are quiet, especially on your bed..."[378]

King James never ceased admonishing his son to be a good Christian. It was a theme he repeated over and over. In fact, he saw being a good Christian as a prerequisite for being a good king! Once again, he instructed Henry,

---

376 Ibid., p. 47.

377 Ibid., p. 47.

378 Ibid., p. 47.

"and ye are a good Christian, so ye may be a good king...establishing good laws among your people: the other, by your behavior in your own person with your servants..."[379]

Once again we see that James felt it was important that a king not take advantage of a servant's natural desire to please his sovereign to the point of any act that would not be considered that of a "good Christian."

Although raised a Presbyterian and head of the Church of England, James enrolled his heir Prince Phillip in Magdalen College at Oxford, which was decidedly of a Puritan bent. In fact, he once orated for **five hours** against the corruptions that had infested the Church of England and, as Lancelot Andrews put it, "...did wonderfully play the Puritan."[380]

James was a great student of Scripture, and it is said that "He was deeply read in the Scripture; he could quote its texts with great facility,"[381]

But like Erasmus, James did not think that the Scripture should be the possession of a privileged few. He knew that the Word of God alone had the power to change the inner man and to advance him spiritually and morally. It was essential that the common man have a copy in easy-to-read English so that he too might benefit from its divine message. He came to the throne of England in 1603 and one of his **first** orders of business was to commission a new translation of the Scripture. But this one would not be for a select few. It would be made available to **all** of his subjects:

---

379 Ibid., p. 48.

380 Opfell, Olga S., *The King James Bible Translators*, (McFarland & Co., London, 1982), p. 93.

381 Coston Sr., Stephen A., *King James the VI of Scotland & I of England, Unjustly Accused*, (Konigs Wort, St. Peterburg, 1996), p. 311.

"He made it clear that he wanted the Holy Word of God to be in the hands of the people and not chained to pulpits or hoarded in cellars to be read only by Greek scholars. He had the deep conviction that the more wide spread the knowledge of God's Word became, the better the spiritual condition would be of his subjects."[382]

"James' own suggestion of adopting the translation was to be made by the most learned linguists, reviewed by the Bishops and other learned churchmen, then presented to the Privy Council and finally, ratified by royal authority. It is evident that James prime motive...was that the Bible should be easily understood by the ordinary people of the day."[383]

As well as his desire that the common man would have his own copy of Scripture, James also has a great burden that all men would come to Christ, both near and far. Writing to George Villiers he encouraged:

"Receive then this New Year's gift from me as a token of my love, being begun on the eve of our Saviour's nativity and ended far within the first month of the year. Praying God that as you are regenerated and born in him anew, so you may rise and be sanctified in him forever."[384]

And just what **was** "salvation" to James? "...white garments washen the blood of the lamb (as St. John sayeth)."[385] And was there

---

382 Ralston, David, *The Real King James, The British Solomon,* Tabernacle Baptist Press, Louisville, 1986), p. 8.

383 Ibid., p. 10.

384 Coston Sr., Stephen A., *King James the VI of Scotland & I of England, Unjustly Accused,* (Konigs Wort, St. Peterburg, 1996), p. 300.

385 Ibid., p. 48.

some religious rite or service required? No. "...all that is necessary for salvation is contained in the Scripture."[386]

Although James knew of the anti-Christian nature of the Roman Catholic Church, he still desired to see them come to Christ. He disputed with the Puritans over their prohibition on Sunday sports because he felt it was a hindrance to the conversion of Roman Catholics![387]

It was this burning desire to see souls saved and God glorified that led James to commission the **first Christian colony** in the New World. The Grant Charter that authorized the colonists to establish the colony of Virginia plainly stated:

> "To make habitation...and to deduce a colony of sundry of our people into that part of America, commonly called Virginia...in propagating of Christian religion to such people as yet live in darkness...to bring a settled and quiet government."[388]

This fact was reemphasized in a later charter:

> "Because the **principle** effect which we can desire or expect of this action is the conversion...of the people in those parts unto the true worship of God and the Christian religion."[389] (Emphasis mine.)

---

386 Ibid., p. 48.

387 Opfell, Olga S., *The King James Bible Translators*, (McFarland & Co., London, 1982), p. 84.

388 Coston Sr., Stephen A., *King James the VI of Scotland & I of England, Unjustly Accused*, (Konigs Wort, St. Peterburg, 1996), p. 16.

389 Ibid., p. 16.

It must be noted and James is to be praised for the fact that the "principle effect" of this endeavor was not to fill the king's coffers (as Spain and France wished) or to enslave the native inhabitants of the new world. It was to teach these people the great soul-freeing truth of the Gospel of Jesus Christ! A further testimony of this relates:

> "...it was published in print throughout the Kingdom of England that a plantation should be settled in Virginia for the glory of God in the propagation of the Gospel of Christ, the conversion of the savages to the glory of his majesty."[390]

Here we see that James was more concerned that the new colony benefit the inhabitants of the New World rather than himself. James was a selfless and loving sovereign who desired that all under his sway should be enriched by his reign.

There were several other areas where James' foresight was truly remarkable. In an age when trials were little more than inquisitions, James was an early advocate of jury trials. In his authorization for the new colony in America he let it be known that trial was to be by jury:

> "Legal procedures were clearly spelled out in some detail by James for example that trials without benefit of a jury were forbidden...James wrote, "...by twelve honest and indifferent persons sworn upon the evangelists, to be returned by such ministers and officers as every of the said presidents and councils, or the most part of them respectively shall assign, and the twelve persons so returned and sworn shall, according to the evidence given unto them...by the verdict of any twelve such jurors, as is aforesaid..."[391]

---

390 Ibid., p. 22.

391 Ibid., p. 334, footnote.

We see then that we **still** have a heritage of this far-seeing king in our courts to this day. In fact, it can safely be said that James has touched the life of **every person on the globe** by his actions while king of England. Is that an overstatement? Read on and see!

"JAMES the INCOMPARABLE"

Christopher Colombus is famous for only one great accomplishment. He discovered the New World. This was not insignificant by any means. But it is this one, single act in his life that we benefit from today.

The Wright brothers basically have one great achievement to their credit, but it is a great one. They invented the airplane. This one, single act has touched us all in some way even if we do not fly personally.

Henry Ford did not invent the automobile. He invented the **affordable** automobile. By so doing, he made it possible for anyone to own a car and not only spawned America's love affair with the car but opened our country up as nothing else could have. His heritage is with us today.

Thomas Edison had numerous inventions to his credit, but it was his incandescent light that has affected our lives the most.

These men were geniuses. They were so great that we can chart changes in civilization from their individual achievements. Yet these men's accomplishments **pale** when compared to those of the greatest sovereign ever to sit on the throne of England. James' greatness literally **altered history**. England alone was not the sole beneficiary of his greatness. America benefitted also. So did Canada, Australia, New Zealand, India, and every nation that ever flew the British flag. Yet James' heritage overflowed even those boundaries to literally affect every man, woman and child on the planet. How so? To understand this singularly great personage, we must review his enormous accomplishments while on the throne.

1. He united the nations of England, Ireland and Scotland to form the foundation of the British Empire. In fact, he was the first to use the term "Great Britain." This would be the power base that would be used to influence the world in the "ways of Britain."

2. He commissioned the translation of the Authorized Version. This single volume was to affect each Briton that came into contact with it in such a way as to fully exploit his individual potential for good (a feat it still achieves today on anyone who will read it!). This effect brought a strain of civilization to England that was lacking in other colonial powers. As a rule, England was more benevolent to its colonies than it contemporaries were to theirs. To this day, independent nations that were at one time British colonies profit from their earlier association with Great Britain. In too many cases these nations' best years were those when they were being "exploited" by this "horrible" colonial power!

3. He established the first Christian colony in the New World. This was the foundation upon which the United States was built. Remember, France and Spain both had colonies here before England did. But their Roman Catholicism forced God to withhold His blessing from their endeavors and then to supplant them with the Bible-exalting British.

James placed the propagation of the Gospel above all else when chartering this new colony. This biblical bias continued throughout the history of the colonies and then prevailed to influence the founding of that new nation, the United States of America. Patrick Henry summed it all up when he stated:

"It cannot be emphasized too strongly or too often that this great nation was founded, not by religionists, but by Christians, not on religions, but on the gospel of Jesus Christ."[392]

Was this Patrick Henry's isolated opinion? Hardly. It was a well known fact that America was **not** founded to promoted either "free enterprise" nor "multi-culturalism". The former was a mere "fringe benefit" of a nation built on Scripture. The latter is a lie perpetrated by public education and the God-hating News Industry in hopes of destroying this nations biblical foundation and enslaving it in New Age paganism. But at the time of it founding everyone knew that America was founded **for God**. The House Judiciary Committee made this fact plain when it stated in 1854:

"Had the people during the revolution had any suspicion of an attempt to war against Christianity that revolution would have been strangled in its cradle...At the time of the adoption of the constitution and its amendments the universal sentiment was that Christianity should be encouraged...That was the religion of the founders of the republic and they expected it to remain the religion of their descendants."[393]

Are these the rantings of a "Right Wing Conspiracy" trying to rewrite U. S. history? Never. Even that cesspool of liberalism Newsweek magazine is forced to admit the truth. In an article entitled "How the Bible Made America" it had this to say about the king's great Authorized Version:

[For centuries the Bible] "has exerted an unrivaled influence on American culture, politics and social life, now

---

392 America's Godly Heritage, video transcript, (Wall Builders Press, Aledo, TX, 1993), p. 5.

393 Ibid., p. 8. (One is forced to wonder what the reaction of our founding fathers would be if they could see this very "war against Christianity" being carried on by the Supreme Court, public education and the News Mafia!)

historians are discovering that the Bible, perhaps more than the Constitution, is our founding document.

"...Bible study was the core of public education and nearly every literate family not only owned a Bible but read it regularly and reverently...Because of this Biblical influence, the United States seemed to europeans(sic) to be one vast public congregation - a nation with soul of a church." (!)[394]

Again, exposure to the King James Bible wrought in America and Americans a goodness that has become famous the world over. No nation is so quick to shed the blood of its young men for **someone's** freedom as America. No nation is as benevolent to its neighbors as America. American soldiers are more famous for their candy bars than for their war crimes. They are viewed by the world as liberators rather than oppressors. Why? Because of the King James Bible. How did that happen? King James!

4. King James' insistence on jury trials has been mentioned earlier. This concept took hold in the colonies and their ensuing states and has been carried around the globe by Western civilization in sharp contrast to the tyrannic kangaroo courts of Muslim and Communist nations.

5. King James exalted womanhood and the sanctity of marriage. He held the institution so highly that he himself spent **fifteen days** in prayer and meditation before entering into that sacred bond with Anne of Denmark.[395] James own words confirm his high regard for this godly institution. In speaking to his heir, he said concerning marriage:

"But the principal blessing that you can get of good company will stand, in your marrying of a godly and virtuous

394 Newsweek, (New York, New York, Newsweek, Inc.)

395 Coston Sr., Stephen A., *King James the VI of Scotland & I of England, Unjustly Accused*, (Konigs Wort, St. Peterburg, 1996), p. 305.

wife...being flesh of your flesh and bone of your bone...Marriage is the greatest earthly felicity...without the blessing of God you cannot look for a happy marriage."[396]

Young couples would do well to follow this worthy man's advice even today!

Here again, James was ahead of his time in advising his son:

> "When you are married, keep inviolably your promise made to God in your marriage, which all stands in doing of one thing, and abstaining from another, to treat her in all things as your wife and the half of yourself, and to make your body (which then is no more yours but properly hers) common with none other. I trust I need not to insist there to dissuade you from the filthy vice of adultery, remember only that solemn promise you made to God at your marriage...And for your behavior to your wife, the Scripture can best give you counsel therein."[397]

Attention must be drawn to the fact that James made a great deal of the fact that the marriage vow was **made to God** and therefore should be kept inviolate. Again, this point could well be emphasized to young couples before they call the caterer.

James himself loved his Anne almost beyond words. The literary assassins have tried to claim otherwise, but James' eloquence speaks for itself: In writing to his beloved wife, he said:

> "...I thank God I carry that love and respect unto you which, by the law of God and nature, I ought to do to my wife and mother of my children...For the respect of your honorable birth and descent I married you; but the love and respect I now bear you

---

396 Ibid., p. 43.

397 Ibid., p. 45.

for that ye are my married wife and so partaker of my honour, as of all my other fortunes..."[398]

(Please note: Bill Clinton has never subscribed to the above!)

Space does not allow me to reproduce all of James' musings about his beloved mate. But he was doubtless in love with **and true to** her until the day she died. At her death he wrote:

> "Her to invite the Great God sent his star, whose friend and nearest kin good princes are, who though they run the race of man and die, death serves but to enhance their majesty. So did my Queen from hence her court remove, and left of earth to be enthroned above, She's changed, indeed, for sure no good prince dies, but like the sun sets only for to rise."[399]

James even rebuked the great Puritan Bible translator Dr. John Reynolds for his opposition to the use of a ring in the wedding ceremony.[400] Dr. Reynolds also took issue with the phrase, "With my body I thee worship" in the ceremony. James responded caustically:

> "Many a man speaks of Robin Hood, who never shot his bow; if you had a good wife yourself, you would think all the honor and worship you could do her were well bestowed."[401]

This high regard for the sanctity of marriage was for years shared by America until the <u>Playboy</u> philosophy became that of public

---

398 Ibid., p. 30.

399 Ibid., p. 42.

400 Puritans did not believe in wearing jewelry. Nor did they celebrate holidays or even birthdays.

401 Coston Sr., Stephen A., *King James the VI of Scotland & I of England, Unjustly Accused*, (Konigs Wort, St. Peterburg, 1996), p. 328.

education and young people were taught to live like dogs, leaping from one mate to the next until the very fabric of our society has rotted down to the standards of Hollywood.

These great testaments of the great King James have been carried around the globe like an unstoppable tide by British and American citizens and thus seen themselves interwoven into the fabric of societies that King James probably never knew existed much less would have thought could be touched by his greatness. This is the legacy he bequeathed to us, and he did us well!

WHO CAN BE AGAINST US?

Who could find it within himself to be against all the good this great king bestowed on the world? What horrible evil could dwell in a heart that it would seek to vilify so benevolent a soul? Well, the sad fact is that there are several. A man of great achievements will be hated, if for no other reason, just because of his achievement. King James' values, along with several other circumstances, guarantee that there will be no lacking of malice for him. The original Solomon explained it best when he wrote: "An unjust man is an abomination to the just: and **he that is upright in the way is abomination to the wicked**" (Proverbs 29:27).

There are many who find in this just king a man to be hated and destroyed. Only two men have stood so fervently for their convictions in modern times as to draw the fire that this great king did. Ronald Wilson Reagan and William Jefferson Clinton are worlds apart politically. But they are the same in one respect. They both stand unapologetically for what they believe to be right. Reagan, the conservative, has been the favorite target of the liberal News Mafia for years. They have done all within their power to vilify him and to diminish his contribution to American history. Clinton, on the other hand, is the shameless liberal. A monument to lies and immorality, he is the focal point of every conservatives' attack. And, just as Reagan

could do nothing to please a Liberal, and Clinton **could do nothing** to please a conservative, King James **could do nothing** to please those, both ancient and modern, who have sworn him to be their mortal enemy.

The haters of King James are best examined by dividing them into two eras; those of his day and those of modern times. I call these the "Then" and "Now" crowds. There are plenty, of both.

Then:

1. The Roman Catholic Church - Although James was baptized against his will into this murderous organization as a baby, he was rescued and subsequently raised a Presbyterian. Rome had lost the throne of England to the Protestants through James and she sought to regain it in any way she could. The "Gun Powder Plot" of 1605 was just one small bit of the tyranny she was guilty of in hoping to eliminate James and restore Roman Catholic rule to England. She absolutely **hated** James with an evangelical fervor, as is observed in the comments made in 1607 by the Spanish Ambassador to his country:

> "He is a Protestant,...The king tries to extend his Protestant religion to the whole island. The King is a bitter enemy of our religion [Roman Catholicism]...He frequently speaks of it in terms of contempt. He is all the harsher because of this last conspiracy [the Gun Powder Plot] against his life...He understood that the Jesuits had a hand in it."[402]

Here we see that the king never forgot the treachery that is part-and-parcel of the Roman Catholic Church. In writing to the Earl of Salisbury, Robert Cecil, James made his distaste for the Roman Catholic organization plain:

---

402 Ibid., p. 40.

"Jesuits, seminary priests, and that rabble wherewith England is already too much infected..., I protest, in God's presence, the daily increase that I hear of popery in England."[403]

His stand on the matter was plain "I am no papist...," he exclaimed.[404]

It is then no wonder that the Roman Catholic Church would stop at nothing to rid herself of this great nemesis. It is also no coincidence that she could not. God protected this soldier of His cross diligently.

2. Opponents of the monarchy - It was unfortunate for James that he came to the throne at a time when there was a rising animosity for the monarchy in England. Within twenty-five years of his death this led to the English Civil War under Oliver Cromwell and the execution of James' son Charles I. James reigned in an age when few kings could please their subjects. In spite of this he is known to have been deeply loved by his subjects. But there would always be an ear ready to hear any demeaning comments about the monarchy and its present representative.

3. Anti-Scottish Racists - It must be remembered that James was a Scot. And he was sitting on the **English** throne. This would be the equivalent of Georgia having a black governor in 1860! As a race the Scots were looked down on by too many English. (They still are in some places.) Add to this the fact that James surrounded himself with Scots in his court to the exclusion of a great many English. This was done for obvious reasons. James knew there were a multitude of plots against his life. He came to England after having reigned in Scotland for thirty-six years. He had a court that he knew and trusted. Bringing this court to England almost intact was no different than we have here

---

403 Ibid., p. 30.

404 Ibid., p. 47.

in the United States when each new President replaces the former President's cabinet with his own.

Be that as it may, James' action wrought no small indignation amongst the English, who felt slighted. Coston documents this English jealously:

> "The English resented having only token representation at this new vital locality.[405] Robert Cecil who agreed to James' terms in this area, was accused of having 'sold out the English to the Scots.'...Argument and debate over English resentment of James' Scottish elite and the resultant English inability to gain unrestricted access to James in his bedchamber was intense."[406]

What did the English think of the Scots? No one could better convey their disdain than James' three most vicious attackers.

1. Anthony Weldon: Weldon wrote a treatise entitled <u>A Perfect Description of the People and Country of Scotland</u>. Wisely, it wasn't printed until 1659, ten years after his death. In it he uses invectives that sound amazingly similar to Fenton John Anthony Hort feelings towards Negroes:

> "First for the country, I must confess, it is too good for those that possess it, and too bad for others to be at charge to conquer it. The air might be wholesome, but for the stinking people that inhabit it."

---

405 Coston is referring to James' bedchamber which, due to the king's poor health, was a beehive of activity and, in fact, his de facto office. Seeing only Scots welcomed there raised the English ire.

406 Coston Sr., Stephen A., *King James the VI of Scotland & I of England, Unjustly Accused*, (Konigs Wort, St. Peterburg, 1996), p. 84.

"Their discourses are full of detraction; their sermons nothing but railing;[407] and their conclusions nothing but heresies and treason's. (sic)"

"Fornication they hold but a pastime, wherein man's ability is approved...at adultery they shake their heads...murder they wink at; and blasphemy they laugh at...,"

"...their flesh naturally abhors cleanness. Their breath commly stinks of pottage; their linen of piss; their hands of pigs t...;...to be chained in marriage to one of them, were to be tied to a dead carcass, and cast into a stinking ditch...I do wonder that...King James should be born in so stinking a town as Edinburgh in lousy Scotland."[408]

2. Frances Osborne: Osborne shared Weldon's disdain for all things Scottish. He considered them "wily," "beggerly," "rabble," and possessors of nothing but, "eggs, barnacles and drugs..."[409] He said of them: "They ruin all about them...None of any other country can prosper that comes to live within the kenning (sight) of a Scot..."[410]

But Osborne had more than mere racial reasons for hating the Scots. He had been born titled (read that "privileged"), in England, in a society that based social standing and privilege on proper birth. Osborne stood well to capitalize on his good birth. But then, down from Scotland came King James and his Scottish court. To Osborne's

---

407 There may be another unexplored reason for Weldon's hatred of James and the Scots; **conviction!** The Scots were Presbyterians. And who hasn't heard of the scalding preaching of John Knox? Could Weldon be nothing more than one more Hell-bound sinner whose best attempt to escape conviction was to vilify its source?

408 Coston Sr., Stephen A., *King James the VI of Scotland & I of England, Unjustly Accused*, (Konigs Wort, St. Peterburg, 1996), pp. 217, 218.

409 Ibid., pp. 226, 227.

410 Ibid., p. 227.

outrage, James elevated a commoner, Robert Carr (or Kerr), to high office. Osborne could not contain his enmity:

> "Robert Carr from a poor page, and to the dishonor of our ancient nobility, raised him to as high a title as most Earls of England."[411]

3. Edward Peyton: Peyton ranked right down there with the worst of them when it came to hating Scots. It almost seem that he and his cohorts were in a competition to see who could think of the most disparaging remarks about the Scots. Peyton's entry in the sweepstakes went like this:

> "...the needy Scots, who, like horseleeches, sucked the exchequer dry; so that honor and offices were set to sale, to fill the Scot's purses, and empty the kingdoms (sic) treasures."[412]

Peyton also had every reason to hate James and his court. He was a baronet who attempted to make the Peerage under James and failed. You can be sure he blamed his fate on "the Scots."

With such hatred seething under the surface, you can be sure that it could only be a matter of time before something burst the bottle and let the venom pour out. Osborne was already boiling over the appointment of Carr.

Then Edward Peyton, who was known for having a violent temper, was removed from his office by George Villiers. Peyton would never forget or forgive this slight and his day for revenge would come.

But most devastating to the "James haters" was the discovery of Anthony Weldon's anti-Scottish diatribe. King James, ever the

---

411 Ibid., p. 226.

412 Ibid., p. 281.

gentleman, dismissed Weldon (rather than quartering him) and at that even gave him a pension. But Weldon had lost a **life** of ease. He too would see his day for revenge.

These are the prime slanderers of the great king. They were known for being vicious, hateful, and dishonest. They were to sow the false charges that others would reap in their own personal effort to assassinate the character of King James and hopefully his Bible as well.

The line was crossed in 1650. King James had been dead for twenty-five years. Weldon then wrote a treatise that incriminated **all** the objects of his, Osborne's, and Peyton's hatred. He did not openly accuse the king of sodomy, but alluded to King James' being an open homosexual with (who else?) George Villiers and Robert Carr! The King was **dead** and unable to defend himself. Moreover, Villiers had been assassinated and then Charles I was executed in 1649. Plus, the English Civil war and anti-monarchal sentiments were at their height. But Weldon still feared what would happen to him when his lies were published. So he performed his utmost act of cowardice. He didn't allow for his charges to be published until **after his death**, when he was safe in Hell!

Even with all this running against the twenty-five year old memory of the benevolent king, his friends and subjects rose with one voice to his defense and Weldon's charges were disregarded. And that is how it would have remained if there had not come a **new wave of hatred** this one led by so-called Christians with as many ulterior motives as Weldon and his hatchet boys.

WHAT DO THEY HOPE TO GAIN?

Why would anyone today pick up the lie of a few disgruntled, bitter men and broadcast it to the world as though it were truth? Why would they not investigate **both sides** of the story? Why are modern

Christians quick **to want to believe** Weldon's scurrilous charge against a man better than he was?

The answer is simple: **they have something to gain by the defamation of King James**. To understand this answer we need to examine who it is that would gain the most from this charge.

1. The Roman Catholic Church - Yep. There she is again. Nearly four hundred years have passed and the Roman Catholic Church still has not regained the throne of England. She still has those designs too. But, sadly, though she would benefit indirectly from the libeling of James, she is not the direct perpetrator of the lie.

2. Marriage and morality haters - Just as there was a air of anti-monarchal fervor in England in the mid-seventeenth century, there is a similar animosity in our country against all that is moral or upholds the sanctity of marriage. You can imagine how "politically incorrect" James' views of marriage and morals are today. But although they benefit from such a libelous fable they are not the purveyors of this lie but they aren't spreading the anti-King James slander.

3. Anti-monarchy/anti-colonialists - I have to admit, as an American I have a natural aversion to defending a monarch. I don't like the idea of one man having absolute rule. I completely understand the biblical teaching of the monarchy. But 50 years of "all men are created equal" has weakened my taste for defending a king who most likely would have assigned me, as a commoner, to serfdom. Be that as it may, King James was a good and benevolent king. He didn't "invent" the monarchy and he certainly didn't abuse the power it gave him. He does not deserve to be vilified just because we don't agree with a form of government that he was born into.

Then, of course, there is the standard educational/News Media diatribe against colonialism. They dare not admit that it is born of nothing more than tired communism's hatred for the West. They know as well as any that most of the nations that were under British rule fared far better then than they do now trumpeting their "divine" independence. (There are exceptions.) But this not-so-dynamic duo has made a religious conviction out of throwing off "the chains" of colonialism and single handedly invented the Third World. They have wrought murder, disease and starvation...but at least they're free of colonialism!

These twisted minds would naturally hate the king that set the entire colonial power of the British Empire in motion by his uniting of those warring nations of England and Scotland and forming the foundation upon which the "dreaded" British Empire was built. But these disseminators of death are not the ones who are breathing new life into Weldon's vicious lie.

4. The haters of America's Christian heritage - The liberals, the atheists and the sex perverts of this country all **hate** the its Christian history. They hate the righteousness that has been preached here for two centuries. Their innate paganism makes them the natural, and mortal, enemy of the only nation in that has **no pagan history.** Every nation in history, with the exception of Israel, God's chosen nation, has been **heathen** and had to be **Christianized**. America is the **only** country that was **never pagan** It was **Christian** and had to be **paganized**. As stated before, that is the goal of the National Education Association. That is the goal of the entertainment world. That is the goal of the News Media. They desire to eradicate America's true history and replace it with one that makes no reference to God, the Bible, or righteousness. They desire to de-emphasize and even eliminate references to the great Christians who had a part in forming this great nation and replace them with "revisionist fabrications" of the "great" parts played by women, blacks, queers, and any and every minority and abstract group they can find in order to alter the character make-up of this nation. They wish for Americans to became addicted to pleasure so they can better control them. Is it working? Yes. Twenty years ago, in doing door-to-door work, you heard some strange things but no one ever stated flatly, "I'm a pagan." That is the result of "higher" (!) education. And the average American used to be referred to as "John Doe," now he's "Joe Six-pack." Yes, these forces of Satan have much reason to hate a pure and moral man like King James and the deep-rooted effect he has had on our society. But they are not the ones parroting the perverseness and hatred for righteousness of Anthony Weldon and his hit-team.

5. The anti-King James Bible crowd - Yes, sadly the purveyors of Weldon's filth are **Christians**. (At least they claim to be.) These people have one goal in mind: Destroy the King James Bible! They hate God's Bible with an unreasonable passion that can **only** be Satanic. They know that if the King James Bible truly is the perfect Word of God, then they are going to have to answer for not reading and obeying it. Their sole defense at the Judgement Seat of Christ is going to be, "But Lord, we didn't have a **perfect** Bible so I **never really knew** just what You wanted me to do!" They realize that the existence of the King James Bible puts the lie to that excuse, so they hate it with all the passion with which the husbandmen hated the son of the owner of the vineyard and realize that the sooner He was dead, the sooner they could go about doing anything they wished. This crowd knows the rules of politics destroy a man's character and he loses his effectiveness. Therefore, they see Weldon's empty charge as a golden opportunity to smear the holy life of a man that they didn't even know just so they can vilify his Bible.

One of the standard bearers of this "Sewer Brigade" has been the former Christian publication <u>Moody Monthly</u>. In 1985 this Christian version of <u>The National Enquirer</u> printed two articles whose sole goal was to smear King James with lies and then disparage his Bible and anyone who used it. The title of these articles were "The Real King James" excreted by Karen Ann Wojohn, and "The Bible That Bears His Name" by Leslie Keylock. Now it is to be noted that this gutter level gossip was perpetrated by two female busybodies. Moody couldn't get a man to voice such empty charges. Now, for all we know these two may be lesbian lovers themselves. No, I didn't say they **were**. I said they **might** be. After all, their minds seem to see homosexuality where it isn't. Since homosexuals seem to dwell on that subject. Why these two women would dwell on it beyond me. But I'm not about to make a charge that they are lesbians. No. Never. If I were going to do that I would be a "Christian" about it, **I'd wait until twenty-five years after they die** just like Anthony Weldon did! I'd have it issued posthumously so that I couldn't be sued just like Anthony Weldon did! This wouldn't be evil. This is, according to <u>Moody Monthly</u> **accepted Christian practice!** So, maybe...just maybe...I'll "practice" on **them** in a few years.

According to this "established Christian practice," we are now free to believe **any filth** we hear about anyone that we didn't like anyhow. Let me give you an example. Many years ago I heard a rumor- I said **rumor**- that Bob Jones, Jr., was a homosexual. I ignored it. Later I was told that he wore women's under-garments. (Right. And you've **seen this**, right?) I ignored it. Then I was told that Bob Jones University has had open homosexuals come to the campus to perform during their "Artists Series," artists who went so far as to bring their queer boy-friends with them. Now please understand. I am no defender of Bob Jones University. That organization has taken a pretty firm stand against God's Bible over the years, no matter **what** they say to perspective students. Now, rumors like these about Bob Jones, Jr., are **perfect** for someone who wants to hurt the university for its stand against the Bible. **But they are rumors!** Just because they attack someone that you may wish to be attacked doesn't mean you delight in them or spread them. Therefore, I will oppose Bob Jones University on the basis of its infidelity to the Word of God. But I will **not** spread such a rumor about its **dead** chancellor in hopes of hurting the university. (Now, of course, **maybe**...after I die...)

6. You - "What!?", you say. "But I'm a Bible-believer. I wouldn't attack King James." That's right. But there are several extenuating circumstances that may cause you to believe, maybe only to yourself, Weldon's disgusting charge. You may not actively wish to believe the lie about King James, but there are some unfortunate circumstances that hold sway over you which work to the benefit of "scum-mouthed" Anthony Weldon and his low-class cohorts at <u>Moody Monthly</u>. These may lead to a difficulty of loyal King James Bible believers not entertaining the secret fear that King James may have, in fact, been a homosexual. Following are the invisible and unsuspected reasons why even some King James Bible believers wonder if Weldon spoke the truth.

1. Distaste for the monarchy: I've already spoken of this, so I won't tarry long. But it is difficult for Americans to defend a **monarch** against charges made by a **commoner**. We simply have a hard time with accepting an absolute ruler.

2. Our natural desire to hear trash: That's right. There is that innate wickedness in all of us that loves to hear an evil report. Even if we support King James and his Bible, we find ourselves naturally wanting to side with his accusers. Add to that what we know about the moral corruption of our own political leaders, and we have a hard time **not** believing an evil report about any leader.

3. We are victims of the "spirit of the age": One thing that is seldom addressed in discussing this issue is the loss of our own innocence as a nation. In the past five years movies, magazines, television, novels and (of course) the News Industry have bombarded us with "Sex, sex, sex!" I have been in the Philippines and seen two teenage girls walking down the street holding hands. Are they lesbians? No. **They're innocent!** They are doing the same thing that girls did in **this country** in the fifties before television had so saturated us with **the spirit** of homosexuality. The News Industry and entertainment industry have so exalted the spirit of sex in this nation that we begin to see **everything** as having sexual overtones. There is **literally** a spirit present in our society that always turns our mind toward sex. Then, when we read about the **common customs** of old England, the evil spirit forces our minds to "read sex" into the context. Watch and I'll prove it. I will relate to you some things that were common customs and practices in the England of King James' time; see if the thought of homosexuality doesn't enter your thoughts **unbeckoned**!

Examples:

A. Kissing: In old England it was a **common practice** for men to kiss each other on the mouth when greeting each other. (I thank God I didn't live in old England!) In my mind I understand that this was accepted then, **and yet I still** have trouble thinking about it. You can't even imagine that two men could kiss **without** anything sexual being involved. (It's not a practice I wish to reinstate.) That is because we are oppressed by the spirit of homosexuality that has been forced on us by New York City and Hollywood and **cannot imagine** this happening **in innocence**. The revulsion we feel for such a practice aids Bible haters' argument in the American mind.

B. Same sex bed sharing: Again, note how **just the mention** of this common practice of James' age forces us to entertain thoughts of homosexual activity. Did men share beds with other men? Yes. Why, even Abraham Lincoln share a bed with a man for years prior to getting married. I can remember twenty-five years ago that two preachers could be at a meeting and both sleep in the same bed in a motel. **Not anymore!** We are so "homosexual conscious" that we wouldn't...no **couldn't**...do it today without vile thoughts entering the picture. No, not thoughts of **having** a homosexual relationship. Simply the presence of the homosexual spirit of our age being present and drawing it to our attention.

The fact is that in James' time medical men thought that by sleeping in the same bed with a sick person, you could take the disease from him and he would get well. Coston illuminates this common practice for us:

> "Of interest, when William of Orange was sick, a page shared his bed in hopes of taking William's sickness upon himself, and such conduct was considered an 'act of bravery and kindness.'"[413]

---

413 Ibid., p. 275.

Sound crazy? So was the practice of "bleeding" which the American medical profession once practiced; to the point of hastening the death of former President George Washington. What courtier who served this beloved king wouldn't have gladly done anything to restore his health to him even it hastened his own death?

C. Terms of friendship: Clich'es change over the years. Also, words subtly change their meanings. An excellent example is the word "gay." When I grew up it meant someone was happy and innocent. Now it has been stolen by sexual perverts and used to describe horrible acts.[414] Here are some terms that were used then that had **a different meaning** than they do today:

"gay": As mentioned before, this was once a testimony to the youthful innocence of an individual, as Stephen A. Coston, Sr., has so well recorded in this reference to James' young...and **innocent** bride-to-be.:

> "Anne, the younger princess, was a gay, good looking girl, barely sixteen, and the more James heard of her attractions, the more resolute he became to marry her."[415]

Was Anne a vile lesbian? No she was innocent and happy. (Innocence the News Industry had already stripped **us** of. Happiness they are still working on.)

With this kind of degeneration in our language, three hundred year hence someone may claim that <u>The Flintstones</u> was about

---

414 "Queer" is much more accurate. If you saw two homosexuals "in action" you **would not** say, "My, aren't they gay?" You would say they were **sick**, or **perverted**, or **abnormal** or **queer**! But of course, that **same spirit** of this age intimidates **you** into using the term that your News Industry masters demand you to use "gay." You would rather **offend God** than the News Industry!

415 Coston Sr., Stephen A., *King James the VI of Scotland & I of England, Unjustly Accused*, (Konigs Wort, St. Peterburg, 1996), p. 346.

homosexuals because its theme song exclaimed, "We'll have a **gay** old time!"

"parts": In James' day a man was praised for having good "parts." (Did that spirit just put a thought in your head?) But this was in no way a reference to a person's **physical** body parts. It was a reference to his **character qualities**. Once again, Coston rescues us from today's vile spirit:

"Sir William Sanderson in describing Sir Walter Raleigh comments 'And for all these his good parts...'"

Sir Anthony Weldon in describing a lady's character: "The honorable esteem I have ever had of you and your brave parts..."

Sir Walter Scott's notation of Sir James Elphington "...a man of excellent parts..."

"Sir Anthony Weldon in describing Sir Thomas Overbury "...a man of excellent parts..."[416]

Does this last statement confirm then that James' chief accuser, Anthony Weldon was a homosexual. Yes! It certainly does...if you're going to misinterpret "parts" as a reference to the physical.

"making love": Whoa! Your mind went off the deep end again didn't it? Hollywood has programed you well. But the "making love" of James' day wasn't the "making love" of movie-saturated America! The "making love" of James' time meant "showing affection" or simply "being nice."

"From there his majesty came to Hyde Park, at the entry whereof he found a fair lady indeed, the fairest Lady Mary in

416 Ibid., p. 177.

398 Gipp's Understandable History of the Bible

England, and he made a great deal of love to her, and gave her his watch, and kept her as long as pleased with him as he could, not without expression to all the company, that it was a miracle that such an ugly deformed father should have so sweet a child, and all the company agreed that it was a great thing to find such a father and such a child."[417]

Now are James' detractors going to claim that the king had sex **in public, BEFORE A COMPANY OF PEOPLE!?** Of course not. But that's the thought that this age's evil spirit would superimpose over so innocent and pure an exchange.

It is to be noted here that James' approach to the monarchy was that he saw himself as the "father" of all of his subject. Thus he loved them all with a father's love. What could be more innocent or pure?

"terms of friendship": In James' day parents called their children by playful animal names...**just like we do today!** Therefore both James and Anne referred to their children by such terms as "dog," "beagle," "hound," or "monkey." Today the term "dog" denotes a homosexual partner. But it didn't in James' day. He often used it when referring to his son Charles. George Villiers was to James like a son. His own father had died when he was young and James somewhat adopted him as his own. Therefore, he too shared the term of friendship "dog." Even Anne wrote to Villiers and called him "my kind dog."[418] (Please don't allow the vile spirit of this age to corrupt even this innocent exchange!)

We see then that **we have been corrupted** with more of a spirit of homosexuality than James was. Our ability to view **anything** through eyes of innocence has been stripped away from us by the decades of "sexualizing" our society has endured at the cruel hands of Hollywood.

---

417 Ibid., p. 38.

418 Ibid., p. 72.

Our innocence has been destroyed. **Our** purity has been destroyed by an entertainment industry and even by a president, who is void of morals and wants us to dwell constantly on the sexual. We are the real victims here. King James is only a minor casualty.

Are you angry yet? Are you angry yet with what television and the News Media have done to you? Sure you are! That's why you'll put this book down and grab the remote and sit down and let them pour more of their filth all over the minds of your and your innocent family!

Remember, King James has not been accused of being a homosexual. He has been accused of being **an open homosexual** and of even defending this perversion before Parliament. This lie is twisted from one more innocent statement the King made to Parliament in defense of the charge that Englishmen were excluded from his inner circle. George Villiers, the Earl of Buckingham, was an Englishman among a sea of Scots in James' court. James was trying to show his critics in Parliament that he was not guilty of hating the English. He loved Villiers as he loved all of his English subjects (his "children"). He claimed to love Villiers more than Parliament loved the handsome Englander. Explaining this before Parliament he said of Villiers:

> "You may be sure that I love the Earl of Buckingham (Villiers had been raised to the peerage) more than anyone else and more than you (Parliament) who are here assembled, I wish to speak in my own behalf, and not to have it thought to be a defect, for Jesus did the same and therefore I cannot be blamed. Christ had his John and I have my George."[419]

Did that vile spirit whisper anything to you?

Now if this is statement defending a homosexual relationship with George Villiers, then James just said that Jesus Christ was guilty of the same thing! We all know that Jesus loved John more than He did

---

419 Ibid., p. 174.

the other Disciples. But this was **by no means** a homosexual relationship. By using this analogy James was in fact making it plain that his love for Villiers was pure. Only someone whose mind is saturated with sex could twist it from its context and try to make it say something that it doesn't.

THE COURTS OF PRAISE

We have examined the charges against King James in light of **the facts** of history and the effect that our involuntary submission to the vile sexual **spirit of this age** has had on the way we view these facts. Now, in closing, let's use a little **logic**. Now, put down your remote and see if you can use your brain without it. As I just mentioned, King James hasn't been accused of being a homosexual. He is accused of being an **open homosexual**. What arguments from logic deny this possibility?

1. Public reaction - Forget the problem between the English and the Scots. Forget the rising tide of animosity toward the monarchy. In the 1600's homosexuality simply was not accepted as "an alternate lifestyle." No amount of fact twisting can alter that truth. If King James had been a homosexual, he would have been driven from the throne...and probably killed. These were not TV-bred Americans who are unable to form a thought independent of an electronic box in the corner of their living room. They knew right and wrong and had never **heard** of "political correctness."

2. Public outcry - If James had been a homosexual, our history books would be **full** of letters, tracts and books written against this sin. Upstanding citizens would have written these while James was on the throne and **alive**. They would not have come slithering out from a few disgruntled outcasts after the king had been dead for a quarter of a century. They would not have cried, "God save the King!" in his presence. They would have instead demanded, "God **kill** this King!"

3. Puritan cooperation - The Puritans were much more strict than the Church of England was in adhering to biblical principles. Do you think for one second that any Puritans would have agreed to help a pervert king translate the Bible?

4. The Anglicans - It must be remembered that whoever sat on the throne of England was automatically the head of the Church of England. Today the Episcopal church is a mere shadow of its former self. Yet even today it is not in favor of ordaining open homosexuals as priests. Do you think that the Church of England of over 350 years ago would allowed the **head** of the church to be a such sex pervert?

5. The Bible Translators - The translation committee was made up of both Puritans and Anglicans. Although the Puritans were the more Bible-oriented of the two groups, neither would have accepted a blatant homosexual's request to translate the most holy of books. Would this astute body join in praise as in the Epistle Dedicatory in the front of the King James Bible and say, "Great and manifold were the blessings, most dread Sovereign, which Almighty God, the father of mercies, bestowed upon us the people of England, when first he sent Your Majesty's Royal person to rule and reign over us."?

Some have claimed that this was just political posturing. In the Bible?! If King James was a queer, he was an abomination to God and would have been to these translators. Do you think they would have allowed **the name of a pervert** to be placed on the Holy Scripture?

6. The Colonists - Throughout their charter, the colonists refer to both God and King James in terms of adoration and praise. Again, these people were indeed Pilgrims. They were unwanted in Europe and sought a home in the New World solely for religious reasons. They were a godly people with standards that would shame and offend us. Yet when this august body of believers joined together to declare the purpose of the voyage in the Mayflower Compact they chose these words to describe their love and respect for their king:

"In ye name of God Amen. We whose names are under written, the loyal subjects of our dread sovereign Lord King James by ye grace of God of Greate Britain, France, and Ireland, King Defender of ye faith, and having undertaken, for ye glory of God, and advancement of ye Christian faith and honor of our King and Country, a voyage to plant ye first colony in ye northern part of Virginia."

Are we to believe that these holy people would so laud a vile homosexual? Do you really believe they would call him the "Defender of the Faith"? Never! They would flee such a despot. And be assured there would never have been a settlement named "**James**town" in his honor!

7. God - We do not want to be guilty of missing the supernatural in all this. Following its publication, the King James Bible found its way **around the world**. Foreign missions were inaugurated from England and God used this Book to carry His Gospel around the world. It cannot be said that the King James Bible was all He had to work with. There were several great translations before it, The Bishop's Bible, the Great Bible, the Geneva Bible. God could have used any one of them. But He chose the Bible of humble King James. If King James was indeed a homosexual, then he was an **abomination** to God. God would not use the Bible of a pervert to evangelize the world.

The fact that God has so totally used the King James Bible and ignored all others is the greatest praise the regal monarch could have garnered. Even **God** said "Amen!" to his Bible.

It can not be said any better than the original Solomon said in Ecclesiastes 8:4:

Where the word of a king is, there is power:
and who may say unto him,
What doest thou?

Chapter 11

Considerations,
Conclusions
and Vindication

ALL books try to lead their readers to a desired conclusion. This one is no exception. Before that conclusion is offered, it will be necessary to consider a broad range of issues. Some are theological. Some are philosophical. Some are simply rational. We have observed the battle which rages in fundamental circles concerning the question of the perfect English translation. We have taken a scriptural look at the localities from which we have obtained the extant manuscripts. We have looked closely at the witnesses and have examined their testimony in light of our two ground rules and in respect to their place of origin and their faithfulness to the Lordship of Christ. We have taken a careful look at the true enemy of the Word of God, the Roman Catholic Church. In so doing, we have examined Rome's efforts and goals concerning the overthrow of the God-honored Universal Text. We have seen that in the past, this organization has been ruthless in her attempt to exterminate both Christians and their Bible. We can be confident that her goals have not changed. We have looked into the lives of the two men who were primarily responsible for the successful overthrow of the Universal Text in textual criticism and have discovered that they were not the "godly conservative scholars" which many brethren claim they were. We have looked at the Authorized Version, a Bible which has lasted through time in spite of major efforts by both fundamentalists and liberals to replace it with the Roman Catholic Local Text of Alexandria, Egypt. We have compared the scholarship and piety of the King James translators to the liberal and infidelic standards of the revisors of 1881 and 1952, who have been faithfully followed by the Lockman Foundation and other modern translators. We have briefly investigated the manuscript readings in a Christ-honoring light. Lastly, we have examined the vile slander that has been heaped on good King James by those who would bear no malice towards him if there was no Bible that bore his name. Now we have some final considerations.

US and THEM

Both sides of this issue will claim sincerity. Some will even do it sincerely. Therefore, the plea to sincerity cannot be our final method of judgement. In Leviticus 10:1-2, Nadab and his brother Abihu **sincerely** offered "strange fire" to the Lord. They **sincerely** died! I believe that many Bible correctors are sincere but sincerely wrong. I don't believe that they all sit around wondering what they can do next to corrupt the Word of God. Yet by their actions of attacking the King James Bible and offering new translations, they "do the devil's work" for him just as effectively as if they did. Although innocent ignorance may prevail for some, there surely must be some who **are not innocent**. Some, somewhere, serve the devil just as clearly in their minds as we serve Christ. I would look for these in the position of the "movers & shakers" of the Bible correcting movement. Before we close this work, there are some points that beg to be made.

1. The Roman Catholic Church - Scholars and their defenders all try to take the moral high ground and put themselves above the issues that common Christians face every day. One of these is the long-standing opposition of the Roman Catholic Church to biblical Christianity. Rome has shed more Christian blood than any overt devil worshippers. Yet unlike the scholars of the King James translation committee, I find modern biblical scholars loath to say anything negative about the Roman Catholic organization. They will elude to it in a negative sense when they try to disparage Erasmus. But they **never** make a public, overt statement affirming the evil of this church. They may try hiding behind the excuse "We deal in manuscripts, not doctrine," but it simply will not wash. If I was on their side, I would find this great silence frightening and suspicious.

Bible-believers, on the other hand, hold a universal revulsion for Rome. We don't like that organization and we certainly don't trust it. I've never heard a modern scholar say that. I've never heard Dan Wallace, James White, Kurt Aland or even the honorable Art Farstad make such a clear statement concerning the evil of this institution.

2. They've been wrong before - Bible correctors offer **nothing** absolute. They refuse to accept the King James Bible as their absolute authority yet admit to being unable to produce any other bible that could wear the title. They take away the faith a Christian has in God's Bible being flawless and replace it with faith in **them**. They yank the King James Bible out of the hands and hearts of Christianity because, according to them, "It's not perfect," and then replace it with an anemic NIV, NASV, CEV, NRSV or whatever is coming out of the oven this week and state, "It's not perfect either." Ask a Bible believers to put the "perfect" Bible he claims to believe in into your hand and he'll hand you a King James Bible. Ask a Bible corrector to put the "perfect" Bible that he claims to believe in into your hand and he'll hand you a modern translation that he will quickly admit isn't perfect, along with a bunch of scholarly double-talk to explain his deceit.

Look at their favored texts. The United Bible Society's text has undergone four editions. Nestle's text has suffered no fewer than 27 revisions. And in the latest they were forced to reintroduce readings that support the King James Bible. Maybe if we wait long enough they'll just throw down their Nestle's and take up the Textus Receptus!

Bible-believers have a much simpler faith. Though many cannot delve into the Hebrew and Greek texts, they still offer an answer to "Where is the Bible of Psalm 12:6, 7?" and "Where is the Bible of Matthew 24:35?" while their opponents offer arguments of vapor.

3. Internal vs. external evidence - Anyone knows that **internal** evidence carries more weigh than **external** evidence. Yet all of the arguments of Bible correctors revolve around vague apparitions of the external. They flee to "ancient manuscripts" and "scholars' opinions" while Bible believers simply turn to a book, chapter and a verse.[420]

More than once in this book you have been guided to an answer that was found **within the pages of your Bible** rather than within the mind of an unbelieving scholar.

4. Man vs God - Bible believers are quick to point out that new versions delete or water down references to "the Lord Jesus Christ." But I have found out that this reflects the approach that Bible correctors have towards our Lord. Although they may make spirited claims, when pressed about their belief in "the Lord Jesus Christ," they don't uphold Him so in their **casual talk** like Bible believers. Are **they** products of new bibles or are the new bible products of **them**? There is an almost scary lack of mention of the Lord in their writings. Yet they claim we should hand them our perfect Bible for their judgement.

---

420 The **internal** evidence offered in defense of the archaic words, Antioch & Alexandria, the italics, inspired translations and many, many more found in this author's work, *The Answer Book* have **never** been refuted by any Bible critic in over ten years.

Furthermore, Bible correctors never make "God" primary in their discussions on the subject of biblical preservation. I am not into the "God showed me this," or "God led me to do this," manner so loosely bandied about by some Bible believers but I do see an intense desire **to be led of God** among Bible-believers that is disdained and mocked by Bible correctors. Their confidence is in themselves rather than **any** higher power.[421] In fact, if you read their writings you will find very few **personal references** to "God."

5. "Doctrines found elsewhere" - In his book *The King James Only Controversy* James White, as so many of his persuasion do, defends the deletion of various Bible doctrines in new versions with the off-handed "But they can be found elsewhere" defense.[422] That may be true. But White is overlooking (innocently, I hope) the sad truth that most Christians, Bible believers or not, are not Bible **readers**. They have a few biblical references committed to memory to defend their doctrinal beliefs. When a new version deletes a doctrinal truth in **one** of these all important references, the Christian, ignorant of its existence somewhere else, will be victimized by some aggressive heretic who **knows** where **his** doctrine is "taught."

In his lame defense of the NIV's elimination of "Lucifer" in Isaiah 14:12, James White gives heretics a welcomed opened door. He admits that the "morning star" of the NIV correlates with Jesus Christ in Revelation 22:16 but then naively states that anyone can see by the context that the two are different. Maybe **he** wouldn't apply the "morning star" of Isaiah to Jesus Christ, but I can assure you that there

---

421. I say that **with apology** to Art Farstad. I **do** believe his sole desire was to be led and used of God. But then, so were Nadab and Abihu's.

422 We saw that this isn't always the truth. As noted earlier, the Ascension of Jesus Christ is only recorded in **three** places in Scripture. Yet more than one modern translation removes one of these references and then casts doubt on another leaving **only one** clear reference to the occurrence. But White will say, "But I **still** believe in the Ascension." True. But he **learned it** out of a King James Bible. So why eliminate the **only Bible** that teaches it clearly?

are some folks out there who absolutely **hate** Jesus Christ and **they** will be standing in line for the opportunity to do so! The NIV translators are guilty of arming the enemies of Christ. Would **you** be proud of the **dubious distinction** of arming the devil's army? Then why would you use such a bible?

The King James Bible presents the strongest and **most familiar** format for teaching Bible doctrine. Turning people away from using it is "doing the devil's work for him." I am convinced that the King James Bible is **word perfect**. But I can **safely** say that if a Christian is **not convinced** of that fact, he should **still** use **only** it because it is simply **superior** to **every** other competitor.

6. Personal involvement - Say what you want to, but we **all** have a certain amount of **ego**. Modern Bible correctors have a personal interest in defending **their** work while Bible believers have **nothing personal** involved in the translation of the King James Bible. How would **you** like to be Dr. Kenneth Barker? He headed the translation of the New International Version and when it was finished, instead of receiving worldwide praise, his **personal** credibility was immediately called into question. This book he offered us in place of our faithful King James Bible was so flawed that he was required to write an entire book, *Accuracy Defined & Illustrated*, in which he had to defend no fewer than **210** changes made by his committee. If that were not enough, he admitted in the Introduction to that one that he would have to write **yet another, larger book** to deal with the weak renderings of his beloved NIV.[423] For **us** it's a **Bible** issue. For **them** it's a **personal** issue. We're trying to save the **Bible**. They're trying to save **face**! They all frightfully realize that if the King James Bible is perfect, that they **wasted** their entire lives pursuing the field of textual criticism. We need plumbers and used car salesmen **more than we need them**!

---

423 Barker, Ken, *Accuracy Defined & Illustrated*, (International Bible Society, Colorado Springs, 1995), p. 18.

There are also the pastors who really never study their Bible. They never delve into the depths of revelation found between the covers of the Book they profess to live by. So **how** do they "feed" their flocks every week when they aren't getting anything from God or His Book? Simple. **Run to the "Greek."** There are a multitude of "study helps" (read that, "Lazy Man's Sermons") available in any Christian bookstore. All the lazy pastor needs to do is pick one up, run a few "Greek word studies," and **snow** his congregation Sunday with his "in-depth knowledge of the original Greek." He hasn't studied his Bible at all. **Greek** study is not **Bible** study. You can study "the Greek" without even having a Bible in the same room! How can it be "Bible" study? But it certainly is quicker and easier than spending hours cross-referencing verse-by-verse Bible revelation. It certainly leaves a lot more time for golf!

Then there are the Christian bookstores whose financial success is predicated on selling a new translation every six months. Go to any Christian bookstore and you will see shelf after shelf filled with modern versions and study helps to go along with them. The regular introduction of modern versions has provided an infusion of hard cash into a million-dollar industry. Didn't you ever notice that **most** new translations are sponsored by a **publishing company**? When the sales of one translation begin to slow down, publishing companies bring out a new one to spark a new influx of cash. It is in the best interests of Christian bookstores to promote **any** new version against the King James. I personally do not believe that a **freestanding** (i.e., not affiliated with a local church) Christian bookstore can stay in business without the new version industry.

7. Who are the "Bad Guys"? - Today's Bible correctors have a perverted way of looking at biblical preservation. They don't claim that heretics deleted Bible truths from the Scriptures but that **orthodox believers** introduced corruptions into the text in the form of the "expansion of piety" phrase which James White wears out in his book in his feeble attempt to defend his scholarly friends. It seems so strange that these men can look at the transmission of the text and believe that only **Bible believers** would alter it. Yet they **never once** suspect heretics. Maybe they believe in a "vast right-wing conspiracy" also.

Furthermore, they seem completely unable to even entertain the thought that the devil would do **anything** to corrupt Scripture. Just as they never speak of God in **preserving** it, they never speak of the devil in trying to **prevent it**. This is totally **humanistic** and leaves the door open to Satan. I don't believe that all Bible correctors are agents of Satan. But I do believe that when they sit down to translate their books they are open to his involvement rather than God's, whether they are aware of it or not. Frank Logsdon realized that too late!

If the devil is going to try to corrupt the Bible, we would have to be able to **see** his handiwork **somewhere**. Are we to believe that **the devil** had complete control of the infallible Word of God in **his** King James Bible? Are we to believe that the devil was the sole proprietor of God's perfect words from 1611 until it was "rescued" by Westcott & Hort in 1871? Are we to believe that **in spite** of the King James Bible being the devil's mistranslation, God was still able to **sweep the world** with Christianity? Are we then to believe that now that God **finally** has had His words "liberated" by modern scholarship in the form of modern translations, He is now somehow **incapable** of inspiring even one revival anyplace in the world? Even James White, high from reading his own reviews, couldn't pretend to believe such an abstract approach to the obvious. If God **had** a Bible, it **had** to be the King James for the simple reason that for almost three hundred years there was no competitor to it. If the devil got into the act he had to enter with the "Modern Version Movement." If we are going to find his fingerprints on the Bible, we **would have to find them among the modern versions**. Some Bible correctors will be quick to proclaim that those fingerprints are evident in such radical translations as the *Living Bible*, *Good News For Modern Man* or *The New World Translation*. But how do they defend the fact that the NIV, NASV, NRSV and others **agree** with these "Satanic corruptions" in so many places? The answer is obvious. **They are all Satanic corruptions**. If you want a Bile untainted by Satanic influence, you have only one choice: the King James Bible.

8. Revisionist history - We are all aware of the practice of liberal historians to "rewrite" American history to the point that young people will never be able to find out the true history of our country. It has been pointed out that some American history books have more references to Marilyn Monroe than George Washington. What is the logical conclusion? Marilyn Monroe is more important in the history of this country than George Washington.

Today I see glimmers of an equally insidious trend among Bible correctors. We saw it in the admission by Kurt Aland that certain manuscripts that agreed with the majority text were no longer quoted in the 27th edition of Nestle's *Novum Testamentum-Graece*. Thus, an upcoming Bible college student will be unaware of valuable manuscript evidence in favor of the King James Bible. There is also a move among biblical scholars to slowly but methodically **reassign** manuscripts of the Byzantine text type to the Egyptian text. Aland teaches that Hesychius first produced his text in Alexandria, Egypt. This was later expanded to become the Alexandrian text. The Alexandrian text was then merged with some Byzantine readings to produce the Egyptian text. Scholars like Dan Wallace, who loathes the majority status of the Byzantine text, are quick to see the opportunity this description provides. Therefore, they have begun **reclassifying** Byzantine manuscripts as "Egyptian" and are quietly "emptying the cupboard" of Bible believers. Thus, slowly but surely, they are whittling down the size of the majority text until they can someday "prove" that there never really was a "majority text" that supported the King James Bible.

9. The rude and the crude - There are people who are "rude & crude" on **both sides** of the issue. That doesn't bother me greatly since **the Apostle Paul** admitted to being "rude of speech." If you follow history, you will be forced to note that God has always had a bombastic defender of truth along the way. Erasmus was one. Luther was one. Zwingli just marched out and killed people. Wesley was confrontational. Even Dean Burgon was less than gentle with the hallucinations of Westcott & Hort. I am certainly not claiming "Divine inspiration" for every rough voice out there to be heard. But I am saying that roughness itself is not a valid reason for rejecting an argument. Even Paul stated that the message of the Cross was offensive. Ruckman and Ross are a good example. Ruckman takes **the facts**, tapes them to a ballpen hammer, and bludgeons the opposition with them. Ross simply bludgeons those that he hates. If there are no facts, he will manufacture them. Bob Ross is one of **our** greatest assets. His smallness, his lack of coherent thoughts, and his manufactured charges **shame** those in the Bible correcting forces. And James White praises him!

10. The "common" argument - Mark 12:37 tells us that during the earthly ministry of Jesus Christ, "the **common people** heard him gladly." God has always reached out to the "common" people. In the New Testament He used the **common** Greek of the day, Koine. He greatly blessed the use of the **Old** Latin "Vulgate" ("vulgate" from "vulgar," or "common"). He greatly used the Peshitto, which is Syrian for "common." Today He uses the "common" language, English. He further has greatly blessed the most common Bible in the world, the King James Bible. Bible correctors all seek to take the Bible **away** from the common people. While claiming to desire to give them a "better" translation, they will plainly state that the common people can have **no perfect Bible** and are **educationally excluded** from the argument. Thus the "common" people need to remove their faith **from a Book** and place it in the fallible hands of a modern translator. And at that they admit that most of their product is **guesswork!**

11. Doing the devil's work - The devil is a destroyer. He cannot build. He can only destroy. Modern Bible correctors **cannot** succeed in their mission of putting new versions into the hands and hearts of God's people **until they destroy** the King James Bible. Their arguments are all negative. They seek to destroy Bible believers by accusing them of being a cult. While **we** claim the Bible is perfect and without error (a

positive position), they say that it isn't and that there is no perfect Bible to be found on earth (a **negative** position).

It must be restated here that **the Church** (**not** Roman Catholic) is the **custodian of Scripture** and **not** education. God trusted His Book to the Church, not scholarship. Scholarship is always a limited number of people controlled by ego and education. The Church is a vast body spread over the globe made up of people of all walks of life. Many within this body do not even agree with each other. Yet the gathering is so vast that it is impossible to control by one central authority like scholarship is. In fact, the transmission and preservation of the Bible across history lacks any logical process. This lack of logic baffles and frustrates modern scholarship.[424] It was the Church that **wrote** the Bible. It was the Church that **copied** the manuscripts. It was the Church that **defined the canon of Scripture**. It was the Church that **shed its blood** to preserve and protect God's Book. And now we are to believe that God has shifted that responsibility to a few egg-headed egotists! The Church, since 1611, has recognized and used only the King James Bible. Not until **education** intimidated the Church through propaganda as incapable of preserving the Bible did the Church humbly apologize and begin to worship **education's** ability to preserve the Bible rather than **God's**.

This shift in responsibility for Scripture's preservation has been a masterful work of Satan. Thus, **every** modern Bible translator, no matter how sincere, is **doing the devil's work for him**. They aren't all a bunch of "demon-possessed" "God haters." Many may love the Lord but are simply deceived by the erroneous belief that they actually have the authority, nay, the responsibility to preserve the Bible. And the Church, like an oppressed prisoner of war, deluded by modern Christian morals and intimidated by the brain power of scholarship, is content to

---

424 It must be remembered that the thought that a group of dry bones, as found in Ezekiel 37, could live again is **horrendously illogical**! But "with God all things are possible." Thus, God could and **did** use the illogical, unorganized fancies of the Church above the educated, methodical and delusional ramblings of scholarship.

humbly accept the twisted declarations of scholarships and to even whimper a "thank you" for to refuse they are given.

12. What if we're wrong? - It is an old truth that, **if they're wrong** they will stand before God and be judged for claiming His Bible was imperfect and for turning His people away from it. **If we're wrong** we will stand before God and be judged for claiming He had given us a perfect Bible and that both it and He could be trusted. Which stand would **you** want to take? Which "mistake" would rather answer for?

YOUR FRIENDS, GOD'S FRIENDS

As a rule, Bible Believers are the friends of the common man and of God. As mentioned above, Jesus Christ was the champion of the common man. Paul, though extremely educated prior to his salvation, never allowed his education to place him above the common people. That's why he himself admits to being rude of speech. The great biblical editor Erasmas desired to see the Bible delivered to the common people. The great Reformer Martin Luther turned his back on the Roman Catholic hierarchy and chose to be a champion of the common man. King James himself desired the Bible to be translated so that the common people of his kingdom could have a copy.

While claiming that they want to put the Bible into "common" English and free the common man of the "old, archaic" English of the King James Bible most, Bible correctors, either due to their superior education or sheer snobbery, place themselves socially **above** those very "common" people they claim to desire to help. They view God's people as ignorant, incompetent bumblers who should leave "the technical stuff" to them.

The Bible states that Jesus Christ spoke as one **"having authority"** and not as the educated Pharisees of His day. Bible believers put the Word of God into the hands of the common people and tell them to turn to its Author who lives within. Bible correctors claim to care for the common people but in fact would **remove this authority** from their hands and hearts and tell them to turn instead to a scholar (read that: "them"!) for authority. Yet that very scholar will hedge his discourse with "We believe..." or "It could be possible..." (Quite authoritative!) Some of them may be sincere. But I'm not going to throw my Bible out on the basis of the sincerity of someone who has no Bible himself!

Furthermore, Bible correctors are not "jealous" for the Bible. They take no attacks on it personally as do Bible believers. This explains the vehemence and violence of most Bible believers' opposition to modern versions. In his book, James White will watch as the RSV attacks the Virgin Birth in Isaiah 7:14, and rather than be angered by it he will **defend** it with the limp claim that this truth is taught in the "*entirety* of the Bible." Yes it is. **But not in the Old Testament!** There is only **one** clear reference to the Virgin Birth in the Old Testament and James White rides to the defense of a rendering wrought by some of the most notoriously liberal translators ever to carve up Scripture! (See Chapter 9.)

James White takes no offense when the NIV alters Micah 5:2 to attack the eternal existence of Jesus Christ. No, even though he admits that there is **no error** in the King James, he still defends the watered down excretion of Ken Barker & company. Of course, Barker is an intellectual with whom White longs to rub shoulders. He has nothing to gain by **defending** the doctrinal truth of the King James Bible. Maybe his good friend Bob Ross should nail White for attacking the "eternal Sonship of Jesus Christ" in his "fine ongoing work"! But don't hold your breath.

Bible-believers take attacks on the Bible as **personal** when in fact they are not. We simply so love and so believe that Book that we feel a oneness with it that makes those attacks hit much harder than intended. Art Farstad did not anticipate this reaction when he produced his New King James Version. I believe he thought it would be welcomed by proponents of the Majority Text as an updated, readable rendition of their "preferred" text. Their uproar and venom against this work was baffling to him. Bible correctors have **everything** personal wrapped up in their position. They have everything to gain by being successful in their attacks on God's perfect Bible. On the other hand, **we** Bible believers didn't translate the King James Bible. If it really had any mistakes in it, it wouldn't reflect on us **personally**. The Bible correctors **did** translate the works they promote or were **personally involved** in the process in some way. They will lose face if their end product is shown to be wrought with errors.

This great love and sympathy for God and His Book leads Bible believers to seek an explanation for problem passages that **preserves** the honor of the Bible. That is why, when we hear of an attack on the integrity of the Bible, we instinctively **turn to its own pages** for evidence that the attack is incorrect. We **love this Book!** We **want** to believe the Bible is right. White, Barker and their ilk regard the Bible with the same feelings that a wolf eyes a helpless baby. Oh boy! Supper!

I am always led to chuckle when I read White or one of his horde whining about not being able to "understand" what they claim is the "obscure language" of the King James Bible. Why is that funny? Think About it! (That's **if** you can think without CNN there to direct the possess for you.) Here are **grown men** pouting about what they claim has them baffled in the King James Bible. These same men think it not unreasonable to spend five, ten fifteen, or more years studying the meaning of some obscure Greek participle yet they refuse to get out of their recliners and seek to understand on the king's English!

In my mind's eye I have often envisioned poor Jack Lewis and James White completely baffled by the King James Bible in the "Laurel & Hardy" vein;

White: Gee Ollie...er Jacky, what does 'chambering' mean?

Lewis: Gosh Stanley, ... I mean Jimmy, I don't have a clue!

White: Oh my, my! I just can't figure it out. How am I going to get through the day?...Pass the popcorn, Jacky.

Lewis: Sure. Here. Eat up...You don't suppose it has anything to do with putting a bad-bad bullet in one of those bad-bad guns, do you?

White: Oh me! I hope not. I can just feel my wrists going limp just thinking about such an awful thing.

But they didn't have guns in 1611. It must mean something else. Do you have a dictionary?

Lewis: Yes. But it's all the way over there on the other side of the room. See it over there next to my bronze statue of Spurgeon?

White: Oh yes. I see it. Too bad it's so far away....How about opening me another cola?

Lewis: Sure. Drink up. There's plenty. You see that's why I hate the King James Bible. There's just no telling the damage that has been done to Christianity because of that one obscure word.

White: Oh I agree, Jacky. I can feel my spiritual growth being stunted even as we speak! Thank god we have so many modern translations. They may omit the Blood of Christ or the Virgin Birth or Christ's ascension or His eternal Sonship, but at least they don't say "chambering." It's a small price to pay to be rescued from the Authorized Version.

Lewis: Right, Jimmy. Pass the popcorn.

White: Err...Jacky. So then what do you suppose 'shambles' means?

Lewis: Beats me, Stanley. Must be a reference to the way a teenage girl keeps her room up.

White: Oh dear. This awful King James Bible just has me beside myself. No one talks like it anymore. I'm at my wits' end.

Lewis: Right on, Jimmy. Nobody talks like that old archaic book. I'm still amazed that it says "sanctum sanctorum"...er...**someplace**...I think. Well, I was pretty sure.

White: Yes Jacky, I know. How did God ever use it for all those revivals all those years? Hand me the remote.

The end product of their stand is that they can hold **no book anywhere** and say, "This is the **perfect** Word of God." We can. I can understand their hesitance. They simply lack the faith to believe that

fallible men could produce an infallible Bible (even though they **claim** to believe that very thing in reference to "The Originals"). They are **philosophical** where we are **spiritual**. They say, "It doesn't make sense." We say, "It doesn't make sense but **God** can do it!"

APPLES OR ORANGES

The Bible is **true**. It is **correct**. It is **accurate**. It is **right**. Whatever it says, it is right. In Matthew 7:17 it says, "Even so every good tree bringeth forth good fruit; but a corrupt tree bringeth forth evil fruit." This brings me to a puzzling situation. It is undeniable that we in America have **more "Bibles" in our language** than any other country. No, even England has not published as many "Bibles"as America. Yet in America we have situations where a six-year-old boy can take a gun to school and shoot a six-year-old girl to death, or a man can have sex with another man and then kill him and eat him! Two teenage boys can go to their high school and shoot fourteen of their fellow students to death. A mother can strap her two infant children into a car and then drive it into a lake, killing them both. High school girls can have babies and then leave them in a dumpster to die. A man can kidnap young girls and video tape himself sexually abusing them and then killing them. This is **not** sin! This is **perversion!** Now how can a nation with so many "Bibles" in its language also be so infested with such repulsively perverted acts? Wouldn't it seem that **all those "Bibles"** would just have to have an overwhelming effect on the spirits that would spawn such horrible acts? How come America is **more spiritually perverted** now than when it had only the "old, archaic King James Bible"?

It is because Matthew 7:17 is **true!** If you sow apple seeds you will reap apples. If you sow orange seeds you will reap oranges. **If you sow spiritually perverted "bibles" you will reap perverts!** James White claims that the past blessings that accompanied the singular use of the King James Bible prove nothing. This is the expected reaction of a man who does not believe in the spirituality of Scripture a man whose

"God" has been neutered. But regardless of his whimpering, **they two are connected!** So also is there a connection between the spiritual perversions that have taken root in this nation and the new bible versions. Since the American Standard Version of 1901, this nation has been subjected to increasingly perverted acts. As these perverted versions have increased, so have the perversions conscious advocates of one are unconscious (I hope) advocates of the other. Barker, Farstad, and the editors of **any** new version can wheel out stacks of letters testifying to the "spiritual superiority" of their particular version. So what? The Mormons and Jehovah Witnesses can do the same. I thought we had enough of "opinion polls" during Bill Clinton's theatrical defense during his impeachment! Public opinion is **not** a standard by which to gauge the value of a version. There will always be people who are in favor of something that is not good for the nation. Didn't this nation "elect" Bill Clinton twice? How's that for a testimony of the value of public opinion?

The test of a translation is what **God** has done with it. The King James Bible was the Bible upon which this great nation was founded. It was the Bible of the to spiritual Great Awakenings. It was the Bible that was used to teach reading and grammar in public schools two hundred years ago. It is the Bible that made this nation great. Now we have many perverted "bibles" and our country is riven with many spiritual perversions. "If the foundations be destroyed, what can the righteous do?" All they can **hope** to do is eliminate as many of the sources of perversion as they can. The only spiritual hope America has is to forsake the multitude of new "bibles" and return to using only the Bible that God used to make this nation great, the King James Bible.

THE END RESULT

The "bottom line" on all this is simple. We you and I are going to be at **somebody's** mercy. We are either going to be at the mercy of the King James translators or at the mercy of modern translators. You decide. You can either pick **one Bible** or many bibles. You can pick a

constant final authority or an ever changing semi-final authority. There is no "none of the above" choice here. It's an "either/or" choice and you're going to have to make it sometime in your life. Think hard. Pray hard. Then jump into one end of the pool or the other.

WHAT IS THE CONCLUSION OF THE MATTER?

Throughout this work we have answered some of the common innuendoes hurled at God's Authorized Version, such as "archaic words," supposed authorization by King James, supposed "better" manuscripts being in favor of new translations, etc.

The conclusion is that first, we Christians who call ourselves "Bible-believing fundamentalists" need to realize that the true enemy to the King James Bible is Rome. Christian colleges should closely examine their curriculum and philosophy of teaching concerning its relationship to the Authorized Version. Preachers should remove all new "Bibles" from their pulpits **and private studies**, realizing that Rome's teaching moves very subtly.

Secondly, it is time to turn away from the teaching that Westcott and Hort were two born-again, Bible-believing scholars. They were not. They and their long-dead theories concerning the Bible should be treated with all the sincerity with which Darwin and his theory are treated in Christian circles.

Thirdly, it is hoped that Christian preachers and teachers would direct their zeal for the Lord in more positive action than in attempting to destroy the Christian's faith in God's perfect Word, and to insult or ruin fundamental brethren who disagree with them concerning the history of the manuscripts. I believe that parties on both sides have been extremely guilty of attacking each other with such zeal as to be a source of never-ending joy for the Roman Catholic Church. Brethren who believe the Authorized Version have been sadly maligned due to a mis-teaching on the part of those who do not believe it. Believers in the

Authorized Version attempted to "fight fire with fire." This has left a sad division in fundamental circles. A faithful return to the Authorized Version will not only be honoring to God, but will be helpful in mending the wounds of nearly one hundred years of warfare with the wrong enemy.

There is **no** Bible that exalts Jesus Christ any higher than the Authorized Version. There is **no** Bible that has ever been more blessed by God than the Authorized Version. There is **no** Bible which is more hated by Satan and the Roman Catholic Church than the Authorized Version. There is **no** Bible which is more clearly translated nor is any easier to read than the Authorized Version. There is **no** Bible which teaches doctrine more clearly than the Authorized Version.

I love the Lord Jesus Christ. I love His Book. I am thankful for His graciousness in giving me a perfect Bible in English. To show my appreciation, I intend to read it, believe it, learn it, memorize it, promote it, defend it, love it, keep it, and (most of all), be in subjection to God's authority through it. In appreciation, I will not change it-not a colon or a comma, not even an italicized word, not a chapter, nor a verse marking. Nor will I condemn the parts I do not understand. I will not "correct" the parts I do not like. I will exalt Jesus Christ and give His Book any benefit of any doubt. I will not worry about "what the Greek says" but will accept the "English" God has given me. The Bible is a spiritual Book. God's hand is on it. I need no more than that. No other version comes close to it nor ever will. There is no reason that it should be replaced, for it is every word of God preserved in English and placed in my hand. **It is up to me to place it in my heart.**

As the very great man of God Lester Roloff once said, "The Bible-we don't need to rewrite it, we need to reread it!"

What more can be said about this grand Book than what it says about itself?

Psalm 12:6, 7 says,

The words of the LORD are pure words: as silver tried in a furnace of earth, purified seven times.

Thou shalt keep them, O LORD, thou shalt preserve them from this generation for ever.

Thank you, Lord, for your perfect Bible, the Authorized King James Bible.

Amen!

Appendix A

When I was doing research on Master's degree, which was later published as *An Understandable History of the Bible*, I wrote to the Lockman Foundation and requested the names of the translators of the New American Standard Version. I received a letter stating that the names were withheld from the public so that no glory would accrue to a man. (Of course, they didn't mind calling themselves the **Lockman** Foundation after Dewey Lockman, the millionaire who financed the project!)

Since then the names of the translator have been revealed. They are listed below.

Peter Ahn
Warren Allen
Gleason Archer
Herman Austel
Kenneth Barker
Fred Bush
David Cooper
Richard Cramer
Edward Dalglish
Charles Feinberg
Harvey Finley
Paul Grey
George Giacummakis
Edward Harrison
John Hartley
F. B. Huey, Jr.
Charles Isbell
David Kerr
William Lane
Timothy Lin

Oscar Lowery
Elmer Martens
Henry Moeller
Reuben Olson
J. Barton Payne
Walter Penner
John Rea
W. L. Reed
Robert Schaper
Moises Silva
Merrill Tenney
Robert Thomas
George Townsend
Bruce Waltke
Lowell Wendt
William Williams
Herbert Wolf
Kenneth Wuest
Fred Young

Appendix B

Following is a list of the major early translations. There may be a few others of lesser importance not listed.

Old Latin -

This was translated around 150 AD and became so popular in the church that it assumed the name "Vulgate" or "common" Bible.

Jerome's Vulgate -

This is the counterfeit "Vulgate" produced by Rome in 380 AD in hopes of overthrowing the true Latin text mentioned above.

Syriac Translations -

1. Peshito - Translated around 157 AD this translation was the Syrian equivalent to the Old Latin and was most widely used by the early church.

2. Thomas Harkel - (Harclean)

3. Palestinian

4. Philoxenus

5. Sinaitic

6. Cureton

Egyptian Translations -

1. Sahidic (Upper Egypt)

2. Bohairic (Lower Egypt)

3. Akhmimic

4. Sub-Akhmimic

5. Middle Egyptian

6. Middle Egyptian Fayyumic

7. Proto-Bohairic

Ethiopic
Slavonic
Armenian
Georgian
Gothic

Bibliography

Sister Mary Agnes, O. S. B., *Nunnery Life in the Church of England*, pp.97-99.

Aland, Kurt. *The Text of The New Testament*. Grand Rapids, William B. Eerdmans, 1989.

Barker, Kenneth L. *Accuracy Defined & Illustrated*. Colorado Springs, International Bible Society, 1995.

Barker, Kenneth L. *The NIV, The Making of a Contemporary Translation*. Colorado Springs, International Bible Society, 1973.

Burgon, John. *The Last Twelve Verses of Mark*. Grand Rapids: Associated Publishers and Authors, Inc., 1881.

Burgon, John. *The Revision Revised*. Paradise: Conservative Classics, 1883.

Clarke, Donald. *Bible Version Manual*. Millersburg: B.T.M. Publications, 1975.

Coston Sr., Stephen A. *King James the VI of Scotland & I of England, Unjustly Accused*. St. Peterburg, Konigs Wort, 1996.

R. W. Church. *The Oxford Movement 1833 - 1845*. London, Macmillan & Co., 1891.

–

Cummons, Bruce. *The Foundation and Authority of the Word of God.* Massillon: Massillon Baptist Temple, 1973.

Farstad, Arthur L. *The New King James Version in the Great Tradition.* Nashville, Thomas Nelson Publishers, 1989.

Fuller, David. *Counterfeit or Genuine.* Grand Rapids: Grand Rapids International Publications, 1975.

Fuller, David. *True or False.* Grand Rapids: Grand Rapids International Publications, 1973.

Fuller, David. *Which Bible?* Grand Rapids: Grand Rapids International Publications, 1970, 1971.

Hills, Edward. *Believing Bible Study.* Des Moines: The Christian Research Press, 1967.

Hills, Edward. *The King James Version Defended.* Des Moines: The Christian Research Press, 1956.

Hort, Arthur. *Life and Letters of Fenton John Anthony Hort.* New York: Macmillan Press, 1896.

Karl, Adam. *The Spirit of Catholicism.* New York: MacMillan, 1972.

King James Dedicatory. Oxford Press, 1611.

Lewis, Jack P. *The English Bible From KJV to NIV, A History and Evaluation.* Grand Rapids, Baker Book House, 1981.

Lockman Foundation. *New American Standard New Testament* Preface. Glendale: Gospel Light Publications, 1971. Volume 6.

Machen, Gresham. *New Testament Greek for Beginners.* Toronto: The Macmillan Co. , 1923.

Maas, Paul. *Textual Criticism*. Oxford, University Press. 1958.

Military History (Cowles Enthusiast Media, June 1997), p.16.

McClure, Alexander. *Translators Revived.* Worthington: Maranatha Publications.

National Council of the Churches of Christ. *Revised Standard Version.* Thomas Nelson and Sons, 1952.

Nestle, Eberhard. *Novum Testamentum Graece.* (26th Edition) United Bible Societies, 1979.

New Standard Encyclopedia. Standard Educational Corporation, 1977.

Newsweek, (New York, New York, Newsweek, Inc.)

Opfell, Olga S. *The King James Bible Translators.* London, McFarland & Co., 1982.

Paine, Gustavus. *The Men Behind the KJV*. Grand Rapids: Baker Book House, 1959.

Paris, Edmond. *The Secret History of the Jesuits.* London: The Protestant Truth Society, 1975.

Ralston, David. *The Real King James, The British Solomon.* Louisville, Tabernacle Baptist Press, 1986.

Ray, James. *God Wrote Only One Bible*. Junction City: The Eye Opener Publishers.

Rice, John. *Our God-Breathed Book--The Bible.* Murfreesboro: Sword of the Lord Publishers, 1969.

–

Riplinger, G. A. *New Age Bible Versions*. Munroe Falls, AV Publications, 1993.

Rockwood, Perry F. *God's Inspired Preserved Bible*. Halifax: Peoples Gospel Hour, 1979.

Ruckman, Peter. *Christian's Handbook On Manuscript Evidence*. Pensacola: Pensacola Bible Press, 1970.

Ruckman, Peter. *Monarch of the Books*. Pensacola: Pensacola Bible Press, 1970.

Ruckman, Peter. *Satan's Masterpiece!* Pensacola: Pensacola Bible Press, 1974.

Ruckman, Peter. *The Bible Babel*. Pensacola: Pensacola Bible Press, 1964.

Frederick Henry Ambrose Scrivener, *A Plain Introduction to the Criticism of the New Testament*, London, George Bell & Sons, 1894.

Smyth, Paterson. *How We Got Our Bible.* New York: James and Pott Co.

Standridge, James. Do We Have an Infallible Bible Today. Mansfield: Cook Road Baptist Church.

Vance, Laurence M. *Double Jeopardy. The New American Standard Bible Update*, Pensacola, Vance Publications, 1998.

Walsh, Walter. *The Secret History of The Oxford Movement*. London, 1897.

Westcott, Arthur. *Life and Letters of Brook Foss Westcott*. New York: The Macmillan Co., 1903.

White, James R. *The King James Only Controversy*. Minneapolis, Bethany House Publishers, 1995.

Wilkenson, Benjamin. *Our Authorized Bible Vindicated*. Takoma Park: 1930.

Index #1

Scripture References

Old Testament

New Testament

Index #2

Individuals

Z

Index #3

General

H

J

–

M

–

–

P

–

R

–

–

Index #4

Modern English Versions

Now go **do something** with what you've learned!

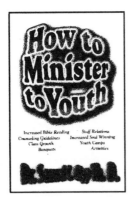

How to Minister to Youth
by Dr. Samjuel C. Gipp, TH. D.
Dr. Gipp now reveals the secret of his success.
If you are a Pastor, Youth Director or Youth
Worker you may find the resources in this book
invaluable.
ISBN: 1-890120-07-3 $14.95

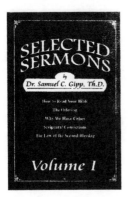

Selected Sermons *Volume I*
By Dr. Samuel C. Gipp, Th. D.
For years people have asked Dr. Gipp about
putting his messages into print. This book is the
first installment of his answer to that request.
Dr. Gipp has been preaching for over 28 years
and has held meeting all around the world. It is
Dr. Gipps intention that these sermons will be
more than a source of "reading enjoyment," but
that they will help you to live more to the glory
of our Saviour, the Lord Jesus Christ.
ISBN: 1-890120-08-1 $14.95

A Practical & Theological Study of the Book of Acts
By Dr. Samuel C. Gipp, Th. D.
Dr. Gipp takes a difficult and sometimes
misunderstood book of the Bible and lays it out in an
easy to understand manner. Great For Bible Studies
or Sunday School Classes.
ISBN: 1-890120-06-5 $14.95

To order these great books or receive a free Catalog please send your order to:
DayStar Publishers • P.O. Box 670587 • Northfield, OH 44067-0587
or call 1 800 311-1823 or your local bookstore.

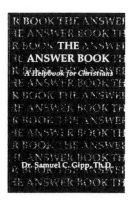

The Answer Book
By Dr. Samuel C. Gipp, TH. D.
The 62 questions most asked by King James Bible critics, and the answers. Layed out so the average Christian can answer attacks against the King James Bible.
ISBN: 1-890120-00-6 $6.95

Living with Pain *A Story of Encouragement*
By Dr. Samuel C. Gipp, Th. D.
Samuel Gipp, 23 years of age, had recently graduated from Bible College and had entered the field of evangelism. Through an unfortunate accident this was postponed for a year with a broken neck. Misdiagnosed, he went almost three months before it was finally corrected, with the broken vertebrae being surgically fused to an undamaged one. With this operation he thought that his ordeal was over. But it was just beginning! Over twenty years have passed and Dr. Gipp is reminded everyday of that hot August Day. Reminded by his constant companion—pain.
ISBN: 1-890120-02-2 $5.95

Reading and Understanding the Variations Between the Critical Apparatuses of Nestle's 25th, 26th and 27th Editions of the Novum Testamentum -Graece
By Dr. Samuel C. Gipp, Th. D.
A technical work to be used with the Nestle-Aland Greek New Testament, suitable for both individual or classroom teaching. The newest edition addresses the changes of the 27th edition. A "must read" for those engaged in the battle of "Textual Criticism."
                                            $11.95

To order these great books or receive a free Catalog please send your order to:
DayStar Publishers • P.O. Box 670587 • Northfield, OH 44067-0587
or call 1 800 311-1823 or your local bookstore.